McGRAW-HILL PUBLICATIONS IN PSYCHOLOGY
CLIFFORD T. MORGAN, *Consulting Editor*

# THE PSYCHOLOGY OF LEARNING

# THE PSYCHOLOGY OF LEARNING

## JAMES DEESE

*Assistant Professor of Psychology*
*The Johns Hopkins University*

FIRST EDITION

McGRAW-HILL BOOK COMPANY, INC.

1952    NEW YORK    TORONTO    LONDON

THE PSYCHOLOGY OF LEARNING

*Library of Congress Catalog Card Number: 52–7436*

# PREFACE

Learning occupies an important place in contemporary psychology. It is a subject matter that the serious undergraduate student in psychology can scarcely afford to ignore. All the divergent interests in learning, however, have never been quite brought together in a book designed for the student. That is what this book attempts to do. It is a textbook, broad rather than exhaustive, that attempts to survey all the present-day problems in the psychology of learning. It is in no sense a monograph; the material is of necessity selected, but the author hopes that the selection will give the student as representative a picture as possible of the contemporary concern with the psychology of learning.

The early chapters attempt to cover the basic problems of learning. Most of the material presented here deals with the acquisition of responses in isolation. These chapters do not concern themselves with the interactions between the different responses that the organism has learned or is learning. The basic problems of reinforcement, extinction, motivation, and punishment are treated here. The middle chapters of the book are concerned with examples of multiple-response learning. The important topic of response interaction is treated in these chapters. The relationships between the learning of different responses is treated under such topics as serial learning, transfer of training, and forgetting. While it is impossible to treat all this material within any "applied" or nonlaboratory context without doing violation to the canons of caution, the author has attempted to make it as realistic as possible to the student. The third portion of the book is concerned with special topics such as individual differences, emotion and learning, and neurophysiology of learning.

The author has attempted to compromise between several alternatives. It is almost impossible to avoid some kind of a theoretical bias, but the book is by and large empirical in approach. Although there is a strong behavioristic flavor, this shows itself in an analytical approach toward learning rather than in a deep involvement with any particular theory. In any case, the author hopes that he has kept his own prejudices to a minimum. The individual instructor is thus free to give vent to his own theoretical views without interference from the textbook.

Secondly, there has been a compromise between what experimental psychologists do and what students find worth while or interesting. For example, the problem of the distribution of practice has intrigued the experimentalists as much as any topic in human learning. If the book were written from the point of view of what psychologists did, an entire chapter would have been devoted to this topic. As it is, only a small section deals with this problem. On the other hand, other problems that have received little or no experimental attention are at least mentioned. The balance is not a perfect one, because there are many more problems that the experimental psychologist finds difficult to tackle than there are problems that are his favorites. However, it must be said in favor of the current trend of experimental work, the basic problems by and large are not the applied ones. We need to know much more about partial reinforcement, for example, before we can approach more adequately the problems of learning a language.

Finally, since the experimental literature is not exhaustively cited, the author has been forced to some arbitrary choices. In most cases he has favored the recent literature over the old. In the case of classical experiments, however, the original studies have been described rather than more recent repetitions of the experiment. In cases where more recent experiments exhibit marked improvements over the older one, both may be cited but only one described. The idea has been to present to the student a fair picture of the problems of learning rather than to assign credit to various investigators.

Although the book is principally addressed to the junior or senior student in psychology, graduate students in psychology will probably find the book useful as well. Students in education, particularly graduate students in educational psychology, will find that the book gives a background to the problems of learning as the educator sees them. Learning is a "basic" topic in psychology, and it is from the knowledge of this that the book has been written.

Dr. E. B. Newman of Harvard University and Dr. J. M. Stephens of The Johns Hopkins University very kindly read portions of the manuscript. Credit for help in clearing muddy passages is also due to the students who have read portions of the manuscript and who have listened to lectures based upon it. The author's wife, Ellin Deese, has been a devoted critic in matters of style and organization. A brief word of gratitude needs to be expressed to the author's former instructors, to O. B. Baldwin who first interested him in the problems of learning, to B. F. Skinner who provided much intellectual stimulation, and especially to W. N. Kellogg in whose laboratory he had the privilege of working. To Miss Elizabeth Ormond he is grateful for the patient and careful typing of the manuscript.

Permission has been granted by many publishers and individuals to reproduce illustrations or passages, and the author gratefully acknowledges these permissions: *American Journal of Psychology;* The American Psychological Association for its several journals; Appleton-Century-Crofts, Inc.; Ralph Gerbrands; *Journal of General Psychology; Journal of Genetic Psychology;* J. B. Lippincott Company; Longmans, Green & Company; The Macmillan Company; Prentice-Hall, Inc.; Ronald Press Company; F. Loren Smith; *Teachers College Contributions to Education;* University of California Press; University of Chicago Press; The Wistar Institute of Anatomy and Biology; and Yale University Press. In each case the original source has been cited with the material reproduced.

*James Deese*

*Baltimore, Maryland*
*July, 1952*

# CONTENTS

# CHAPTER 1

# INTRODUCTION

Most human behavior is learned. This fact in itself would make the study of learning one of the most important parts of psychology. Those of us who are interested in the "pure" problem of finding out what makes animals and men tick find the study of learning one of the most fascinating of the areas of psychological research. Why do we learn some things easily and others only with great difficulty? Why do we forget some things easily and always remember others? What are the factors which contribute to rapid and easy learning? How is learning related to the physiology of the organism? There are many more questions we can ask, some of which we can answer and some of which we cannot.

If we are people who look at the practical side of things, we should find learning a fascinating study too. A very large number of the applied problems in psychology are concerned with finding out how to teach organisms new responses efficiently and how to eliminate old ones easily. The redirection of behavior is the major problem of the psychotherapist. The complexity of the modern industrial and military world makes it essential that men learn difficult tasks with the most efficient expenditure of time and energy. In short, it is not difficult to find reasons why learning is an important part of psychology.

## LEARNING THEORY

It is probably more difficult to convince the student that *learning theory* is of general enough interest and importance to warrant study. Theory, even to the fairly sophisticated student of psychology, often means fussy disputes about matters of no importance. We must admit, alas, that there is a certain amount of truth in this view. There are large areas of the psychology of learning where we are simply lacking the basic facts; this lack has been supplied by theory. Two unfortunate consequences have resulted. First of all, when the facts are discovered, theory more often than not turns out to be wrong. Secondly, it suggests the notion that psychologists are given to theorizing because they simply do not know enough.

Theories, however, serve useful functions. They supply hypotheses and hunches about unknown areas. Theories also serve to integrate and lend coherence to a science. Because theories help us to organize factual information, there will be a good deal of emphasis upon various theories in this book. Often we shall find it necessary to treat very hastily the problems which are purely applied. This is done for a very practical reason, however. Applied problems often have very local settings that are of little general importance. This is particularly true of problems in learning. A good working theory, on the other hand, should enable us to "think through" many of the specific applied problems which come our way.

There is no better way to make the student appreciate the value of a theory than to ask him to read a survey of the experimental literature upon some aspect of learning. He would find hundreds of experiments which overlap, duplicate, and frequently contradict one another. If the student had no theory to guide him, he would find it difficult to tell the important experiments from the unimportant experiments. If he were to memorize the contents of such a survey, he would have at his command a mass of highly specific information which was limited to narrow examples of behavior. Theory should serve to lift the student beyond the confines of a single experiment into an awareness of some general principles about learning and behavior. The purpose of this book is to give the student a grasp of some of these important principles of learning, as they are now understood, together with the experimental background necessary for the student to approach the problem critically. It is the task of the student to take these principles out of the confines of a textbook on learning and to apply them to the problems of personality, perception, and social behavior.

## THE POINT OF VIEW OF THIS BOOK

To be sure, a complete devotion to a given theory is apt to be a dangerous thing. In this state of our psychological knowledge (or ignorance), we are apt to overlook important facts because they may contradict the particular theory in which we have a vested interest. It is safe to say that there is no theory now in existence which will be ultimately correct, but a good theory may be modified to fit some new group of facts. It is certainly inevitable that some of the principles emphasized in this book will be in need of revision within the next few years. This, however, is the mark of a healthy, growing science and not the mark of utter confusion.

Because we should have a healthy skepticism in the area of theorizing, it should be made clear to the reader from what point of view this book was written. First of all, it is important to note, the subject matter of this book is the behavior of organisms. No matter what we may think about the kind of stuff of which the human mind is made, the only thing we, as psychologists, have to study is observable behavior. Certainly we may have theories about the things not observable at present which may cause the observed behavior, but our theories must be well grounded in the subject matter and methodology of the sciences. We may consider thinking as an example of behavior which we cannot observe directly, but the fact that someone has thought can only be revealed when he speaks or does something else which indicates that the thinking took place.

No matter how much we may desire it, we cannot consider the subtle intangibles of the philosopher's *mind* to be the subject matter of a science. This does not mean that we are going to limit our study of behavior to the conditioned reflex. Behavior means all sorts of things; it means the skilled behavior involved in motor performance; it means verbal behavior and language skills; it means thinking, problem solving, and attitude formation.

This book is behavioristic chiefly in the sense that it emphasizes observable animal or human behavior. We must see an organism do something before we can talk about how it learns. Measurements or qualitative records which show us what the organism does under a certain set of conditions are needed. From these records we may infer unobserved processes, but it is of paramount importance that we have records of behavior in the first place.

In the second place, the theoretical framework of this book is one which has wide application. A great many examples of learning will be covered with a relatively economical set of principles and concepts. This introduces an assumption that much of behavior is made of the same stuff. If this assumption is correct, then rats, pigeons, dogs, and men are controlled by many of the same behavioral mechanisms and learn new behavior in much the same way. We are more interested, of course, in the behavior of men than in the behavior of rats. Aside from this anthropocentric value, however, man in many respects is the more interesting animal. Thus, while we shall draw many examples of learning from rat behavior, our ultimate interest will be in man.

The rat is used in the psychological laboratory for very good reasons. The behavior of the rat is relatively simple. The past history and environment of the rat are comparatively easy to control. The rat is small and easy to care for. Consequently, it is just about the best subject we can find for a study of the simple, basic mechanisms of learning. To be sure, it may seem to be of more immediate importance to do experiments upon sixth-grade children learning about life than to do experiments upon rats pressing levers in small wooden boxes. However, even as early as the sixth grade, the primary learning processes have already been obscured by a host of secondary processes. If the aim is to study the primary processes, it is usually necessary to turn to the subhuman. We can control, to a very considerable extent, the past history and experiences of our laboratory animals. We must accept human subjects as they are. There are, of course, many problems in learning which are peculiarly human. So, for some purposes, we must accept the human being as an experimental subject, poor though he be in this respect.

## SOME EXAMPLES OF LEARNING

It is customary, to the point of obligation, to begin an account of some psychological subject with a definition of the field to be covered. What is learning? Most certainly this is the wrong place to give an answer to such a question. At this point it would be necessary to formulate a definition in terms of conditions not yet examined. An arbitrary definition could be stated, but it would have little meaning in terms of the important conditions of learning which will be examined later. Perhaps it would be more sensible to begin with some simple examples of learning. These examples are necessarily simple because they are meant to demonstrate some fundamental conditions of learning which are very often obscured in more complicated examples.

Learning, like many of the psychological processes, is so ever present before our noses that we habitually ignore it. We frequently overlook what is basically important, and we may be surprised when it is called to our attention. The known empirical—this simply means experimental or observational—principles of learning are so simple that any patient, though not necessarily ingenious, individual can demonstrate a great many of them to his own satisfaction in a single afternoon of teaching tricks to Fido. However, teaching tricks to Fido does not in itself lead to an understanding of the principles of learning, any more than playing croquet leads to an understanding of the laws of motion. Just as it would be a mistake to assume that a good automobile mechanic is a competent physicist, it is a serious mistake to assume that a competent animal trainer (or schoolteacher) knows all about learning simply because he is a good trainer (or teacher).

*A simple example of human learning.* In a book about learning and social problems, Miller and Dollard (1941) [1] use a very simple example of learning in a human child to illustrate some basic principles. The same example will serve us well.

Suppose that we have a six-year-old girl who is very fond of candy. Suppose that we send her out of the room, and while she is absent, a piece of very enticing candy is hidden under the edge of the center book in the lower shelf of a large bookcase consisting of several shelves. She is brought back into the room and told that there is a piece of candy hidden under one of the books and that she may eat the candy if she finds it. She immediately begins to search for the candy, and after looking for 210 seconds and examining 37 books she finds the candy. She is then sent out of the room a second time, and a new piece of candy is placed under exactly the same book. When she returns this time she goes directly to the lower shelf, instead of examining the higher shelves first, and this time it takes her only 87 seconds, and she looks under only 12 books. The third time she finds the candy under the second book examined, and it takes her only 11 seconds. It is obvious that in this brief period of time the girl's behavior with regard to that particular book has changed considerably. Her behavior has become efficiently "adaptive" in this situation.

The problem which this example poses for the psychology of learning is to find out just what conditions are essential for the girl's behavior to change in the way indicated. A look at a second example will suggest two fundamental conditions which are important to learning.

*A simple example of learning in the rat.* This example of learning in the rat involves an experimental situation which the reader will meet very frequently in the first few chapters of this book. A white rat is introduced, for the first time, into a relatively soundproof box about 8 by 12 inches and about 12 inches high. At one end of this box a small lever projects from the wall, and beneath the lever is a small opening. The lever is connected to an automatic recording device and to a magazine filled with small pellets of food. The lever and the magazine are so arranged that when the

---

[1] Complete citations, indicated in the text by author and date, will be found in the References section at the end of the book.

lever is depressed slightly, a pellet of food is dropped through the opening into the box containing the rat. The lever is the only conspicuous feature of the inside of the box. The walls are painted a uniform neutral color and the box is entirely bare. This apparatus, which was designed by B. F. Skinner (1938) for an exhaustive study of the behavior of the rat, is shown in Fig. 1.

If the rat is hungry when it is introduced into the box, it will explore the box very readily. One of the things characteristic of the behavior of the

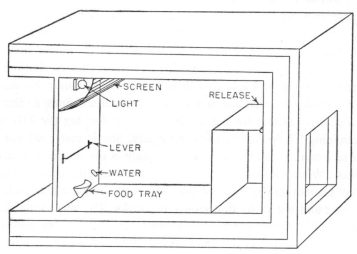

FIG. 1. An example of the Skinner box. One side has been cut away to show the interior. When the animal depresses the lever, a device automatically delivers a pellet of food into the tray below. (*Skinner, 1938.*)

rat following deprivation from food is an increase in activity and exploratory behavior. The rat will sniff the air, paw the walls of the box, bite here and there. Eventually, simply because of the lack of things to do in the box, it is inevitable that the rat will manipulate the lever in some way. Sooner or later it will depress the bar far enough to release a pellet of food. The rat may not discover the food immediately, but when it does, it will certainly eat the food. We may be assured that the rat's interest in the box will now increase. Exploration and manipulation of the environment will become more intense. It is inevitable again that the rat will press the lever a second time. This time, perhaps, it will discover the pellet of food immediately. At this point the behavior of the rat will appear to become markedly altered. Instead of resuming its casual exploration of the box, the rat will now proceed to press the lever repeatedly. As a matter of fact, if it is hungry enough, it will press the lever at a rate determined only by the time it takes to put its nose down and eat the food before pressing the bar a second time. This will continue for as long as the rat is hungry.

A casual observer might say that the rat has learned that there is a connection between pressing the bar and obtaining food. The rat has certainly "learned" a new response.

*Two fundamental conditions.* These two examples reveal some of the fundamental principles of learning. Especially important are two conditions which appear in both examples. First of all, it seems that both individuals, the girl and the rat, were hungry in some fashion. The girl was hungry for candy and the white rat, with its less specialized tastes, for Purina Chow. Secondly, it appears that learning took place when the girl's desire for candy and the rat's desire for food were satisfied. From these two examples we certainly cannot conclude that these two conditions, desire and satisfaction, are fundamental to learning. If we did so we would be violating the logic of experimental inference, for the experimenter did not take the very necessary trouble to find out what would happen if the rat were not hungry or the girl were not given candy. In other words, the proper experimental controls necessary to support such a conclusion are missing. You may be assured that these experimental controls, however, have been performed in many other experiments.

From a large number of experiments it most certainly appears that hunger and satisfaction of the hunger are among the most important conditions for learning. Just why this is so is still a matter of considerable dispute, and, as always, there are important exceptions to this rule, some of which we shall consider in later chapters.

## OPERATIONAL DEFINITIONS

These terms, "hunger" and "satisfaction," are taken from the common, everyday vocabulary. They have been used, I think the reader will agree, in a very broad sense. We do not ordinarily speak of a hunger for candy; we would more often say a "desire" or "craving" for candy. Generally we seek to imply some subtle shade of difference in meaning between these words. Unfortunately, however, these words from our everyday vocabulary, which we use to describe psychological conditions, have very fuzzy meanings. They communicate something to nearly everyone, but nearly everyone has a different idea as to their exact meaning.

One of the first requirements of a scientific vocabulary is that the terms used be capable of exact definitions which may eventually be referred to objects and conditions in the natural world. The definitions of many of our everyday words, even when they are explicitly set forth in the dictionary, depend not upon experimental operations, but upon casual observation, tradition, and the opinion of authorities. Of course, there can be as many definitions of this sort as there are dictionaries.

In order to make our language as explicit as possible, it will be necessary to introduce many new words as well as exact definitions of old words. This will involve the use of *operational* definitions (Boring, 1945). These definitions are in terms of operations performed by an experimenter or an observer which result in changes of behavior in the organism under study. Desire, motives, etc., may be given precise definitions in terms of observable operations. A hungry rat, by this sort of definition, is one which has been deprived of food for a period of time. We have no assurance, however, that operational definitions of these psychological terms parallel the definitions found in everyday discourse. Sometimes we find that we can extend the use of these definitions to all varieties of human behavior, but such extensions must be very carefully examined.

*The circularity of operational definitions.* Operational definitions will very often appear to be circular. Rewards are defined in terms of their effects upon behavior. Thus we must know the effect upon behavior before we can class a certain stimulus as a reward. Frequently, we turn the definition around. We know that a certain change in behavior has taken place; from this we infer a reward.

In brief, the operational definition of a reward tells us nothing about *why* a reward operates in the way it does. An operational definition goes no further than to describe an observed relationship between a change in behavior and the presence of certain conditions. That such definitions are *not* circular has been strenuously proposed from time to time (Meehl, 1950). Whether we agree or not that such definitions are circular, it is apparent to most people that these definitions are not completely satisfying.

Because these operational definitions are not completely satisfactory, people have proposed, from time to time, definitions of psychological variables (such as reward) in terms of *hypothesized* events. Thus a reward may be defined as some stimulus which serves to reduce the internal stimulation associated with a drive or motive state (Hull, 1943). Such a definition is not an operational one, at least at this point, for there are no operations for measuring such a reduction in internal stimulation.

Operational definitions serve merely to order facts in a clear and unambiguous way. They do not serve to "explain" things. Definitions in terms of hypothesized events attempt to explain observed events in terms of unobserved events which might possibly occur. Such hypothetical definitions are an important part of the paraphernalia for extending the boundaries of knowledge. They help us to make guesses about new relationships which may be tested experimentally. However, lest we get lost in the maze of modern theories of learning, it is important to realize that there is a difference between these hypothetical definitions and operational definitions. We know so little about the whys of learning that this distinction is a very important one.

## THE NATURE OF EXPERIMENTS

Because most of our information about learning is drawn from experimental studies, it is necessary to know something about the nature of an experiment. Whenever possible, scientists prefer to do experiments rather than just observe natural events. The reason is simple enough; experiments are *controlled* observations. It is always easier to infer *causal* relations when the events under study are controlled.[2]

*Independent and dependent variables.* There is a particular way in which events are controlled in an experiment. In the classical experimental design, all conditions are held constant but one, and this one condition is allowed to vary in known quantities. Thus we may wish to study the effect of amount of reward upon the acquisition of a response. In this case it is necessary to observe separately the effects of different amounts of reward when all other conditions—such as motivation, previous history—are held constant.

In this example, amount of reward is an *independent variable*. It is independently controlled by the experimenter. Changes in the independent variable are accompanied by changes in behavior. The resulting changes in behavior constitute the *dependent variable*. Sometimes in an experiment there may be more than one independent variable. The joint effects of amount of reward and length of food deprivation may be studied, for example. In this case the experimental design is much more complicated, though the interpretation of the resulting change in the dependent variable

---

[2] The most important paper devoted to the methodology of the study of learning is that of Melton (1936). This paper is a bit out of date, but it is still important for its concise summary of many important problems.

is the same. There will be one set of results which will tell us how behavior changes when reward is varied independently of food deprivation, and there will be another set of results which will tell us how behavior changes when food deprivation is varied independently of reward. In addition, from such an experiment, we shall be able to tell something of the *interaction* between amount of reward and food deprivation, *i.e.,* we shall be able to tell how they modify each other in their effects upon behavior.

*Functional relationships.* When the dependent variable shows changes as a result of variations in the independent variable, it is said that the dependent variable is a *function* of the independent variable. In the example above, change in behavior is a function of the amount of reward. This is of fundamental importance, since the aim of this book is to analyze the conditions of which learning is a function.

Much of the data discussed in this book will be presented in graphs. Graphs are useful because they show at a glance the nature of a functional relationship. In graphical presentation of data the independent variable is always placed on the horizontal axis (the abscissa) and the dependent variable is always placed on the vertical axis (the ordinate). A good example is Fig. 4 on page 17. Here the per cent of times a conditioned response occurred (dependent variable) is plotted against the number of trials of training (independent variable).

*Motivation and reinforcement as variables.* The two conditions which were pointed out as important to the two examples of learning discussed earlier are usually called "motivation" and "reinforcement." Reinforcement as an independent variable will be discussed in Chap. 2. It will be difficult to discuss reinforcement without reference to motivation because this is a good example of an interaction between two independent variables. A definition and analysis of motivation will be postponed to a later chapter, however.

Then, the next five chapters will concern themselves with some fundamental questions concerning the effect of reinforcement upon learning. The student whose primary interest is in finding out about human learning may be a bit impatient with these chapters. If he is persistent, however, his persistence should be rewarded with a little better insight into the building blocks of behavior and personality.

# CHAPTER 2

# REINFORCEMENT AND LEARNING

Reinforcement is perhaps the most basic notion in the whole of the psychology of learning. Like many other basic notions, there is little or no agreement about the exact definition of reinforcement. In practice, however, the term "reinforcement" most frequently corresponds fairly well to the layman's term "reward."

A reward is a bonus which is given to someone for doing something we like or approve. We generally give such a reward because we want that individual to continue the rewarded behavior. It is fairly evident from casual observation that rewards are indeed major determiners of behavior. Most behavior theorists believe that rewards are *the* most important determiners of learned behavior. At any rate, reinforcement or reward is certainly one of the most important concepts in the psychology of learning.

We cannot call reinforcements rewards and simply let it go at that. Different people have too many meanings for the term reward; consequently, it is necessary to present a definition of the concept of reinforcement. This definition of reinforcement will be an operational one (pp. 7–9); that is to say, it will refer only to events which can be observed and measured. It is important to point this out, since reinforcement has been frequently defined theoretically in terms of entities or constructs which are hypothetical or unobservable. Such definitions embody theories of reinforcement, and since we do not wish to examine theories of reinforcement at the moment, we shall do best to stick to the operational definition.

## AN OPERATIONAL DEFINITION OF REINFORCEMENT

Recall, for a moment, the case, cited in the first chapter, of the rat which learned to press a bar. Each time the rat pressed the lever it got a pellet of food. Pressing the bar is a response, and the pellet of food is a stimulus. After the rat had been presented with the food pellet a few times after pressing the bar, the rate at which the rat pressed the bar increased greatly. If we had followed pressing the bar with the sound of a buzzer instead of the pellet of food, would the rat have increased its rate of pressing the bar? It is very unlikely that it would, at least to such a great extent. The pellet of food is a reinforcement and the buzzer is not. The pellet of food is a reinforcement simply because it increased the rate at which the rat pressed the bar while the buzzer did not. This example embodies a definition of reinforcement. *A reinforcement is any stimulus which can increase the strength of a response when it is presented in close temporal conjunction with the occurrence of that response.*

The inquiring student will want to ask some questions about this definition of reinforcement. What is strength of response? Do reinforcing stimuli have properties besides being reinforcing which make them clearly different from nonreinforcing stimuli? In other words, why do some stimuli reinforce and others do not? Another question might be: How close does the temporal conjunction between the response and the reinforcing stimulus have to be? It is such questions as these which will be the main concern of this chapter.

## THE CONDITIONS OF REINFORCEMENT

Experiments have given us a good deal of information about the conditions under which reinforcement occurs. These experiments do not tell us much about the basic mechanisms of reinforcement, but they do tell us where and when and how much reinforcement takes place under a given set of conditions. These experiments are important because they tell us how behavior is determined by reinforcement when other variables are held constant.

### Strength of Response

Before we can go very far in an analysis of the conditions of reinforcement, we must specify what is meant by "strength of response." When an organism learns a new response, it usually learns rather gradually. There is a change in performance which takes a period of time to develop. It is this change in behavior which is an increase in the strength of response. In the examples in Chap. 1, the rat pressed the bar more frequently and with greater force after a few reinforcements; the girl found the candy much more quickly and with fewer mistakes after a few reinforcements. These are examples of increasing the strength of response.

In a general sort of way, it is easy to see that there can be many ways of measuring the change in behavior which results from reinforcement. There is no particular way of measuring this change which we can unequivocally call the measure of strength of response. We assume that strength of response is related in particular ways to direct measures of behavior, however.

Strength of response is an example of an *intervening variable* (see Mac-Corquodale and Meehl, 1948). An intervening variable is not something we measure directly, but we postulate it as some factor or variable that determines the observed change in behavior.

*What we measure directly.* Because it is important, the difference between *measured* variables and *intervening* variables needs emphasis. We measure directly such things as reaction time (latent period) of a response, the rate or probability of occurrence of a response, or the magnitude of a response. These are all easily observed dependent variables in experiments on learning.

These different measures are all used to evaluate how much learning has taken place. In one experiment, magnitude of response may be used to indicate how much learning has taken place; in another experiment the probability of occurrence of a response may be used. There are many different measures of behavior used in the experimental laboratory; the reader of this book will become acquainted with a fair number of them.

*What is inferred.* In one way or another it is usually assumed that all of the measured variables are indirect indicators of the strength of response. There is nothing unusual or suspicious about this assumption; a change in the color of a piece of litmus paper and a change in taste may both be indicators of the change in pH of a solution.

Perhaps what is unusual about strength of response is that there is no way of measuring it directly. This is why strength of response is an intervening variable. It is related on one hand to various independent variables in an experiment, such as deprivation of food, reinforcement, and punishment, and on the other hand it is related to the various dependent variables, such as reaction time and probability of occurrence, etc.

This chapter deals with reinforcement; consequently the next few pages will deal with the effects of various aspects of reinforcement upon both direct measures of behavior and the inferred intervening variable, strength of response.

*Strength of Response as a Function of the Number of Reinforcements*

The greater the number of reinforcements, the greater the strength of response. This is a generalization which is apparent to everyone. The more often a response is rewarded, the more thoroughly it is ingrained. Thus it is apparent that there is a summation of the effect of reinforcement from trial to trial or from occasion to occasion. An examination of learning as a function of the number of reinforcements will yield some information about the way in which this summation takes place.

*Latent period and the number of reinforcements.* Latent period is one of the indicators that is changed by a change in the strength of response. Latent period (or latency) is the time which intervenes between a stimulus and the beginning of a response. Thus it is the same thing as reaction time. Latent period is inversely related to the strength of response; when latent period is short, response strength is high; when latent period is long, response strength is low.

We have an experiment at hand that illustrates how the number of reinforcements affects latent period. The experimenters (Graham and Gagné, 1940) prepared a small runway for rats. This runway was about 3 feet long and just wide enough for the rats to run along without turning around. At one end was a goal box with food in it. On the first trial a hungry rat was placed in the starting box and the door to the runway was opened. The time that it took the rat to get started after the door was opened was measured. This procedure was repeated a large number of times; each time the rat was allowed to traverse the runway and to enter the goal box and eat the food.

Figure 2 shows what happened to the latent period. It gradually decreased. It changed most between the first and second trials. Thereafter, between each successive trial, there were smaller decreases in the latent period, until after quite a few trials the latent period hardly decreased at all. From such data, we can infer that it was the first reinforcement that increased response strength the most and that each successive reinforcement thereafter added less and less to the total response strength.

*Magnitude of response and number of reinforcements.* Magnitude of response is a second measure of the strength of a response. As you might expect, it increases with the number of reinforcements. We can see that fact in an experiment by Hovland (1937c) in which the amplitude of the galvanic skin response was the measure of magnitude. This response (abbreviated GSR) is a change in the electrical resistance of the skin which is due to the activity of some effectors in the skin (probably the sweat glands; see McCleary, 1950). In the experiment, Hovland gave some subjects a mild electric shock at about the same time he applied a vibrator to the skin. Originally the vibrator did not elicit very much of a GSR, though the electric shock did. After a few pairings, however, the vibrator alone came to elicit a good-sized GSR. As the number of reinforcements

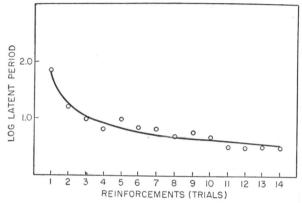

FIG. 2. Latent period as a function of the number of reinforcements. Latent period decreases with reinforcement. (*Graham and Gagné, 1940.*)

(pairings) increased, the magnitude of the GSR to the vibrator increased. This you can see in Fig. 3.

As in the case of the measurement of the latent period in the runway, this experiment with the GSR shows that the first reinforcement (pairing of the vibrator and shock) contributed the greatest increase in response strength. Each successive reinforcement added less and less to the increase in response strength. So, in this experiment, as in the first, the strength of response increased rapidly at first, then more slowly with more reinforcements.

*Correct responses and number of reinforcements.* A third measure of the strength of response is the percentage of correct responses which occur in a given number of trials. To illustrate this measurement we shall look at an example which, like the last one, is much like the classical studies of the conditioned salivary response by Pavlov (1927), who first described simple conditioning.

A dog is placed in a lightly restraining harness. The experimenter fastens a pair of electrodes to the right rear paw of the dog, so that a mild shock may be delivered to the leg. When the dog is shocked, it responds by flexing the leg. The apparatus is so arranged that if the dog flexes its leg before it gets shocked, it will avoid the shock. A buzzer is sounded a brief moment before the shock. After a number of occasions when the buzzer is paired with the shock, the dog learns to flex its leg to the buzzer.

The reader will perhaps recognize that the shock is what Pavlov called an unconditioned stimulus, and the buzzer is a conditioned stimulus. The

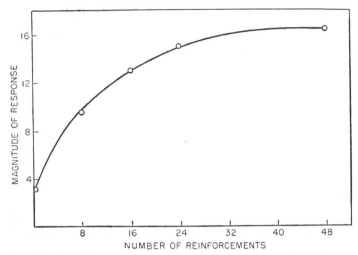

Fig. 3. Amplitude of the galvanic skin response as a function of the number of reinforcements. (*Hovland, 1937c.*)

response to the shock is an unconditioned response, and the response to the buzzer is a conditioned response. The conditioned stimulus acquires the ability to elicit the flexion response by result of its pairing with the electric shock. Thus the electric shock is a reinforcement (perhaps, more strictly speaking, removal of the electric shock is a reinforcement), and at the same time it is the unconditioned stimulus. As a matter of fact, Pavlov used these terms interchangeably, though strict usage today probably would not permit this.

But no matter what terms we use, the experimental fact is that the percentage of conditioned responses becomes more and more frequent as we increase the number of reinforcements. To illustrate this point, Fig. 4 gives the results in a specific experiment (Deese, 1948); the percentage of conditioned responses is plotted for each successive group of twenty trials during the course of learning. As you can see, the curve looks very much like those we saw in the case of latent period and amplitude of response. Early in learning the percentage of conditioned responses increased rapidly; later on, it increased more slowly.

Some psychologists have thought that curves like this one should be S-shaped (Culler, 1928). Sometimes they are, and when they are, the greatest change in per cent of conditioned responses takes place in the

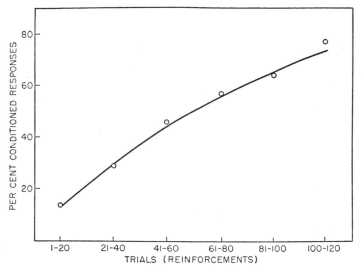

FIG. 4. Per cent of correct responses (probability of occurrence) of conditioned withdrawal response as a function of number of reinforcements. (*Deese, 1948.*)

middle of learning, not at the beginning, and much smaller increases in per cent of conditioned responses occur at the beginning and the end of learning. More often than not, however, learning curves are not S-shaped but like those in Figs. 2, 3, and 4. As we shall see in a moment, such curves are roughly exponential in shape.

*A theoretical curve.* This matter of the shape of the learning curve is more than one of idle curiosity. It makes a difference in one's theory of learning. Learning theorists, in fact, put great stock in the shape of learning curves and attempt to predict them or deduce them from their theories. They reason that if there are certain quantitative similarities among various curves, these similarities probably reflect similar underlying causes. In the three curves of Figs. 2, 3, and 4, for example, we can extract characteristics that are common to all of them:

1. Response strength is an increasing function of the number of reinforcements.

2. Response strength increases to a limit; beyond this there is no further increase unless the conditions of the experiment are changed. This limit, or *asymptote,* varies, we may note in passing, with different kinds of learning situations, the level of motivation of the organism, and several other factors.

3. As response strength steadily approaches its limit, or asymptote, each reinforcement brings a smaller and smaller increment in response strength.

All three of these characteristics of the learning curve are represented in one mathematical function, the *exponential function.* This function, stripped down to its bare essentials, may be written as

$$y = e^x$$

when $y$ is the independent variable, $x$ the dependent variable, and $e$ a constant (which the student of mathematics will recognize as the base of Naperian logarithms). And, as we shall see in a moment, this basic equation takes more elaborate forms when constants are inserted in it in various ways.

Such a function is well known to many people because it seems to apply to many different kinds of data. Many important physical and chemical systems are described by exponential equations. For example, it describes an autocatalytic chemical reaction, and it frequently fits quite well the growth of simple plants and animals—just to name two of many possible examples. It is no wonder, then, that psychologists have asked the question whether it will do the job of describing the learning curves we have examined in Figs. 2, 3, and 4.

The derivation of an exponential equation for the learning curve proceeds as follows. First let $R$ be response strength (the dependent variable on the vertical axis) and let $N$ be number of reinforcements (the independent variable on the horizontal axis). Then, remember characteristic 1 above, that, for every increment in reinforcement, there is an increment in response strength, and put this in the form of a ratio that the mathematician would write as $d(R)/d(N)$.[1] Next, consider characteristic 2 above, that each learning curve has its limit or maximum; this we may

---

[1] Obviously, values of number of reinforcements are discontinuous. For purposes of quantitative treatment, it has been implicitly assumed that they are continuous (Hull, 1943; Deese, 1950a). No serious error seems to have resulted from this assumption.

call *M*. Finally, note characteristic 3, that increments in reinforcement get smaller and smaller as response strength reaches its limit *M*. This is another way of saying that the ratio $d(R)/d(N)$ gets smaller as *R* approaches *M*.

The student who shies away from mathematics may have gotten lost by this time. In that case, he may find it convenient simply to take our word for the rest. At any rate, all that has been said in the preceding paragraph may be written down simply in the differential equation

$$d(R)/d(N) = k(M - R)$$

in which *k* is a constant of proportionality. This expresses what we have been saying in words. All we need to do, to get a curve that looks like the learning curves of Figs. 2, 3, and 4, is to integrate this differential equation. The result is
$$R = M - Me^{-kn}$$

This is an exponential equation written in the form that can apply to a learning curve.

This equation, or something very close to it, has frequently been embodied as a fundamental assumption in a theory of learning (Hull, 1943; Estes, 1950). It is not a rational equation in the mathematical sense, for it is not based on known factors in the learning process. Instead, it has been chosen because it happens to fit learning curves with the three characteristics that we considered above. This much, however, is an important first step in learning theory, for it does give us a generalized description of many of the facts of learning. In the future, however, we seriously need a rational explanation, in terms of what goes on in learning, of the factors that make the exponential equation a good fit for the experimental facts (see Estes, 1950).

## Time of Reinforcement and Secondary Reinforcement

In the preceding section, we considered the way in which *number of reinforcements* increases strength of response as seen in (1) decreasing latent period, (2) increasing magnitude of response, and (3) increasing per cent of correct conditioned responses. Now we turn from number of reinforcements to *time of reinforcement* and consider its effect upon strength of response. In doing this, we shall be introduced to some new concepts, namely, gradient of reinforcement, secondary reinforcement, and the goal gradient, for it was experiments on time of reinforcement and its effect on strength of response that in part led psychologists to formulate these concepts.

How close in time does the reinforcement have to be to the response before it will increase the strength of that response? Psychologists long ago saw that this is a fundamental question, so they have carried out a good many experiments that are designed to answer it.

*The gradient of reinforcement.* One experiment by Perin (1943) makes use of rats in a Skinner box and demonstrates the relation between the time of reinforcement and strength of response. To do this experiment, Perin slightly modified the lever in the Skinner box; he simply projected a rod into the box and used it for a lever. He began the experiment with a period in which the rats were habituated or made accustomed to the box, and during that period the rat could move the rod either to the right or to the left to get a pellet of food. After the animal had learned to move the rod in both directions and had displayed its preference for one or the other, the apparatus was changed. It was changed so that a movement of the rod in the preferred direction would give no food, and a movement of the rod in the nonpreferred direction would cause the rod to be withdrawn and the food pellet to be delivered.

The important point of the experiment is that the reinforcement (food pellet) was given some time after the response (lever pressing); this time ranged from 30 seconds down to 0 seconds. As you can see in Fig. 5, the results were clear: The rate of learning was faster when the reinforcement was delivered closely after the response. As a matter of fact, the rats learned so slowly with the longer time delays that the experimenter predicted that they would not learn at all if the time between response and the reinforcement were extended to about 40 seconds. Figure 5 shows the whole relationship of the delay between response and reinforcement and the speed of learning. Because this curve is typical of such experiments, it is convenient to have a name for it, the *gradient of reinforcement.*

*Secondary reinforcement.* There is a curious fact about Perin's experiment. Of all the experiments which have demonstrated the gradient of reinforcement, Perin's is practically the only one which shows the gradient to reach zero after such a short delay. Wolfe (1934) reports an experiment, for example, that shows a gradient of reinforcement just as does Perin's, but in his case the gradient is longer and much more gradual. Indeed he finds that food reinforcement is effective with rats even after a delay of 20 minutes between response and reinforcement.

What is the explanation of the difference between these results? In answer to this question, we meet one of the most important principles of learning, that of secondary reinforcement. Hull (1943) gave it an explicit formulation in terms of modern learning theory, but Pavlov was its discoverer. So it is appropriate to illustrate the principle by drawing on an experiment from Pavlov's laboratory (1927).

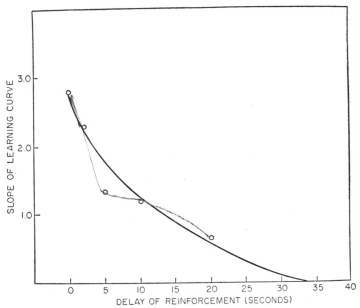

FIG. 5. Slope of learning curves as a function of the time between response and reinforcement. The curve is extrapolated, on the basis of the five plotted points, to show zero learning at a delay between 30 and 35 seconds. (*Redrawn from Perin, 1943.*)

As in nearly all his experiments, Pavlov did this one with the salivary response of the dog. As we all know, this response, salivation, occurs when foods are put in the mouth, but it does not happen ordinarily when other stimuli, such as lights and sounds, are used. To measure the salivary response, Pavlov rigged up a special device that would measure quite accurately the amount of saliva the dog would secrete each time he presented a stimulus. His now famous conditioning procedure was to present some neutral stimulus, like the ticking of a metronome, then follow it by giving food to the dog. Of course, after a few reinforcements with food, the dog soon became conditioned to the sound of the metronome and secreted saliva when it heard the sound. This, of course, is simple conditioning. For our purposes here, however, we should specify it more precisely as *first-order conditioning*.

But Pavlov carried the experiment a step further. He presented a black cardboard square to the dog. As we might expect, no saliva flowed to this stimulus. The black cardboard square was then paired ten times with the ticking metronome, given without food. By the tenth trial, the black square made the dog give a salivary response, *even though it had never been paired with the unconditioned stimulus or received any reinforcement*. This procedure, Pavlov called *higher order conditioning*. It is an illustration, however, of what we nowadays call *secondary reinforcement*. In the procedure, the conditioned stimulus not only gives a conditioned response, but it also acquires the ability to act as a reinforcing agent (Hull, 1943). It is this acquired reinforcement that is the *secondary reinforcement*. Indeed, any example of higher order conditioning is an example of the operation of secondary reinforcement.

*Secondary reinforcement and the gradient of reinforcement*. We are now in a position to understand the reason why Wolfe's and Perin's experiments concerning the gradient of reinforcement came out with such different results. Wolfe made use of a simple maze shaped like a T. The animal in this maze must make only one choice on each trial, so that it is just about the simplest kind of maze problem. The goal box at the end of one arm of the T contained food, the goal box at the other end did not. Otherwise, both goal boxes and both arms of the T were exactly the same. The maze had doors just before the goal boxes, so that the animals could be retained in the arms of the T for a period of time before they were allowed to enter the goal box. Thus the arms of the T served as retention chambers.

It was the retention chamber that accounts for the difference between the experiments. Because it was regularly associated with food, which is a primary reinforcement, it came to be a conditioned stimulus, and, as such, could serve as a secondary reinforcing agent. That is to say, the retention chamber in itself served to reward the animals to some extent; hence, the animals learned to turn in one direction to reach the retention chamber associated with food even when they had to wait afterward for food. Thus, no matter how long the animals were delayed before they entered the goal box, they could learn to turn to the side with food—simply because of the secondary reinforcement associated with the retention chamber. Of that we can be sure, for Saltzman (1949), in an experiment that ties in well with Wolfe's, has clearly demonstrated that rats can learn a simple T maze entirely on the basis of secondary reinforcement.

It is interesting that Perin's experiment, unlike Wolfe's, had in it no stimuli that could provide secondary reinforcement. In fact, Perin went to a good deal of trouble to make certain of it. He built his apparatus so that the rod the rat pushed to get food was withdrawn as soon as it was pushed. So the rod, which otherwise might have become a conditioned stimulus that could serve in secondary reinforcement, was never present except when the delay between response and primary reinforcement was zero. Thus there was minimal opportunity for the lever to acquire the power of secondary reinforcement. As a result, the amount of delay between the primary reinforcement and the response had to be very short if the animal were to learn, for there was little or no secondary reinforcement to bridge the gap.

*The gradient of reinforcement and the goal gradient.* By this time, you can probably see that there are two types of gradients of reinforcement. If no opportunity for secondary reinforcement is present, there is a very small range of delays between response and reinforcement which will result in learning. This small gradient, exemplified in Perin's experiment, Hull (1943) has called the *gradient of reinforcement.* This is really a gradient of *primary* reinforcement. If, on the other hand, there is an opportunity for animals to bridge delays through secondary reinforcement, there will exist a longer gradient which, following Hull, can be called the *goal gradient.* This term refers to a gradient of *secondary* reinforcement.

Using Wolfe's and Perin's data as models, Hull has formulated the relationship of the goal gradient to the gradient of reinforcement. With any particular amount of reinforcement, he states, maximal response strength decays with time separating the response from the reinforcement. The limit of this decay, of course, is zero response strength. As opportunities for secondary reinforcement are added, however, the slower will be the rate of fall of the gradient. Such a gradient, resulting from the addition of cues for secondary reinforcement, Hull calls the *goal gradient.*

So far we have supposed that there are two gradients of reinforcement, one primary and the other secondary. Against this notion, however, Spence (1947) pits a rather radical suggestion, that the gradient of primary reinforcement may not exist at all. That is to say, when all cues for secondary reinforcement are entirely eliminated, there may be no learning unless the response and the primary reinforcement occur at exactly the same moment.

If this proposition be true—and Spence makes a good case for it—then any gradient of response strength that we obtain with delay in reinforcement would mean that some secondary reinforcement is present. Whether Spence is right or not we do not know.

The important thing, however, is that there is a temporal gradient of the effectiveness of reinforcement which varies as a function of the opportunity for secondary reinforcement. When the opportunity for secondary reinforcement is small, the gradient is short; when the opportunity for secondary reinforcement is large, the gradient is long (Perkins, 1947).

### Amount of Reinforcement

Do different amounts of a reinforcing stimulus have differing abilities to increase response strength? This, like the question of the time between reinforcement and response, is one of the fundamental questions which can be answered experimentally. Of especial interest is the effect of amount of reinforcement on magnitude of response and on time of response.

*Amount of reinforcement and magnitude of response.* An experiment by Gantt, which Hull (1943) makes use of, will give us some notion of the relationship between amount of reinforcement and magnitude of response.[2] This was a study with the conditioned salivary response of the dog. The dog in question was conditioned to four different stimuli, one of which was reinforced by ½ gram of food, one by 1 gram, one by 2 grams, and one by 12 grams. These four conditioned responses were reinforced in a random order. After a long period of training, the animal apparently learned to respond differentially to the four different stimuli, according to the amount of reinforcement associated with them. Figure 6 shows that the conditioned stimuli associated with the larger amounts of reinforcement resulted in larger conditioned responses.

*Amount of reinforcement and time of response.* Another experiment by Grindley (1929) shows a similar relationship between amount of reinforcement and response strength. Grindley used a runway, and chickens were his subjects. He measured the rate at which the chickens ran down the runway for different amounts of rice. To put his results briefly, 1 grain of rice, he found, resulted in much slower rates of running than did 6 grains of rice.

[2] Gantt supplied Hull with some unpublished data from an earlier experiment (Gantt, 1938).

A similar experiment, however, complicates the picture. In this experiment (Wolfe and Kaplon, 1941), ¼ kernel of corn, 1 kernel, and 4 kernels were used as the different amounts of reinforcement. As in Grindley's experiment, the largest amount of reinforcement led to the greatest response strength. But an interesting paradox turned up. Four quarter kernels of corn proved to be distinctly more reinforcing than a single kernel of the same size as the four put together. Just why this happened we do not know,

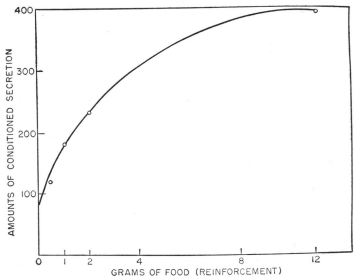

FIG. 6. Amount of conditioned salivary secretion as a function of amount of reinforcement. (*Data supplied by Gantt, redrawn from Hull, 1943.*)

but it is possible that the amount of activity involved in eating may have something to do with it, for it takes more activity to eat the four quarter kernels than it does to eat one whole kernel.

More recent experiments add some new information. One of them (Crespi, 1942, 1944) confirms the earlier experiments: the greater the size of the reinforcement, the greater the response strength. Another one (Zeaman, 1949b) turns up a new point. To understand it, one should go back to the equation (p. 19) describing the typical learning curve. In this equation there are two constants besides the fixed constant e. One, M, sets the limit of learning or, put another way, the maximum response strength; the other, k, reflects the rate of increase of response. In this experiment (*i.e.,* Zeaman, 1949b), it was the *limit* of response strength that was affected by the amount of reinforcement; the limits were different for different amounts of reinforcement. The *rate* of approach to these limits, however, was the same for different amounts of reinforcement.

There is no certain interpretation of these results, but there is one that has a considerable amount of logic to it. We can think of the limit, $M$, as a measure of *performance* that reflects principally the degree of motivation of the subject and of the rate, $k$, as the rate at which learning takes place. If that be the case, we can then say, from these results, that amount of reinforcement affects motivation or willingness to perform, but not the rate of learning (increase of response strength) per se (see Crespi, 1944; Seward, 1951).

## THEORIES OF REINFORCEMENT

Little has been said thus far about any theory of reinforcement. In fact, the whole issue was avoided at the beginning of this chapter by accepting an operational definition that said nothing about the causes of reinforcement. The question of why reinforcement occurs, however, is an important one and one that has attracted considerable attention. The attempt to find the basic cause of reinforcement has led to several theories of reinforcement, and it is these we shall examine now.

Unfortunately, like many other basic problems in psychology, the exact nature of reinforcement remains an unsolved problem. In the absence of any definite information we must content ourselves with examining the alternative theories of reinforcement and what evidence bears on them. At this point, the reader will do well to remember the importance of keeping fact and theory separate, for we cannot accept, with any degree of finality, any theory at the present time. Indeed, the operational definition of reinforcement must serve as our mainstay for a while yet. That should not discourage us, however, from trying to develop a sound theory of reinforcement.

There are alternative theories of reinforcement, and these seem to fall rather distinctly into two classes, what we may call *effect theories* and what we may call *contiguity theories*. Because we cannot stop to treat separately each slightly different twist on these two basic notions, a sort of composite picture of each type of theory must be attempted. To achieve this, it will be necessary to draw a little from this theorist and something else from that theorist. It is well to remember that what comes out is not necessarily the view of one man, but a sort of montage of slightly different aspects of the same view.

## The Effect Theory of Reinforcement

One answer to the question why some stimuli are reinforcing and others are not is to say that some stimuli have a special *effect* upon the person or animal and that it is this effect which is important to learning. There are many notions as to just what this effect may be, and we shall examine them in some detail.

*Natural selection and learning.* The principle of effect in learning is historically related to Darwin's theory of natural selection in evolution. Darwin and his successors undertook to explain the process of species evolution in terms of natural selective breeding. The characteristics of organisms that are adaptive survive, said Darwin, but the characteristics that are unadaptive die out. The early theorists of evolution pointed out all sorts of examples of anatomical and physiological characteristics that were adaptive and that seemed to make for selective breeding. Thus in evolution, biological changes in organisms have "good" and "bad" effects, and, according to the natural selection theory, only the changes with "good" effects survive.

Behavior patterns provide many good examples of the survival of adaptive, instinctive mechanisms. Thus natural selection can be extended to the behavior of animals, on the phylogenetic or species scale. Certain kinds of stereotyped mating reactions, for example, have a survival value, and it is not difficult to see why the early theorists in evolution thought that they had survived as a result of natural selection.

In an ontogenetic scale, that is, within the lifetime of the individual, as well as in the evolutionary scale, there appears to be a process of selective adaptation. Organisms seem to learn those things which are useful—they learn the location of food supplies, water, hiding places, etc.—and investigators of animal behavior who followed Darwin presented us with many examples, some a little fanciful, of such adaptiveness in animal learning. It is not surprising that the first experimental studies of animal learning were conceived from this point of view (Hobhouse, 1901).

The successors of Darwin argued that behavior that preserved the organism from harm and kept it fed and sheltered survived, whereas unadaptive behavior did not survive. This basic notion was combined with the theory of hedonism. Pleasure, it was held, is associated with adaptive responses and pain with nonadaptive behavior. Thus pleasure and pain became mechanisms in the theory of evolution.

*The principle of effect.* E. L. Thorndike, now famous for his work in this field, gave us the first statement of the principle of effect that was based upon experimental observations (Thorndike, 1898). Thorndike had worked with animals and their ways of learning for many years, and the principle he stated was firmly based on his observations. He called this principle the *law of effect.* What the law said was that responses were learned or fixated because of their effects or consequences.

When he first stated his principle, Thorndike put it in terms of satisfaction. Responses which have satisfying effects, he said, are fixated or stamped in, but those which do not have satisfying effects are dropped out or eliminated. Since the term "satisfying" is vague and a little subjective, Thorndike was very careful to specify exactly what he meant by it. A satisfying object was something that an organism would exert effort to achieve.

Since Thorndike's original statement, the principle of effect has been restated in many different ways; each was an attempt to be more precise or objective. One of the best of the modern statements of the principle was made by McGeoch in his book on human learning (McGeoch, 1942). McGeoch (1942, p. 574) subdivides the principle into three statements:

"Acts are fixated and eliminated as functions of their effects.

"Acts followed by a state of affairs which the individual does nothing to avoid, and which he often tries to preserve and attain are selected and fixated, while acts followed by states of affairs which the individual avoids or attempts to change are eliminated.

"Other things being equal, acts leading to consequences which satisfy a motivating condition are selected and strengthened, while those leading to consequences which do not satisfy a motivating condition are eliminated."

*Need reduction.* The first two of McGeoch's three statements are purely operational, for they refer to events we can observe. The second statement, for example, talks about animals avoiding things or striving to attain things, and we can easily point out such events. The third statement, however, goes a good deal beyond a purely operational statement. It gives a reason why reinforcing stimuli are reinforcing. It says that they are reinforcing because they satisfy a motive state. Thus we have a new idea, the idea that reinforcing stimuli have their effects upon motive states.

Of those who have been working on the problem of learning, C. L. Hull (1943) has given us the most complete theory of the relationship of motivation to the effect theory of reinforcement. He points out that organisms can be regarded, in one sense, simply as bundles of needs. These needs are a result of the continuously active processes of the body. Hunger, for example, gradually comes about because stores of food in the tissues of the body become depleted, and thirst is a result of the continuous loss of water from the body. Needs also arise as a result of things in the environment. A dog, for example, that steps on a thorn has a need to remove its tissues from injury. Similarly, cold or rain or other kinds of "uncomfortable" stimulation set up needs.

Now, says Hull, the function of behavior is to satisfy these needs, that is, to get the organism back into a state of equilibrium. Thus needs bring about responses. The dog, for example, that steps on a thorn flexes its leg in order to remove the painful stimulation. Stimuli, such as dryness in the throat, that are associated with thirst bring the organism to drink.

The basic point to Hull's theory concerns the effect of behavioral responses upon the need. Some kinds of behavior serve to reduce the need state of the animal. If the need is for water, for example, then drinking responses alleviate the need. Naturally, when behavior succeeds in reducing a need, the stimulation that arises from the need is also reduced. This characteristic of need reduction, according to Hull, is the defining characteristic of reinforcing stimuli. Reinforcement is reinforcement because it has the effect of reducing needs in the organism. In Hull's own words (1943, p. 80): "Whenever an effector activity occurs in temporal contiguity with the afferent impulse, or the perseverative trace of such an impulse, resulting from the impact of a stimulus energy upon a receptor, and this conjunction is closely associated in time with the diminution in the receptor discharge characteristic of a need, there will result an increment in the tendency for that stimulus on subsequent occasions to evoke that reaction."

*Need-reduction theory and the Skinner-box example.* We can see how this principle would work out in the example of the rat in the Skinner box. The rat is made hungry by deprivation of food for several hours before the experiment begins. So the rat has internal stimuli which are the result of the need for food. The rat is placed in the box, and eventually sees the bar (stimulus), then depresses it (response). As a result it gets a pellet of food (reinforcement), and when it eats the food, in due course it satisfies its hunger and reduces the internal stimulation. Thus the reduction of internal stimulation is closely associated with the stimulus-response unit of sight-of-bar—pressing-bar. According to the principle of need reduction, it is this association which is reinforcing and which makes the rat have a greater tendency to press the bar in the future.

*The operational view of effect.* Thus far it has been very difficult to obtain any direct test of the assumptions of the need-reduction theory. There are some grounds for distrusting the notion, at least in its present form. We are not sure that needs always act to influence behavior by producing stimuli. It is possible that some of the primary needs, such as sex and hunger and thirst, act directly through chemical effects upon the nervous system (Morgan and Stellar, 1950). If that be the case, only by stretching the definition of stimulus can we still think of needs as stimuli. Far more important, however, is the fact that we have no direct evidence that reinforced responses, as operationally defined, actually do serve to reduce needs.

For this reason, those who want to stick as closely as possible to observable events and to operational definitions have rejected or ignored the need-reduction theory of effect. They represent several gradations in their viewpoints—McGeoch's statement was closer, and Thorndike's original conception even closer, than Hull's to an operational definition—but the modern psychologist who holds most closely to an operational view is Skinner. He is content to point out observable facts. He has evidence which leads him to believe that hungry rats learn to press bars while satiated rats do not. This fact, says Skinner, makes it clear that the reinforcing value of a stimulus does depend upon motivation, and it permits us to hold on to the *adaptive* aspects of an effect theory. Knowing little more than this, however, Skinner feels that he is not justified in assuming specific mechanisms for effect.

## The Contiguity Theory of Reinforcement

It seems fairly obvious, although it may not be true, that some stimuli are reinforcing and some are not. Food, for example, appears to be reinforcing for a hungry person or rat, but lights and bells are not—unless they have acquired secondary reinforcement. To effect theorists this difference is accepted as fact and taken as something to be explained. It is not so obvious, however, to another group of theorists, the contiguity theorists. Indeed, they deny that certain stimuli are intrinsically reinforcing while others are not. Instead they assert that *all* stimuli have, potentially, the property of reinforcement.

This radically different kind of theory is called the contiguity theory or association theory because it lays its entire emphasis upon the contiguous association of stimuli and responses. Contiguity theory has its origins in the philosophy of associationism, but its modern application to the psychology of learning is largely due to the efforts of E. R. Guthrie (1930, 1935). Consequently, we shall draw our account of contiguity theory largely from the work of Guthrie.

*The principle of contiguity.* A definition of reinforcement according to the principle of contiguity is very simple. Guthrie's definition says: "A combination of stimuli which has accompanied a movement will on the recurrence tend to be followed by that movement" (Guthrie, 1935, p. 26). This means that any stimulus which happens to strike the organism at the same time it is making a movement will have the ability to elicit that movement in the future. According to Guthrie, nothing is necessary to define reinforcement except that stimuli and movements occur together.

Now we come to the question: If that is what the contiguity theorist thinks reinforcement is, how can he explain the fact that some stimuli are much better than others in reinforcing responses? In answering this question, he reasons thus: Motives bring out certain responses to certain stimuli; for example, an animal must be hungry before it will respond to the stimulus of food by eating it. Then, of course, in addition to motivation, there must be a reward, that is, the reinforcing stimulus, to bring out the particular response, say, eating. So motivation and reward are important because they make responses occur, but that is all that is important about them.

To see how this idea works out, let us take our stock example of the Skinner box. Moreover, let us take two different kinds of situation. The first one is the conventional one. The hungry rat in the Skinner box sees the bar at the same time it presses it. This, of course, produces a pellet of food which it promptly eats. When it finishes the pellet, it looks at the bar again. In the past, looking at the bar has been associated, through contiguity, with pressing the bar, so it presses it again. And so on.

Now to understand why this situation, according to the contiguity theorist, makes the rat learn to press the bar, let us take a second case. Suppose when the rat first pushed the bar—while looking at it—it heard the sound of a buzzer instead of getting a pellet of food. The buzzer would not have made it do anything in particular and it would have wandered away from the bar. Then, at some distance from the bar, it would look at it again but not be able to press it. So it would learn to do something else besides pressing the bar when it saw it.

In either case, the rat learns to do whatever it is it has done. If it always, or nearly always, pushes the bar when it sees it, the response of pushing it is associated with seeing it. If it is somewhere else and doing something else when it sees it, it learns to do that something else instead of pushing the bar.

All this means, in the view of the contiguity theorist, that motivation and reward simply determine what the animal does. The pellet of food keeps the rat in the vicinity of the bar where it can push the bar when it sees it. It also keeps the rat from doing other things, like wandering around the cage, after it presses the bar, and thus it keeps the rat from learning the "wrong" responses. So, in a word, reward or reinforcement has no unique or intrinsic effect; it determines what responses the animal makes and thus what responses can become associated, through contiguity, with stimuli that are present.

*Contiguity theory and one-trial learning.* One important point made by Guthrie in his contiguity theory of learning is that an association between any stimulus and a movement is an all-or-none affair which takes only one trial. What, then, does Guthrie do about the common observation that it takes several reinforcements to bring to full strength even a simple conditioned response? The answer is very simple, and it hinges on the definition of the word "response." Response, as we have used it thus far, is not the simplest unit of behavior. As a matter of fact, from the physiologist's point of view, it is a very complicated thing. Some examples will make this clear.

If you ask someone to move his right arm in an arc from right to left very slowly, several times, each attempt will be slightly different. Different muscle groups will be involved to different degrees in each repetition. There will be minute differences in the patterns of muscular activity. Guthrie takes something like the physiologist's view. He considers the minute response of a muscle to be the unit of response.

There are many examples of everyday responses, for which functionally equivalent repetitions are vastly different in detail. A response of opening a door may be accomplished in several ways. The doorknob may be turned with the right hand or it may be turned with the left hand. The hand may push the door open or the shoulder may help. Yet these are all equivalent when considered from the point of view of getting the door open. A rat in pressing a lever in the Skinner box may do it in several different ways; the definition of a response in the Skinner box is exactly like the definition of the response of getting the door opened; the definition is in terms of an effect upon the environment.

It is the movements involved in a response which are important. In order for a response, such as lever pressing, to be performed correctly on every trial, it is necessary for many different movements to be learned while other movements are unlearned. Thus, while association by contiguity is an all-or-none affair, learning in practice appears to be a gradual affair.

Very recently, at least one theorist (Estes, 1950) has concerned himself with the problem of generating theoretical equations, like that on page 19, from a consideration of the statistical problems involved in this view of the unit of response. He considers what would happen mathematically if a given movement were contiguous with different samples from an available population of stimuli. All the potential stimuli in the Skinner box, for example, constitute a population of stimuli; at any one moment the rat is stimulated only by a sample of these. Sometimes these samples will overlap with one another a great deal, and occasionally not at all. From the laws of probability, Estes generates learning curves based on the frequency with which successive stimulus samples will contain common elements. The mathematics of Estes's treatment is rather complex, but the interested student will find it very worth while to consult his paper.

*Varieties of contiguity theory.* There are many other kinds of association theories besides Guthrie's. Some are in entirely different settings and actually appear to be opposed to Guthrie's views, but their notions of reinforcement are not basically different. One such theory, propounded by Tolman (1932) and his students, takes the view that rewards are important in performance but not in learning. By this distinction the theory says that learning is basically a matter of association of stimuli and responses, but that these associations do not show themselves unless motivation and reward are present. For example, a rat in a bar-pressing box may learn that the sight of the bar and pressing the bar go together, but it will not demonstrate that it has learned this unless it is hungry and gets food when it presses the bar.

## A CHOICE BETWEEN THEORIES

Which of the theories of reinforcement is correct? We do not know at present, for if we did it would not be necessary to present both of them at such great length. We can, however, look at some experiments which have been designed as tests of one or another of the theories. These experiments do not provide crucial tests, of course, but they may help us to decide which of the theories is the one we can put the most stock in at the present. In some ways it is not necessary to make such a decision, but on the other hand, because reinforcement is so basic to learning, a decision would make some difference in how we go about other problems in learning.

## The Latent-learning Experiments

There are a whole group of experiments which grew out of Tolman's particular version of contiguity theory. These experiments, known as latent-learning experiments, have been less concerned with demonstrating the correctness of the contiguity theory than with demonstrating the incorrectness of the effect theory.

According to the effect theory, some psychologists have reasoned, a reinforcing stimulus is that which will satisfy the prevailing motive state. This would be food to the hungry rat, and water to the thirsty rat. If that is true, animals that do not have an opportunity to satisfy their drives in a situation ought not to learn. This line of reasoning has led to the so-called latent-learning experiments. Since these experiments have been among the most important grounds for arguments between the effect theories and the contiguity theories, we shall examine them in detail.

*Blodgett's experiment.* The classical latent-learning experiment is one performed by Blodgett (1929). He allowed one group of hungry rats to explore a maze, but without food in the goal box. This group, therefore, had no reinforcement in the sense that the effect theorist speaks of reinforcement. In addition, Blodgett allowed a second group of hungry rats to explore the maze, but this group was given food in the goal box, and it therefore received conventional reinforcement.

There was a difference between the behavior of these two groups. The group which was reinforced with food seemed to learn on schedule, but the other unreinforced group showed no signs of improvement. After seven days, the rats in this group were entering just as many blind alleys in the maze as they did on the first day. At this time, however, Blodgett introduced the food into the goal box. Their performance suddenly and dramatically improved, so that almost immediately they made as few errors as the rats which had been reinforced all along.

These results can be seen in Fig. 7. They show us that the rats which did not receive food as reinforcement were able to profit from their "experience" in the maze, though the results of such experience did not show up until a reward or goal was introduced. Since the evidence of learning taking place during the nonrewarded series did not occur until food was present, the learning was said to be "latent."

*Other latent-learning experiments.* Several investigators have repeated Blodgett's experiment. One such early repetition (Tolman and Honzik, 1930), with a better controlled situation, showed striking confirmation of Blodgett's results. Proponents of the principle of effect, however, showed that there were many defects in these experiments. It is possible, for example, that removing the animals from the goal box could provide rein-

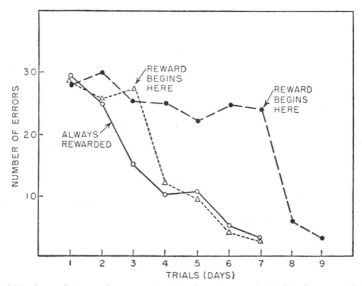

FIG. 7. Number of errors in rewarded and nonrewarded trials in maze learning. When the reward is introduced, errors drop to a level comparable to errors made by animals continuously rewarded. (*Redrawn from Blodgett, 1929.*)

forcement by effect. Critics also pointed out that the great improvement in behavior that showed up as soon as food reward was introduced was not much greater than the difference between the first and second trials for the control group. You see this point in Fig. 8. Therefore, it has been argued, the improvement which resulted from the introduction of reward for the latent-learning group is just about the order of magnitude one would expect at the beginning of learning.

These criticisms have been effectively answered in another experiment (Buxton, 1940). In this one, rats were permitted to live in the maze for a period of several days. They were placed in the maze at different positions and removed from it at different positions. Consequently, the animals explored all parts of the maze to about the same extent, and they were not differentially rewarded by being removed from any particular part of the maze.

The really important result of this experiment is that it was not necessary to give the rats one rewarded trial before the sudden improvement in performance occurred. Instead of allowing the rats to run through the maze in order to discover the food for the first time, the experimenter put the

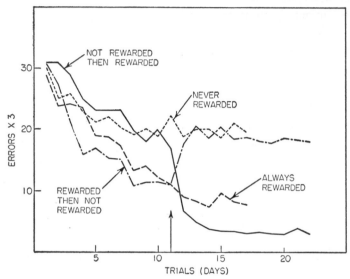

Fig. 8. Number of errors in rewarded and nonrewarded trials in maze learning. The results of this study are in exact confirmation of those shown in Fig. 7. (*Redrawn from Tolman and Honzik, 1930.*)

rats directly into the goal box, so that they had a chance to see that food was there. After that, when they were put at the beginning of the maze, most of the rats were able to find their way to the goal box without making very many errors. This experiment, then, provides one of the best examples of latent learning, and it must be admitted that it is a very difficult experiment to interpret within the framework of the effect theory of reinforcement.

A subsequent experiment (Seward, 1949), moreover, confirms it. This made use of the same technique of prefeeding the animals in the goal box just before the test trial. The two experiments taken together present excellent evidence that animals can learn to find their way about, even though their behavior is not differentially rewarded. There are many other experiments besides these two, and the interested reader can find a good review of them in a paper by Thistlethwaite (1951).[3]

*Tolman's interpretation of latent learning.* The latent-learning experiments have been strongest ammunition for the type of contiguity theory sponsored by Tolman (1932). He maintains that there must be a clear separation between learning and performance. To him, a *learned* act— which he describes as a "learned environmental cognition"—may be used when the animal is motivated and rewarded, but motivation and reward are not always essential to the learning process. This means, by inference, that drive reduction is not always essential to the learning process. The latent-learning experiments support this view very well. In the first place, they show that animals learn even when it is not immediately evident in their performance at the moment. Secondly, they appear to learn whether they are rewarded or not.

The cognitive version of contiguity theory advanced by Tolman is a little different from the contiguity theory advanced by Guthrie. Tolman does not put so much emphasis upon rigid stimulus-response bonds. Tolman's contiguity theory is a theory of stimuli as signs which lead to other stimuli (stimulus-stimulus bonds) rather than a theory of stimulus-response bonds. From this point of view, animals learn "what leads to what" rather than stimulus-response connections. Because the latent-learning experiments were conceived within the framework of Tolman's theory, this theory has an easy job interpreting them (see Spence, 1942b).

### Some Conditioning Experiments

There is another group of experiments which have been designed to test the adequacy of the effect theory of reinforcement. These experiments are more directly concerned with Guthrie's version of contiguity theory than are the latent-learning experiments. A review of a few of these experiments will give us a look at another aspect of the problem of effect theory and contiguity theory.

*Avoidance conditioning and reinforcement theory.* One experiment, now a classical one, is by Brogden, Lipman, and Culler (1938). They set it

[3] It is only fair to mention that some investigators (Reynolds, 1945c; Meehl and MacCorquodale, 1951) have failed to find latent learning in experiments designed like Blodgett's.

up to test whether need reduction is or is not necessary for learning. To make the test they used the guinea pig as an experimental animal and put the animal in a revolving cage that had electrodes attached to it, so that the animal could be shocked. The standard procedure was to sound a tone, which the animal could plainly hear, then turn on the shock.

There were two different groups of animals, each of which got somewhat different treatment. In one group, if the animals learned to run to the tone (thereby anticipating the shock) they did not get a shock. In other words, they could learn to avoid the shock by responding to the tone. The other group of guinea pigs got shocks irrespective of what they did. They could not accomplish anything by running; they did not reduce the need to avoid painful stimulation. In a word, the first group could learn by the effect principle or by the contiguity principle, but the second group could learn only by the contiguity principle.

The question is how well these two groups of animals learned to run when they heard the tone. They both learned, but one did not learn so well as the other. The animals that could avoid the shock by running to the tone learned fairly quickly to run 100 per cent of the time. The other group, which could not avoid the shock, learned to run about 50 per cent of the time. Thus the results of the experiment appear to be ambiguous. On the face of it, both kinds of learning seem to take place, but pure contiguity learning is not nearly so effective as learning by the principle of effect.

Unfortunately, this experiment, like the latent-learning experiments, is not crucial. It is plain to see that shock makes animals emotional, just as it does people. Some people seem to relieve their emotional tensions by running or engaging in activity, and perhaps guinea pigs do, too. If that is the case, even though the animals in the contiguity group could not get away from shock, they might have been reducing their emotional needs. If we were to accept this possibility, we would then conclude that there was effect learning in the second group as well as in the first.

*Sheffield's experiment.* Unfortunately, this problem of tension reduction in the contiguity group (the second group above) has never been settled. A second experiment (Sheffield, 1948), however, removes some of the ambiguity. In this experiment, the investigator noted very carefully exactly what the animals did when they were shocked. He observed that running was not always the response that occurred when the animals were shocked; in fact, some animals made responses that were incompatible with running.

Some animals crouched to the shock rather than ran. Within the group of animals who were not allowed to avoid the shock, the animals that did not learn to run were those that did not run when they were shocked in the first place. Those that did learn to run were those whose natural response to shock tended to be running.

This result, of course, puts a different light on the experiment by Brogden, Lipman, and Culler. It tends to account for the difference between the 100 per cent and the 50 per cent conditioned responses in the two groups. Animals associated with the stimulus whatever they did at the moment the stimulus came on. If they happened to be crouching when the tone came on, they learned to crouch to the tone. This accounts for the fact that only 50 per cent of the animals in the pure contiguity group learned to run. Since learning in the avoidance situation also can be explained by contiguity or association, it makes us think that contiguity may indeed be all that is necessary for learning. The experiment is not crucial, but like the latent-learning experiments, it points to the possibility that the principle of effect may be unnecessary.

*Seward's experiment.* A third experiment is an attempt to test the contiguity theory rather than the effect theory. To understand it, you will recall that the function of a reward, according to Guthrie, is to prevent the behavior from being unlearned, or to keep the "wrong" thing from being learned. With this point in mind, Seward (1942) attempted to substitute something for a reward, according to the way a reward acts in Guthrie's theory, that would still permit learning. Instead of rewarding the animal with a pellet of food for pressing the lever in a Skinner box, Seward removed the animal from the box after it had pressed the bar. This ought to preserve the response from being unlearned, argued Seward, just about as well as a reward. Seward compared the *time* that it took the animals to get around to pressing the bar (*a*) when they were rewarded with a pellet of food, (*b*) when they were removed from the box, and (*c*) when nothing happened after the response occurred. According to his measures, the animals that were removed from the box did learn to press the lever, since they did much better than the group which had nothing as a consequence of the bar-pressing response. They did not do so well, however, as the group which was rewarded with food for pressing the bar. So, the results of this experiment appear to be just about as equivocal as those of the Brogden, Lipman, and Culler experiment. Further, effect theorists might argue, it is conceivable that removal from the box constitutes a reward (need reduction). This is not a very great possibility, but the mere fact that it can be suggested prevents Seward's experiment from being a crucial test.[4]

## A Choice Between the Theories

Though the experimental evidence leans toward the contiguity theory, the weight of common sense seems to be on the side of the principle of effect. People and animals do seem to learn things when they get what they want or avoid what they do not want. That tends to place the burden of proof on the contiguity theory to prove that it is right. Yet, when we turn to physiology, the need-reduction version of the effect theory has its drawbacks. Indeed, it is becoming less and less plausible as we learn more and more about how needs affect the nervous system and behavior. This point is against the effect theory.[5] In contrast, the contiguity theory is simple and direct. It requires only one basic principle, while effect theory is frequently complex and cumbersome.

*Need we choose between the theories?* We have already seen that there is no crucial evidence on one side or the other. The weight of the experimental evidence seems to be against the effect theory, but this is only by inference. We shall examine some additional evidence at a later point, some of which seems to be against the effect theory and some in favor of the effect theory, but none of it is crucial.

The difficulty of finding a situation which seems to favor one theory or the other has led some psychologists to question seriously whether or not there is a real difference between these theories. In the main they seem to lead to the same predictions. Contiguity theory predicts that animals will learn when they are rewarded, but for different reasons than does the effect theory. On the other hand, effect theorists have a ready answer when animals seem to learn when there is no apparent reward in the situation, but to do that they suggest all sorts of rewards which might not occur to us at first glance. That, in itself, is a shortcoming. And since the theories do lead to nearly the same predictions, if one can get beneath the different words they use, must they not be essentially the same?

[4] Of course, there are many other experiments that could be cited as being in favor of either contiguity or effect theory. For example, the studies of sensory preconditioning (Brogden, 1939, 1947) are some that can most easily be interpreted in terms of contiguity theory. Again, however, none of these experiments is crucial.

[5] Miller and Dollard's (1941) distinction between drive reduction and need reduction tends to get around this objection.

Several psychologists have taken this point of view. Skinner (1950) underscores it and goes further. To him the important function of psychology is to predict and control behavior. If one theory does this about as well as another, let us ignore theories—we will never learn anything new by theorizing anyway—and let us get on with studies that will help us to predict and control behavior.

It seems very likely at this moment that the only way out of this dilemma lies in the direction of new evidence, rather than elaboration of present theories and the recapitulation of already tried experimental designs. It is very probable that the most fruitful source of new evidence will be on the border line between psychology and physiology, because it is here that the answers to the whys of learning seem to be. Perhaps in the area of physiological psychology we may assess the adequacy of the assumptions of one or another of the theories, or perhaps a new and unthought-of notion may arise.

As things stand now, we shall probably do best to go along most of the way with the operational approach. The latent-learning experiments tell us that we must insist upon a distinction between learning and performance. Learning, of course, does not always show up immediately in performance, but because performance does eventually change as the result of stimulation, even in the latent-learning experiments, we must insist that the latent-learning experiments fit the operational definition of reinforcement. The important point is that the change in behavior which is a function of reinforcement may not show up immediately but may await the introduction of an incentive.

CHAPTER 3

# THE NATURE OF EXTINCTION

It is a fundamental property of all simple conditioned responses that when the reinforcing stimulus is withdrawn, the response will gradually diminish in strength. This is a common enough observation. Parents are sometimes admonished to avoid picking up their babies when they cry, because "then they will not cry in order to be picked up." It is doubtful whether many parents last out this process, but then the advice itself is testimony to the widespread knowledge of the effects of withdrawal of the reinforcement.

## EFFECTS OF WITHDRAWAL OF REINFORCEMENT

When the reinforcement of a particular response is withdrawn, that response declines in strength. The term "extinction" refers to both the withdrawal of the reinforcement and to the resulting decline in response strength. It is necessary to specify that the loss in response strength occurs as a function of the withdrawal of reinforcement, since there are other variables which also may produce a decline in response strength.

Typically, we condition an animal by reinforcing every correct response it makes. Ordinarily, each time the rat in the Skinner box presses the lever, it receives a pellet of food. Under these conditions, the latencies between successive lever pushes will be small and the force with which the lever is pressed will be at least strong enough to activate the feeding device each time. If we now withdraw the reinforcement, the result is a decline in strength of response; the latencies between responses will get longer and longer, and the force with which the lever is pushed will get weaker.

*The effect of extinction upon rate.* In Chap. 2 we saw that the latent time or reaction time of a response was an excellent measure of the strength of response. But latent period can be measured directly only in a situation where we have discrete trials, that is, where we can time the interval between a certain stimulus event and the response. In the Skinner box we

42

cannot do this, since there is no definite stimulus which sets off each response. We can, however, time the interval between successive responses; this is usually done by measuring the rate of pushing the lever.

The rate of response in the Skinner box can be measured by simply counting the number of pushes that occur in a given unit of time, say, 1 minute. A rat, for example, after it has learned the lever-pressing response, may continue to respond at the rate of seven pushes per minute. The rate is an important measure of behavior, since it is sensitive to a number of different variables.

For most purposes we get an excellent idea of the rate of emission of responses at any given moment by looking at a graph. The graph in Fig. 9 is an example. The vertical axis is plotted as the *cumulative* number of responses, that is to say, it shows the number of responses which have occurred up to any given time. The horizontal axis is time. If we read over to 1 hour in time we see that approximately 200 responses have been given up to that time. The rate itself is given by the slope of the curve at any point, and it can be specified as

$$\frac{\Delta N}{\Delta t}$$

where $\Delta N$ is an increment in number of responses and $\Delta t$ an increment in time. Where the slope of the curve is steep (as it is in the beginning), the rate is high; where it is flat, the rate is low.

The curve in Fig. 9 happens to be a curve of the rate of response of a single rat in a Skinner box during extinction. This curve shows the number of responses that occurred after reinforcement had been withdrawn. There are two things to notice about this curve: (1) The rate declines as a function of time in the absence of reinforcement. The rate is quite high in the beginning (about the same rate as that under reinforcement). Eventually the rate of response approaches zero (the curve becomes almost flat). The relationship appears to be an exponential one. That is to say, the rate of response during extinction depends upon the difference between the number of responses that will take place before extinction is complete and the number of responses that have occurred at any particular moment (Ellson, 1939). (2) The rate during extinction is also much more variable than the rate during continual reinforcement. Under optimal conditions the rate of response during reinforcement should be practically a straight line, with only imperceptible deviations. You will notice in Fig. 9 that the rate during extinction is quite irregular. The rat may press the bar rapidly for a few seconds, then cease to press it altogether for a brief time.

*The effect of reinforcement upon resistance to extinction.* Resistance to extinction is another important indicator of the strength of response. Resistance to extinction is defined as the total number of responses emitted between the time the reinforcement is withdrawn and the time at which rate of response reaches zero. This measure has sometimes been called the "reflex reserve" (Skinner, 1938) in order to imply the idea that reinforcement creates a definite potential or reserve for emitting responses, and that this reserve is exhausted during extinction.

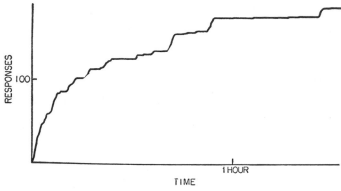

FIG. 9. A typical extinction curve for the lever response in the Skinner box. Cumulative number of responses is plotted on the ordinate. Thus, where the curve is level, no responses occur. (*Skinner, 1938; data from F. S. Keller and A. Kerr.*)

If the reflex reserve, or resistance to extinction, is plotted against the number of reinforced responses during conditioning, one gets a curve like that in Fig. 10 (Perin, 1942). The shape of this curve is like that for other measures of response strength that we took up in the last chapter; it seems to be exponential. Like other exponential curves, it approaches a limit and, after 90 or so reinforcements, additional reinforcements will not appreciably increase the reflex reserve—in this case for the lever response in the Skinner box.

*Failure to respond as a measure of extinction.* The Skinner box has the advantage that it yields a picture of behavior much like that in nature, that is to say, the organism is free to respond when it chooses. For purposes of control, however, most experimenters prefer to administer discrete trials to the organism under study. To do that, they like to pair a conditioned stimulus with an unconditioned stimulus a number of times until they observe that the conditioned stimulus evokes a conditioned response.

In such a procedure, of course, the unconditioned stimulus provides the reinforcement, and when the unconditioned stimulus is removed, the organism will soon fail to respond to the conditioned stimulus. The measure of extinction one can use in this situation is the number of times the organism responds to the conditioned stimulus, after the unconditioned stimulus has been discontinued. This measure, too, can be used as an index of reflex reserve.

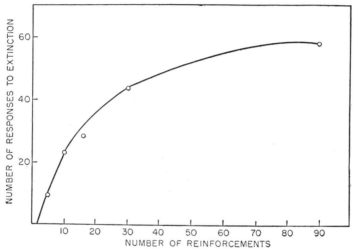

FIG. 10. Number of lever responses to extinction as a function of the number of reinforcements. (*Redrawn from Perin, 1942; data from Perin, 1942, and Williams, 1938.*)

## VARIABLES WHICH AFFECT EXTINCTION

The *speed* with which a response is extinguished is determined by a number of conditions, some of which we shall want to examine. In addition, there are a number of important factors which affect the *permanence* of extinction which are of theoretical importance.

*The effect of massed trials during extinction.* One of the main advantages of giving discrete trials during an experiment on learning is that the experimenter can control the rate at which the trials come. This is sometimes a very important variable. Pavlov (1927), for example, showed that extinction of a conditioned salivary response is affected by the rate at which the extinction trials are carried out. If the extinction trials were given in very rapid succession, response strength declined very much more rapidly than if the same number of unreinforced trials were given at a slower pace. Thus massing of extinction trials appears to reduce response strength more rapidly than does distributing extinction trials through time.

Several investigators, however, have doubted Pavlov's results on this point (Guthrie, 1934), and they have done some more experiments on it. Let us consider two. Rohrer (1947) used a modified Skinner box in which the bar was presented before each response and then withdrawn right after each response; in this way, he managed to give discrete trials in a Skinner box. His results agreed with those of Pavlov in that massing of trials during extinction quickened the extinction process. This was true, however, only after a large number of reinforcements had been given. After a very small number of reinforcements, it did not seem to make much difference whether extinction trials were massed or distributed.

Sheffield (1950) found exactly the opposite to be true in the case of extinction of the habit of running down an alley to food. In other words, extinction with massed practice took longer than extinction with distributed practice. In view of the fact that this experiment disagrees with the two earlier experiments as well as with a number of experiments which bear on the problem indirectly (Gagné, 1941; Reynolds, 1945b), a clear-cut decision cannot be made. Tentatively we can decide that in many, if not most, situations massing of extinction trials produces faster extinction. There must be some exceptions, however, and it is very possible that these exceptions may be of theoretical interest.

*The effect of effort upon extinction.* The effort required to make a response is another important factor in extinction. Fortunately, results of studies dealing with the effect of *effort* upon extinction are rather unequivocal. The classical study is that of Mowrer and Jones (1943). They trained rats to press a lever for food in a Skinner box. During acquisition the lever was counterweighted with a number of different loads, so that different amounts of work were required to press the bar. The effect of the different amounts of effort required upon acquisition is not important at the moment. During extinction, however, the bars were counterweighted in the same way. For one group of rats the bar required 5 grams to activate the feeder, for another group it required 42.5 grams, and for a third it required 80 grams. The results are given in Fig. 11. They clearly show that additional effort makes it much easier to extinguish a response. Put in quantitative terms, there is a simple negative relation between resistance to extinction and the amount of effort the task requires.

This study receives ready confirmation in one by Solomon (1948a). Using food for reinforcement, Solomon trained rats to jump from one platform to another. After that, the rats were extinguished when they had to jump a distance either of 16 inches or of 8 inches. The animals which were required to jump the longer distance extinguished much faster than did the animals which jumped the shorter distance.

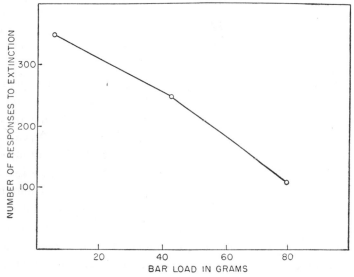

FIG. 11. The number of responses emitted by rats during extinction as a function of the amount of work required for the response (counterweight on lever). (*Mowrer and Jones, 1943.*)

The influence of work on behavior is a topic of very general interest, and these experiments upon extinction seem to be a small part of a quantity of data, both from animals and from human beings, which have a common theoretical basis (Solomon, 1948b). It is not surprising that some theories of extinction are closely related to theories of work and fatigue.

*Spontaneous recovery.* Spontaneous recovery is the name Pavlov assigned to one of the most interesting and important properties of extinction. It means what it implies, that extinction does not always permanently and completely abolish the conditioned response, and that after extinction, learned responses may recover.

An example from Pavlov's laboratory will demonstrate the basic principle of spontaneous recovery. Pavlov (1927) produced a conditioned salivary response by allowing a dog first to *see* some meat powder, then allowing the dog to eat it. After the dog had learned to salivate to the sight of the meat powder, Pavlov began to extinguish him by no longer putting food in his mouth following the sight of food. It took only a few trials of this sort to extinguish completely the conditioned response. The animal was then removed from the experimental room for about 2 hours. When the dog was brought back to the experimental room and the visual stimulus of meat powder presented, the conditioned response occurred again. True, the amount of saliva flow was not so great this time as it was before the extinction process was begun, but there was no doubt that the conditioned response had recovered to a considerable extent—actually, about one-sixth the original amount.

An experiment by Ellson (1938) very neatly shows the quantitative properties of spontaneous recovery. Four groups of rats were trained to press a lever in the Skinner box. Following the conditioning procedure, all animals were permitted to operate the lever without reinforcement until they had failed to respond for a period of 5 minutes. One group of rats was then removed from the box and allowed to rest for a period of 5 minutes. The rats were then replaced in the box and additional unreinforced responses were counted. A second group of rats resumed extinction after a pause of 25 minutes, the third group resumed extinction after 65 minutes, and the fourth after 185 minutes. All animals showed an immediate tendency to press the lever when replaced in the box, even though all of them had failed to press the lever for a period of 5 minutes prior to their removal from the box. Figure 12 shows that the amount of recovery, or number of responses after rest, is an increasing function of the length of the rest period. Like most of the phenomena associated with the learning process, this function also seems to have its limit, so that an extremely long rest period yields no more spontaneous recovery than a moderately long one.

It is probably obvious by now that spontaneous recovery is a very important part of the extinction process. We may, for example, try to stop our dog from begging at the dining-room table by ignoring it when it begs, and we may find by the end of a meal that we have been successful; the dog has retired to the living room. The next evening, however, it will probably be back, begging again. The experimental results on spontaneous recovery tell us that it will not be so persistent this time, and it will retire earlier. Repeated extinctions will finally eliminate the response.

*Disinhibition.* Another interesting effect connected with extinction is that which Pavlov called "disinhibition." This term stems from a special theory of Pavlov's (1927), which need not concern us at the moment. In Pavlov's original demonstration of disinhibition, he established a conditioned response to the sight of meat powder. Once the conditioned response was well established, he extinguished it by presenting the meat powder in the dog's sight without letting it eat it. When Pavlov had com-

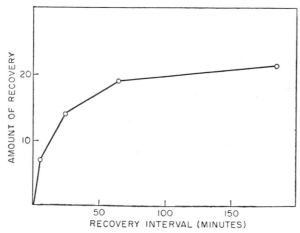

FIG. 12. The number of responses in a second extinction period after different lengths of recovery period. (*Redrawn from Ellson, 1938.*)

pletely extinguished the conditioned response, he paired a new stimulus with the conditioned stimulus. This new stimulus was a neutral one; it was vibration to the skin at the same time food was brought in sight. The dog salivated to this novel combination of stimuli—it showed disinhibition. Thus, the salivary response to the sight of food, which had been completely extinguished, came back again when the new stimulus, vibration, was presented along with the food.

Such disinhibition is very easily observed, particularly in the type of conditioning that involves a definite conditioned stimulus. As a matter of fact, if experimenters do not want to get it, they must be very careful to control extraneous stimulation in order to prevent it. For example, it can be most disconcerting to an investigator to get an animal completely extinguished and then have someone slam a door out in the hall—the animal usually starts responding again.

## PARTIAL REINFORCEMENT AND EXTINCTION

In Chap. 2, we considered the effects of reinforcement upon response strength when a reinforcement is given for every response—the procedure in a conventional learning experiment. As has been frequently noted (Jenkins and Stanley, 1950), however, this condition is seldom met in nature. More often an organism will be reinforced only occasionally for a particular response. When mice come out to explore for food, they may occasionally find crumbs under the breakfast table, but it is the poor housekeeper who reinforces them for every try. In most cases there are intermediate conditions between reinforcement and extinction. The mice may find food on Monday evenings when the floor gets neglected in favor of the family wash, but not on Tuesday or Wednesday evenings.

So we may conceive of a kind of continuum from 100 per cent reinforcement for every given response to no reinforcement for any response. Any condition in between, where the reinforcement is given only occasionally, is known as *partial reinforcement*. This term is in some senses a misnomer, but it is a term so widely used that we cannot avoid it. The conditions of partial reinforcement are of considerable importance; consequently, they have been studied in considerable detail.

*Partial reinforcement and rate of response.* As in many other cases, Pavlov originally discovered the effect of partial reinforcement, but he seemed to overlook its great theoretical and practical importance. It was Skinner (1933, 1938) who was one of the first experimenters to give it serious attention. He used a somewhat unusual procedure to analyze the effects of partial reinforcement. He first conditioned animals to press a lever by reinforcing them 100 per cent of the time with a food pellet. He then extinguished this response and reconditioned it, this time by giving the animals a reinforcement on a time schedule. In one example, Skinner reinforced the lever response by giving a pellet of food every 5 minutes; the responses which occurred during the 5-minute periods between food pellets went unreinforced. After any one reinforcement, he found, the rate of response would increase slightly, then gradually decrease, as it does during extinction. When the next reinforcement came, the rate, which by this time was relatively low, would immediately go up again. Then again there would be a decrease in rate, but this decrease would not be so severe as the preceding one. Eventually the rate of response would smooth out, so that the little extinction curves between reinforcements would disappear.

Thus he could maintain a response with only a small fraction of the usual number of reinforcements. With the particular time intervals he used, however, the rates of response would be lower, on the average, than when responses are reinforced every time.

Skinner also studied in great detail the effect upon the rate of response of "fixed ratios" of reinforcement. In this procedure for reinforcement, a reinforcement is given every so many responses. For example, one response out of ten may be reinforced. This may be done on a rigid schedule or it may be done more or less at random. By various techniques of either fixed-ratio or period (time-schedule) reinforcement, Skinner was able to get fantastically high rates of response (Skinner, 1938, 1950). Perhaps the most important difference between fixed-ratio and periodic reinforcement that he found can be summarized by saying that fixed-ratio reinforcement puts a premium on responding rapidly in order to get the reinforcement, while periodic (time-schedule) reinforcement simply keeps the animals working away at the lever.

*Partial reinforcement and resistance to extinction.* One of the most important discoveries Skinner made about partial reinforcement is that this procedure greatly increases resistance to extinction. After periods of reconditioning with partial reinforcement, Skinner (1938) found that the extinction curves were very much larger than following conditioning with 100 per cent reinforcement. Also, the extinction curve after partial reinforcement was very much more regular than it had been after reinforcement of every response. These results of Skinner's suggest that partial reinforcement accumulates much greater response strength per reinforcement than does simple reinforcement.

This last point was dramatically made in another study by Humphreys (1939). This investigator conditioned the eyelid response in human subjects. As we all know, human beings (as well as animals) will blink their eyelids when a puff of air is suddenly blown at the eye. Humphreys took advantage of this unconditioned response by pairing it with a flash of light. His subjects quickly learned to react to the light. In the conditioning trials, however, he divided his subjects into three groups of 96 individuals each. One group had the conditioned stimulus paired with the puff of air on every trial. A second group had the light paired with the puff on only 50 per cent of the trials. In this condition, the pairings of the light with the puff of air occurred more or less at random. A third group was like the first in having a reinforcement on every trial, but like the second group in having only half the number of reinforced trials. To accomplish this, he had rest intervals for the third group at the times when the second group was getting unreinforced trials.

Humphreys found that there were no differences in the rate of acquisition between the 100 per cent and the partial-reinforcement groups. There was, however, a striking difference between these two groups in the resistance to extinction. The partially reinforced group extinguished much more slowly than did the groups with reinforcement every trial. This conclusion has been well supported by a number of studies (Sheffield, 1949; Grant and Hake, 1949; Jenkins, McFann, and Clayton, 1950; etc.).

Humphreys pointed out that his findings were inconsistent with the effect theory of reinforcement. After all, his partially reinforced group exhibited greater strength of response, in terms of resistance to extinction, than his normal group that had twice as many reinforcements. Yet, if it is effect that is important, response-strength should be considerably less in the practically reinforced group. So Humphreys felt that the effect theory was hard put to explain his results. Instead he put forth a common-sense, "expectancy" theory of conditioning, and this we should consider in some detail.

*Expectancy.* The theory of expectancy can be stated very briefly. Organisms come to respond to conditioned stimuli because the conditioned stimuli lead them to expect the unconditioned stimuli. Humphreys's subjects, for example, blinked to the light because they expected the puff of air; and rats press levers because they come to expect food as a result.

This notion was not discussed in Chap. 2, which dealt with reinforcement, because it had little to offer in that context. It is when we consider partial reinforcement, however, that the theory of *expectancy* becomes important. Expectancy, Humphreys thought, could explain the results he obtained with partial reinforcement. Subjects, he reasoned, come to expect the puff of air after every light signal when the light is reinforced 100 per cent of the time. Consequently, when extinction begins they quickly come to expect that the puff of air will not follow; thus they extinguish rapidly. When the puff is given only occasionally during acquisition, however, the subjects are not so sure during extinction that it will not appear again; consequently they respond for a much longer time and extinguish more slowly.

The theory of expectancy has been roundly criticized on a number of scores. Some critics have claimed that it is an anthropomorphic notion. Others have pointed out that the definition of expectancy is vague and ambiguous. Certainly, the criticism of anthropomorphism is justified.

Human learners seem to be capable of "expectancy" principally by way of verbal cues. We can tell ourselves when we ought to expect something to happen. It is doubtful that any animals are capable of expectancy in this sense.

The most serious criticism of the notion of expectancy is that it is an *ad hoc* explanation. The notion of expectancy is acceptable if it is defined as the ability to respond to a conditioned cue before the unconditioned stimulus appears. When the buzzer sounds the dog salivates; *then* the meat powder is placed in the mouth. If all one means by expectancy is this ability to react in a manner appropriate to the unconditioned stimulus before it appears, there can be no question about it; practically all animals can so react. If, on the other hand, expectancy means the ability to react to a conditioned stimulus by means of a mediated symbolic response, such as that which a human subject might use when he tells himself that the conditioned stimulus means the unconditioned stimulus is coming, then it is doubtful whether the notion applies to simple animal behavior at all.

*Alternate theories of partial reinforcement.* Because of the ambiguity of the notion of expectancy, other theories have been put forward to explain the effect of partial reinforcement. Particularly prominent have been notions which attempt to make the effects of partial reinforcement upon extinction compatible with the effect theory.

Denny's (1946) approach is in terms of derived, secondary reinforcement. As he puts it, neutral stimuli that cannot serve in primary reinforcement acquire secondary reinforcing properties during the learning process. These secondary reinforcements increase strength of response. Thus, in partial reinforcement, during the trials in which the primary reinforcement is absent, response strength is increased through secondary reinforcement. From this idea, Denny argues that when the cues for secondary reinforcement are reduced to a minimum, the superiority of partial reinforcement ought to disappear. He actually found, when secondary reinforcements were reduced as much as possible, that 100 per cent reinforcement gave slightly greater resistance to extinction than did 50 per cent reinforcement, and this experimental fact seems to confirm his notion.

In a sense, Denny's notion is but a more elaborate treatment of Humphreys's original idea, for the notion of expectancy could be considered to be a kind of anthropomorphic analogue to secondary reinforcement. There are difficulties, however, with the idea that secondary reinforcement explains the effects of partial reinforcement. Secondary reinforcements are usually much weaker than primary reinforcements. They take quite a few trials to become established. So, in Denny's experiment, the first few unreinforced trials must have had little or no secondary reinforcement. Even when the secondary reinforcement was well established, it must have been weaker than the primary reinforcement. It is very surprising, then, to find that a schedule of 50 per cent reinforcement sometimes results in extinction curves which are more than twice as large as those found after 100 per cent reinforcement. Thus, while secondary reinforcement may well be a factor in producing increased resistance to extinction after partial reinforcement, it cannot be the only factor at work.

Another possible explanation of the effect of partial reinforcement can be made by redefining the unit of response. One can, if he wishes, call all of the activity that occurs between reinforcements one response. Mowrer and Jones (1945) show that when responses are counted according to this scheme, actually *fewer* responses show up in the extinction curve after partial reinforcement, although more single bar depressions may happen. The reader may well ask what justification Mowrer and Jones have for counting responses in this way. Actually little justification is needed, since the definition of a response is somewhat arbitrary anyway. Most psychologists use "response" ambiguously. Sometimes they use the term to mean a unit of behavior which is terminated by a reinforcement—this is the sense in which Mowrer and Jones use the term—and sometimes they use the term to mean a specific piece of behavior. If we accept the first definition, then Mowrer and Jones have a good point. If, on the other hand, we accept the second definition, their treatment seems a little unjustified.

*The present status of the problem of partial reinforcement.* In the final analysis, the effects of partial reinforcement are probably multiple. There is probably an effect of secondary reinforcement, and probably the definition of the unit of response has something to do with it. If my neighbor's child has to cry twice as long as my child in order to get an ice-cream cone, then the response which gets him the reinforcement is twice as long. All other things being equal, it should take twice as long to extinguish the neighbor's child on crying for ice cream.

It appears to be almost certain that there are other explanations of the effect as it applies to human adult behavior. Through the mediation of verbal behavior, human adults may adopt hypotheses. These hypotheses themselves may be learned according to the principles governing simple behavior, but their mere presence means that factors are at work which are not present in the behavior of animals incapable of a high-level symbolic performance.

The effect of partial reinforcement is of great importance from a practical point of view. Learning is not greatly retarded by partial reinforcement, as Jenkins and Stanley point out (1950), and on the other hand, one can use it to get the greatest amount of learning for the least cost in reinforcement. Conversely, this effect presents a puzzle to the parent who attempts to eliminate undesirable behavior in his offspring by extinction, for the parent often does not realize that even an occasional reinforcement —reward for bad behavior—can preserve and maintain the behavior as effectively as continuous reinforcement. Thus the one time that the parent gives in during the extinction process defeats the whole carefully planned strategy. It is a hard point for parents to understand—and a harder one to carry out—never to give any reinforcement during attempted extinction. It is equally hard to understand, but equally true, that if one wants to keep behavior going for long periods of time in the absence of direct reinforcement, partial reinforcement is the best technique to use.

## THEORIES OF EXTINCTION

To the layman, a theory of extinction may seem to be superfluous. An animal stops responding because he is no longer rewarded. This simple explanation is hardly sufficient, however, because it fails to account for many of the particular features of extinction. Actually, theories of extinction have been quite complicated, and interesting as well, since there seem to be some fairly straightforward issues.

### The Theory of Response-induced Inhibition

This is one theory of extinction. Its most important statement comes from Hull (1943), though Hull, in turn, derived many of his notions from Pavlov. Because of the importance and generality of Hull's theory, we shall consider it at some length.

*Reactive inhibition.* Hull starts with the assumption that whenever an organism makes a response it also generates some inhibition to that response. To say this means that, all other things being equal, once a response takes place, it is somewhat less likely to occur in the immediate future. Such inhibition may be thought of as a kind of analogue to fatigue; it makes the next response more difficult. Like fatigue, this inhibition will disappear after a period of rest; if not enough rest is allowed, however, the inhibition will accumulate from response to response. If it accumulates rapidly, it may eventually stop the response, which in turn, of course, is said to produce the inhibition. This kind of inhibition Hull calls "reactive inhibition."

Hull advanced the hypothesis that the amount of inhibition that results from a series of responses is a positively accelerated function of the amount of work involved in the performance of the response. That is to say, as the response requires more and more effort, the inhibition accumulates at an ever-increasing rate. Further, he specified, the inhibition generated by each response decays progressively with the passage of time at rest, in a way that is described by a simple negative exponential function. And eventually, with enough rest, the response will completely recover its strength.

Reactive inhibition is said to accumulate whether the response is reinforced or not. If the response is reinforced, the positive effects from the reinforcement must overcome the negative effects from the reactive inhibition in order for the response to occur again. Most of the time the positive effects will keep the animal responding, but there is an interesting exception—a matter of experimental fact—which lends a good deal of plausibility to Hull's notion. If, during conditioning, trials are massed very close together, the animals may slow their rates of responding and even stop altogether, even though the reinforcement is still present (Hovland, 1936). This effect has been called "inhibition of reinforcement."

The most important aspect of the theory of response-induced inhibition, however, concerns the results of extinction. When responses are no longer reinforced, reactive inhibition is thought to accumulate without being counteracted by any positive effects of reinforcement. The result is that the animal eventually ceases to respond. Since reactive inhibition disappears with time, we would predict spontaneous recovery of the response after a period of rest. You will remember, however, that in the example from Pavlov's laboratory, spontaneous recovery was only about one-sixth the value of the original response strength. At best, spontaneous recovery only goes to the extent of about 50 per cent of response strength at the end of conditioning. Because of this fact, that spontaneous recovery is incomplete, Hull postulated a second factor to account for the permanent effects of extinction. This second factor is "conditioned inhibition."

*Conditioned inhibition.* According to Hull, reactive inhibition is a kind of negative motivational state, or tissue injury. Presumably animals are motivated to avoid reactive inhibition just as they are motivated to avoid an electric shock. If we accept the need-reduction theory of reinforcement, it is easy to see how escape from or avoidance of reactive inhibition would constitute a reinforcement. Thus when an animal ceases to respond, his fatigue state or reactive inhibition is reduced. This, in keeping with the need-reduction notion, is reinforcing. Reduction of reactive inhibition then reinforces the animal for doing nothing. This inhibition that is learned by the supposed reinforcement of reducing reactive inhibition is conditioned inhibition.

The notion of conditioned inhibition does not entirely depend upon the need-reduction theory of reinforcement even though Hull presents the notion in this context. Reactive inhibition could bring about a state of failure of response. Simply by contiguity, failing to respond could become conditioned to the cues which previously brought about the response. Thus learning not to respond could just as easily be the result of simple association as it could be the result of reinforcement by the principle of effect.

*How reactive and conditioned inhibition account for the phenomena of extinction.* The theory of extinction that is based on reactive and conditioned inhibition seems rather complicated, but its essentials are simple. Extinction involves an active suppression or inhibition of the learned response. This inhibition is composed of two parts, one of which recovers with rest, the other of which does not. Thus spontaneous recovery is predicted, as well as the fact that spontaneous recovery is never complete. The theory accounts for inhibition of reinforcement by massed trials during conditioning, and it would predict a more rapid extinction by massed trials during extinction. The fact that extinction is more rapid when the amount of work is great is accounted for by the hypothesis that reactive inhibition is a function of the amount of work required for a response. It is apparent then that most of the simple, classical phenomena of extinction are accounted for by this two-factor theory.

## The Theory of Competition

An alternative theory of extinction features competition between various responses involved in learning and extinction. For this reason, it may be called the "competition theory." This is very straightforward and direct. The clearest exposition of it comes from Guthrie (1935) and Wendt (1936). Guthrie's development of the theory is more widely known, so we shall draw largely upon it.

As we have already seen, Guthrie is the principal advocate of the notion that reinforcement is simply a process of association by contiguity. If a response occurs in the presence of a certain stimulus, he says, that stimulus will have the tendency to evoke that response in the future.

*Explanation of the theory.* We have already gone into this contiguity theory in some detail in the last chapter. There is one feature of it, however, that needs emphasis if we are to understand how it manages to explain extinction. This is the notion that contiguity learning in its bare essentials occurs in one trial. We must stress "in its bare essentials" because there is a problem here of defining what responses are learned and extinguished.

Most psychologists are accustomed to defining responses in terms of their end effects. We say, for example, that there is a response of opening a door or pressing a lever. Guthrie, however, when he uses the term "response" in his contiguity theory, does not mean these goal-defined units, but rather he means separate and discrete muscular movements. It takes many of these separate movements to make up the usual goal-defined response. This distinction permits one to assume that the association of a movement may occur in one trial, if at the same time it is understood that it may take many trials to condition all the movements necessary to the performance of an act. Furthermore, in the course of learning a goal-defined act it is obvious that many faulty movements which do not lead to the final act must be unconditioned. This last statement contains the germ of Guthrie's notion of extinction.

According to Guthrie, competing responses learned to the same stimulus are responsible for extinction. If lever pressing is a response conditioned to certain proprioceptive cues, the same proprioceptive cues may become conditioned to the movements involved in running. The next time these cues occur, the animal will tend to run rather than press the lever, since the most recent response is the one now conditioned to the cues. This process has been called "associative interference" or "competition." Through it, organisms learn, during the course of extinction trials, to perform new responses to old stimuli (p. 198), and this is responsible for extinction. To put this statement another way, we may say that if we desire to eliminate a conditioned response, it is only necessary to cause other movements to occur in the presence of the conditioned stimulus. Thus the conditioned stimulus will be associated with the new movements.

*How Guthrie's theory works in practice.* From this theory of extinction, Guthrie is able to draw many practical suggestions about the control of behavior. For example, he gives three different methods of breaking a habit in real-life situations. The first method consists of introducing the conditioned stimulus subliminally so that a response will not be elicited.

This is what is done when we train a horse to saddle by first putting on only a light blanket, and then gradually working up to full gear. The light blanket is not a sufficient stimulus to set off bucking, and the horse is not disturbed by the gradual addition of heavier loads. A second method of breaking a habit is to repeat the conditioned stimulus until the original response is exhausted, so that the organism is too fatigued to respond to the conditioned stimulus. This is the bronco-busting technique. In much milder cases, this technique suggests Hull's two-factor theory of extinction. The third method is to present the conditioned stimulus when it is mechanically impossible for the organism to make the response.

It is important to notice that the use of these three methods as examples of competition rests upon the assumption that the theory of competition is correct; they do not demonstrate the theory to be correct. This, in fact, has been one of the major criticisms aimed at Guthrie's theory. The theory does not lend itself readily to the prediction of experimental results; rather its strength lies in its appeal to common sense and to anecdotal example. Or, in a word, the theory is difficult to test.

There is a second, serious criticism of Guthrie's theory. The theory is not specific enough to predict many of the facts about extinction which are already known. For example, as far as can be seen at present, Guthrie's theory would predict extinction to be the mirror image of conditioning (Hilgard and Marquis, 1940), since it considers extinction and conditioning to be essentially the same processes. That is not the case, however, as can be seen from an inspection of many examples. Extinction and conditioning always seem to be different—*e.g.,* one may take a longer or shorter time than the other—depending upon the specific situation. Moreover, the theory does not predict the phenomenon of spontaneous recovery. Finally, if one takes spontaneous recovery for granted, one might expect from Guthrie's theory that the reverse of spontaneous recovery would be found in the conditioning process. This does not happen, although there is, of course, a superficial analogy between forgetting and spontaneous recovery, but in simple conditioned responses forgetting is not nearly of the order or magnitude of spontaneous recovery.

These criticisms of Guthrie's theory mean that it has serious weaknesses because they mean that, as the theory stands now, it is either incorrect or incomplete. On the positive side, however, Guthrie's theory is to be commended for its simplicity. It demands only one mechanism to account for both conditioning and extinction. Certainly the theory demands attention.

Finally, it should be mentioned that there is very little difference between Guthrie's notion of *interference* and Hull's concept of *conditioned inhibition*.

### The Present State of the Theories of Extinction

Response-induced inhibition is undoubtedly a factor in the decrement of response strength observed during extinction. It is the only way we can account at present for many of the phenomena of extinction. Further, the concept applies to many problems in human behavior (p. 157).

For example, even such an esoteric condition as disinhibition occurs in human behavior. During the Second World War British psychologists studied in great detail the breakdown of vigilance during continuous visual search. They found that many of the results of such continuous search as are involved in plane spotting, for example, could be accounted for in terms of response-induced inhibition. Ability to spot targets gradually declines as a function of time at search, but the ability to identify targets correctly can be improved by "disinhibiting" the inhibition accumulated by continuous search; almost any stimulus that wakes up the searcher—a telephone message, for example—will do (Mackworth, 1948).

*Nonresponse extinction.* There is evidence, however, that leads us to be almost certain that response-induced inhibition and conditioned inhibition cannot be the sole factors responsible for the decrement we see in extinction procedures. As a matter of fact, the principal source of the *permanent* decrement found in extinction may be something quite removed from response-induced inhibition. The evidence for this statement comes from studies in which a specific response is extinguished without ever being performed—in a word, from studies of *nonresponse extinction.*

Our first experimental example of such extinction comes from Seward and Levy (1949). They trained rats to run down a runway to secure food that was placed in a goal box at the end of the runway. After it was conditioned, one group of rats was placed directly in the goal box without there being any food in it. In other words, these rats were permitted to see that the reinforcement was no longer in the goal box. A second group of rats did not have the benefit of this "preview." The next day, all rats were given a series of extinction trials. The group that had been able to see beforehand that the food was not there any more extinguished in about half the time required for the other rats. So it was evident that the response of running down the runway had been reduced in strength by the "look" and thus extinction took place without the running response.

A second experiment points to the relative roles of response-induced inhibition and other factors in extinction. This second experiment (Deese, 1951) was quite similar to Seward and Levy's; rats were trained to go to one side of a one-choice T maze. After the animals had been trained, half of them were placed directly in the empty goal box to let them see that

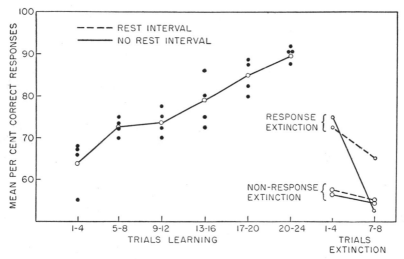

FIG. 13. Learning and extinction of a simple response in a T maze. "Response" extinction obtained following usual extinction procedure. "Nonresponse" extinction following animals being placed in foodless goal box. (*Deese, 1951.*)

there was no food in the box. All animals were then given a series of extinction trials. As in the previous experiment, the animals that had been allowed to see that food was missing extinguished more rapidly than did the other animals.

In addition, however, a test was made for spontaneous recovery from this kind of "nonresponse" extinction. The half of the animals that had been permitted to see the empty goal box before extinction were given their extinction trials immediately after the "look"; the other half were given their extinction trials 24 hours later. If there were spontaneous recovery from inspection of the empty goal box the group tested 24 hours later should have shown greater resistance to extinction; however, there were no differences between these groups. A test of spontaneous recovery from ordinary extinction in the same maze showed that there was indeed spontaneous recovery when the rats had to run through the maze in order to get to the empty goal box (Fig. 13). These results suggest that there was little or no response-induced inhibition developed by the nonresponse technique of extinction, while there was response-induced inhibition developed by the usual way of producing extinction. From this reasoning it is possible to conclude that response-induced inhibition is not essential to extinction.

*Where do we stand?* We have fairly good evidence that there is a kind of response-induced inhibition—some sort of negative feedback from responses; performance of a response does induce a temporary kind of inhibition. The studies of nonresponse extinction, however, make it appear that this inhibition must play a minor role in the permanent effects of extinction. The more permanent effects of extinction may be due in part to conditioned inhibition, in part to the acquisition of competing responses, and in part to other factors. About all we can say at present is that, in the simplest cases, all that seems to be necessary for extinction is for the organism to *perceive* the absence of reinforcement.

CHAPTER 4

# STIMULI IN LEARNING AND THE
# PROCESS OF DISCRIMINATION

As we have seen in the past two chapters, one important function of stimuli is their property of reinforcement. We know, however, that stimuli serve purposes in learning other than reinforcement. They serve as signposts which lead rats to make the correct turns in mazes; they serve as signals which tell dogs of the approach of electric shock in the conditioning apparatus. And there are many more subtle functions of stimuli as well. They serve for discriminations in social situations. At least some adults, for example, make rapid discriminations, on the basis of differential reinforcement, about the appropriate company in which to tell salty stories. It is the social boor who is impervious to obvious signs of discomfort on the part of his audience during a tedious anecdote. The appropriateness of our behavior in such situations is based upon our ability to learn to discriminate between various signs or stimuli in our world.

## OPERANTS AND RESPONDENTS

In many situations it is difficult to see the stimuli which give rise to the behavior in question. While walking down the street, a person may suddenly change his pace from a leisurely stroll to a brisk walk. It would be difficult for the casual observer to put his finger on the exact set of stimuli which brought about this change. This inability to identify the stimuli responsible for some kinds of behavior has led to an important distinction between kinds of responses. This distinction is based upon whether or not we can determine with some degree of certainty what the stimulus was which led to a response.

*Respondents.* Respondents are responses, the stimuli for which we can readily identify. Many of the examples of learning used thus far in this book have been examples of responses to easily identifiable stimuli. All of

63

the examples of learning from Pavlov's laboratory are of this sort. Salivation is the direct result of some substance going into solution in the mouth. By a process of pairing, this stimulus-response unit is associated with the sound of a buzzer, so that a new conditioned stimulus-response unit is developed. This kind of stimulus-response unit has been named the "respondent," because the behavior is a response to a definite stimulus (Skinner, 1938).

*Operants.* Operants are responses, the stimuli for which we cannot easily identify. Thus far in this book, there have been many more examples of operants than respondents. And for that there is good reason: Operants are much more common than respondents.

The rat pressing a lever in the Skinner box is the classical example of the operant as it has been studied in the psychological laboratory. When the rat first presses the lever, we call it an unconditioned response. The rat is reinforced by the pellet of food. The rat, at least to the observer, appears to learn that pressing the bar leads to food. The response is now a learned or conditioned response. As in the case of the respondent, the unconditioned response and the conditioned response are essentially the same. In the case of the respondent, we can easily see why we make a distinction between an unconditioned response and a conditioned response; each is to a different stimulus. In the case of the operant, however, we cannot so easily see a difference in the unconditioned response and conditioned response because we cannot easily identify the conditioned stimulus and unconditioned stimulus.

We do not know why the rat pressed the bar the first time. We assume, as a fundamental postulate of psychological theory, that there must have been some stimulus, or some energy change, which led to the response. Our present techniques do not allow us to measure this stimulus, however. This unidentified stimulus is exactly analogous to the measurable unconditioned stimulus in the case of the respondent. Because we cannot identify it, however, it cannot enter into our experimental description. Thus, to the casual observer, the operant is a sort of a free response which has the appearance of spontaneity. Because it appears to *operate* upon nature to produce consequences, this free response was named the "operant" by Skinner (1938).

The respondent can be diagrammed this way:

$$S \to R$$

because we know what the stimulus is that elicits the behavior in question. In the case of the operant the diagram becomes

$$(s \rightarrow) R$$

In this case, we indicate the stimulus by a small $s$ in parentheses because, while we know there must be a stimulus, we cannot identify it.[1]

*Conditioned stimuli for operants and respondents.* Just as we cannot identify the *unconditioned* stimulus in the case of the operant, we usually cannot identify the *conditioned* stimulus. Ordinarily, we do not attempt to determine exactly what stimuli in the Skinner box become associated with lever pressing. We rely entirely on changes in *rate* of response to tell us when the animal has started to learn something. Before its responses become conditioned, the rate of response is very low; the rat hardly presses the bar at all. After it has become conditioned, the rat will press the bar at a relatively high rate.

It is apparent, however, that operants do come to be performed in the presence of some stimuli and not in others. Skinner (1938) trained some rats, for example, to press the lever in the Skinner box only when the light was on. Superficially, the light in this case appears to be a conditioned stimulus. Skinner (1931, 1935, 1938), however, presents some cogent theoretical arguments against considering it to be a conditioned stimulus in the same sense that the stimuli used by Pavlov are conditioned stimuli. In the case of the Pavlovian or respondent conditioned response, the conditioned stimulus is paired with each occurrence of the response. In the case of the operant conditioned response, the response is free to come out in a very large number of stimulating situations; it is, however, reinforced only in the presence of some definite stimulus—in Skinner's example, in the presence of light.

Because these two procedures are quite different, Skinner has avoided

---

[1] Distinctions similar to that between operants and respondents have been made by other investigators. Konorski (1950) makes one which is very close to Skinner's. Better known to American investigators is a distinction made by Hilgard and Marquis (1940). They suggest the terms "classical conditioning" and "instrumental conditioning." Classical conditioning occurs in any situation in which the conditioned response has no effect upon the delivery of the unconditioned stimulus. In Pavlov's laboratory, for example, the unconditioned stimulus was delivered regardless of whether or not the animal salivated to the conditioned stimulus. In the case of instrumental conditioning, the conditioned response has an effect upon the appearance of the unconditioned stimulus. In avoidance training, for example, if the animal responds to the conditioned stimulus, it will avoid the electric shock.

the use of the term "conditioned stimulus" in connection with the operant. He prefers to use the term "discriminative stimulus." There is considerable merit to this term, since the operant does come to be attached to particular stimuli by a process of discrimination. Other learning theorists, however, have used the term conditioned stimulus to apply to any stimulus which elicits or sets off a learned response, whether it is an operant or respondent. We shall follow the more widely accepted terminology, and thus use only the term conditioned stimulus. The reader, however, should remember that a conditioned stimulus for an operant may have been established by a procedure very different from that used in the establishment of a conditioned stimulus for a respondent.[2]

With the distinction between operants and respondents behind us, then, we are ready to examine the processes of generalization and discrimination. The processes of generalization and discrimination are exactly the same, or at least very similar, for operants and respondents, though the means by which they arise may be somewhat different in the two cases. In respondent conditioning, discrimination is usually begun after the response has become conditioned to a specific stimulus. In operant conditioning, discrimination is begun after the response has become established in the presence of *all* the stimuli in the environment of the animal. Thus a dog is conditioned to salivate in the presence of a tone signal. The rat in the Skinner box merely learns to press a lever; there is no particular stimulus which is a signal for the response.

## GENERALIZATION AND DISCRIMINATION

If a dog is conditioned to make a salivary response to some stimulus, the familiar buzzer, for example, he will make that response to stimuli

[2] For most cases, the distinction between operants and respondents is clear enough. There are, however, some borderline cases. Avoidance conditioning (p. 110) is one. Skinner (1938) argues that avoidance conditioning is really operant conditioning, though superficially it looks very much like respondent conditioning. In avoidance conditioning, there is a definite unconditioned stimulus (usually electric shock) which elicits the response. The unconditioned stimulus is paired with some conditioned stimulus (a tone, for example) until the tone itself comes to elicit the response in question. Skinner's arguments as to why this should be considered an example of operant learning are too complicated to present here, but the interested student may want to consult his book (1938). In passing, it should be noted that Skinner advances the hypothesis that respondents are limited to smooth-muscle and glandular responses, while operants are limited to skeletal responses.

other than the one specifically conditioned. For example, the dog conditioned to the buzzer may also give a conditioned response to the beat of a metronome (Pavlov, 1927). To some extent, then, the dog fails to discriminate between a stimulus to which he has *not* been conditioned and one to which he has been conditioned. This failure of discrimination is known as "generalization" or "induction."

The tendency to give a conditioned response to a stimulus not specifically conditioned is usually not so strong as the tendency to respond to the specifically conditioned stimulus. Thus there is usually some degree of differentiation or discrimination to begin with. One of the first things we want to know about generalization of conditioned responses to various stimuli is the amount of such generalization. If a response is conditioned to a particular stimulus, how strong is the tendency to make that response to other stimuli?

*Generalization of the galvanic skin response.* The best known studies of generalization of the conditioned response are the studies of Hovland (1937a, 1937b) on the conditioned galvanic skin response (abbreviated GSR). This response is a sensitive change in the electrical resistance of the skin, and it is an autonomic reflex that is relatively easy to condition. Hovland used electric shock as the unconditioned stimulus and a pure tone of 1,967 cycles as the conditioned stimulus. After the GSR had been conditioned to this tone, Hovland measured the magnitude of the conditioned response that occurred to other tones of the same intensity but of different frequencies. The other tones were spaced a certain number of just-noticeable differences apart, on the assumption that equal JNDs provided a sensory scale with equal intervals [an assumption apparently correct only in the case of pitch (Stevens and Davis, 1938)]. Hovland found that the magnitude of the conditioned response was at a maximum for the tone specifically conditioned and that it fell off in a negatively accelerated function for frequencies both above and below the tone specifically conditioned. These results are shown in Fig. 14.

In addition, Hovland performed a second experiment. This time he held frequency constant and varied the intensity of the stimulus. He found essentially the same kind of gradient, but in this case the difference between the responses to the generalized stimuli and the response to the specifically conditioned stimulus was smaller. In other words, his subjects seemed to generalize pitch less than intensity.

The existence of generalization, as well as some degree of differentiation, has been confirmed in numerous studies (Littman, 1949). The specific form of the generalization gradient found by Hovland, however, has not always been confirmed (Schlosberg and Solomon, 1943; Hake, Grant, and Hornseth, 1948). This is understandable, because we would expect the amount of generalization to be dependent upon a number of conditions: the response used, the pattern of reinforcement, the degree of motivation, the intensity of the unconditioned stimulus—to name only a few

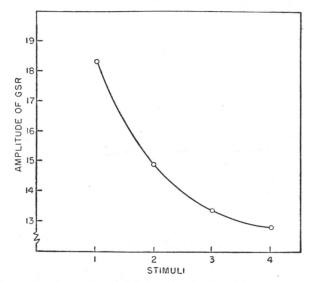

FIG. 14. Generalization of a conditioned galvanic skin response to different stimuli. Stimulus 1 was actual conditioned stimulus. Other stimuli were tones of different frequencies. (*After Hovland, 1937a.*)

factors. The importance of studies like Hovland's is that they have established gradients of generalization as fact. These gradients are of fundamental importance, because many of the phenomena of forgetting, transfer, and problem solving depend upon the process of generalization.

*The process of discrimination.* If we wish to break down generalization, we can do it by differential reinforcement. This is a matter of reinforcing responses to one stimulus while failing to reinforce responses to other stimuli.

It has been suggested, perhaps not too seriously, that very early in infancy all organisms exhibit almost complete generalization; that is to say, almost any stimulus will elicit almost any response. If this idea be so, it is only through a laborious process of differential reinforcement that organisms are brought to the point where they can show the degree of discrimination we can measure in the laboratory. Thus all learning reduces to a kind of discrimination. At any rate, it is easy to see from casual observation that man and animals show high degrees of discrimination. The well-trained hunting dog, for example, will easily recognize and respond only to its master's voice. The process whereby this discrimination is developed can be studied in the laboratory to great profit.

Extinction, as well as conditioning, will generalize (Hovland, 1937a). This fact is of fundamental importance to the process of discrimination. The fact that extinction generalizes makes discrimination a very complicated and slow process. An example will show us something of the interaction of the generalization of conditioning and the generalization of extinction.

Suppose, for example, that we condition an animal to avoid shock by pairing a 1,000-cycle tone with an electric shock. The animal must learn to flex its forepaw to the tone in order to avoid the shock. After we have trained the animal to the point of avoiding the shock almost 100 per cent of the time, we change the conditioned stimulus to a tone of 500 cycles. The animal will give a conditioned response to this stimulus, but, since it is not reinforced, it will soon extinguish. When we return to the 1,000-cycle tone we find that the animal has generalized the effects of extinction to the 500-cycle tone, so that it will not respond to the 1,000-cycle tone nearly so well as before. It will take only a few trials, however, to bring the response to the 1,000-cycle tone up to full strength. This will, of course, tend to raise slightly the strength of the response to the 500-cycle tone, and so it will have to be extinguished again. A number of such alternations of conditioning and extinction will eventually bring the animal to the point where it can discriminate between tones, *i.e.,* respond positively to the 1,000-cycle tone and not respond to the 500-cycle tone.

*The algebraic-summation theory of discrimination.* The best theory about discrimination which has been advanced to date is the algebraic-summation theory. This theory has been most adequately presented by Hull (1943). Hull has made the simple assumption that conditioning and extinction interact algebraically. The amount of generalization of extinction is simply subtracted from the amount of generalization of conditioning at any point. If we let $R$ stand for response strength (from conditioning) and $I$ for inhibition (from extinction), the following equation expresses the notion:

$$R_a = R - I$$

$R_a$ is the *net* response strength left after the inhibition due to extinction is subtracted.

The theory is illustrated in Fig. 15. Here, the solid curve represents the generalization of conditioning $(R)$, the dashed curve represents the generalization of extinction $(I)$, and the dotted curve represents the net response strength $(R_a)$ after $I$ has been subtracted from $R$ for every stimulus.

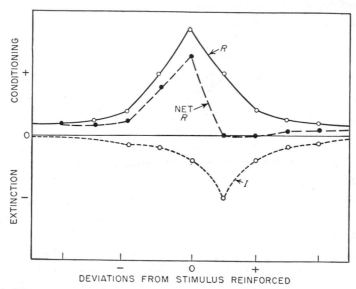

Fig. 15. Illustrates algebraic summation theory of discrimination. Net response strength is a result of subtraction of generalized extinction from generalized conditioning. (*After Hull, 1943.*)

The algebraic-summation theory of discrimination is probably the most adequate we have at the moment. It is possible that the generalization of conditioning and extinction do not interact in this simple manner, but there is no direct evidence against the notion. Certainly, the algebraic-summation theory has very adequately handled a great deal of data in discrimination learning.

*The effect of motivation upon discrimination.* Pavlov (1927) reported that he was able to obtain almost perfect discriminations after long and careful training. When a difference was above threshold, animals could always tell the difference between two stimuli, which they indicated by responding positively to one stimulus and not responding to the other stimulus. Skinner (1938), however, has pointed out that this apparent absolute degree of discrimination will be altered by a change in the motivation or drive of an animal. Under a fairly low degree of motivation (animals which have been fed not too long before), it is possible to obtain almost perfect discrimination in the Skinner box. Rats will learn to press the lever when the box is dark and not press it when the box is lighted. If, however, the animals are made hungrier, the discriminations will become imperfect; there will be a "leaking" of responses in the dark to responses in the light. It is reasonable to suppose that, under very high motivation or in highly charged emotional situations, even the best of discriminations will break down.

*Spence's analysis of transposition.* Talking about discrimination naturally leads us to the phenomenon of transposition, for this is the term that is used for the apparent ability of organisms to make *relational discriminations*. It implies that animals, and people, respond to relations between stimuli rather than their absolute values. Transposition is an important problem for the learning theorist—as well as for the more practical individual—and we should therefore consider some examples of it and how it is understood in learning theory.

An example of transposition is given by an experiment of Köhler's (1915). Chickens were trained to respond (with food as reinforcement) to the darker of two gray surfaces. They were never reinforced when they responded to the lighter of the two surfaces. When this discrimination had been perfected, the animals were presented with a new choice. They were made to choose between the *original* reinforced gray and one *darker,* rather than lighter, than the other. The animals, by and large, immediately chose the darker of the two grays, even though they had always been reinforced in the presence of the other stimulus. In other words, argued Köhler, the animals had learned the relationship "darker than" rather than the association of the originally darker stimulus with the reinforcement.

For a theoretical treatment of this phenomenon, we turn to Spence (1937a). He analyzed this behavior in terms of the mechanisms of generalization and discrimination. To follow his reasoning, let us suppose that we have trained an animal to discriminate between two stimuli, to which we can assign the arbitrary intensity values of 256 and 160. The response to stimulus 256 is reinforced and the response to stimulus 160 is extinguished. Then, after we have established a discrimination between stimuli 256 and 160, we shift the values of the stimuli to 256 and 409. We find that the animal chooses stimulus 409, a stimulus to which the response has never been reinforced. This is an example of transposition or relational discrimination.

Spence's theoretical analysis of this case is illustrated in Fig. 16. He points out that we know that the extinction to stimulus 160 generalized to some extent to stimulus 256. Furthermore, the conditioning to stimulus 256 generalized somewhat to stimulus 409. To arrive at the value of response strength to a particular stimulus, Spence assumes that the inhibiting effects of extinction may be subtracted from the positive effects of condi-

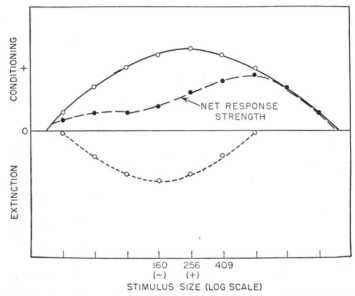

Fig. 16. Illustrates how algebraic summation theory of discrimination can account for "transposition." The net response strength is strongest not at stimulus specifically conditioned (256) but at higher ones (409, etc.). (*After Spence, 1937a.*)

tioning. Under these conditions it is quite possible that the net response strength to stimulus 409 may be greater than that to stimulus 256. Stimulus 256 will have suffered some reduction in response strength as the result of the generalization of extinction, but stimulus 409 will have suffered much less reduction, because it is farther away—in stimulus value—from stimulus 160 than is stimulus 256. Figure 16 shows how it is possible under these conditions for stimulus 409 to have the greater residual response strength.

With this type of analysis, Spence can also predict that some of the time transposition will fail; *i.e.*, the animals will appear to respond to the absolute properties of stimuli. This will happen, he deduces, when the new stimulus is so far away from the positively conditioned stimulus that little or no positive generalization will have occurred. In this case, despite the effects of generalized extinction, the animals will continue to respond to the old stimulus. And Spence's prediction is supported by the data. When the new stimulus is too far away from the previously conditioned stimulus, transposition does fail (Klüver, 1933; Gulliksen, 1932; Spence, 1937b; and Webb, 1950). Spence (1942a) also finds failure of transposition in a case in which chimpanzees were required to choose the middle of three stimuli.

Several studies of transposition in children (Kuenne, 1946; Alberts and Ehrenfreund, 1951) show that as children progress from preverbal to verbal stages of development, they change their solutions to transposition problems. In the preverbal stage, they seem to solve transposition problems in a manner indicated by the analysis of Spence; however, when the children become verbal, they tend to use verbal techniques in the solution of the problem. Here again, as in the previous chapters, we have evidence that human behavior in its more rudimentary aspects is controlled by the basic mechanisms of learning, but that verbal behavior tends to short-circuit these mechanisms.

*Stimulus generalization and transfer of training.* Stimulus generalization is a basic component in the ability of organisms to transfer what they have learned from one situation to another, similar situation. The relationships between stimulus generalization and even very simple examples of transfer of training are quite complicated, however, and we must postpone a discussion of these relationships until some other important factors in human learning have been examined. Suffice it to say at present that stimulus generalization of verbal responses to symbols has been well established in human learning (Yum, 1931; Gibson, 1941). The generalization curves obtained with verbal material seem to be similar in most respects to those obtained by Hovland and others. Response strength is at a maximum to the stimulus involved in original learning and falls off as the stimuli become more and more different from those used in original learning.

## SIGN LEARNING

Most of the learning problems we have examined thus far have dealt with cases in which organisms learn new responses or learn to modify old responses, cases in which they learn to emit responses under some stimulating conditions and not to do so under others. However, an equally important aspect of behavior concerns the way in which organisms learn relationships between certain aspects of their environments. Organisms—rats included—seem to learn stimulus relationships in the world without the mediation of specific responses. Rats appear to be able to learn the location of food in a maze as well as to learn the responses necessary to get to the food.

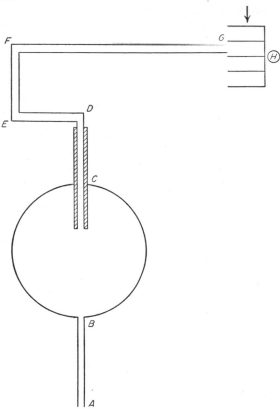

FIG. 17. Floor plan of training maze used by Tolman, Ritchie, and Kalish. The rats must learn the location of G. (*Tolman, Ritchie, and Kalish, 1946a.*)

*Spatial learning experiments.* Demonstration of this last point is provided by some experiments on spatial learning. In one such experiment (Tolman, Ritchie, and Kalish, 1946a), rats were trained to run a rather peculiar elevated maze (a maze in which the paths were elevated runways without walls). As you can see from Fig. 17, the animals, which were required to start at *A,* had to run across a round, open platform, then take a roundabout path to reach the goal box at *G.* After the animals had learned to run directly to *G,* the maze was changed to the even more peculiar pattern shown in Fig. 18. In this maze, the animals found that the pathway that led from the round platform was blocked a short distance away. This made them return to the round platform and then tentatively explore the radial pathways leading out from all sides. The question was: What pathways would they choose? The result was that a preponderance of the ani-

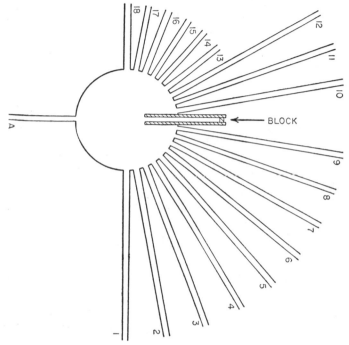

FIG. 18. Floor plan of test maze used by Tolman, Ritchie, and Kalish. Shows that they have learned the spatial location of goals by choosing correct pathway. (*Tolman, Ritchie, and Kalish, 1946b.*)

mals chose to run all the way down the radial path which led in the direction where the goal box should have been. Thus the experiment seems to indicate that, in addition to learning the pathway *A* to *G,* the animals had learned the general spatial position of *G,* and as a result, when the situation was changed, they knew how to start out in that general direction.

Despite the outcome of this experiment, Kendler and his associates have questioned the extent to which rats are capable of this kind of spatial learning (Kendler and Gasser, 1948; Kendler and Mencher, 1949). Instead of the open elevated maze described above, they used an enclosed alley. In that case, they found only a slight tendency for spatial learning.

This finding raises the question whether it is easier in some situations than in others for animals to learn locations rather than to learn specific responses. On the positive side, we have evidence that learning to make a particular turn (to the right, say) is much more difficult than learning the spatial location of the goal (Tolman, Ritchie, and Kalish, 1946b). The relative difficulty of space vs. response learning seems to be a function of the number and kinds of cues available. Under some conditions, learning the spatial location of the goal is very much easier than learning specific responses, but under other conditions, there is little difference between the two (Blodgett and McCutchan, 1947). In experiments in which rats must learn to make specific responses (turning to the right, irrespective of what the visual cues might be), learning is very much retarded, because the spatial cues are in opposition to the specific responses (Blodgett and McCutchan, 1947). Apparently, when rats learn mazes, they acquire both directional and response dispositions, and if these support one another, learning will be facilitated; if they oppose one another, learning will be disturbed (Blodgett, McCutchan, and Mathews, 1949).

It is not clear, however, what these comparisons prove at this stage. There is abundant evidence to show that rats can learn without the mediation of specific responses (Honzik and Tolman, 1936; Seward and Levy, 1949; Deese, 1951). Whether there is a real difference in place or directional and response learning is another question. Some people have considered place learning to be a complex case of stimulus-response learning, while others have considered it to be an example of pure stimulus-stimulus (sign) learning. Tolman has amplified this latter view in a long series of papers, of which his "cognitive maps" paper is typical (Tolman, 1948).

*The relation of response learning to place learning.* We need to find, if we can, some scheme or concept that will let us understand better the respective roles of place and response in the learning processes of organisms. Of considerable help in this matter are some ideas put forth by Hebb (1949). These ideas are not about place learning and response learning, but about the relation of learning early in life to that later in life. From them, however, we are led to a fruitful hypothesis about place learning and response learning.

Hebb makes the observation that the rapid learning of the mature animal depends upon a slow and difficult process of learning how to learn in the infant organism. (It is the more elementary type of infant learning with which most of the early chapters of this book are concerned.) Spatial learning seems to be an exception, however. Hebb points out that rats may require a lot of experience with visual stimuli in order to be able to solve visual discrimination problems. He suggests that a great deal of perceptual organization, by way of learning, goes on during the early life of the rat. This early learning is a slow incremental process, which is in contrast to the frequently obtained evidence of rapid, insightful learning in the older organism.

From these general notions of Hebb, we can now frame a hypothesis about the specific problem of place learning vs. response learning. The studies reviewed above suggest that the adult rat can learn perceptual relationships (place) independently of any particular responses employed. Indeed, the adult rat's use of what it has learned does not seem to depend upon a rigid sequence of stimulus-response units. This ability to behave independently of sequence of responses seems to be acquired. Very likely, in early infancy, the rat learns simple stimulus-response units, in the manner suggested by the classical conditioning experiments. It is only after a considerable amount of generalization and subsequent discrimination that the rat can free itself from pure stimulus-response learning. Therefore, "pure" spatial learning would occur only in the experienced, adult organism.

We should be quick to admit that there is little direct evidence in support of this hypothesis. It ought to be an easy one to test, however. Young animals should find it more difficult than older animals to learn the relationships between various cues and reinforcement; animals with less perceptual stimulation in their histories should find it more difficult to learn about relations between cues. Perhaps very young rats would not be able to learn at all in the pure spatial situations described earlier.

*Set and learning.* Another important question that comes up when one considers discrimination learning is the problem of set or attention. Everyone agrees that animals do not indiscriminantly perceive all stimuli which happen to come into range of their sense organs (Spence, 1950). So there must be some kind of a selector mechanism at work which enables the animal to pick out certain important features of the environment. However, the exact nature of this selector mechanism in discrimination learning has been the basis of a long and rather fruitless controversy (Blum and Blum, 1949). We shall consider only the main experiments and ideas that it has produced thus far.

Krechevsky (1932) suggested that this selection process takes the form of the rat testing and rejecting "hypotheses" about the problem at hand. For example, a rat, when presented with a discrimination problem that requires it to distinguish between a large and a small white circle, might take the hypothesis that turning to the right is the correct solution to the problem. The rat might find that this solution works at about the level of chance. Consequently, it would have to find a new hypothesis, and this one might be that the stimulus card with the experimenter's thumbprint on it leads to food. This, too, might be wrong. If the rat tries one hypothesis after another, it should happen sooner or later upon the right one, which, for example, might be the difference in the size of the circles. Perhaps all this sounds anthropomorphic, but it does essential justice to Krechevsky's notion.

Krechevsky's notion of "hypothesis" in discrimination learning has sometimes been called the noncontinuity theory of learning. The alternative to it is a continuity theory. Those who adhere to this alternative consider discrimination learning to be an essentially continuous process. They believe the rat, for example, probably directs his attention over the environment more or less at random. Of course, some stimuli, bright objects for example, are probably prepotent in capturing the rat's interest (Spence, 1940). Moreover, from one trial to the next, the rat may respond to different aspects of the stimulus situation. Nevertheless, these various responses are reinforced or not, depending on whether they are correct, and the process of learning is one of gradually building up response strength according to the principles of reinforcement we have already considered.

Even the continuity theorists, however, recognize that rats sometimes react consistently to one aspect or another of the stimulus situation. When they do, they might seem to be showing hypotheses. The continuity theorists explain such behavior, however, on the basis of generalization from previous learning. If the rat has learned something before that will help in learning the new discrimination, they speak of positive generalization (or transfer). If the generalization hinders the new learning, they call it negative generalization (or transfer). In any event, they explain hypotheses, when they appear, as generalization from previous learning, and they consider that original learning is otherwise a continuous process.

The bulk of the experimental evidence seems to be on the side of the continuity theorists. One technique which has frequently been used to test the continuity hypothesis has been the use of training reversal. Animals are trained to make some simple discrimination, with one stimulus reinforced and the other not reinforced. After a number of trials, the stimuli are reversed so that the one which was previously reinforced is no longer reinforced, and the stimulus originally unreinforced is now reinforced. If training on the original discrimination resulted in a gradual accumulation of response strength to the reinforced stimulus irrespective of any "hypotheses" the animal may have had, then there ought to be a lot of negative transfer or interference when the discrimination is reversed. Furthermore, the amount of interference should be roughly proportional to the amount of original training. This was found to be so in several experiments (McCulloch and Pratt, 1934; Spence, 1945). Several other experiments, however, find this not to be the case (Krechevsky, 1938; Lashley and Wade, 1946). More recently a number of well-controlled experiments (Ehrenfreund, 1948; Ritchie, Ebeling, and Roth, 1950; Grice, 1951) have shown negative transfer with reversal training, so it appears that the evidence in favor of the continuity hypothesis is a little better than that in favor of the noncontinuity hypothesis.

As further evidence in favor of the continuity hypothesis, Spence (1937b) found a high correlation between the response strength of stimuli used in pretraining experiments and rates of learning of those stimuli in a final training test. Lashley (1942) confirmed this observation, but he suggested that this correlation may have been a spurious one, and that it really did not demonstrate that stimuli which had frequently been reinforced in the past were more easily learned in a new problem. Blum and Blum (1949), however, have recomputed some of the correlations, taking into account Lashley's objections, and they find that the correlations most certainly do indicate a relation between previous reinforcement and the rate of learning on a new problem.

It appears, then, that the experimental evidence favors the continuity theory. Furthermore, the continuity theory fits in a little better with other data obtained upon simple learning in animals. We can conclude, with a reasonable degree of assurance, that response strength in discrimination learning proceeds in much the same way that it does in other, simple learning problems. Each reinforcement adds a small but finite amount to the response strength already accumulated.

*Some concluding remarks about sign learning.* One of the most controversial issues in the present-day theories of learning is that of the role of perceptual or sign learning in the behavioral processes. The issues involved are difficult to understand because the views expressed are by no means clear. The gestalt psychologists have taken the view that learning is to be conceived as perceptual organization. Tolman (1932) has elaborated this position at great length. He has emphasized the development of perceptual memory pictures of the environment that are used when the organism is in an appropriate state of need. This view has been contrasted with the view that the organism learns only specific stimulus-response connections, which get chained together in a complicated way. Theorists at one time or another have announced ideas ranging all over the continuum between these two notions. Furthermore, theorists in these matters change their views from time to time.

At the present time, there seems to be evidence which supports the view that organisms can learn about their environment without the mediation of specific responses. We have no idea, however, how important this kind of perceptual learning may be in the life of the organism as a whole. It probably varies with the kind of organism; the living conditions of some animals probably make it necessary for them to do much more perceptual learning than other animals. Intelligence may be related to the ease of perceptual learning. These are all things, however, for which we have no good data. It would seem that a question as to which is most important, sign learning or stimulus-response learning, is probably irrelevant.

It is possible, however, that stimulus-response learning may be more fundamental or primitive than sign learning. It may require a considerable substrate of stimulus-response learning before an animal is capable of sign learning. We do not know whether or not this is so; it is only suggested as a hypothesis.

## TIME RELATIONS BETWEEN STIMULI

A rather prosaic question about stimuli in learning concerns the time intervals between stimuli. Usually this means the time which elapses between the presentation of the conditioned stimulus and the unconditioned stimulus. Pavlov studied this problem at great length, and we can summarize, very briefly, some of his principal findings.

*Pavlov's studies on time intervals in conditioning.* Pavlov (1927) made use of two different techniques in his studies on the conditioned response. In one technique, the conditioned and unconditioned stimuli overlapped one another in time. The conditioned stimulus may come on before the unconditioned stimulus or the two may be simultaneous, but the essential point is that they overlap. In the other technique, the two stimuli do not overlap. Usually the conditioned stimulus is presented first, followed by an interval of time and then the unconditioned stimulus.

Pavlov thought that the simultaneous conditioned response was the easiest to form, and in all the basic experiments in Pavlov's laboratory the conditioned and unconditioned stimuli were presented simultaneously. Following this basic conditioning procedure, Pavlov would then gradually lengthen the time interval between the conditioned and unconditioned stimuli, or gradually allow the conditioned stimulus to be on longer and longer before presenting the unconditioned stimulus.

With a delay in the presentation of the unconditioned stimulus, Pavlov found that animals could learn to delay the onset of the conditioned response for very long periods of time. Pavlov took the ability of the animals to delay the conditioned response in the presence of the conditioned stimulus to mean that the conditioned response was actively inhibited. He used the *delayed* conditioned response as an example of what he called "internal inhibition." He also found that animals could delay the onset of the conditioned response when the conditioned stimulus was presented and then withdrawn before the unconditioned stimulus came on. This Pavlov called the "trace" conditioned response, and he also considered it to be an example of internal inhibition. He also found that it was more difficult to establish the trace conditioned response than it was to establish the delayed conditioned response.

Most of Pavlov's observations upon delayed and trace responses were directed toward his concept of internal inhibition. He did not study the *rate* of learning with different delay or "trace" periods; he was interested only in the fact that delay or trace conditioned responses could be established. More recently, investigators have concerned themselves with the rate at which learning takes place with different periods of delay between the conditioned stimulus and unconditioned stimulus.

*Rate of learning and delay of the unconditioned stimulus.* A number of studies agree in showing that the highest rate of conditioning occurs when the onset of the conditioned stimulus *precedes* the onset of the unconditioned stimulus by a very brief period of time. The most recent of these studies (Spooner and Kellogg, 1947) summarizes the data from some earlier experiments as well (Wolfle, 1930, 1932). In these studies the conditioned response studied was a withdrawal of the hand (human subjects) produced by an electric shock and paired with an auditory signal. Figure 19 shows the results of these studies. You can see from this figure that the largest percentage of conditioned responses seems to occur when the conditioned stimulus precedes the unconditioned stimulus by about a half a second. The conclusion is almost exactly duplicated by two studies of the conditioned eyelid response (Reynolds, 1945a; Kimble, 1947).

*Backward conditioning.* One curious case of the time relationships between the conditioned and unconditioned stimuli has frequently been investigated. This is the case of backward conditioning. In backward conditioning, the unconditioned stimulus *precedes* the conditioned stimulus. Pavlov thought that conditioning could not take place in this case; how-

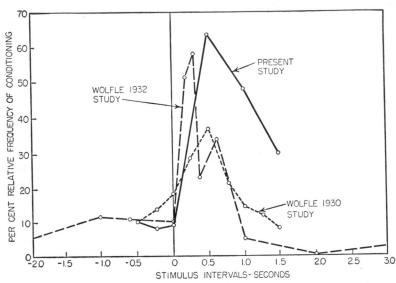

FIG. 19. Results of Spooner and Kellogg (1947) and Wolfle (1930; 1932) studies on the time interval between conditioned and unconditioned stimuli. Notice that the greatest per cent of conditioned responses occur when conditioned stimulus precedes unconditioned stimulus by some fraction of a second. Backward conditioned responses occur in low frequency. (*Spooner and Kellogg, 1947.*)

ever, several investigators (Wolfle, 1930, 1932; Spooner and Kellogg, 1947) have been able to obtain some slight evidence of backward conditioning (see Fig. 19). It has been frequently claimed, however, that backward conditioning is not true conditioning but is kind of a sensitization. The unconditioned stimulus (usually an electric shock in the cases where backward conditioning is found) "sensitizes" the subject so that he will give a response (usually a withdrawal response) to almost any stimulus. This interpretation is in accord with the data found by Spooner and Kellogg (1947). They find that the percentage of backward conditioned responses is initially high, but *decreases* during training. This may be because the subjects become "adapted" to stimuli other than the electric shock.

*Simultaneous conditioning.* Practically all studies agree in showing that conditioning is less efficient when the conditioned and unconditioned stimuli are presented together than when the conditioned stimulus precedes the unconditioned stimulus. Spooner and Kellogg (1947), as a matter of fact, find that when the conditioned and unconditioned stimuli are given simultaneously, the percentage of conditioned responses decreases during training, just as in the case of backward conditioning. For this reason, Spooner and Kellogg have tended to classify simultaneous conditioning with backward conditioning.

Just why strict simultaneity in conditioning is not so efficient is a matter of considerable dispute. It would appear that this fact is inconsistent with Guthrie's contiguity theory of conditioning (p. 57). Guthrie, however, is able to explain this away by pointing out that the external conditioned stimulus may not be the actual stimulus that sets off the response. Guthrie places great emphasis upon movement-produced stimuli as stimuli in learned behavior. If the conditioned stimuli and unconditioned stimuli are presented simultaneously, the movement-produced stimuli will not synchronize properly with the unconditioned stimulus. On this basis, a good case can be made for the notion that Guthrie's contiguity theory is very much in accord with the fact that the conditioned stimulus should precede the unconditioned stimulus by a brief period of time.

Hull (1943), in his theory of conditioning, has made much of the concept of the *stimulus trace*. The stimulus leaves an aftertrace in the organism, and it is this aftertrace which is conditioned. While the trace is building up, conditioning will be very rapid, but after the trace begins to decline, conditioning will be at a slower rate. In this way, Hull is able to account for the curves found in Fig. 19.

CHAPTER 5

# MOTIVATION AND LEARNING

There are certain well-defined relations between the need state of an organism and how it behaves. Hungry rats, for example, are almost always more active than well-fed rats. Just why this is so is a problem for physiological psychology. What are the physiological characteristics of the animal when it is hungry? How does the physiological effect of hunger produce an increase in activity? These and similar questions are important ones for the physiological psychologist to deal with. Right now, however, we are not directly interested in the physiological problems of need states, except in so far as solutions to these problems may contribute indirectly to our understanding of the process of learning. The problem at the moment concerns the relationship between the states of need and learning.

In order to solve this problem we do need some clear way of indicating when an organism is in a state of need. Fortunately, we do not always have to infer a need state from behavior, as we find it necessary to infer a reinforcement from behavior. We can, in fact, define some need states independently of what the animal does. In hunger, for example, there is a continuum from fasting to feeding. An animal which has eaten just an hour ago is less hungry than one which has eaten 24 hours ago, provided both animals are on their accustomed feeding schedules. We can therefore measure the strength of a drive in hours that the animal has been deprived of the needed substance. In some cases, we may wish to know something about the physiological conditions (such as level of blood sugar) brought about by a certain period of fasting, but for most purposes, in the study of learning, it is adequate to know how long it has been since an animal has ingested a certain substance.

This operational definition of drive in terms of feeding and fasting works best with the various hunger drives and with thirst. As a matter of fact, with the possible exception of sleep, it may not work at all with other drives. Consequently, most of the work on the relationship between drives and learning has made use of hunger and thirst. In such work, there is often the implicit assumption that other drives act in the same way as hunger and thirst. That, however, may not be true even for the other, simple primary drives (such as sex), and it is most certainly not true of many of the derived or secondary drives. Nevertheless, there are some general relationships between hunger and thirst and learning. From these relationships, we may not be able to make a very specific statement about, say, the development of the secondary sexual drives, but we do derive some hypotheses that may help solve such problems as those of sexual motivation and learning.

A brief word is in order about another drive frequently used in psychological experiments. This is the need to escape tissue injury. Frequently we "motivate" animals to learn by the use of an electric shock. Escape from or avoidance of the shock is usually considered to be the reinforcement in these cases. We shall examine this kind of motivation in Chap. 6, which deals with punishment. It needs to be mentioned here, because the need to escape tissue injury, superficially, seems to have quite a different relation to learning than the other drives.

## THE RELATIONSHIP BETWEEN MOTIVATION AND PERFORMANCE

*Activity.* Animals are more active when they are hungry. As a matter of fact, there are a number of fairly precise relationships between activity and hunger. These can be summarized as follows: (1) Activity increases directly as a function of hours of food deprivation (Siegal and Steinberg, 1949). (2) There is some point, when the deprivation becomes severe enough, at which activity drops off (Skinner, 1938). This is near the point of complete starvation. (3) Rats, when allowed to exist upon a free feeding schedule, will show regular cycles of activity and eating. A period of quiescence is followed by some activity which culminates in eating (Richter, 1927). (4) Eating itself is followed by a period of subnormal activity (Finger, 1949).

These cycles in activity brought about by different conditions of motivation are important to learning in that animals learn only when they are active. A sleeping animal is inert as far as learning is concerned, and an inactive but waking animal is scarcely better. It is easier to teach a hungry animal to run a maze simply because he is more active. An indifferently motivated rat may sit down in an alley and refuse to go further. So in the sense that drive or motivation is an important determiner of activity, motivation is indirectly important to learning.

There are, of course, many other drives besides hunger that produce activity. Sex, maternal drives, hoarding, and a lowered temperature are all factors which will produce increased activity in the rat (Morgan and Stellar, 1950). So we see that the determinates of activity are of consider-

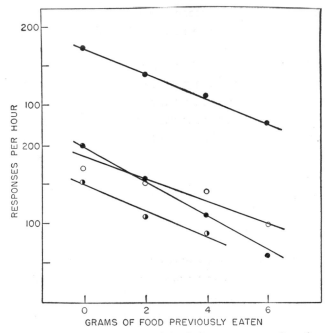

FIG. 20. Rate of responding under partial reinforcement as a function of amount of food previously eaten. The lower curves represent averages of four rats each. The upper curve is an average of the lower curves. (*Skinner, 1938.*)

able complexity. To make matters as simple as possible and to avoid unnecessary confusion, we shall treat the behavior of the rat as though it were entirely determined by drives manipulated in a given experiment. This is a convenient fiction which will considerably simplify our analysis.

*Performance of learned acts and drive.* As you might expect, unmotivated animals in almost any kind of learned task will make many more mistakes than motivated animals. Indeed, even after animals have been trained for a large number of trials, they will choose the alley in a T maze that leads to food only about 50 per cent of the time if they are not hungry (Strange, 1950a). Similarly, the rate at which rats in a Skinner box will press the lever depends upon their state of hunger at the moment. Illustrating this point is Fig. 20 (Skinner, 1938), which shows the rate of responding after the rat has eaten various amounts of food. The more food the rat eats before the experiment, the lower his rate of response. And this is true in extinction just as it is during reinforcement, as you can see in Fig. 21 (Skinner, 1938). Animals not fed before extinction show the highest initial

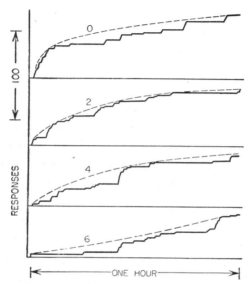

FIG. 21. Each curve is an extinction curve for lever pressing in rats. The number shows how much food (in grams) was fed to the rat before extinction. Notice that the initial rate during extinction is very much higher after no food than after 6 grams of food. (*Skinner, 1938.*)

rate of response; animals fed 6 grams of food before extinction show the lowest initial rate.

So we see that there is a definite relation between learned behavior and motivation. The higher the drive state, the more activity, the higher the percentage of correct responses, and the higher the rate of performance of the specific responses which will satisfy that drive. There is a limit, of course, to this relationship. If an animal is deprived of food or water too long, debilitation results, and this may reduce performance and activity.

*Performance of a learned act and irrelevant drives.* We have just seen that increased motivation results in greater activity, and higher drives increase the tendency to perform responses which satisfy these drives. Now what about the effects of drives *irrelevant* to the behavior in question?

Suppose we have trained a rat to press a lever in order to obtain food. Will increasing the rat's thirst drive increase his tendency to perform the response appropriate to satisfaction of the hunger drive? The answer to this question seems to be an unequivocal "no."

Several studies show that increasing the strength of an irrelevant drive at the time of extinction does not increase the resistance to extinction (Strange, 1950; Siegal, 1946). In both of these studies, the relevant drive, as well as the irrelevant drive, was present in some strength at the time of extinction. For example, the animals may have been trained under hunger to obtain food, then extinguished under both hunger and thirst, but the addition of thirst did nothing to increase the tendency to respond during extinction.

An apparent exception has been found in the case where the relevant drive is very low at the time of extinction; in this study (Webb, 1949), addition of an irrelevant drive did seem to increase slightly the tendency to make the response appropriate to the other drive. This result can be explained, however, by an interaction between hunger and thirst. The animals were trained when they were hungry. Before extinction they were made thirsty by deprivation of water and they were given complete access to food. We know, however, that rats will not eat very much food when they are thirsty, and so during extinction they are slightly hungry as well as thirsty. The tendency to perform the response appropriate to hunger, therefore, can be attributed to the slight degree of hunger drive present.

*Drive and learning jointly determine performance.* Performance is determined both by what and how much an organism has learned and by its drive state. There seems to be a simple way to specify the relationship between drives and learned behavior. When drive is absent, learned behavior does not occur. Furthermore, for most of the complicated behavior of the waking adult, there will be no organized performance unless learning has taken place. In other words, when learning is "zero," the act in question cannot be performed; when drive is "zero," the response in question cannot be performed.[1] This simple conclusion must be tempered, however, by the knowledge that learned drives are possible, so that even

---

[1] Zeaman and House (1950) have some data which seem to show that the performance of a learned act is not zero when drive is reduced to zero. Zeaman, however, worked with the light-aversion drive, and this may be somewhat different from other drives. Furthermore, in Zeaman's experiment, a residual *secondary* drive was probably operating when the primary drive was absent.

in the absence of a "physiological" drive, behavior may occur. Hull (1943) has put this conclusion in the form of an equation:

$$R = f(D) \times f(H)$$

where $R$ is response strength, $D$ is drive, and $H$ is habit. The equation means that response tendency is some function of drive times some function of habit, and it expresses the joint effects of drive and learning on performance.

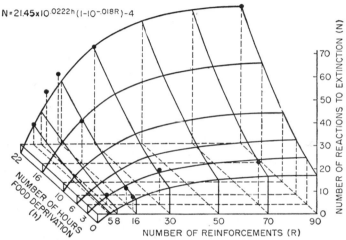

FIG. 22. Resistance to extinction as a joint function of number of reinforcements and hours of deprivation. The dots are the obtained, empirical points. The curves are extrapolations from these points. (*Perin, 1942.*)

Hull (1943) has shown how the joint determination of response strength by drive and learning works by summarizing some data from other investigators (Perin, 1942; Williams, 1938). The measure of response strength used in these investigations was resistance to extinction. As we saw in Chap. 3, the number of responses in the extinction curve increases as a function of the number of reinforcements. And, as we can see from Fig. 22, the number of responses in the extinction curve also increases as a function of the hours of deprivation. Figure 22 shows the relations of both number of reinforcements and drive to response strength. This figure cannot be taken too literally, for if an extinction curve is obtained after a very short period of food deprivation, the curve rises more rapidly than would be expected from Fig. 22 (Saltzman and Koch, 1948). The curve probably also does not hold for very long periods of deprivation.

It is very important to realize that this curve shows nothing of the way in which drives *modify* learning. This can clearly be understood if we examine the way in which the data were obtained which went into Fig. 22. All the animals in two experiments summarized in this graph were *conditioned* after they had been deprived of food for 23 hours. They were *extinguished* after various amounts of deprivation, ranging from 3 to 22 hours. The learning in these experiments was under a constant level of drive, but performance during extinction was under different levels of drive. The effect of different levels of drive upon *rate* of learning is an important problem, and we shall deal with it next.

### THE EFFECT OF MOTIVATION UPON LEARNING

As we have just seen, performance is determined in part by the level of drive. For the subject matter of this book, a more fundamental question concerns the relation between the *rate* of learning and the level of drive. This question has received a lot of experimental attention; consequently we are able to offer a fairly clear picture of the relations between the rate of learning and drive strength. The experiments which bear on this question are of two types: (1) latent-learning experiments in which drive is the principal variable; and (2) studies of the effect of drive level during learning upon resistance to extinction.

*Latent-learning experiments.* In Chap. 2 (p. 34) one kind of latent-learning study was examined. This was one in which hungry rats were allowed to explore a maze before the introduction of a reward. In general, the results of several such experiments showed that learning was independent of the kind of *specific* reinforcement employed. Rats allowed to explore a maze without food reward eventually showed that they learned the maze as well as animals that had been rewarded all along.

The kind of latent-learning experiment which is important to the question of motivation and learning is a little different. In this kind of experiment, satiated rats are allowed to explore a maze which contains a reward. If the reward is food, the animals are satiated with food before they are allowed in the maze. The result is that they will not nibble at the food in the maze; indeed, they may seem to pay no attention to the food whatever. The question we now ask is: Do the satiated (nonhungry) rats learn the maze as well as rats which are hungry? Many experiments have been designed to answer this question, and we shall attempt to review a few of them.

The best known of these studies is one by Spence and Lippitt (1940). In one of their experiments, animals were trained in a T maze which contained food in one goal box and water in the other. The animals were satiated for food and motivated for water. After a number of trials in which the animals were forced to go to each side of the maze an equal number of times, the motivation was changed so that the rats were now hungry instead of thirsty. If the animals had profited from being in the presence of food even though they were thirsty and not hungry, they should now choose the side leading to food rather than the side leading to water. If, however, learning depends on the level of drive and the relevance of a drive to the reinforcement, the animals should continue to choose the water side, even though they were now hungry. As it happens, the rats chose the side leading to water. Though the reasoning upon which the experiment was based is far from foolproof, the results suggest that the effect of a reinforcement is somehow dependent upon the level of drive present.

Spence and Lippitt, however, went on to perform a second experiment, and this turned out to complicate the picture. This time the rats were treated to food on one side of the T maze and to nothing on the other side. Otherwise, the rats were thirsty, but they had continuous access to food. In contrast to the first experiment, when the animals were switched from water deprivation to food deprivation, they chose the food side about as often as animals which had been trained under high hunger motivation all along. Thus it appears that when the thirst drive is not reinforced, the animals learned the location of food, though not motivated for food.

Many subsequent experiments have contributed to the ambiguity of the situation. Some studies indicate that learning is dependent upon the animals being motivated to reach the goal in question (Kendler, 1947; Kendler and Mencher, 1948; Walker, 1948). Some studies are just plain ambiguous (Spence, Bergmann, and Lippitt, 1950), and some indicate that animals can learn the location of a goal even though they are not specifically motivated to achieve that goal (Meehl and MacCorquodale, 1948, 1949; Frank and Deese, 1949; Strange, 1950; and Thacker, 1950).

Various theorists have tried to explain these conflicting results. Among those who believe learning not to be dependent upon motivation, Leeper (1948b) has pointed out that the results which seem to show that learning the location of food cannot take place when the animal is not motivated for food may be explained by failure to control the attention of the animals. That is to say, in these experiments, the animals may never have noticed the goal objects irrelevant to their thirst drives. Various subsequent experiments have attempted to test this idea of Leeper's, sometimes with results in favor of Leeper's view (Frank and Deese, 1949) and sometimes with results opposed to it (Kendler and Mencher, 1948).

Leeper's criticism of those experiments which fail to find latent learning is but one of many criticisms which have been leveled at these experiments (Thistlethwaite, 1951). If we tentatively accept the conclusion that animals *can* learn the location of a goal object when they have an irrelevant drive, it would mean that rate of learning does not depend upon motivation. To this conclusion, however, we are forced to believe that the experiments which show opposite results are contaminated by some sort of experimental artifact. Even this assumption, however, does not solve our problem, because it has been frequently pointed out that thirsty animals are always somewhat hungry. But this criticism of the latent-learning experiments has sometimes been answered by saying that the rats may be *physiologically* hungry, but they are not really hungry in a behavioral sense, for they do not eat and they are not interested in food. Thus, as you can see, the results of the latent-learning experiments in which drive is a variable are highly inconclusive.

*Resistance to extinction and drive at the time of learning.* Fortunately, however, there is another approach to the same problem. It is to find out how conditioning animals under various levels of drive affects resistance to extinction. To do that, a number of investigators have measured the extinction of responses learned under different levels of drive. In their experiments, rats were conditioned to press a lever after various periods of deprivation of food, and then they were all extinguished under the same level of drive. One group of rats, for example, was conditioned after 12 hours of food deprivation and another after 24 hours of deprivation. Both groups were then extinguished after a period of 24 hours of food deprivation. If the rate of learning were affected by the level of drive under which it occurred, the group conditioned after 24 hours of food deprivation should show more responses in the extinction period than the group conditioned after 12 hours of food deprivation.

But experimental results in this type of situation are almost all negative (Kendler, 1945; Reynolds, 1949; Strassburger, 1950). With extinction as the measure, it appears that the effect of reinforcement is independent of the level of drive under which it is given. An earlier study (Finan, 1940) showed that animals conditioned after 12 hours of deprivation gave significantly more responses in extinction than did animals conditioned after

1 hour of deprivation. However, animals conditioned after 24 hours of deprivation and animals conditioned after 48 hours of deprivation showed *less* resistance to extinction than did animals conditioned after 12 hours of deprivation. These results are in conflict with the later studies, but the differences are very small, and the conclusion probably holds that rate of learning in the Skinner box is independent of the level of drive over a very considerable range.

Finally, a recent study (Deese and Carpenter, 1951), which combines some of the features of the latent-learning studies with some of the features of the resistance-to-extinction studies, shows the same results. When the drive under which animals have learned to run in a simple runway is suddenly *increased,* the change in behavior is what would be expected if learning were independent of the level of drive (Deese, 1950a). These animals, in fact, do as well as animals which had learned under high drive. When the drive is suddenly *reduced* in strength, however, some residual effect of the high drive is present. Even though the animals may now be working under low drive, they act as if they were working under high drive. This residual effect found in the switch from high drive to low drive is very much like something called "externalization of drive" (Anderson, 1941a; see p. 96) which we shall consider later, in another context. We can safely conclude, however, that learning seems to be independent of drive in this situation.

*The implications of the independence of learning from drive.* This conclusion, that learning, within limits, does not depend upon the level of drive, has several implications. For one thing, it is an additional bit of evidence against the drive-reduction theory of reinforcement (p. 28). One would expect from this theory that the amount of drive reduction per reinforcement would depend upon the absolute level of drive because the stronger the drive, the more reinforcement should be able to reduce drive stimuli. That, however, is not what happens, so this deduction from the need-reduction theory appears to be incorrect. It is possible, of course, that need reduction could operate independently of the absolute level of drive, but from our present understanding of the hypothesis, this would not be likely.[2]

There is one very serious qualification to the conclusion that learning does not seem to depend upon the level of drive. We have already seen

[2] Hull, the principal advocate of the need-reduction theory, originally took the view that learning was a function of drive (Hull, 1943). Later, however, he postulated learning to be independent of drive (Hull, 1950).

that drive is necessary for performance. Inasmuch as organisms must do something in order to learn, learning depends upon drive. This is a most indirect sort of dependence. It means that if an animal is motivated enough to move about, increasing his motivation will not appreciably increase his ability to learn. This fact may account for the apparent disagreement of Finan's (1940) experiment with the other experiments on rate of learning and drive. You will remember that he found that the animals conditioned under very low drive (after 1 hour of food deprivation) showed a little less resistance to extinction than animals conditioned under a higher drive. It may well be that this group simply was not active enough to learn properly.

If these conclusions are correct and if they apply to human learning as well, they should change our ways of looking at motivation in human learning. To be sure, little Johnny must be motivated in order to learn to read, but this may simply mean that he must go through the proper motions of reading in order to learn what they are. The rate at which he learns may not depend upon how motivated he is, except in so far as motivation may determine the degree of attention he will give to the task.

### SECONDARY OR DERIVED DRIVES IN ANIMAL LEARNING

Thus far we have dealt only with examples of primary or unlearned drives; of these we have used only hunger and thirst. The reason for that is that the simple, primary drives are easily and quantitatively handled in the investigation of certain problems. Obviously, however, we cannot deal with all learned behavior in terms of these simple drives. In human behavior, for example, at least in civilized human behavior, these drives probably play a minor role in all but very early learning. Indeed, it is difficult to see the motivation of the scientist or politician or artist in the same light as the motivation of the hungry rat. So there are certainly more complex drives to consider before we can understand all kinds of learned behavior.

In order to understand what these drives are, it is necessary to see how drives can become acquired. That is the subject of this section. In considering it, we should admit that we are just beginning to find out how the complicated, learned drives of the daily lives of men and rats come into existence. To date, our knowledge in this area has come principally from the study of simple, secondary drives in animals. If we wish, for example, objects to which animals will normally be quite indifferent can be made to assume great importance in their lives. The process by which this change is brought about is the development of secondary or conditioned drives. We can gain some notion of the nature of these secondary drives by studying the way in which they originate and are maintained.

*Token-reward studies.* An interesting example of a secondary drive comes from studies of token rewards. The general idea of such studies is to choose some primary drive, such as hunger, and some stimulus, such as a poker chip, and to give the stimulus secondary reinforcement. This is done by making the animal use the stimulus (the poker chip) to satisfy his primary drive (*e.g.,* to get food). In time, the animal comes to work, indeed to learn new habits, in order to get the stimulus. At this point we say that a secondary drive has been set up because the animal is now motivated to get, and is rewarded by getting, the stimulus that received secondary reinforcement.

To be more specific about such secondary drives, we may take Wolfe's (1936) experiment with chimpanzees. First of all, he trained them to insert poker chips, *i.e.,* the tokens, in a slot machine in order to obtain food— much as rats were trained in a Skinner box to press the lever to obtain food. Then he trained the animals to discriminate between poker chips of different value. With a fine disregard for the rules of poker, he gave them two grapes for a red chip, one grape for a blue chip, and no grapes at all for brass chips. The final and important step was to train them in other tasks, such as pressing a lever, in order to obtain the poker chips. In learning such tasks, the chimpanzees showed that they had developed a secondary drive for poker chips.

*Strength of secondary drives.* Secondary drives built up in this way, however, do not seem to be very strong. For one thing, animals will not go to any great limits in piling up tokens. In an experiment somewhat similar to Wolfe's, for example, Cowles (1937) was finally able, after a long process of training, to get chimpanzees to accumulate as many as 20 poker chips without first being paid off in food. That is not very many chips. A second sign of the weakness of such secondary drives is the ease with which they extinguish. In studies of this point (Smith, 1939; Mitrano, 1939), token-reward habits extinguished very quickly when they were not given primary reinforcement.

This aspect of experimentally produced secondary drives makes something of a stumbling block for people who would like to interpret the intricate motivation of human learners in terms of secondary drives. What prevents the money-hoarding behavior of the miser from being subject to either satiation or extinction? We can supply a number of hypothetical answers to this question, but I am afraid that we cannot be very confident of any of them. The reason for this caution is that no one has ever satisfactorily demonstrated the existence of a secondary drive acquired in the laboratory which was very resistant to extinction, much less one that increased in intensity with repetitions of the learning situation without primary reinforcement, as seems to be the case in human behavior. This fact should make us a little cautious in making use of the hypothesis that all higher order drives are derived from simple, biological drives by a process of conditioning. We have demonstrated that drives can be developed through conditioning, but we are far from a perfect understanding of human motivation in terms of secondary drives.

*Specificity of secondary drives.* Experimentally produced secondary drives not only seem to be weak in strength, but there is some question about how general they are. The token-rewarded habit, in Wolfe's (1936) experiment, for example, seems to be specific to the drive to which it was conditioned, for the chimpanzees were not interested in the tokens when they were satiated for food. On the other hand, Estes (1949a, 1949b) finds that rats trained to associate the click of a feeding magazine with water will still work for the "click" when they are given access to water but deprived of food. You will remember, however, that rats deprived of food will tend also to be somewhat thirsty, and it may well be that Estes's animals continued to respond on the basis of a residual thirst drive.

The conclusion that secondary drives are not limited entirely to the presence of the primary drive, however, is bolstered by some studies of Anderson's (1941a, 1941b). Anderson arranged his experiments so that rats had to learn a new maze solely on the basis of secondary reinforcement. He found that these rats would learn the new maze whether or not they were deprived of food or whether or not food was present in the maze, so long as the new maze contained cues which had been associated with food in the past. He called this behavior "externalization of drive," and by this he meant that a motive had become established to an external object rather than an internal state of need.

*A broad basis for secondary motivation.* Unfortunately, one of the most important questions about secondary motivation has received no experimental treatment at all. This is the problem of what would happen if a cue or token were conditioned to two, three, or more primary drives. How stable would the secondary drive be if, for example, the click of the magazine in the Skinner box were associated with reinforcement of the thirst drive, the hunger drive, and the sex drive? Would the drive to hear the click then be more resistant to extinction?

There is no experimental answer to these questions. An experimental program in this area is badly needed, since this may well turn out to be one of the crucial missing links between the elaborate secondary drives of ordinary living and the secondary drives of the laboratory. Perhaps, too, if a secondary drive paired with a large number of primary drives were acquired under a schedule of partial reinforcement, the results would approximate the stronger learned drives of everyday life.

Before leaving this point, we should note that Anderson's notion of externalization of drive, mentioned above, corresponds fairly closely to a concept developed by Allport (1937) in a discussion of human personality. Allport calls this concept the "functional autonomy of motives." As he put it, a functionally autonomous motive is a self-sustaining motive; it is not dependent upon the satisfaction of some basic biological need. Functionally autonomous motives develop from primary motives by a process of learning; thus, on a superficial level at least, the concept appears to bear close resemblance to the concept of externalized drives. Indeed, if one wished to go out on a limb, one could say that Anderson's externalized drives in the maze are prototypes of such involved autonomous drives of human life as what Thorstein Veblen called the "instinct of workmanship." As Allport points out, good workmanship to the skilled craftsman is an end in itself, aside from all monetary rewards the workman may receive as the result of his effort. The comparison to the rat who learns a maze for its own sake, rather than because it is hungry, provides an interesting parallel. Perhaps future experimental work will bridge the gap between the human's functionally autonomous motives and the rat's externalized drive.

*Fear as a drive.* A word needs to be said about fear or anxiety as a secondary drive. Fear may be called a secondary drive which develops by a process of association with situations which are injurious or painful to the organism. For example, in flexion conditioning (p. 110), the tone, which is the conditioned stimulus, tends to become feared by the animal because it is associated with shock, which is painful. If fear is a secondary drive, it should be possible to teach animals to avoid such conditioned stimuli in themselves; that is, to develop a secondary drive of avoidance. Miller (1948), in fact, demonstrated that animals can be trained to avoid such secondary cues. In this way, as Miller points out, cues associated with painful stimulation can acquire the functional properties of a drive, and escape from, or avoidance of, such secondary cues can acquire the functional properties of a reward.

Fear as a drive is of very great importance in human and animal behavior; consequently, it has received rather thorough experimental treatment (Miller, 1951). Some of these experiments are covered in Chap. 6, which deals with punishment, so they will not be reviewed here. It is only necessary to point out that fear is, to a very considerable extent, a simple secondary drive based upon association with noxious situations.

### MOTIVE-INCENTIVE CONDITIONS IN HUMAN BEHAVIOR

Our operational definition of drives in animal behavior is in terms of such simple measures as the number of hours of deprivation of, say, food. When we come to use this definition with human beings, we are confronted with the obvious fact that human behavior is much too complicated. To be sure, some of the complicated behavior of people is motivated by primary biological drives, such as hunger, thirst, and sexual need, but even when that is true the connection between the behavior and the drive is rather indirect. As a consequence, the operational definition of drives that serves us well in animal learning will not do for human learning.

Even when we can identify the primary drive in human learning, it is usually interwoven with secondary, acquired drives. A person works for the promise of satisfaction of a primary drive. This promise may be in the form of money, praise, social status, or security, which only indirectly and after some delay satisfy the primary drives. That fact makes us think primarily in terms of secondary drives when we consider human learning. We cannot, in fact, always be sure that the motives we see are actually acquired from primary motives, for occasionally learning seems to take place because of some intrinsic interest or some sort of motivation which may, in the end, prove to be "built in" rather than acquired.

*The origin of human motives.* There are many theories about the origin of human motives. One comes from the psychoanalysts who like to tell us that the origin of most, if not all, human motivation is in a vital urge most intimately bound up with the sexual drive. Another comes from experimental psychologists who work with secondary reinforcement; they suggest that our motives come from a lot of basic, biological urges. Others have suggested that there are many kinds of motivation, but that in a sense they are all unlearned.

Probably, as with nearly all theories, there is some truth in each of these views. The sexual drive, both because it is strong and because repressive measures against sexual behavior are found in most societies, probably is responsible for a tremendous amount of motivated activity. Personal adornment, courtship behavior, speech patterns, physical labor, all may owe a great deal to the sexual drive. Yet the picture is obviously a complicated one, for people indulge in physical labor for reasons other than to satisfy a sexual urge, either directly or indirectly. There are undoubtedly many primary drives which get transformed by a learning process, and there is good reason to believe that many of the complicated actions of life are motivated more or less directly by simple, unlearned drives. It has been suggested, for example, that alcoholism in part may be due to a genetically determined inability to metabolize certain vitamins (Williams et al., 1949).

Fortunately, for many of the problems of learning, it is not necessary to be concerned about the origins of motives. We can study the relationship between certain incentives and learning, for example, without knowing just why the particular incentives we use are effective. We have already seen (p. 94) that motives can be learned; we are now concerned with the relationship of motivation to the learning process and behavior per se.

*The nature of incentives.* In animal behavior we can easily distinguish between motives and incentives. We can make an animal hungry without promising it food. Alternatively, as in Anderson's experiments, we can offer an animal an incentive (food) without the animal's being hungry.

An incentive is something which an organism will actively attempt to obtain; it is a goal object. This notion of incentive is very close to the notion of reinforcement as defined by the effect theory of reinforcement. It is necessary to keep the distinction clear between the operational definition of a reinforcement (a stimulus which will increase the strength of a response) and the operational definition of an incentive. McGeoch's definition of reinforcement according to the principle of effect (p. 28) is a definition of an incentive; thus, according to the principle of effect, an incentive and a reinforcement are the same, but it is important to remember that they are the same *only* if we accept the theory of effect.

In the case of human behavior, it is not so easy to distinguish between motives and incentives. Frequently, in laboratory studies of learning, we will tell the subject that he will receive something in return for behaving in a certain way. The subject may be offered a bonus for learning a maze; in life most people operate on the assumption that their employer will properly reward them at the end of a pay period. The incentive in these cases is what is offered the learner. His motivation is the desire to obtain this incentive.

Human motivation cannot easily be manipulated, so frequently we end up by manipulating the incentive and calling it a change in motivation. Most of the time this is justified; people, by and large, have a greater desire to receive $10 as the bonus for a laboratory experiment than $1. Strictly speaking, however, this example is one of the manipulation of the value of the incentive. Because changes in incentive value are nearly always accompanied by changes in motivation, the incentive becomes just about the most suitable device for studying human motivation in the laboratory. There are cases where this relationship does not hold, however, and we must be on the watch for them so that we do not misinterpret some notions about human motivation.

Thus the value of an incentive depends upon two aspects: (1) The learner must have a desire for the incentive—the motive part of the picture. (2) The learner must have the ability to understand the nature of the reward or incentive. While most of the time we cannot separate motives and incentives in human behavior, in theory at least we can parallel the action of motive and incentive in animal behavior by the cases in human behavior. Whenever we offer a human learner an incentive, we assume that there is a motive to go along with it. In the case of the rat, we create the motive by depriving it of food or water. In human learning, instead of making the learner go through the task once to find out that he will actually be rewarded, we tell him beforehand and rely on the knowledge that he has already learned enough about the way the world works to accept our word.

*Incentives and performance.* There is a large literature in industrial psychology on the relationship between various incentives and output. Most of the literature is irrelevant to learning, but two examples will demonstrate a point. Kitson (1922), in a classical study, showed that industrial workers of long experience may not necessarily be working at top efficiency. Despite the fact that the typesetters whom he studied had ample opportunity to learn their trade to perfection, the addition of a monetary incentive resulted in a great improvement in output. Similar studies (Mace, 1935) have shown that the addition of an incentive may delay or eliminate fatigue (work decrement) due to continuous work. Thus, incentives operate to increase performance of a goal-directed activity.

Various incentives which are used in industrial work create many problems of a psychological and sociological sort. While these problems are of interest to a general understanding of human behavior, they are not directly important to the psychology of learning. Consequently, the use of incentives in industry will not be stressed here. Suffice it to say that the use of incentives such as piece-rate payments or special bonuses does not always work as it should. The motivations of workers in modern industrial society are very complicated. It is true that the human being in our civilization seems to be almost universally motivated for the acquisition of coin, but this is frequently obscured by other motives. He may be motivated to earn a certain, minimum amount of money with the least possible effort. He may be motivated by such things as security, social approval, or "feelings of self-respect," all of which have been indicated as important in industrial performance. Thus, the manipulation of one kind of motivation, the desire to earn money, may not always lead to the expected results, because of the fact that the other motives of people may lead them to act in different ways.

We do not need to dwell upon the learning and performance of people at work to see how incentives affect human learning, for there are a host of experimental studies dealing directly with this subject. In these studies, psychologists have employed a wide variety of incentives, and there are several possible ways of classifying them. For our purposes, the following classification will do: praise and reproof, promise of reward, rivalry and competition, and ego involvement. We shall now consider how these incentives affect human behavior.

*Praise and reproof as incentives.* A particularly important group of incentives are those *verbal* incentives which can be classified as praise and reproof. Such incentives are present, whether we realize it or not, in almost all our learning and education, both in school and in everyday life.

The classical study of praise and reproof as incentives is that of Hurlock (1924). She used four groups of school children who were of approximately the same level of ability. These children practiced addition problems under different conditions. One group worked by itself without comment from the teacher. Three other groups worked together under different incentive conditions. Of these, one was given praise and encouragement for its work; another was reproved or dressed down for its careless and inferior work; and a third group heard and saw praise and reproof given to other children but received none itself. At the beginning of the experiment, all four groups were about equal in their scores on the addition test. As it went on, the control group—the one that worked by itself—did not gain at all from practice. Of the three groups working together, the one that was praised gave evidence of large and consistent gains throughout the examination period; the one that was reproved gained early in practice but could not maintain its gain; and the group that was ignored, like the reproved group, gained slightly at first and then fell back to its original level.

The early gains evidenced by all three of the groups that worked together may be the result of an increased motivation early in practice which resulted from the complex conditions of rivalry, etc. It is interesting, however, that the reproved and ignored groups, who did not receive a positive incentive for their increased performance, soon fell off in performance. Most important is the fact that the praised group, which was motivated both by the situation and by reward for its progress, consistently gained throughout the experiment.

It is important to note in this experiment that the increased scores were not necessarily a result of learning, but they may have been similar to the effects of drive upon performance in animal behavior. Looked at in this light, the increased motivation and incentive could have maintained the children at higher levels of efficiency in the use of the skills they had already acquired.

This interpretation of the effects of praise and reproof is borne out in a subsequent study (Brenner, 1934). Brenner's study shows that the novelty of the experimental situation can provide motivation in itself. Brenner did not confirm the specific form of Hurlock's results, however, and we probably ought to attribute this lack of agreement to a fundamental difficulty in this type of experiment, namely, the fact that the experimenter himself is a variable. Whatever praise and reproof are given must be given by a person, and characteristics of this person undoubtedly have a good deal to do with the results. Indeed, a more recent study has shown that the type of individual giving the incentive may be much more important than the nature of the incentive (Schmidt, 1941).

Despite this problem, however, the conclusions concerning the relative effects of praise and blame probably stand. These conclusions probably can be generalized to say that motivated behavior should be positively rewarded. Thus, reproof or blame probably is adequate for motivation, but in order to ensure a continued high level of performance, the improvement which results from reproof should be immediately rewarded. If it is not rewarded, the individual's desire is not satisfied; he has not eliminated the source of the blame or won praise in its place.

Because human learners are intensely "ego-involved" in what they are doing, praise and blame are powerful incentives. There are wide individual differences in the effects of praise and blame, however, because human personalities differ in the type and degree of ego involvement (Thompson and Hunnicutt, 1944). Thus, on one hand, there is the unbalanced high-school student who commits suicide because he is criticized by his teacher, and, on the other hand, there is the blithe psychopath who persists in antisocial behavior despite the stern disapproval of the entire community.

*Promise as incentive.* Several studies indicate that a *promise* of a reward, usually money, is effective in improving efficiency in the classroom (Thorndike and Forlano, 1933; Forlano, 1936). One of these, an early study by Leuba (1930–1931), indicates that it does not matter too much what kind of an incentive is promised or in what amount the incentive is given.

These studies raise an interesting question: How does the promise of reward work as an incentive? The principle of effect suggests that rewards actually act to preserve behavior which they follow. This is Thorndike's view (1932). As a matter of fact, Thorndike cites the results of the effects of rewards and their promise upon human behavior as proof of the principle of effect. It is obvious, however, that the effects of rewards could be interpreted entirely as an effect of motivation upon performance. Motivation increases the efficiency of performance. The promise of a reward raises a motive to achieve that reward, so performance may be improved. To be sure, Thorndike (Thorndike and Forlano, 1933) has claimed that rewards increase the *rate* of learning, but this is not clearly established. Even if it were, rewards could still work by increasing the efficiency of performance and hence the efficiency of what is learned, rather than through the principle of effect (stamping-in). In other words, individuals may learn better under a promised reward simply because they are more attentive to what they are doing, and that, in turn, lets them more readily correct their mistakes.

*Rivalry as an incentive.* Another incentive that is greatly emphasized in our culture is rivalry or competition between individuals and between groups. Rivalry is obviously not a simple incentive, and it has something in common with other incentives that we are considering here. Nevertheless, it is one we can label and use in various situations, including learning experiments. In such experiments, both group and individual rivalry have been used as incentives. Hurlock (1928), for example, has studied the effect of group rivalry upon children. Children quickly catch on, she finds, to the spirit of group rivalry and they perform better in order to see the group to which they belong come out ahead. The effectiveness of group rivalry as an incentive, however, seems to decrease with intelligence. As a matter of fact, with high mental ages (adults) the effectiveness of group rivalry almost entirely disappears (Sims, 1928; Whittemore, 1925). Zubin (1932) has shown with school children that rivalry between individuals is a potent way to increase performance.

These various forms of competition are effective in practice, provided they can be made genuine. Indeed, they may be very useful as a social technique for improving performance. However, rivalry frequently results in other things besides increased performance. It may produce undesirable changes in attitude, such as antagonisms and feelings of inferiority for those who do not "win." In any learning situation, decisions have to be reached about these possible effects, and it may be these decisions rather than decisions about the effects of rivalry as an incentive per se which are of fundamental importance.

*Ego involvement and motivation.* Many of the incentives mentioned thus far depend to some extent upon the individual learner being motivated to defend and expand his ego. Motivation which involves any use of the individual's own estimation of his status in the world is called "ego involvement." The effectiveness of an incentive in a situation may depend to a very considerable extent upon the willingness of the learner to defend his ego in that situation. For example, I would not be at all dismayed to be ribbed about my inability to read Babylonian cuneiform, but I would feel very sheepish indeed about any slight to my ability to read the psychological journals.

The degree of ego involvement is one of the factors most responsible for variations in the effectiveness of various kinds of incentives. Failure does not mean the same thing to an individual who is indifferent to his performance on that task as it does to an individual who is highly motivated to succeed. Likewise, praise is ineffective as a motivating device unless the individual is motivated to achieve recognition for his work.

The importance of ego involvement as a source of motivation in human behavior cannot be underestimated. Sometimes, ego involvement may be so great that threat of failure disorganizes performance on a task (Alper, 1946b). It is indeed surprising that this very powerful source of motivation is frequently ignored by those who must deal with people in a practical way. It has been pointed out (G. Watson, 1939) that the correlation between the employer's estimate of the worker's needs and wants and the worker's own statement of his wants is just about zero. The employer believes that wages and security are the dominant motives, whereas it is apparent that ego satisfaction is of primary importance to many individuals.

*Intrinsic versus extrinsic motivation.* The kinds of incentives we have been talking about thus far are what have been called "extrinsic incentives." They are motivating devices to get people to do tasks irrespective of the inherent satisfaction from doing the task. From the point of view of the sort of social theories upon which our society operates, we may view these kinds of incentives with a little distaste. After all, we ought to do things because we can see that they are worth while in themselves or that they lead to some desired end. Intrinsic motivation is then the kind of motivation that comes from a knowledge that accomplishment of a task is going to satisfy some goal in itself. We seldom need an extrinsic motivation in teaching an adolescent how to drive an automobile.

It is important to remember that this distinction is one that is critical primarily to society and social ethics. It is important to the psychology of learning only in so far as motivation is important to learning and in so far as there are any real differences between the strengths of motivation associated with intrinsic and extrinsic incentives.

In some cases, there are, no doubt, real differences between intrinsic and extrinsic incentives. Such incentives as praise and incidental rewards may begin to pall after a while, whereas intrinsic motivation remains constant or even may increase. These differences are not clearly established, however, and it is well to remember that society does recognize the importance of extrinsic motivation in getting people to do things.

The relative values of extrinsic and intrinsic incentives are important to theories of education, but, at least in this stage of our knowledge, it makes little difference to the psychology of learning.

## MOTIVE-INCENTIVE CONDITIONS AND RATE OF LEARNING

Earlier in this chapter when we took up the relationship between drives and learning in animal behavior, we saw that amount and rate of learning do not seem to depend critically upon degree of motivation. If an animal is motivated enough to be active, it does not seem to be important how motivated it is. This is an interesting and important point, and in thinking about human learning we may ask: Is the same true of human learning? Within limits, it probably is. In human learning, as in animal learning, it is necessary for the learner to do something in order to learn. In human learning this means attending to the business at hand and actually going through the proper motions. Beyond determining these effects, motivation may be of little importance in human learning. Unfortunately, however, we cannot be as positive that this conclusion applies to man as that it does to animals, for there are only a few scattered experiments on the problem.

*Incidental learning in human learners.* First of all, there is some evidence that humans *can* learn when they are not specifically motivated to do so. Perhaps the most familiar of the studies concerned with this problem is one by Lepley (1935). Lepley tested for recall of class names in a group of college students who had heard the roll called 45 times. It is apparent from the results Lepley attained that the students learned the names of the people who immediately preceded and followed their own names. There is no good reason for people to learn these names, particularly those which occur after their own names; it appears as though these students simply learned these names incidental to other activities.

Another example of incidental learning is provided by a demonstration of Jenkins (1933). Jenkins had a student, who thought he was serving as an experimenter, read a list of nonsense words to another student, who was instructed to learn the words. After the learner had reached a certain criterion, both the subject and the experimenter were dismissed and told to return 24 hours later. At this time both subject and experimenter were asked to recall the list of words. It turned out that both the learner and the experimenter recalled a great many of the words from the list; the learner, however, recalled more words than did the experimenter. Upon asking for reports from the subjects, Jenkins found that some of the experimenters did deliberately try to learn, but even those who did not deliberately try to learn recalled a good many of the words.

This experiment shows that (1) even without specific instructions to learn, human beings will form a set to learn; (2) even without this specific set to learn, humans will learn. In this connection we may note that, in Jenkins's experiment, as the set to learn decreased, the amount of material retained 24 hours later decreased. So, while it appears that subjects can learn without a specific set to learn, they seem to learn more adequately when they do have such a set.

In a third experiment, the investigators (Biel and Force, 1943) attempted to control for lack of attention in incidental learning. One group of subjects was told that the experiment was one in the legibility of type face. The subjects in this group were instructed to mark the most legible of nonsense syllables which appeared in different styles of type. A control group was given instructions to learn. Immediately after being given 12 trials of practice with the nonsense syllables, both groups were tested for recall. It turned out on this immediate measurement of retention that the group which had practiced without intent to learn recalled slightly more syllables than did the group which practiced with intent. On a delayed retention test sometime later, the same result was found. The results of this experiment imply very strongly that once the learner's attention is focused on the material to be learned, the particular set or motivation he has is unimportant. They imply, too, that the incidental learners ("experimenters") in Jenkins's experiment did not learn as much as the learners because they did not pay enough attention to their work.

*An analogue to latent learning.* This question of incidental learning, which we have been considering, is very much like the question of latent learning in animals. When we took up latent learning (p. 90) we noted two main points: (1) animals are capable of learning something without having a specific incentive to learn it; and (2) once they are motivated enough to keep them working at a task, increased motivation and increased rewards do not make them learn any faster. These are the two main points supporting the notion of latent learning. We have just seen above that one of them, namely, learning without an incentive to learn, may also hold for human beings. We may now go on to ask whether the second point, namely, that *additional* incentives do not increase learning once there is enough motivation to perform, also applies to human learning.

Unfortunately, there are no crucial and conclusive experiments on this point, and all that we have is a preliminary experiment (Deese and Bowen, 1950) that tends to confirm it. In this experiment, subjects were required to learn a series of letters from the International Morse Code. These subjects were willing and cooperative students who were paid for their work. Subjects in one group were told at the beginning of the experiment that if they made a certain score (the exact score was never specified) on a final recall test, they would receive an additional bonus of two dollars. Thus, one group of subjects received a promise of reward before learning began. A second group of subjects learned the code signals without the promise of a bonus; before the final recall test, however, this group was also told that if a certain score were made, an additional two-dollar bonus would be given. Thus both groups were motivated on the final test, but only one of the groups had the additional incentive during learning. As it turned out, the group which was promised the bonus before learning began showed a higher number of correct responses during learning; so it is clear that the two groups differed in performance as a result of the motivation. On the final test, however, both groups did equally well. The conclusion seems to be that the additional incentive affected performance, but that learning, as measured by the final test, was just as good without the additional incentive. Unfortunately, the number of subjects was small and the results cannot be pushed too far. It is harder to establish a negative conclusion than a positive one, so a bigger number of subjects is necessary before we can be content with the results of this experiment.[3]

*Some conclusions about motivation and human learning.* Superficially at least, human learning seems to have about the same relationship to motivation as does animal learning. Motivation operates chiefly upon performance. In so far as better performance forces better learning, motivation operates upon learning. Beyond a critical level of motivation which establishes good performance, it is not clear that additional motivation makes for better learning. If this is true, the place of motivation in animal learning is exactly paralleled in human learning.

It is important to remember that we can learn only what we do. Thus motivation is of practical importance for human learning. To be on the safe side, it is better to make sure that learners are motivated. In the schoolroom, a child who is unmotivated can go through the superficial motions of performance without really doing what we want him to. The author recently saw an example of this point in a youngster who had completely failed to learn how to do subtraction. He was a bright young boy, and evidently during the school hours devoted to this subject he had hit upon the effortless expedient of writing down numbers at random as a means of satisfying the superficial requirements of the schoolroom. This activity did not get him to learn subtraction. When really put to the task, however, he learned subtraction with no difficulty at all. In the vernacular, this boy had been "just too lazy," but his trouble was that he had not been motivated to do subtraction.

There is an important question whether certain incentives are more effective than others in getting people to perform and thus to learn. We do not have clear evidence, however, with which to answer it. In practical situations, what is the most effective incentive probably depends a lot on the personality of the learner and the social and ethical situation. So, for

---

[3] A recent experiment by Saltzman (1951) supports this conclusion. In an incidental learning experiment, Saltzman found that specifically telling the subjects to "try to learn" did not increase amount learned.

the present at least, these are things which are best left to the parent or teacher. The skillful teacher, for example, will be an artist at fitting the proper kinds of motivating devices to the needs of the moment, but the unskillful teacher will go on using all the incentive devices she can find in the textbooks and teaching manuals—probably without any noticeable effect upon her pupils.

# CHAPTER 6

# NEGATIVE REINFORCEMENT AND PUNISHMENT

In the first few chapters of this book, we occasionally saw examples of learning in which the reinforcement was avoiding or escaping some painful stimulation. In a flexion-conditioning experiment (p. 15), for example, a dog learns a new conditioned response when a buzzer and shock are paired together, and eventually the dog comes to raise its leg when it hears the buzzer and thus avoids shock. This is an example of *negative reinforcement*. Up to this chapter, however, we have had no occasion to consider punishment. An everyday example, of course, is spanking a child for getting into the cooky box. That, at any rate, is the kind of situation in which we speak of punishment. Negative reinforcement and punishment have much in common, but they also differ in important respects. The purpose of this section is to consider these similarities and differences.

*Anxiety.* Both punishment and negative reinforcement involve anxiety. Although this term is used somewhat differently from time to time by different people (Mowrer, 1939, 1947; Estes and Skinner, 1941), it refers in general to an emotional disturbance that has become conditioned to a neutral stimulus by some process of pairing the neutral stimulus with painful stimulation. For example, in flexion conditioning of the dog, the first application of electric shock produces an emotional disturbance in the dog; later, because the buzzer comes on just before the shock, the buzzer becomes conditioned to the disturbance. When it sounds, it is said to produce anxiety in the dog; and when we use anxiety in this sense, we are summarizing the fact that organisms will act toward a neutral stimulus which has been associated with a painful stimulus as if the neutral stimulus were itself painful.

*Negative reinforcement.* The notion of anxiety is important, at least in learning theory, in understanding secondary reinforcement. When secondary reinforcement is used, as in the flexion-conditioning experiments, anxiety is generated. As some theorists see it (Mowrer, 1947; Skinner, 1938), the conditioning of anxiety is a simple matter of contiguity learning—simple learning by association. Once established, however, anxiety takes on the role of a need, a sort of unpleasantness or discomfort, and thus becomes a secondary drive. This drive can now be reduced by the appropriate behavior, for example, by the dog lifting its leg when it hears the buzzer. So it introduces a second stage of learning which some theorists regard as taking place through the principle of effect. The need-reduction theorists (Hull, 1943; Mowrer, 1947) consider the reduction of anxiety to be the reinforcing state of affairs. More operational theorists (Skinner, 1938) simply liken the learning that takes place because of anxiety to other types of operant learning. In any case, the basic notion of negative reinforcement is that anxiety is acquired by contiguity conditioning and this, functioning as a secondary drive, is responsible for the further learning that negative reinforcement produces.

There is an interesting theoretical consequence of this notion of the role of anxiety in negative reinforcement. If anxiety functions as a secondary drive, then it ought to be possible to use it to produce new learning without the presence of the primary incentive originally used to built it up. To be more specific, one would predict that once animals had been taught to avoid a painful stimulus such as shock and also had been presented with pairings of a tone and shock, they would learn to avoid the tone, even if the shock were not present. This prediction has been tested with an experiment, and the experiment confirms the prediction (Miller, 1948). So we have some direct evidence that anxiety functions as a secondary drive.

*Punishment.* Now punishment, like negative reinforcement, produces emotional disturbances, and thus it comes to produce anxiety. Punishment and negative reinforcement are not alike, however, in two important respects: (1) For one thing, negative reinforcement is painful stimulation for *not* doing something, and consequently it is an incentive to the organism to change its behavior. For example, in flexion conditioning, shock is administered when the animal does *not* lift its paw, but it avoids or escapes shock when it does. In punishment, on the other hand, the organism gets painful stimulation for doing something, and the punishment is an incentive to stop or suppress a response. In punishment, for example, an animal gets shocked for pushing the wrong lever or the child gets spanked for making noise. (2) Secondly, negative reinforcement is applied to poorly motivated behavior; punishment is applied to moderately or highly motivated behavior. The child bangs the floor or gets into the cooky jar, not simply at random, but because he has some motive to do so. Punishment must suppress a response that has a motive and an incentive. In the experimental case of negative reinforcement, on the other hand, it is the more or less random behavior of the animal, or perhaps behavior elicited by the negative reinforcement itself, that it is designed to change. In this case, the reinforcement does not have to combat some other motive or incentive—at least not a strong one.

With this much of a background concerning the use of the terms "negative reinforcement," "punishment," and "anxiety," we can go on to an analysis of the experimental work on punishment.

### THE CLASSICAL EXPERIMENTS ON PUNISHMENT

Thorndike, for many years, dominated the theory of punishment. Because his influence is still felt to a very considerable degree today, it is best to begin with his notions concerning the effects of punishment.

*Thorndike's earlier views.* When Thorndike promulgated his original statement of the principle of effect (1898), he believed that there was a simple, common-sense solution to the problem of punishment. Punishment was simply the exact opposite of reward. Thorndike said for reward learning that if a modifiable connection is made and is accompanied by or followed by a satisfying state of affairs, the strength of the connection is increased. At the same time, he also said that if a connection is made and is followed by an annoying state of affairs, its strength is decreased. Thorndike defined an annoying state of affairs in terms of its effect upon the animal. By an annoying state of affairs he meant one which the animal does nothing to preserve, often attempting things which put an end to it. This definition, incidentally, will serve us as an operational definition of painful stimulation.

*Thorndike's later views.* Over a period of years which followed this statement of the dual law of effect, Thorndike came to the conclusion that the effects of an annoying state of affairs were not quite so simple as this common-sense view would make it appear. He decided this after a long series of experiments, on both animal and human learning. In brief, Thorndike accumulated evidence which convinced him that the effects of reward and punishment were not mirror images of one another. "The results of all comparisons by all methods tell the same story. Rewarding a connection always strengthened it substantially; punishing it weakened it little if at all" (Thorndike, 1932a, p. 58).

The way in which Thorndike came to this rather surprising conclusion makes an interesting story. This is particularly true since the interpretation of his experimental work, especially that on human subjects, has become a very controversial issue (Postman, 1947; Stone, 1948a). Both the logic and generality of his conclusion have been challenged. An analysis of the experimental work promoted by Thorndike's views will make some of the controversial issues clear.

*Thorndike's experiment.* Thorndike's most characteristic experiments upon the problem of punishment made use of a rather mild form of "painful stimulation." Most of his work on human subjects concerned a comparison of the effects of the experimenter saying "wrong" as opposed to "right" following certain responses of the subject. The effects compared were the relative frequency of repetition of the punished or rewarded responses.

In one of his experiments, Thorndike (1932b) asked subjects who were not familiar with Spanish to guess the correct English word to a Spanish word, given in the form of a multiple-choice test. If the word chosen were correct, the experimenter informed the subject by saying "right"; if the chosen word were incorrect, the experimenter said "wrong." It was possible to determine the effect of "right" or "wrong" upon the frequency of repetition of the subject's first response by finding out, on further testing, if the subject gave the punished or rewarded response with a frequency greater or lesser than that expected by chance. Since there were five alternatives for each item on the test, the frequency of repetition by chance would be 20 per cent. This was the base line against which Thorndike measured the effect of saying "right" or "wrong" upon the tendency to repeat a response. As it turned out, the consequence "right" did increase the tendency to repeat the initially given response. The consequence "wrong" had no weakening effect at all; as a matter of fact, it seemed to Thorndike that it may have had a slight strengthening effect.

Many repetitions of similar experiments by Thorndike (1935) led to the same results. But other investigators have leveled some serious criticisms at Thorndike's experiments. In the first place, the use of "chance" as a base line against which to measure the effects of reward or punishment has been called into question. It is extremely unlikely that responses of subjects in such a situation are at the chance level "when nothing happens"; rather there seems to be evidence that responses go in "runs" or sequences to which the one-in-five chance expectancy would not apply.

Stephens (1934*b*) used an empirically determined probability of repetition, rather than chance, in an experiment much like Thorndike's. The empirically determined frequency of repetition without any consequences turned out to be about 36 per cent instead of 20 per cent. When the effects of punishment were measured against this base line, there was a weakening effect of saying "wrong" (Stephens, 1934*a*, 1934*b*). The situation is complicated by the fact, however, that an earlier experiment by Lorge and Thorndike (1933) failed to find such a weakening influence even when the effects of punishment were measured from an empirical base line.

*Some indirect effects of punishment.* Thorndike has argued that in some situations punishment may indirectly weaken a response. This occurs because, according to Thorndike, punishment produces variability of behavior. Thus a painful stimulus, or what Thorndike called an "annoyer," may lead the organism to make a new response. In maze learning, for example, punishment of an error may lead the learner accidentally to make the correct response, and this response indirectly eliminates the punished response, because it will always be performed hereafter.

This notion was advanced by Thorndike to account for the cases, in both animal and human learning, in which punishment of incorrect responses does seem to facilitate learning (Postman, 1947). In addition, some evidence has been gathered which more directly supports Thorndike's position. Bernard (1942), in a study of human learning, showed that punished errors, per se, were not eliminated faster than errors which were not punished. Punishment did facilitate learning, but it did so by producing greater variability of behavior and thus increasing the probability of the subject's discovery of the correct response.

Stone (1948*b*) has recently performed an experiment which does not seem to confirm this notion altogether. He finds that when subjects are under instructions to learn, the mere occurrence of a particular response increases the probability of its repetition above that expected by chance. Measured from this empirical base line, Stone found that saying "wrong" following a response not only failed to reduce its strength, but actually increased the strength of the response. Thus, in this case, punishment could hardly have been said to produce greater variability of behavior. According to Stone, the effects of punishment are very complicated and depend upon the interaction of punishment with other factors.

*Other factors which may influence the effect of punishment.* In a move to bring some order out of chaos, Stephens (1941) has advanced the hypothesis that the effect of punishing a response depends upon the strength of the response at the time of punishment. To test this hypothesis, Stephens had a group of schoolboys indicate their choice of the correct response in 84 items on a multiple-choice test. He also asked them to indicate, on a three-point scale, their degree of certainty. This was done for three days; on the third day the correctness of that day's choice was indicated. A fourth day was used to test for the repetition of responses which were supplied with "right," "wrong," or no information. Stephens discovered that "wrong" had little effect where the subjects were not sure of their choices and had shown little consistency in the first three days, whereas "wrong" very definitely reduced the repetition tendency of responses which were consistent the first three days and of which the subjects were sure. Stephens points out that Thorndike and his supporters almost universally had used such weak associations that the effect of symbolic punishment upon these associations was of little significance. Further experimentation is needed to establish this point. However, the hypothesis serves to reconcile the opposing results found by different workers.

A further criticism of Thorndike's interpretations concerns the intensity of the punishment he used. Stephens (1934a) has argued that the failure to find a weakening effect of punishment may be due to "wrong" functioning more as a positive reinforcement than as a punishing stimulus. The influence of "wrong" as a fixative agent may be greater than its influence as a punisher. Consequently, Stephens (1934a) compared the effects of a flash of light as a stimulus with the effects of symbolic punishment. The flash of light apparently is slightly reinforcing, since it increased the frequency of repetition over that frequency found when nothing happened after the response. Measured from the repetition frequency to the flash of light, punishment had a weakening influence. This may account for the findings of Stone (1948b) cited above, which showed that punishment seems to increase the strength of response.

*Other stimulus effects of punishment.* Muenzinger and his associates (Muenzinger, 1934; Muenzinger, Bernstone, and Richards, 1938) have shown that shocking the correct response in discrimination learning with rats will result in some facilitation of learning, though not so much facilitation as if the wrong response were shocked.[1] Thus it is possible that a punishing or negatively reinforcing stimulus may act in several ways. In addition to the possible inhibiting effects upon behavior, it may serve the

---

[1] It is only fair to mention that Wischner (1947) obtained opposite results. This is apparently due to a difference in the way of measuring trials (Muenzinger, 1948; Wischner, 1948).

opposite function of *emphasizing* those responses with which it is temporally contiguous. Because responses near to the punishment in time are emphasized, they may be remembered and possibly consciously avoided on the next trial, not because they are shocked, but because they are incorrect. That shock as a purely informational stimulus is of value in the elimination of errors has been demonstrated for human learning by Bunch (1935). Shock could serve to tell the subject that the response it follows is correct. Thus learners could deliberately ignore the punishing aspects of a painful stimulus and use it as a cue to the correct response.

*A summary of the experiments stemming from Thorndike's work.* The author believes we can safely conclude that in general punishment *does* have a weakening effect. This is not universally true, however; many experiments indicate that punishment may actually serve to increase the strength of a response. This is probably because the punishing stimulus has some function other than punishment. It may serve to reward subjects or to give them information or to emphasize the responses which it follows. Furthermore, it is probable that the effects of punishment depend both upon the strength of the punishment and upon the strength of the response at the time of punishment. In the main, punishment has the effect of at least temporarily suppressing responses which it follows, but a host of particular conditions may make this generalization incorrect for any given situation.

### THE EFFECTS OF PUNISHMENT WHEN ONLY ONE RESPONSE WILL SATISFY A DRIVE

One of the most important conditions of punishment has been all but completely ignored in the classical experimental work. This concerns the effect of punishment upon a response when that response is the only one which will satisfy a drive. It is easy to see that in the Thorndikian type of experiment, the learner may have his "drive" satisfied by responses other than the specific responses punished. The learner is seldom interested in defending his original response as the "right" one, and he will readily abandon it when he knows it is "wrong." Thus, in this case, the effect of punishment is to produce variability of behavior, as Thorndike suggested.

But what happens when the response which satisfies a drive itself is punished? The child who is punished for stealing from the cooky jar knows no other way to satisfy his craving for sweets. No matter how many raps on his knuckles the child may receive, the cookies lose none of their attraction. There are some very interesting experiments upon rat behavior which tell us a good deal about this situation.

*Skinner's experiment.* Skinner (1938) studied the effect of punishment upon the lever-pressing response in the Skinner box. In his experiment, the punishment was a sharp slap on the paw of the animal, delivered as a result of a lever-pressing response. The slap was automatically delivered by the lever itself.

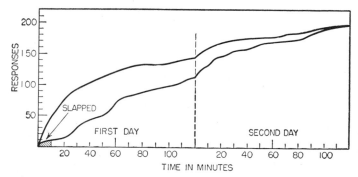

FIG. 23. The effect of punishment upon the number of responses to extinction. The initial effect of punishment is to reduce the rate of responding. There is, however, a recovery from this effect. (*Skinner, 1938.*)

To measure the effects of such punishment, Skinner obtained extinction curves following periodic reinforcement with food from four rats. Of these rats, two were slapped at the beginning of the extinction period and two were not. The result was that the rats that were slapped at the outset of extinction showed a much lower rate of response during extinction. As a matter of fact, the punishment seemed to inhibit the response entirely for a brief while. The curious thing, however, is that by the time extinction had been about completed, the slapped rats had caught up, in the total number of responses emitted, with the rats that were not slapped. These results can be clearly seen in Fig. 23.

Skinner interpreted the results of this experiment to indicate that punishment has only a temporary inhibiting effect. It does not affect the "reserve" of responses which the animal has to emit; it only affects the rate at which that reserve will be emitted. Early in extinction, the animals that are punished show a lower rate of response, but eventually the rate for these animals accelerates so that they show a total number of responses equal to that of the animals that have not been punished. Thus punishment does not weaken the tendency to perform a highly motivated response; it only inhibits it for a time.

*Estes's experiments.* Estes (1944) has made a very extensive study of the effects of punishment in the Skinner box. In these experiments he substituted an electric shock for the slap. The shock was delivered through the lever in the Skinner box, so that rats that had been used to receiving food as the result of pressing the lever received a shock instead. Estes came to conclusions which are very similar to those of Skinner. The effect of punishment was permanently to weaken responses only slightly, if at all, but there was a temporary inhibition of the tendency to respond as a result of the punishment. Estes found that even if he continued the punishment for long periods of time, there was always some recovery of response strength after the punishment stopped.

Estes did find, however, that there was some permanent depression of the reserve of available responses, even though the punishment never completely eliminated the extinction curve of the food-getting response. When the punishment was administered according to a periodic schedule, the effect of depression of the rate of response was not nearly so severe, but the depression lasted longer. You will recall that in periodic administration, a stimulus—the punishment in this case—is not delivered for every response, but is delivered for only an occasional response. It is interesting that the results of periodic punishment parallel almost exactly the results of periodic reinforcement (p. 50).

*Estes's suggestions about the use of punishment.* Estes's experimental work has led him to make some statements about control of behavior through the use of punishment. His principal point has already been mentioned. It is difficult, he says, to eliminate a response permanently from an organism's behavior by the use of punishment. Permanent weakening of a response can apparently come about only by pure extinction, that is, by evoking the response without any reinforcement. To put this conclusion in Estes's own words: "A response can be permanently weakened only by a sufficient number of unreinforced elicitations, and this process of extinction cannot proceed while a response is suppressed as the result of punishment" (Estes, 1944, p. 37).

This conclusion, Hilgard (1948) points out, is in accord with the clinical findings about forms of aggressive behavior that have been punished by parents or some agent of society. These behaviors are not eliminated until they "can be brought to free expression when the behavior can be appropriately redirected" (Hilgard, 1948, p. 140). The behavior can be redirected, Hilgard points out, by positively reinforcing some behavior incompatible with the undesired behavior. The reader will recognize that this suggestion is similar to ones made by Guthrie (1935, 1938).

In addition to his general statement of the effects of punishment on learned responses, Estes has several specific suggestions about the use of punishment. Punishment, he says, may be used to hold a response down for a period of time. But if the repression of the response is to be permanent, some means must be found to readminister punishment perpetually. Parents who contemplate sending their offspring to boarding school or college would do well to bear this in mind. The effects of such continuous readministration of punishment, however, might well involve drastic effects upon the individual's personality. It might be possible, on the other hand, as it was suggested above, to take advantage of the period of suppression following punishment to strengthen one of the alternate responses which might satisfy the basic drives of the organism.

*The conditioning and extinction of anxiety.* Another important point Estes makes is that the effects of punishment seem to be correlated with the stimuli which set off a response rather than with the response itself. That is to say, the anxiety (p. 110) aroused by the shock itself becomes conditioned to the stimuli of the experimental situation. This anxiety, which results in the animal's withdrawal from the situation, becomes prepotent over the lever-pressing response, and consequently the lever-pressing response disappears for a time. Thus, the effect of punishment upon the rate of response seems to work by interference of anxiety responses with the responses being punished (Webb, 1949).

But the fact that punishment works by interference has other consequences. Since, as a result of the interference, the animal does not press the lever again for a while, it does not get the punishing stimulus. Thus the anxiety response to the stimuli of the experimental situation becomes extinguished, because the stimuli are always present but only the punishment itself reinforces anxiety. Then, after extinction of the anxiety response has progressed, the strength of the lever-pressing response again becomes prepotent over the anxiety response. The net result of this cycle is that punishment tends not to have permanent effects because these effects get extinguished.

This interpretation of punishment can be made quite real by looking at the example of punishment in the Skinner box in detail. Suppose a hungry rat has just been shocked on the lever response. It is very frightened as a result and shies away from the lever with signs of great emotional disturbance. At this stage, the effect of the punishment is very obvious; the rat spends all its time exploring the possibilities of leaving the box. Eventually, however, the rat calms down a bit, since its anxieties are not reinforced, and it is not shocked again. The rat is still hungry, and it has learned no new method of obtaining food. It must still press the lever in order to obtain a pellet of food. So the rat reapproaches the lever. The sight of the lever may reintroduce the anxiety response, but since the lever does not reach out and bite the rat, it approaches a little closer to the lever. At length, the rat reaches out and presses the lever again; it gets shocked again, and the whole cycle is repeated as a result.

We may well ask: How long does it take for anxiety to extinguish? This is an important question, for if the interpretation given above is correct, it means that the period of suppression of a response which results from punishment will last as long as the anxiety exists in some strength. Miller (1946, 1948) has performed some experiments in which he has measured extinction of conditioned responses based upon anxiety. His results show that in some cases anxiety may be very slow to extinguish. This suggests that the period of suppression may last for a long time under some circumstances. It is to be noted, however, that Miller found no evidence for "functional autonomy" of anxiety.

*Using the suppression period produced by punishment.* It was suggested earlier that it may be possible to make use of the temporary period of inhibition-of-response produced by punishment to teach an organism a new method to reach its goal. An experiment by Whiting and Mowrer (1943) suggests that this may be a very valuable technique in the control of behavior.

Whiting and Mowrer studied ways of getting rats to abandon old, preferred ways of adjustment in favor of new adjustments. They used three groups of rats. All three were taught to run a simple maze. After the habit of running to the goal box had been acquired, they extinguished one group of rats by discontinuing the reinforcement. They continued to reinforce the second group, but placed a barrier in the path leading to food. In the case of the third group, they punished the response of running to the goal box with an electric shock. All three groups were then presented with an alternative way of reaching the goal. The animals that had been punished on the original habit, they found, showed the fewest errors in reaching the goal by way of the alternative pathway. These animals also showed less regression to the original habit after the second habit (the alternative route) had been learned.

This experiment suggests strongly that teaching an alternative response during the period of suppression induced by punishment is a very effective means of redirecting behavior. Of course, as we might expect, if the second habit is extinguished, there will be a tendency to revert to the original, punished habit.

*The effect of very strong punishment.* Is it possible that punishment which is very traumatic in nature may be sufficient to completely eliminate a response? The punishment used by Estes was not very strong, so this question is not answered by his experiments. Indeed, there are very few experiments from any source that bear on it. One of them (Masserman, 1943), however, gives an affirmative answer; that is to say, it indicates that a really traumatic punishment may completely eliminate a learned response. In fact, it goes even further; it suggests that traumatic punishment may eliminate almost all behavioral adjustments in the situation.

This finding brings up another and important point, namely, the relation between punishment and neurosis. Neurosis, as most psychologists conceive it, is an anxiety response that generalizes to all sorts of behavior and stimulus situations. Moreover, it has some of the earmarks of functional autonomy for it may persist for a very long time after the time it was produced without receiving any further reinforcement. The fact then that traumatic punishment may eliminate or suppress not only a specific learned response but other responses as well is, in a sense, an experimental production of neurosis through traumatic punishment (p. 305).

With this thought in mind, let us look a bit more closely at the way negative reinforcement or punishment may set up more or less permanent symptoms of anxiety and neurotic behavior. Take our case of dogs conditioned to avoid an electric shock by flexing their paws to a tone. The conditioned stimulus may give rise to inhibition of respiration, acceleration of heart rate, pupillary dilation, etc. (Kellogg, 1941; Gantt, 1944). Thus the tone is an anxiety producer. The onset of the tone may set up an attempt on the part of the animal to escape from the situation. This may take the form of struggle in the experimental stock. Once this struggle starts it is almost impossible to eliminate. The dog will always struggle to the tone. The struggle itself, because it is frightening and painful to the animal, reinforces the anxiety. Thus, even though the dog may never receive another shock, the anxiety responses continue indefinitely. So we can see that in this instance anxiety has become "functionally autonomous" from the shock, because it is reinforced by behavior of the animal itself. Thus, it is possible for the anxiety associated with punishment or negative reinforcement to become almost permanently established.

*Punishment applied to the presentation of the reinforcement.* Another interesting exception to the principle that punishment does not have a permanent suppressive effect upon behavior seems to occur when punishment is simultaneous with positive reinforcement. Lichtenstein (1950*a*, 1950*b*), for example, inhibited eating in dogs by shocking the animals *as food was delivered to them* by an automatic feeder. When they were no longer shocked, however, the anxiety responses extinguished, and the animals went back to eating after a few trials. When, on the other hand, the animals were shocked *as the food was actually in the mouth,* the animals refused to eat again in the experimental situation. Despite repeated trials over a period of days, the eating behavior in the experimental situation was completely inhibited. As a matter of fact, in some cases the disturbance generalized to cases outside of the experimental situation, and the animals refused to eat in their home cages.

This experiment suggests that perhaps the most effective way of administering punishment would be to make the positive reinforcement itself something to be avoided. This point has interesting clinical and theoretical implications, and it certainly deserves further attention.

## THE ROLE OF ANXIETY IN HUMAN BEHAVIOR

The importance of anxiety as the motivating device which suppresses punished behavior has been emphasized by Estes (1944). In an earlier section, we saw how Mowrer (1951) and Miller (1951) have gone on to show how anxiety states are formed as secondary drives. In their theory of punishment, whenever such anxiety drives are present and are stronger than the goal-oriented drive, goal-oriented behavior is suppressed. Whenever, on the other hand, anxiety drives are satiated or extinguished, goal-oriented behavior recovers its strength. Thus the rat that has been punished for pressing the lever presses the lever again when its anxiety in the situation has disappeared.

Anxiety, of course, is of tremendous clinical importance in human behavior (Dollard and Miller, 1950; Mowrer, 1951). Society demands that we learn at an early age to suppress much goal-oriented behavior because such behavior often is apt to lead to punishment. The child, for example, who has been punished in the process of toilet training may have a whole series of anxiety responses connected with the eliminative functions. By stimulus generalization, these anxieties may spread to aspects of life not directly connected with eliminative functions, and we may have as a result what psychoanalysts call an "anal-compulsive" individual. Indeed, a very large portion of the clinical problems of behavior seem to be connected with anxiety or fear of punishment.

In the matter of anxieties, the rat seems to have an advantage over the human being. The rat does not seem to carry its anxieties around with it. The rat's anxieties are conditioned to relatively specific stimuli, and it shows signs of anxiety only in the presence of these stimuli or stimuli much like them. The human being, however, through the mediation of verbal behavior, is able to carry his anxieties about, and he is able to make use of implicit verbal behavior to reinforce these anxieties. Society tries to make sure that the individual uses these verbal cues, in the absence of a more direct threat of punishment, to keep him from doing that which is forbidden though desirable.

It is obvious that society is only partially successful in this respect. People can learn to disregard these verbal cues. The very fact that an individual may on one occasion transgress some taboo without being struck dead on the spot makes it more likely that he may try the same thing in the immediate future. Those who deal with clinical problems in human behavior, however, tell us that this disregard may only be superficial and transgression may lead to deep-seated conflicts. The adolescent boy may tell himself that the apparently omniscient and omnipresent father who watches over all his behavior—thus acting as a conscience—does not actually exist, but unconsciously he may still believe in this father figure. When he disregards his voice of conscience, he may find himself in a serious conflict that stems from anxiety over an unconsciously felt threat of punishment.

Does all this mean that punishment is an undesirable and ineffective way of controlling behavior? In a theoretical sense, the answer is probably "yes," but so many practical problems arise that this statement must be heavily qualified. Punishment is certainly an unsure and awkward way to control behavior. Furthermore, we do not know enough about its consequences to be sure that it might not get out of hand and cause serious behavioral maladjustments. It is most obvious, however, that it would be well-nigh impossible, not to say foolish, to attempt to rear children in our world totally without punishment. Since society, in the last analysis, is to a large extent a punishing and anxiety-producing agent for the control of behavior, children should learn to accept the discerning use of punishment (Jenkins, 1945). Those who make use of punishment as a method of controlling behavior, however, should not be surprised at its failure or the maladjustments it may produce.

## A SUMMARY OF THE NATURE OF PUNISHMENT

Because of the practical importance of the problem of punishment, a concluding summary, in which the relevant principles are brought together, is probably in order. These conclusions point up the essential notions concerning the nature of punishment in learning and behavior.

1. Punishment may reduce the tendency to make a particular response if the organism has available other responses which satisfy its current motivation. Society does not have too much trouble with its average citizens in suppressing the tendency to steal food, since there exist other channels for satisfaction of the need for food.

2. Punishment does not permanently reduce the tendency to make a response when that response is the only available avenue for satisfaction of the organism's current motivation. The effect of punishment in such a case is to depress temporarily the tendency to perform that response. As long as the positive motivation and habit strength induced by positive reinforcement remain, it will be necessary continually to readminister the punishment in order to keep the response suppressed.

3. Theoretically at least, the most effective and least harmful technique to eliminate a response is to subject that response to extinction.

4. Punishment is not always to be identified with the application of a painful stimulus. Stimuli which have become conditioned to a painful stimulus may also act as punishers. Such stimuli give rise to what is called anxiety, and anxiety in turn sets up a motivation to escape such stimuli. Anxiety-producing stimuli may be used either as punishing stimuli or as negative reinforcements.

5. The use of punishment as well as negative reinforcement may be the source of some abnormalities of behavior. This is a special problem, and it has received some experimental treatment which will be covered in a later chapter.

A final word of caution might be added. These conclusions are not above dispute, and further experimental evidence may render them obsolete.

They represent our present accomplishment in the understanding of punishment as it is obtained from experimental evidence. They serve to lend some coherence to a large body of observations on behavior found in the laboratory and in real life, but they may well be supplanted by a new set of conclusions sometime in the future.

# CHAPTER 7

# SERIAL LEARNING AND THE CHAINING OF RESPONSES

One of the most fundamental questions in the study of learning concerns how organisms learn to perform organized sequences of responses. Many of the examples of learning discussed in the earlier chapters involved sequences of responses rather than single responses in isolation. These examples were treated, however, as if they involved only a single response by itself. In the Skinner-box experiments, for example, the behavior was characterized as a "lever-pressing" response. Actually, a very elaborate chain of responses is involved in pressing the lever in the Skinner box (Skinner, 1938). The rat must see the lever; this may lead to lifting the paws. The rat cannot begin the actual depression movements until he feels the lever. The food must then be seen, seized, and eaten. Skinner characterizes at least four separate responses as part of the chain involved in pressing the lever.

This behavior was treated as a single response, however, because at the time we were not interested in the constituent members of the chain of responses and how the chain got organized. The "response" was defined as something which produced a definite effect upon the environment (moving the lever through a certain excursion). After so defining the response, it was possible to study the effects of a number of different variables and to treat these variables as if they were affecting only one response in isolation. Before reaching a complete understanding of the nature of learning, however, it will be necessary to examine the available evidence on the organization of response sequences.

In one sense, the larger part of the remainder of this book will be devoted to this problem of the organization of sequences of responses, since response interactions provide the basis for much of forgetting, problem solving, and transfer of training. Therefore, when we consider these prob-

126

lems separately, we shall examine special examples of the effects of certain response sequences. The problem in this chapter is to find out what is known about the way in which responses get hooked up together so as to make a sequence of behavior.

## SERIAL LEARNING IN ANIMALS

*The maze.* There are many examples of complicated, organized response sequences in the experimental studies of animal behavior. The best known and most thoroughly studied example of such sequences is maze learning. Maze learning in animals was studied very early in the history of experimental comparative psychology. This is particularly true of the rat, for which the maze is both convenient and representative of the kind of activity rats engage in when in the wild state. In a word, maze learning represents the sort of thing rats do best.

A floor plan for a typical maze for rats is shown in Fig. 24. The rat must learn to make an appropriate series of turns in the right order; it must learn to turn first to one side, then to the other, etc. These responses are always required to be in the same order; in this sense the maze represents the simplest kind of serial learning. For this reason, the maze has persisted as the most frequently used example of serial learning in animals. Serial learning of the sort required in the typical laboratory maze is not very characteristic of behavior in nature, because the maze represents serial learning stripped down to its essentials. Various kinds of mazes have been devised to study such special problems in serial learning as resemblance between responses in the chain, resemblance between stimuli in the chain, and number of responses required in the chain.

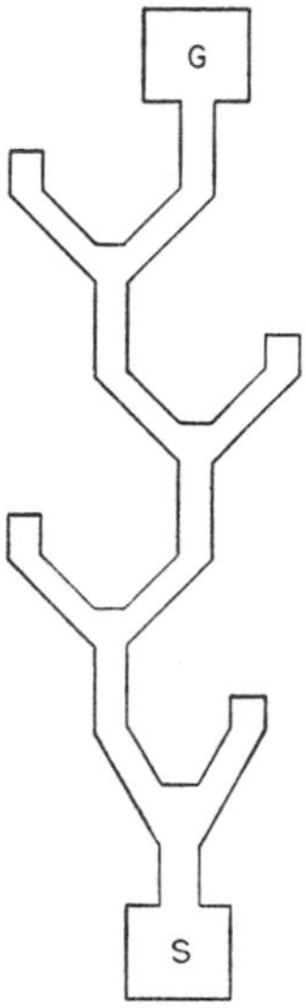

*Watson's theory of maze learning.* Perhaps the earliest attempt to outline the theoretical basis of serial learning in the maze is that of J. B. Watson. Watson was one of the great pioneers in the study of learning, and he was one of the most important figures in the beginning of behavior theory. Among other things, Watson was one of the first psychologists to advocate seriously the study of simple processes in animal behavior as a means of understanding

FIG. 24. The floor plan of a multiple-choice - point maze. The number of choices is p r o b a b l y smaller than would be used in practice. Each entry into a blind alley would contribute one error.

basic principles of behavior that may apply to human beings as well as to animals.

Watson assumed that the basic unit of habit was the classical conditioned response (Watson, 1924). That is to say, the fundamental process involved in habit was that by which a neutral stimulus comes to elicit a response when it is paired with a stimulus which already has the power to elicit that response. Watson's position in this respect was so important and fundamental that we can do no better than look at a quotation from the second edition of his famous textbook (Watson, 1924, pp. 293–294).

"Certainly at birth or shortly thereafter the elements or units out of which every habit is formed can be noted. We mention the contraction and flexion of the fingers, of the lower and upper arm, raising and lowering of the hand, rotation of the head, bending the trunk from side to side, the backward and forward, well-systematized movements of the legs, and a host of others. The conclusion is forced upon us that in habit no new elementary movements are needed. There are enough present at birth and more than will ever be combined into complex unitary acts. . . . One needs only to examine the five or six day old infant to be reasonably convinced that there is no need for the formation of additional reflex arcs to account for all later organization. The new learned element in habit is the tying together or integration of separate movements in such a way as to produce a new unitary activity. And by unitary activity we mean nothing more than the everyday acts of life, such as reaching out the hand for an object that stimulates the eye, picking the object up and carrying it to the mouth or laying it on the table. . . .

"We can define habit then as we did instinct as a complex system of reflexes which functions in a serial order when the child or adult is confronted by the appropriate stimulus."

Watson applied this general notion to the analysis of maze learning in rats. Maze learning is an example of how a whole series of discrete movements get organized into a unitary act. In a complicated maze, the animal must learn a series of responses; for example: run 5 feet, turn left, run 3 feet, turn left again, etc. Watson thought of the animal which had learned the maze correctly as having synthesized a whole chain of conditioned responses. Each movement that the animal made was the response to a kinesthetic stimulus produced by the preceding movement. Thus each response provided a conditioned stimulus for the next response.

If this notion of Watson's is correct, the whole chain of responses in the maze ought to be a very mechanical affair; each response should be exactly the same each time it is made, and each response should follow exactly in its proper sequence. Experimental support for this view was offered by Watson (Carr and Watson, 1908). Rats were trained in a maze in which the alleys could be lengthened or shortened without changing the pattern of turns which the animal had to make. Carr and Watson noticed that animals trained on short alleys (a turn required after a relatively short straightaway) attempted to turn at the same place when the alley was lengthened. Thus it looked like the animals had learned a sequence of movements, in which the nth movement was a turn. Apparently they had not learned to turn right when the first opening presented itself, but to turn right after so many movements.

Such observations supported the notion of kinesthetic chaining as the basis of maze learning. Subsequent experimental work, however, has shown that this cannot be the only, or indeed the principal, way in which rats learn mazes. Macfarlane (1930), in an experiment that helped refute Watson's simple idea, trained rats to run a maze in which the passages contained water to the depth of 8 inches. The rats were thus forced to swim the maze. He then switched them to walking by putting a false floor in the maze a little below the surface of the water. There was no increase in errors when the animals were transferred from swimming to running; so the learned maze pattern did not consist entirely of a chain of kinesthetic conditioned responses.

*Hull's analysis of maze learning.* Aware that Watson's approach was a little too simple, Hull has formulated a conditioned-response theory of serial learning that is a little more complicated and is less easy to disprove. Hull (1930) differs from Watson in that he believes external cues from the maze are conditioned to each response. The visual stimuli at a choice point, he would say, provide the cue for the response of turning to the right. In addition, however, Hull follows Watson to the extent of assuming that kinesthetic cues can provide part of the chain that keeps the responses in their proper order. Moreover, since animals are usually motivated during runs through the maze, he posits a drive stimulus which is conditioned to every response the animal makes (Hull, 1930, 1931); that is to say, because the animal is equally hungry at every point in the maze, the stimuli from the drive are conditioned to every part of the maze.

Another feature of maze learning, according to Hull (1932), is the *goal gradient,* which we have already considered (p. 23). It states that, all other things being equal, the part of the maze that is nearest to the goal will be the part that is learned the fastest. From this principle we may deduce that one factor in maze learning is nearness of correct turns to the goal; correct turns are learned because, on the average, they are closer to the goal than incorrect responses. By the same principle, we may deduce that animals will learn to choose the shorter of two alternate routes to the goal. Hull also predicts that entries into blinds that are close to the goal should be eliminated first.

In practice these deductions are not always verified, and for that there are many reasons. One of them is that the hypotheses do not apply to all mazes, because there are other factors in maze learning besides the goal gradient. If, for example, the last choice point in a maze points in the same direction as the alley leading to the goal, it will be the hardest blind to eliminate, even if it is nearest to the goal. This is because we must reckon with the factor of stimulus generalization between this blind alley and the alley leading to the goal. In this case, stimulus generalization has produced negative transfer that cancels out the goal-gradient effect.

Besides the goal gradient, we should mention another principle that Hull has listed among the mechanisms which govern maze learning. This is the *fractional anticipatory goal response.* You will recall that Hull suggested that a persisting stimulus, probably arising from the drive state, is conditioned to every response in the maze. It is most strongly conditioned to the goal response, that is, to the response of eating the food at the end of the maze. It is possible, however, that this persisting stimulus may prematurely elicit the goal response at some point earlier in the maze. This fractional anticipatory goal response allows Hull greater freedom in accounting for the data of maze learning. For example, Hull can explain quite readily the fact that when maze behavior is extinguished, it does not extinguish serially as one would expect, but seems to disintegrate all at once (Spence, 1942*b*).

These and other concepts have allowed Hull to account for the data on maze learning more adequately than any theorist before him. It is obvious that maze learning is very complicated, and even the elaborate schemas of Hull are too simple to account for all of the data. There are many secondary principles of maze learning, such as "centrifugal swing" (Schneirla, 1929), that are not of much general value to the psychology of learning but are necessary for a complete account of maze learning in animals.

*Studies on the linear maze.* A particular kind of maze, the linear maze, has enabled Hull and his students to make a very thorough analysis of several factors in maze learning. Actually the linear maze represents a much greater simplification of the problems of serial learning than does the ordinary maze, and it has the additional advantage that it is more analogous to the problems of serial learning in human learners.

The linear maze, as shown in Fig. 25, is just a long alley which has been divided into three or four compartments. There are anywhere from two to four doors between each compartment. Only one of the doors between each compartment will be free to swing open; the others will be locked shut. The rat must learn which door is free to open and to run to it. Since the doors between each of the compartments look very much alike, the rat must "remember where he is" in the maze and choose the

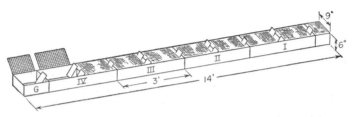

FIG. 25. A simple linear maze. There are four choice points with two choices at each. There is a "centering" door between each choice point to prevent favoring of one door over another by virtue of the previous correct response. (*Smith, 1949.*)

door appropriate to the particular compartment he is in. If all the choice points have the same door the open one, the problem is an easy one for the rat, but if all the choice points have a different door which is open, it is a difficult problem. Thus, while the stimuli are much the same from compartment to compartment, the responses can be all the same or all different or anything in between.

When we study learning in this type of maze, there are two aspects of the rat's behavior that are particularly striking. One is anticipation, and the other is perseveration. *Anticipation* is a response which is incorrect at the choice point where it occurs but which is correct later on. For example, the rat may choose door 1 when he should have chosen door 2, but when door 1 is correct at the next choice point. In this case, the rat has anticipated the second choice point. Likewise, *perseveration* is a response which is incorrect where it occurs, but which was correct at some earlier choice point.

It is easy to see that, when a *different* door is correct at each choice point, the anticipation and perseveration produce nothing but errors. Moreover, they tend to produce the greatest number of errors in the middle of the maze (Hill, 1939; Hull, 1947), because only anticipation can work at the beginning of the maze and only perseveration can work at the end of it, but both can operate and thus multiply errors in the middle. If, on the other hand, the same door is required at every choice point, anticipation and perseveration are beneficial to learning, for however the animal anticipates or perseverates at any choice point, he still makes the correct choice. Moreover, in this case, because anticipation and perseveration are greatest in the middle of the maze, the fewest number of errors occur at the middle choice point (Sprow, 1947).

These statements we have just considered are statements of both theory and fact. They are deducible from Hull's theory, and experiments have been carried out that verify them (Hill, 1939; Hull, 1947; Sprow, 1947). In addition, we have an experiment (Smith, 1949) that undertakes to investigate the cases where the choice points are neither all the same nor all different. In this experiment the point at which the maximal errors occurred was exactly in accord with the hypotheses put forward by Hull. For example, if the first three choice points are all the same, but the last choice point different, then the maximal number of errors occurred at the next-to-the-last choice point, since the animal anticipated the last choice point here.

You may have noticed by now that anticipation and perseveration are but special cases of stimulus generalization. The rat in the linear maze, when faced with a choice point, will not always be able to tell which compartment he is in. This is a failure of discrimination and is therefore stimulus generalization. Therefore, these studies on the linear maze tell us that the principles derived from a study of simple conditioned responses are useful for an analysis of a relatively complex form of behavior. These studies show the way in which generalization of stimuli associated with particular responses may interact to produce a complex pattern of behavior. To be sure, the linear maze is a highly artificial and formalized variety of a serial learning problem, but then, it is necessary in experimental investigation to study situations which, while they may be of no practical importance, provide a proof for certain hypotheses which are important. For example, no one is very much interested in the eye structure of *Drosophila* in itself, but no one would reproach the geneticist for using variations in eye structure as a function of the fly's heredity as a tool for experimental study.

Perhaps in justification of the study of rat behavior in the linear maze, it might be mentioned that principles arrived at in the study of the rat's serial learning processes have been of value in analyzing some of the problems in human learning.

## SERIAL LEARNING IN HUMAN LEARNERS

Serial learning in human beings is a topic which probably gets closer to the interests of most students in psychology. It is still woefully far, as the reader will see, from the kinds of things that the practical man of human affairs would like to study, but a study of serial learning is a necessary step in our comprehension of the mechanisms at work in human learning and behavior. In addition, a discussion of serial learning in human subjects allows us an opportunity to examine some of the techniques used generally in the study of human learning. This discussion of techniques will save many pages of explanation in the later chapters of this book.

### Maze Learning in Human Subjects

That maze learning is a task in which the rat is at its best is indicated by the fact that neither human adults nor children are much better at it than the rat is. As a matter of fact, the major difference between human adults and rats is in the number of times a given blind alley will be entered on any one trial (Hicks and Carr, 1912), but the over-all efficiency of learning is not very different between the two species.

Most frequently, when human subjects are asked to learn mazes, they are blindfolded, so that the serial aspects of the problem can be emphasized as much as possible; otherwise the subject might learn it by "seeing it as a whole." In one study of human maze learning, Warden (1924) analyzed the way in which human learners attacked mazes which they traced with their fingers while blindfolded. Different subjects had different ways of approaching the problem. Some of his subjects used verbal cues to guide them. Others tried to develop spatial schemas of the maze, and some made little or no use of symbolic cues at all. Thus there are widely differing techniques which people use in learning mazes. For this reason, perhaps, there has been no good analysis of the exact pattern of human maze learning. The problem is not a practical one, so there is no reason to attack it for applied reasons. Indeed, human maze learning is no better as an example of serial learning than are many other more characteristic problems, and the variability between learners in approaching the task makes human maze learning of little theoretical interest.

*Rote Verbal Learning*

Of much more practical and theoretical interest is the case of verbal learning. After all, a great deal of our education and of our everyday behavior is learning and using words in various orders and combinations. In attempting to study verbal learning experimentally, however, we run into some problems of technique and of control of learning that we must solve in order to make sense of the data we get.

In practical situations, when we are faced with the task of learning some new verbal responses, such as memorizing a poem, we sit down with the material in front of us and, by a somewhat hit-or-miss procedure, learn the thing. We seldom learn a poem by starting at the beginning and going through it line by line. More often we skip around, read one line several times, try learning several lines together, or learn only part of a line at a time.

While this hit-or-miss procedure is characteristic of verbal learning in general, it will not do for laboratory procedure. In the laboratory we are interested in the problems created by the relations between the parts of the material to be learned. In order to study these relations, it is necessary to hold constant the serial order of acquisition. Thus, in laboratory learning, the learning method is controlled by presenting to the subject only one unit of material at a time, and the units are always presented in some predetermined order.

This technique reduces the variability in methods of learning between subjects; that is, it makes our subjects learn more nearly in the same way. Because the technique permits a control of the serial order, it also makes an analysis of the serial interaction effects possible. The serial interaction effects are among the most important conditions of human learning and retention, so it is essential that laboratory studies of human learning be well controlled in this respect.

*Nonsense syllables.* Such serial (or rote) verbal learning was actually the first kind of human learning to be studied in the experimental laboratory. Ebbinghaus (1885) launched a series of studies on human verbal learning as the first experimental assault on the citadel of the "higher mental processes." The methods which Ebbinghaus used are the basis for the methods used today, so they will be discussed in some detail.

Ebbinghaus apparently discovered very early that there is one great difficulty in the study of human verbal learning, namely, that it is impossible to control the amount and type of verbal learning which the subjects have done in the past. We cannot maintain human subjects in a laboratory colony, free from the burdens of everyday life and motivated to work on an experimental schedule. Human subjects come into the learning laboratory with a long history of verbal learning behind them. Ebbinghaus showed, however, how we can make use of the previously acquired verbal skills of human beings and at the same time eliminate previous learning for the specific material we wish to have the subjects learn. This can be accomplished with nonsense syllables as learning material. Nonsense syllables are sufficiently strange and novel to the learner so that a uniform minimum amount of the subject's verbal skills is called upon. Indeed, if our material is complete "nonsense" to a subject, he cannot bring into the experiment a large assortment of acquired reactions to the specific words to be used.

The nonsense syllable itself is usually constructed of two consonants and a vowel; the vowel is sandwiched in between the consonants. Thus, SYL or NEP is a nonsense syllable. Some nonsense syllables resemble English words more than others (for example, compare XYQ and CET). For this reason several investigators have "calibrated" nonsense syllables in terms of their association value (Glaze, 1928; Hull, 1933). Such calibrations have resulted in classifications of nonsense syllables according to the degree of meaning or familiarity. So nowadays, if an investigator wishes to study a problem in which it is important that all the materials be of the same level of difficulty, he may choose the nonsense syllables from appropriate classes of the calibrated lists.[1]

Sometimes meaningful material is used in the study of rote verbal learning. The degree of meaningfulness may range all the way from connected sentences down to the nonsense syllables. Thus meaningfulness itself can be a variable in the study of rote verbal learning. Material other than nonsense syllables has been calibrated for various things, such as meaningfulness, association value, and degree of resemblance (Hovland, 1951).

*The anticipation method.* In rote verbal learning the serial order of learning is imparted by the order of presentation. In addition, the subject is instructed to learn the material in a particular way. The nonsense syllables, if they are to be used, are exposed to the subject in a small window,

---

[1] Sometimes all-consonant nonsense syllables are used, such as NXG. The consonant nonsense syllables have been brought together and calibrated by Witmer (1935).

behind which a drum revolves, and on this drum is the material to be learned (see Fig. 26). Thus only one syllable is exposed at a time. Furthermore, the syllables are exposed at a constant speed, so that the same amount of time is spent on each item. The subject is asked to *anticipate*

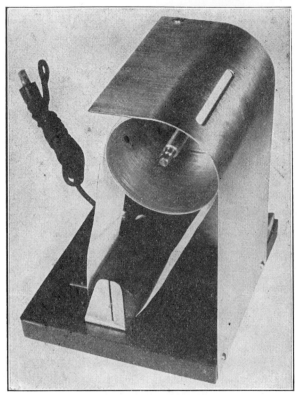

FIG. 26. A simple memory drum. Syllables are printed on the drum behind the shield. The syllables appear in the aperture one at a time. The drum does not move continuously but moves the syllable into place and then waits for a brief time before moving the next one into place. (*Courtesy of Ralph Gerbrands.*)

each syllable before it appears in the window. There is a blank space between each syllable, which allows the subject time to anticipate. Usually the subject is instructed to spell rather than pronounce the syllables, and in this way he can avoid having difficulty with the pronunciation of the syllables.

In the anticipation method, each item or nonsense syllable serves in turn as a stimulus and as a response. For example, the first nonsense syllable might be SYJ. When the list begins on each trial, the stimulus for this syllable is provided by the symbol which may indicate the beginning of the list. The next syllable might be LOZ. SYJ is the stimulus which tells the subject that LOZ is coming up. LOZ in turn might be followed by NEP. Thus, SYJ is the stimulus for the response "L–O–Z." LOZ is the stimulus in turn for the response "N–E–P," and so on.

Table I shows the results of an experiment on rote verbal learning with one subject. In the columns are given the syllables in the list, in this case twelve. The rows represent the trials, and there were 20 trials given to this subject. Note that a trial is defined as one repetition of the entire list. The plusses represent correct responses, the zeros represent incorrect responses or no responses at all. The first time through the list, of course, the subject can get no responses right, since this is the first time he has seen the material. Notice that this particular subject guessed at the first syllable on the second trial and got it right. On the third trial he correctly anticipated the first syllable, the second syllable, and the last syllable. On the nineteenth and twentieth trials the subject anticipated all the syllables correctly.

*The paired-associates method.* For many purposes, there is one grave defect in the anticipation method. It is the fact that each item serves as a stimulus and response in turn. Sometimes it is very important to sort out and independently vary the stimulus and response aspects of a task to be learned. This cannot be done with the anticipation method; consequently a modification of the anticipation method, known as the "method of paired associates," has been developed.

In using this method, as its name implies, pairs of items are presented to the learner. He is instructed to learn the pairs in such a way that when the first member of a pair appears, he is to attempt to recall the second. Thus the first member of a pair is a stimulus item and the second member a response item. Unfortunately, in this method, the serial order of presentation cannot be retained, since if it were, subjects could make a connection between response items and the stimulus items which follow. Therefore, in this method, the pairs of stimulus and response items are presented in some random or prearranged order which is different for every trial. As you can see, the method of paired associates has the disadvantage of destroying the simple serial characteristics of rote learning, but it enables the investigator to distinguish between stimulus material and response material. For some problems the simple anticipation method is more suitable; for other problems the method of paired associates is better.

## TABLE I

### Subject's Record Sheet from Serial Learning Experiment

| Trial | Syllable | | | | | | | | | | | | Number correct |
|---|---|---|---|---|---|---|---|---|---|---|---|---|---|
| | CEX | MOQ | RUY | GAF | LIQ | KOC | QUZ | DEJ | TAH | WOG | FIK | VUS | |
| 1 | 0 | 0 | 0 | 0 | 0 | 0 | 0 | 0 | 0 | 0 | 0 | 0 | 0 |
| 2 | + | 0 | 0 | 0 | 0 | 0 | 0 | 0 | 0 | 0 | + | + | 3 |
| 3 | + | + | 0 | 0 | 0 | 0 | 0 | 0 | 0 | 0 | 0 | + | 3 |
| 4 | + | + | 0 | + | 0 | 0 | 0 | 0 | 0 | 0 | + | 0 | 4 |
| 5 | + | + | 0 | + | 0 | 0 | 0 | 0 | 0 | 0 | 0 | + | 4 |
| 6 | + | + | + | + | 0 | 0 | 0 | 0 | 0 | 0 | + | 0 | 5 |
| 7 | + | + | + | + | 0 | 0 | 0 | 0 | 0 | 0 | 0 | + | 5 |
| 8 | + | + | + | 0 | 0 | 0 | 0 | 0 | 0 | 0 | + | + | 5 |
| 9 | + | + | + | + | 0 | 0 | 0 | 0 | 0 | 0 | + | + | 6 |
| 10 | + | + | + | + | 0 | 0 | 0 | + | 0 | + | + | + | 8 |
| 11 | + | + | + | 0 | 0 | 0 | 0 | 0 | 0 | 0 | + | + | 5 |
| 12 | + | + | + | + | + | 0 | 0 | 0 | 0 | + | + | + | 8 |
| 13 | + | + | + | + | + | 0 | 0 | 0 | 0 | + | + | + | 8 |
| 14 | + | + | + | + | 0 | 0 | 0 | + | 0 | + | + | + | 8 |
| 15 | + | + | + | 0 | 0 | 0 | 0 | 0 | + | + | + | + | 7 |
| 16 | + | + | + | + | + | + | + | 0 | + | 0 | + | + | 10 |
| 17 | + | + | + | + | 0 | + | + | 0 | + | + | + | + | 10 |
| 18 | + | + | + | + | + | + | + | + | + | 0 | + | + | 11 |
| 19 | + | + | + | + | + | + | + | + | + | + | + | + | 12 |
| 20 | + | + | + | + | + | + | + | + | + | + | + | + | 12 |
| Number correct | 19 | 18 | 15 | 14 | 6 | 5 | 4 | 5 | 6 | 8 | 16 | 17 | |

*The Nature of Associations in Rote Verbal Learning*

One of the basic problems about simple serial learning, in which the items are always presented in the same order, is the degree to which different items become associated with each other. We know that successive items are associated, since otherwise the learner would not be able to anticipate. Learners also make connections between items which do not adjoin. These associations of items that are not adjacent to one another are called "remote associations."

In a typical experiment, nonsense syllable A becomes a cue or stimulus for the response of nonsense syllable B. B is a cue for the response C, etc. The subject learns the list in order. In addition, however, syllable A is connected to some degree with syllable C, so that A will occasionally give rise to the response C. Such responses, of course, are exactly analogous to anticipatory errors found in the studies on the linear maze (p. 130). In verbal learning these anticipatory responses are called "remote forward associations."

Since perseverative errors are found in the linear maze, it might be supposed that perseverative errors would be found in rote verbal learning as well. Indeed, they are. If the learner responds with A when he should have responded with D, this is a perseverative response. In verbal learning, such perseverative errors are called "remote backward associations."

It was Ebbinghaus (1885) who first detected these remote associations. The method by which he did it is known as the "method of derived lists." First he learned a list of nonsense syllables—Ebbinghaus always used himself alone as a subject—then learned a second list derived from the first list in such a way that if remote associations within the first list had built up, they would help him learn the second list. By various control procedures it was possible for Ebbinghaus to measure the relative strength of different degrees of remote forward associations. He found that the number of trials necessary to learn a derived list varied directly with the closeness of the derived associations. For example, relearning the original list in exactly the same order as it was originally learned took a minimum of trials, but relearning it in a random order was extremely difficult.

Ebbinghaus's results are not too easy to interpret. For one thing, because he worked on only one subject, it is hard to tell how reliable they were. For another, the method he used tells us very little about which specific remote associations had been formed. Nor, finally, does his method tell us how frequent remote associations are.

A method used by McGeoch (1936) has been much more informative about remote associations. After a list of syllables had been practiced for a brief time (not learned to a perfect criterion), the syllables were given to the subject one at a time, and he was instructed to respond with the first syllable which came to mind. Figure 27 (McGeoch, 1936) shows the frequency of association as a function of degree of remoteness. You will

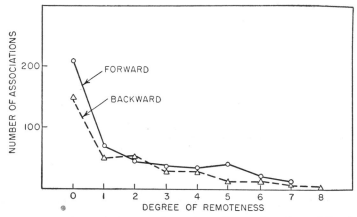

FIG. 27. Number of associations at time of recall as a function of the degree of remoteness (syllables spanned). (*After McGeoch, 1936.*)

notice that the number of remote associations, both forward and backward, falls off abruptly after zero degrees of remoteness; in addition, it is apparent that the forward associations are somewhat more numerous than the backward associations.

There is still another method which has the advantage of giving directly measures of remote associations during the course of learning. This method comes from an analysis of the errors which the subject makes during learning. If in response to syllable A the subject should give syllable C, an anticipatory error is made, and this is counted as a remote forward association. This method is directly analogous to the method used to discover anticipatory and perseverative responses in the linear maze.

*The theories of remote associations.* All sorts of associations are formed during serial learning. Associations between adjacent items are the most common, and the frequency of associations falls off as a function of the degree of remoteness of the items. As might be expected, remote associations are more common early in learning than they are late in learning, and anticipatory (forward) associations are more common than perseverative (backward) associations.

There have been several theories advanced to account for these remote associations. One theory has it that the earlier items are still being responded to when the later items appear. Thus there is an association between the trace of the earlier item and the occurrence of the later item. This theory has been greatly elaborated by Hull and his associates (Hull *et al.,* 1940).

Another theory interprets remote associations in terms of mediated connections between two items in a list and a third, common one. The mediating factor might be anything in the subject's general environment to which the specific items on the list to be learned become conditioned. McGeoch (1942) discusses this hypothesis at some length and compares it with the trace hypothesis.

In view of the great similarity between remote associations and the kind of anticipatory and perseverative errors found in studies on the linear maze, it seems very likely that the causes are similar. Anticipatory and perseverative errors in the linear maze are attributed to stimulus generalization; it seems to be quite possible that remote forward and backward associations might have a similar cause. To be sure, the gradients of generalization would have to be more complicated than those discussed in Chap. 4, but in other connections it has become apparent that human behavior shows many examples of stimulus generalization along complex stimulus gradients. Generalization could be simply on the basis of the time sense; that is, errors could occur because the subject "loses his place." Certainly most lists of nonsense syllables offer ample opportunity for generalization based upon the items themselves. If, for example, in a list of nonsense syllables, DOX is followed by CET, and DOQ is followed by ZYM, it is very possible that the similarity between DOX and DOQ could cause the subject to respond with ZYM instead of CET. There does not seem to be any direct experimental evidence to support the notion, but it is highly probable that the number of remote associations will increase directly as the similarity between items in a list is increased.

## STATISTICAL BEHAVIORISTICS

Very recently an entirely new technique has been developed for the analysis of the sequential, serial characteristics of behavior. This technique, called "statistical behavioristics" by its authors (Miller and Frick, 1949), was not devised specifically for the study of learning, but rather to study the dependencies between responses after learning has taken place. The notion involved in statistical behavioristics is sufficiently fundamental and important to warrant treatment here.

Its starting point is the theory of dependent probabilities. In the sort of probability theory we learn in the freshman algebra course, events are considered to be independent. That is to say, it is a fundamental proposition of this kind of probability theory that one toss of a coin, for example, is not influenced by another. We learn that the probability of a coin turning up heads is ½. We also learn that the probability of a composite event is the product of the separate probabilities of its constituent events. Thus the probability of two coins on the same toss both coming out heads is ½ × ½, or ¼.

In dependent probabilities, however, the occurrence of one event is said to influence the probability of a second event. This would be the case, say, if the first coin coming out heads made it more likely that the second coin would come out heads. This is an absurd example, of course, since the coins represent independent physical systems. Dependent probabilities apply to the behavior of organisms, however, and the analysis of the degree of dependency is the business of statistical behavioristics.

An example will help make the matter clear. For written English it is possible to state the probability of occurrence of the letter Q. In order to do this it would be necessary to find out, in a very large sample, just how many times Q occurred. The probability of the occurrence of Q would be given by the ratio of the frequency of occurrence of Q to the frequency of occurrence of all symbols in the English language. Obviously Q would have a small but finite probability of occurrence. If we now ask: What is the probability of occurrence of A following Q, we can give a simple and straightforward answer. The probability is zero, for A never follows Q in the English language. On the other hand, U always follows Q. So the occurrence of Q immediately changes the probability of occurrence of all other letters that might follow it. Q is a special case, but it illustrates the fact that in any language there are dependent probabilities between letters. Given any letter, we can predict at a greater than "chance" level what the next letter will be. It is also easy to see, furthermore, that the probability of occurrence of a given letter can be influenced by the letter which occurs two or three spaces back, and so on. In English, for example, two consonants are more likely to be followed by a vowel than by another consonant.

So we see that the basic notion in dependent probabilities is very simple, even though the mathematics are mysterious and imposing. Without going into the theoretical background, a few examples of dependent probabilities in behavior will show the possibilities of this kind of analysis in understanding the serial characteristics of behavior.

*Dependent probabilities in trial-and-error behavior.* Miller and Frick (1949) show how the analysis of dependent or conditional probabilities can apply to sequences of responses in trial-and-error behavior. In one case, for example, they compared the behavior of a rat and of a child in a multiple-choice experiment. The problem for the rat and the child was to find a way to get out of an enclosure with four doors. The door which permitted an exit varied from trial to trial, so it was useless for the learner to attempt to try again the door which had been correct on the previous trial. The original purpose of this experiment, which is part of an older study (Hamilton, 1916), was to get an extended sample of trial-and-error behavior.

Miller and Frick point out that if one attempts to predict which of four possible doors the child will pick on any one trial, the best guess is chance —unless information is available about what the relative frequency of responses has been and what response immediately preceded the response in question. Once we have these two pieces of information, however, we can increase our prediction over chance. If, for example, a sequence of two responses in the child is considered, we find that of the sixteen possible sequences (four doors times four doors), six sequences appear 80 per cent of the time. Thus a knowledge of the choice just before the response we wish to predict greatly increases the accuracy of our prediction.

When Miller and Frick analyzed the data involved in sequences of three responses, they found great regularity in the third choice. It was nearly always a response which was different from the preceding two. Thus if the child chose doors 1 and 2, there was a very low probability that either doors 1 or 2 would be chosen on the next response. Miller and Frick point out that this is one respect in which the child differs markedly from the rat. The rat was much more likely than the child to go back to one of the doors chosen on the preceding two responses. It could be said that the child has a longer memory span than the rat.

*Dependent probabilities in verbal behavior.* One of the best opportunities for the use of statistical behavioristics is to be found in verbal behavior.

Miller and Selfridge (1950) show that an analysis of serial dependencies in verbal behavior is one way of making a distinction between easy and difficult material. This is the kind of distinction we make when we say that nonsense material is hard to learn and connected, logical material is easy to learn. Miller and Selfridge show that it is not the "sensibleness" alone which is responsible for the ease of learning and retention, but the nature of the dependent probabilities in the verbal material. When a talker says "children like to," his choice of the next word is limited; it is not likely to be *elephant, loud,* or *punished.* Though language is determined by the intention and needs of the speaker, it is also determined by what has gone before—verbal context (Miller, 1951).

All this is a way of saying that sensible language may be approximated by chains of serial dependencies. The order of approximation to sensible English may be defined by the number of preceding items which determine the present item. Thus, if we select words at random from the dictionary or a word list, we would have a *zero-order approximation* to English. An example of a zero-order sequence might be: "pack byway phosphor kettle hypermetrical gloat." A *first-order approximation* would select words according to their relative frequencies in English usage. Thus common words like "the" and "before" would most likely show up. If we gave a word to an individual and took the next word in the sentence he constructed, gave it to another individual for him to construct a sentence, etc., and then put the second choices of all the individuals together, we would have a *second-order approximation.* An example of a second-order approximation taken from Miller and Selfridge looks like this: "was he went to the newspaper is in deep and." For *higher order approximations,* individuals may be given sequences of words to use. In this case, they add a word directly after the sequence and drop the first word of the sequence. This new sequence is then given to another individual, etc. An example of a seventh-order approximation obtained in this manner looks like this: "then go ahead and do it if possible while I make an appointment I want to skip very much around the tree and back home again to eat dinner after the movie early so that we could get lunch because we liked her method for sewing blouses and skirts is."

You see that seventh-order approximation appears to make a vague kind of sense—a sort of stream-of-consciousness sense. This is because it preserves the ordinary dependencies of speech in a chain of considerable length. Miller and Selfridge show that it is this chain that determines how

easy it is to learn and remember verbal material. Up to a point, the longer
the chain, the easier it is to learn and remember. With adult subjects, however, there is no difference in the recall scores for a seventh-order approximation and for good, sensible English. So, though the seventh-order approximation is essentially nonsense, it is recalled as well as the sensible
material.

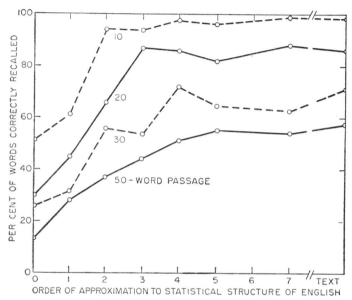

FIG. 28. Accuracy of recall as a function of the order of approximation to the
statistical structure of English. (*Miller and Selfridge, 1950.*)

A summary of Miller's and Selfridge's results is given in Fig. 28. This
shows the relation between order of approximation and ease of recall.
You will notice that above fifth-order approximations there seems to be
little improvement in recall. This apparently is because the fifth-order and
higher approximations preserve the short-range dependencies which the
individual can remember. Put another way, the fifth-order or higher approximations connect material within the individual's immediate memory
span, and it seems to be this immediate memory span which is the unit of
retention. As long as the material is connected for as long as the immediate memory span, the individual can remember it as well as textual
material.

Thus it appears that the easier learning of meaningful material is because
meaningful material preserves the short-range associations of ordinary

language. The units are phrases. The results of Miller's and Selfridge's study indicate that the phrases which can be put together are fairly short. We can assume that these are the combinations of words that can be grasped as a unit by the learner. These units, then, are put together by the learner in complex serial learning.

# CHAPTER 8

# FACTORS AFFECTING RATE OF COMPLEX LEARNING

Of the great amount of experimental work that has been done in human learning, a large share has dealt with the question of how learning progresses and of how various factors affect progress in learning. The first step in answering this question is to study the so-called learning curve— the way performance changes from trial to trial—and to find, if possible, some general ways of describing it. Further steps include the study of how specific factors, such as the distribution of practice and inhibition in learning, affect the course of learning. These are the steps we shall follow in this chapter.

## LEARNING CURVES

Perhaps the earliest interest which psychologists showed in the learning process was in charting the day-to-day or trial-to-trial improvement in performance. In fact, a very large portion, often as much as a third, of the early textbooks on learning were devoted to the measurement of improvement and the learning curve. The early interest in this topic is certainly understandable, since one of the first things to do when a new set of events comes into the laboratory is to measure them as extensively as possible.

We may be excused from the same devotion to learning curves today on several grounds. First of all, we know what the earlier investigators suspected: there is no single type of learning curve. Rather there are curves which show a decrease in errors with practice, curves which show an increase in accuracy with practice, etc. There is no such thing as *the* learning curve; there are simply curves which show how various aspects of performance change as a function of practice. About the only thing that can be said about the various kinds of learning curves is that they are not straight lines; they are usually represented by some more complicated mathematical function.

From time to time there have been attempts to obtain rationally derived learning curves of various sorts. Thurstone (1930), for example, has derived a rational equation for an error curve. He has done this by making the assumption that all acts involved in learning can ultimately be classified into correct and incorrect responses. Others have attempted to develop theories of learning based upon mathematical functions which represent unobservable processes, then have attempted to relate these functions to particular kinds of learning curves which embody measurement of a particular aspect of behavior.

A learning curve, then, is any curve which shows improvement in performance as a function of practice. The word "improvement" is a stumbling block in this definition. How do we know when a learner is improving? The only answer which can be given to this question is an operational one. Improvement means a change in behavior toward some standard or goal set up by the experimenter or teacher. There is no other way to evaluate learning than in terms of some arbitrary standard set up by the experimental conditions. If a learner increases the number of nonsense syllables which he gets right from trial to trial, this is improvement in performance by our definition, since the standard set for the learner is to get all the syllables right.

*Types of learning curves.* Learning curves can be classed roughly into three types, which depend upon what aspect of improvement in performance is measured. One type of learning curve is an *error curve,* a second type is a *time curve,* and a third type is an *accuracy curve.* The characteristics of each type are as follows:

Error curves: Error curves show a decrease in errors as a function of practice or number of trials. In many cases it will do just as well to plot the reverse, the number of *correct* responses as a function of practice. In rote verbal learning, for example, we can plot either the number of syllables which the subject anticipated correctly on each repetition of the list, or we can plot the number of times the subject failed to anticipate correctly for each trial.

Time curves: Time curves show a decrease in time per trial as a function of practice. This is the kind of curve one would obtain if the length of time it took an individual to assemble a jigsaw puzzle were measured. Each time the puzzle is assembled, the time of assembly is lessened. Both time curves and error curves can sometimes be obtained from the same task. In maze learning, for example, we can plot both number of errors and time per trial as a function of practice.

Accuracy curves: A third way of charting improvement with practice is to plot some measure of a change in accuracy with an increase in the number of trials. If an individual were to fire at a stationary target, we might plot his deviation from the center of the target for each trial. Or, if the individual were tracking a constantly moving target, we might plot the amount of time he stayed on the target for each trial.

Each of these functions measures a somewhat different aspect of performance. There is no ultimate kind of plot; the nature of the curve will simply depend upon what the investigator is interested in showing. This point is an important one, since the effect of an experimental variable frequently will not show up with one way of plotting the learning data while it will show up with some other method. You can find many examples of each kind of curve scattered throughout this book. You will see that not all curves of the same type look alike; the curves will vary somewhat from task to task and will depend upon the specific conditions of learning.

It might be mentioned that there is a different classification of learning curves based on the direction of the change measured. According to this classification there are two types of learning curves, decreasing-score curves and increasing-score curves. Error curves and time curves are decreasing-score curves. Accuracy and correct-response curves are increasing-score curves.

It should be noted that the measures of improvement are not all necessarily independent of one another. In maze learning, for example, number of errors and time per trial will be very highly correlated. This is simply because the fewer the entrances into blind alleys, the less the time it takes to go through the maze. There are less mechanical correlations as well. In general, for example, an increase in accuracy will go along with a decrease in the amount of time necessary to accomplish a unit of work. In other words, improvement in one aspect of a task is usually accompanied by improvement in other aspects as well. This is not necessarily so, but it is generally true of learning outside of the laboratory.

In addition there are many other changes in behavior through the course of improvement of performance which do not very often get charted. Usually there is a change in the attitude of the individual toward the task. A task may be regarded as very difficult at the outset of learning and then regarded as very easy after much practice has been obtained. There may be a change in the degree of emotional tension which an individual shows during learning. At the outset of learning there may be much tension and anxiety which may be reduced by the learning of the task. Finally, the mode of attack of the learner most surely will vary throughout the course of learning. Thus it is clear that there are many aspects of the change in performance with practice, and some of these are often ignored.

*Plateaus.* There is one feature that is characteristic of many learning curves; this is a place somewhere in the curve where there is little or no measurable improvement. A classical example of such a curve is shown

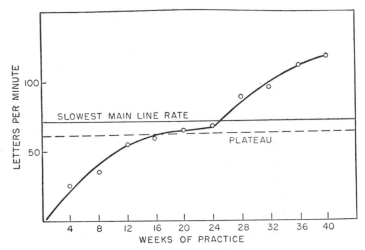

FIG. 29. Learning curve for receiving telegraphic code. Plateau occurs in the middle of the curve, just before the minimum main-line (railroad) rate is reached. (*After Bryan and Harter, 1897.*)

in Fig. 29. This represents a curve of learning to receive a telegraphic code. You will notice that there was a period of about 6 weeks during which the learner did not appreciably increase in his ability to receive code signals. After this period of little or no improvement, there was a sudden spurt in letters received per minute which gradually leveled off to a final asymptote. Such a period of little or no improvement is known as a "plateau."

The particular curve in Fig. 29 comes from a famous old study by Bryan and Harter (1897, 1899) on the acquisition of skill in telegraphy. In learning to receive telegraphic code, Bryan and Harter found that learners come to receive individual letters first, then words as units, and finally phrases or sentences as units. They put forward the notion that plateaus occurred when learners made the transition from the lower order of units to the higher ones. They were able to justify this interpretation by a study of the way in which their subjects learned jumbled letters, disconnected words, and meaningful phrases. They found that the plateau occurred at just about the point where there was no further improvement in the ability to receive disconnected letters and words. Thus the plateau occurs where

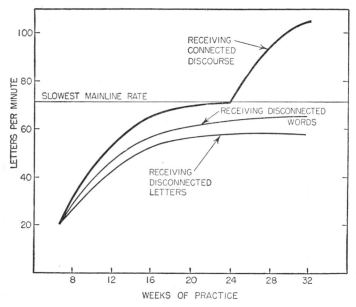

FIG. 30. Learning curves for receiving connected discourse, disconnected words, and disconnected letters. Notice that the plateau in the curve for connected discourse occurs at the point where there is no further improvement in curves for disconnected material. (*After Bryan and Harter, 1899.*)

the limit on the lower order habits has been reached and where the higher order habits have not yet begun to appear. The results of the comparison of disconnected and connected material are shown in Fig. 30.

It is apparent from other sources that there are many other causes of plateaus in the learning curve. Swift (1918) argued that plateaus are caused by a decline in the learner's motivation. He pointed out that plateaus for all learners occur in about the same place; furthermore they occur in many tasks which do not involve a hierarchy of habits. Book (1925), in his handbook on learning to typewrite, located the lapses in attention and drop in motivation at the point where letter habits were making a transition into word habits. Thus the failure to improve may generate discouragement, which furthers the failure to improve. Individuals get discouraged when they reach a plateau; this discouragement prevents them from attempting further practice. Book also points out that it is possible that the failure to improve may force the learner to attend to the wrong things; the learner may change his mode of practice to a less efficient way in order to overcome the plateau.

We can see that plateaus are complicated. Sometimes they cannot be avoided; they occur because it takes us a while to learn how to put simple habits together into more complicated ones. Sometimes, as Book points out, careful instruction can minimize plateaus by keeping the learner interested in what he is doing despite a lack of improvement. Plateaus are undoubtedly one important factor which keeps adult learners from acquiring such skills as playing the piano or playing tennis. A well-motivated adult can learn the fundamentals of these skills quite easily, but there then follows a long period of time when devoted practice brings no fruits of improvement. At this point interest drops and the individual will cease "taking lessons."

Sometimes plateaus can be overcome simply by resting for a while. Thus an individual who takes a semester of typing in high school is often agreeably surprised when he or she comes back to school in the fall and finds that his performance at typing actually seems better than it was in the spring, despite a lack of practice during the summer.

Very frequently, the asymptotic limit which learners finally reach is a plateau. The author doubts that his typing has improved very much in the past ten years, but there is certainly room for improvement. A little practice would eliminate some bad habits and bring in some new levels of organization which would no doubt quickly raise his level of typing from its present position to a higher one. Thus, while he is currently at his "asymptotic limit" of performance at typing, a little practice would raise that limit. There are surely real "physiological" limits to our ability to perform specific skills; we cannot type faster than our fingers will move. Most of us, however, seldom push ourselves to this limit.

## DISTRIBUTION OF PRACTICE

One of the most important conditions which determines an individual's rate of acquisition of a new habit is the way in which he distributes practice through time. We may ask the question: Is it better to practice a new task with as little interruption for rest as possible, or are frequent rest intervals beneficial to learning and performance? Almost without exception we can say that well-spaced and frequent rest intervals increase the rate of learning and are beneficial to performance. The distribution of practice is one of the most important specific variables which determines the course of acquisition.[1]

The specific effect of a certain method of distributing practice will, of course, depend upon the specific task involved and the other special techniques of practice. There is, however, enough generality to the effects of distributed practice so that the results of a number of experiments can be discussed as if they applied universally in learning. This is not quite true, but it is true enough to make it possible to arrive at some fairly general conclusions about the distribution of practice.

There are three important variables in the distribution of practice. These are (1) the length of the rest period, (2) the length of the practice period, and (3) the place where the rest intervals occur. These variables interact to some extent with the other conditions of practice, the method of measurement of performance, etc. These three variables and their interactions with other features of performance will be discussed first, and then a brief discussion of the theory of the distribution of practice will be undertaken.

*Length of the rest period.* A well-known experiment by Lorge (1930) demonstrates the most important point about the effects of the length of the rest period in distributed practice upon performance. Lorge studied the effects of continuous practice for 20 trials compared with the effects of practice in which a rest period of 1 minute and a rest period of 1 day intervened between each trial. The tasks he used were mirror drawing, mirror reading, and code substitution. He found that either case of distributed practice resulted in better learning than massed practice. Figure 31 shows the results for the mirror-drawing task. You can see that the time curve for the two groups with distributed practice dropped very much more rapidly than the curve for the massed-practice group; the difference is apparent almost from the very beginning of practice. You will also notice, however, that the difference between the group that rested for 1 minute between each trial and the group that rested for 1 day is very small.

---

[1] Strictly speaking, the distribution of practice does not seem to affect the *rate* of learning so much as it affects some other constant of the learning function.

This last point is emphasized by a more recent experiment (Kientzle, 1946). Kientzle studied the effect of various lengths of rest period on the learning of an alphabet-coding task. Figure 32 is obtained from some of her data, and it tells the story very well. This illustration shows that small rest periods resulted in great improvement over no rest between trials, but that beyond 45 seconds, not much advantage is gained by increasing the rest interval.

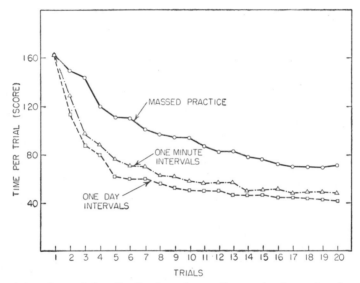

FIG. 31. The effect of the distribution of practice upon mirror drawing. Notice that the group with no rest between trials (massed) does consistently worse than the other two groups. (*Redrawn from Lorge, 1930.*)

We know, too, that the optimal length of the rest period varies with the specific task and conditions of practice. Travis (1937) found, for a target-tracking task, that a 20-minute rest period was better than a 5-minute rest period or any periods longer than 20 minutes. This optimal length is a good deal longer than that found in Kientzle's experiment, and it is possible that some kinds of tasks and conditions of practice would show optimal rest periods even greater in length.

In a repetition of the essentials of Kientzle's experiment, Kimble (1949) found the advantage of distributed practice to increase with rest periods up to 30 seconds. Kimble's and Kientzle's data are presented in such a way that they are not easy to compare, but Kimble's findings seem to confirm Kientzle's. We seem justified in concluding, therefore, that increasing the length of the rest interval over *relatively* small periods does not appreciably increase the rate of learning. Most of the advantage of distributed practice is in the advantage of some distribution over none at all (McGeoch, 1942).

*Length of the practice period.* How long should the practice period be when the rest period is held constant? A very early experiment provides an answer to this question (Jost, 1897). Jost used nonsense syllables as his

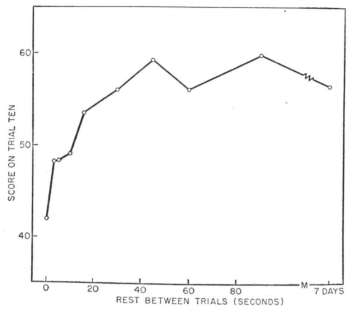

Fig. 32. The effect of time between trials on performance of a learned act. Notice that rest intervals greater than 45 seconds do not appreciably increase performance on this particular task. (*Data from Kientzle, 1946.*)

learning material. Learning was for 24 trials given at a rate of 2, 4, or 8 trials per day. Jost measured the ability to recall after a 24-hour rest period, and his results showed that the shorter the practice period (the fewer the repetitions of the list in any one day) the better the recall scores.

A recent experiment was concerned with the joint effects produced by the concomitant lengthening of the work period and shortening of the rest period (Kimble and Bilodeau, 1949). In this experiment it was found that shortening the work period is much more important than lengthening the rest period, as might be expected from the earlier experimental results.

Thus the more important variable appears to be the length of the practice period. If the rest period exceeds a certain critical length, which for most tasks is probably very short, a further increase will not increase the rate of learning or performance, whereas almost any variation in the length of the work period will produce an effect upon learning and performance. It appears as though using the shortest work period which is compatible with the nature of the task to be learned is the most efficient way to practice. This does not mean, of course, that practice should be broken up into unnaturally short intervals, but it does mean that short practice periods interspersed with frequent, brief rest periods will be beneficial to learning and performance.

*When are rest periods of greatest benefit?* There is considerably less agreement on the question of where, in practice, the rest periods are of greatest benefit. An early experiment by Carr (1919) on maze learning shows that distribution of practice is of greater benefit early in practice than it is later in practice. Snoddy (1935) finds the same thing to be true of mirror drawing.

There is probably a flaw in both of these experiments, however. In maze learning as well as mirror drawing, the earlier trials take longer than the later trials. This is because the learner makes more mistakes early in learning. Therefore, a learner who has had the same amount of rest early in learning as another learner has had late in learning will benefit more from the rest periods, because the effectiveness of the rest period depends upon the amount of work that has gone on. It is quite possible, then, that the findings which show that rest early in learning is the more beneficial are an artifact of the nature of the tasks used to study distribution of practice.

This interpretation is borne out by some additional evidence which shows that later rests may be more beneficial than early rests for some kinds of tasks. Doré and Hilgard (1938) studied the relative advantage of distributed practice early and late in the acquisition of a target-tracking task. In this experiment, each trial lasted the same length of time, so that amount of work did not appear as an uncontrolled variable. The length of the rest period was progressively increased in one group and progressively decreased in the other. The group which had the progressively increasing rest periods showed a higher rate of learning. A later study (Cook and Hilgard, 1949), which was very similar in design, showed the effects of early and late distribution to be about the same.[2]

---

[2] The issue is still not clearly settled. Renshaw and Schwarzbeck (1938) found early distribution to be better than late distribution for the same kind of target-tracking task as that used by Hilgard and his associates.

*Retention after distributed practice.* Does the advantage of distributed practice show itself after an opportunity for forgetting has been allowed? Some early experimenters (Austin, 1921; Robinson, 1921; Gordon, 1925) showed that the beneficial effects of distributed practice actually increased relatively when a time interval of a day or more was interpolated between learning and test of retention. In one study (Gordon, 1925), a test given several weeks after learning showed that the advantage of distributed practice actually increased over this retention period. A more recent study (Epstein, 1949) shows a small but positive advantage of distributed practice over massed practice after a retention interval of two weeks.

From these data, it seems clear that the advantages of distributed practice are not temporary in nature. These advantages show themselves when a long enough time has intervened between learning and a test for retention to permit forgetting to take place. There is even some evidence that suggests that the relative advantage of distributed practice increases after an interval of rest (Robinson, 1921). These long-time effects of the distribution of practice are important practically as well as theoretically, because they tell us that the distribution of practice will be of permanent value to the learner. Kimble (1949) presents evidence which seems to show that the optimal rest period during learning is much smaller for measures of retention than measures of learning.

*Theory of distributed practice.* Since the beneficial effects of distributed practice are so widespread and important, several theories have been advanced to account for them. The fact that the amount of work per unit of practice seems to be the major determiner of the effectiveness of distributed practice (Hovland, 1940b; Kimble and Bilodeau, 1949) makes those theories that are based upon the notion of an inhibitory feedback from performance seem the most plausible.

The idea that work produces a feedback that makes subsequent work more difficult is a very useful one in psychology. You will recall that one of the theories of extinction makes use of this idea. While work-induced inhibition does not explain all the effects found in extinction, it certainly is an important concept for the temporary effects of extinction. The notion of an inhibitory feedback from behavior finds many other applications of which one is the explanation of at least part of the distributed-practice effect.

There are several variations in theories about the effects of inhibition upon behavior, but all these variations have certain fundamental notions in common. Perhaps the most basic of these is the idea that the tendency to respond is a function of the algebraic interaction of two factors, an excitatory potential and an inhibitory potential. The excitatory potential [3] makes for a greater tendency to respond; it is the result of reinforcement, drive, etc. The inhibitory potential makes for a tendency not to respond, and it is analogous to fatigue.

It is usually assumed that the amount of excitatory and inhibitory potential associated with a response reaches a peak just after the response

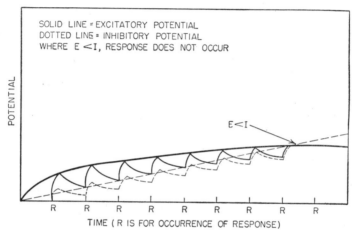

FIG. 33. The growth and decay of excitatory and inhibitory potential.

takes place, and then slowly declines. This conception is shown graphically in Fig. 33. Here you will notice that the amount of excitatory potential is greater than that of inhibitory potential; this will be so any time the response actually occurs. If the inhibitory potential is greater than the excitatory potential, the response will not occur. Notice also that the inhibitory potential declines very much more rapidly than the excitatory potential.

A second assumption about inhibitory and excitatory potential is that they add up from response to response. Inhibitory potential adds up in a linear fashion while excitatory potential adds up exponentially. When we put this assumption together with the first one, we predict that the excita-

[3] This use of the term "excitatory potential" makes it exactly the same as "response strength," a term used earlier. This use of excitatory potential does not exactly follow Hull *et al.* (1940), the author of the notion, but it makes a continuity between our present and earlier discussion.

tory effect does not add up very much faster no matter how close together in time the responses are, but that the inhibitory potential adds up very much faster the closer the responses are in time. Indeed, the inhibitory potential may add up fast enough to completely cancel the excitatory potential. In this case the response would not occur. It is easy to see how the distribution-of-practice effect can be deduced from such a theory.

Hull and his associates (1940) have developed this theory at great length. From the theory, they have carefully developed many hypotheses about rote learning, and they have put many of these hypotheses in precise, and sometimes complicated, form. In general, their predictions from the theory have been verified. For example, Hovland (1938c, 1940b) has shown that the greatest beneficial effect of distributed practice is in the middle of a series of nonsense syllables learned by rote. This conclusion was derived from the theory. The interested student will want to examine this theory in greater detail as an example of the use of deductive methodology in learning theory.

McGeoch (1942), like Hull, subscribes to an inhibition-excitation theory, but he has reframed it in terms of differential forgetting. He points out that when an individual learns, he learns not only correct responses but also incorrect and conflicting responses. The incorrect responses are less well fixed during the learning process and consequently are forgotten sooner. This notion, as you can see, is exactly parallel to the notion of the differential rate of decay of excitatory and inhibitory potential and leads to just about the same predictions. In addition, however, to some of the hypotheses advanced by Hull's version of the theory, the differential-forgetting version of the theory is supported by a few other facts. For example, McGeoch points out that fewer repeated errors in maze learning are found when learning is by distributed rather than massed practice.

*Implications of the theory.* The principal implication of the inhibition-excitation theory of the effects of massed and distributed practice is that the amount of work involved in a task determines to a great extent the relative effectiveness of distributed practice. In other words, tasks which involve a great deal of work should clearly show the beneficial effects of distributed practice. Of course, work does not necessarily mean physical work; it may also mean "mental" work. Thus, the theory can account for the fact that the advantage of distributed practice over massed practice in rote serial learning increases as the amount of material to be learned is increased (Lyon, 1914; Hovland, 1940b).

### THE SERIAL POSITION EFFECT

There is one special effect upon the course of learning when the material is learned in a rigid serial order. This is known as the "serial position effect." It refers to the fact that the rate at which a given item in a serial list of items is learned depends upon the location of that item within the

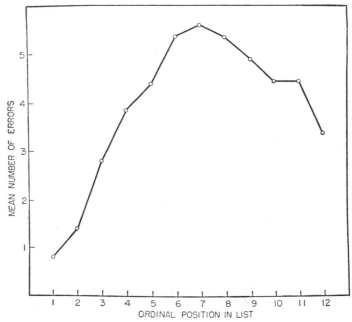

FIG. 34. Number of errors at each syllable position for learning nonsense syllables by the method of anticipation. (*Hovland, 1938b.*)

list. Items which are at the beginning of a list of nonsense syllables are learned more quickly than items anywhere else within the list. Items at the end of the list are next easiest to learn. For this reason, the serial position effect has sometimes been called the "primacy-finality" effect, to emphasize the point that items at the beginning and end of a list of items are easiest to learn.

*The serial position curve.* A curve that shows the number of correct responses made during the learning process as a function of the order of the items in the list is known as a "serial position curve." A typical example is shown in Fig. 34 (Hovland, 1938b). You can see from this curve that the greatest number of failures of anticipation occurred at the seventh syllable position, which is just past the middle of the list. This finding, as it turns out, is a general one; the most difficult part of a list of serial items to learn is the part just past the middle of the list.

We can say then that the most general serial position curve is a bow-shaped curve, skewed slightly to one side. This basic curve may vary as a

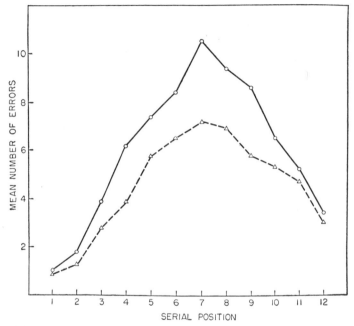

FIG. 35. The effect of distribution of practice upon the serial position curve. Massed practice is indicated by the dotted curve and distributed practice by the solid curve. Notice that massed practice has its greatest effect in the middle of the curve. (*Hovland, 1938c.*)

function of conditions of learning, but if the items are all of the same difficulty and of the same degree of resemblance to one another, some form of this curve will appear.

*The serial position curve and distribution of practice.* One of the most important variables which determines the magnitude of the serial position effect is the distribution of practice. Figure 35 shows that with massed practice the serial position effect is much greater than it is with distributed practice. Another way of putting this point is to say that nearly all the beneficial effects of distributed practice in rote verbal learning come in the quicker learning of the items in the middle of the list (Hovland, 1938*b,* 1938*c,* 1940*b*). This relationship is of great importance because it suggests that the inhibition due to massed practice and the serial position curve have a common cause, at least in rote verbal learning.

The common cause, we might assume, is the active inhibition of items during learning. This notion receives very strong support from the phenomenon known as "reminiscence" (p. 174). In serial learning this phenomenon shows up in the form of better recall for items in the middle than for other items, when a rest interval is allowed before a test for retention. This and other points lead us to expect that theories of the serial position effect should be quite similar to theories of distributed practice. And they are. But let us see specifically what they are.

*Theories of the serial position effect.* The most elaborate of them stems from a concept derived from Pavlov. Pavlov (1927) was able to establish, in salivary conditioning, what he called a "trace conditioned response." To get such a response, he first presented the conditioned stimulus and then delayed some time before presenting the unconditioned stimulus. Thus the animal had to learn to delay the conditioned response for a period of time after the conditioned stimulus had disappeared. The ability to achieve this delay, Pavlov believed, was made possible by an active inhibition of the conditioned response during the delay period.

From the concept of the trace conditioned response, it is but two steps to the serial position effect. The first step is to liken remote forward associations (p. 139) to trace conditioned responses; Lepley (1934) did that. An association between an item at the beginning of the list and the end of the list, said Lepley, is inhibited by a process analogous to Pavlov's inhibition of delay. The second step, made by Hull (1935*a*), was to take this similarity and to expand it to account for the serial position effect. Hull argued that the inhibiting effect of the delayed association between the first item and successive items ought to affect intervening items. For example, if there is an inhibition of the association between item 1 and item 9 in a series, it should make the association between items 6 and 7 more difficult. Consequently, the items in the middle should be inhibited in proportion to the number of delayed associations which span them. This notion is illustrated in Fig. 36 (Hull, 1935*a*). You will notice in this figure that the greatest number of delayed associations spans the middle items, and this is a way of representing the point that the most difficult item to learn should be the middle item.

In actual fact, however, the middle item is not the most difficult to learn; the items just past the middle are the most difficult. So, while Hull's notion could be right in general, on this specific prediction it is wrong. Aware of this fact, Hull *et al.* (1940) has developed a much more elaborate treatment of inhibition and the serial position effect.

This treatment is so complicated to explain in detail that we shall note only its main points. It assumes, just as the older theory does, that a stimulus trace extends from any syllable to the remaining syllables in the

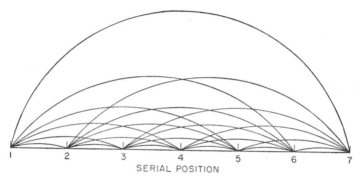

FIG. 36. This illustrates how remote forward associations could account for a symmetrical serial position curve. The "inhibition" at each position is proportional to the number of associations spanning that position. (*After Hull, 1935a.*)

list. Hull goes on, however, to assume very exact values for the strength of this trace at the time each remaining syllable has its turn. With the values he assumes, together with the assumption of excitatory and inhibitory potentials outlined earlier, Hull and his associates were able to generate, after suitable mathematical treatment, a serial position curve that fits very well the empirically obtained data. The theoretical curve is skewed, as are the empirically obtained curves, and it shows that there is less efficient learning of the last half of a list of items than the first half.

*The serial position curve and anticipation and perseveration.* You have probably noticed that there is a similarity between the serial position curve and the effects of anticipation and perseveration in the linear maze (p. 131). In the case of the linear maze, when the correct responses required at each choice point are all different, the effects of anticipation and perseveration are to make the middle choice point of a linear maze the most difficult choice point to learn. Similarly, in rote verbal learning, anticipation and perseveration make the middle items the most difficult to learn.

In both cases of serial learning, we observe a serial position effect and we can attribute it to remote associations.

Although this general theory seems quite plausible, it is obviously desirable to show, experimentally if possible, that remote associations are actually responsible for the serial position effect. Unfortunately, there is no study in the literature which directly makes the necessary comparison. Bugelski (1950), in a recent paper, points out the relationship between anticipatory intrusions and the serial position effect, but he does not compare directly the number of such intrusions occurring at each syllable position and the difficulty of learning that syllable position.

### THE CONCEPT OF INHIBITION

We have just seen two examples, in the effect of massed practice and in the serial position effect, of conditions which can best be explained by an active inhibitory process in learning. The exact nature of the inhibition involved in each of these examples is not clearly understood, but it seems to be well agreed upon that inhibition as a concept is needed to explain the experimental data bearing on these two effects. These are not the only cases, however, in which the concept of inhibition is useful. Inhibition, of essentially the same variety, is used as an explanatory concept to account for some of the data in experimental extinction. And there are many other examples of the use of the concept in the theories of learning.

Moreover, the concept of an active inhibitory process is not limited to learning but seems to be involved in any sort of activity that requires repetitive work. Accordingly, in a learning situation, the difference between massed and distributed practice may be the result not only of what the individual learns but a difference in what he is able to do at the moment. Here again we meet the distinction between learning and performance, and the point is that inhibition may be at work in performance as well as in the learning process. If, however, the effect of inhibition were entirely a temporary one on behavior alone, that is, upon performance, we might expect that there would be complete recovery after a period of rest. Such is not the case, for the effects of massed practice, for example, are still apparent after a period of time has elapsed (p. 157). This is probably because individuals learn what they do. If performance during learning is made inferior by massed practice, this inferior performance is what is learned and what will be retained later. Therefore, a measure of retention after massed practice will show what is retained after massed practice to be inferior to what is retained after distributed practice.

*Inhibition in mental work.* When individuals are allowed to work at their own pace on repetitive tasks, there is evidence that they introduce their own rest pauses, and that these increase in length as the time at work increases (Bills, 1931). In fact, these brief rests or "blocks" increase in both frequency and length as work continues (Fig. 37). Semiregular blocks

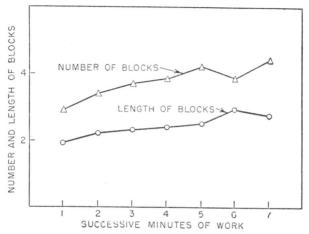

Fɪɢ. 37. The number of "blocks" and duration of blocks increase as a function of time at continuous work on a repetitive task. (*Data from Bills, 1931.*)

of this sort are characteristic of repetitive work. These blocks seem to be caused by inhibition that has built up during work, and the block is a device, we may assume, for allowing inhibition to dissipate itself.

Experimental evidence supports this inhibitory idea of blocks. Such evidence, moreover, indicates that amount of inhibition built up depends on the repetitive nature of work. Take, for example, an experiment by Robinson and Bills (1926). Subjects were instructed to write certain letters of the alphabet as rapidly as possible. One group of subjects wrote repetitively only two letters, like this: abababababab. The other group wrote repetitively six letters, like this: abcdefabcdef, etc. The group which wrote only two letters showed more blocks and a faster decline in rate of work than did the group which wrote six letters.

These experiments suggest that merely changing activity may serve to dissipate some of the inhibition involved. Thus, working on varied and nonrepetitive activity is apt to generate less inhibition than work on monotonous and repetitive activity.

*Kinds of inhibition.* It may well turn out that there are several kinds of inhibition. One may be a matter of interference. Certainly there seems to be a certain class of disruptive effects which are due to interference. One example of this kind of inhibition may be the serial position effect; another example seems to be the kind of inhibition produced in retroactive experiments (p. 187). A second kind of inhibiting effect seems to be more like the classical notion of fatigue than one of interference. In this case, inhibition seems to be the accumulation of something that produces a tendency not to respond. This kind of inhibition fits the data on massed and distributed practice and experimental extinction, though some theorists have applied the notion of inhibition through interference to these phenomena. At the present time, there does not seem to be data available which can tell us whether there is one kind or many kinds of inhibition, and if there are many kinds, which kind specifically applies to a certain class of data. Probably the best guess we can make now is that two or more kinds of inhibition are at work in most situations. The serial position effect, for example, may be due both to interference and to a tendency not to respond as a result of the repetitive nature of the learning task.

## THE NATURE OF LEARNING MATERIAL

In addition to the factors we have already considered, there are many other variables that affect the rate of learning either the material as a whole, as in the massed-distributed practice effect, or parts of the material, as in the serial position effect. Most of these variables seem to have something to do with the nature of the material learned. Indeed, next to the nature of the learner, that of the material to be learned is probably the most important variable in the psychology of learning. At this juncture we are not prepared to examine all that is known on this point, but we can look at a few ways in which the material to be learned affects learning.

*Meaningfulness of material.* It is obvious that a person will learn something meaningful to him much more rapidly than he will nonsense or completely unfamiliar material. It is less obvious perhaps that this effect is due, in part, to sequential dependencies between parts of material—the kinds of dependencies we took up in the last chapter under the heading of "statistical behavioristics" (p. 141). But meaningful material, almost by definition, contains a lot of short phrases which go together. For example, it is probably easier to remember the phrase "the man who can is the man who will" than the phrase "six birds catch tubes which new ghosts will not," principally because the first phrase contains a lot of words which go together frequently in ordinary English. So sequential dependencies constitute one factor that makes meaningful material easier to learn than meaningless material.

Another element in the picture is the "idea." If we do not ask learners to learn the letter of what is being taught, but only the "idea," obviously learning will be somewhat the easier. For this there are many reasons. One is that, in the nature of things, the criterion of having learned is a lot more lax for ordinary verbal ideas than it is for rote learning of specific words. Secondly, the idea is probably a smaller unit of learning than a lot of words put together in a meaningful or meaningless pattern. Unfortunately, we are not yet to the stage where we can actually determine the units of ideas, so this statement has to go untested for the moment.

We do know, however, that ideas in themselves differ with respect to their ease of learning. Reed (1938) attempted to compare two passages of prose, each of which contained 67 different ideas, on an immediate recall test. One of the passages contained a lot of abstract ideas, while the other passage was a simple narrative. The subjects recalled many more of the ideas from the simple narrative than they did from the abstract prose. Unfortunately, this comparison is only suggestive, since these passages probably differed in very many other important ways.

A third and important factor in learning of meaningful material is the degree of transfer of training (p. 214) that the learner is able to bring to bear upon his task. That is to say, what the learner has already learned is what makes material meaningful, and if he has learned more, especially more that is relevant to the task, he will learn more rapidly than he would otherwise. Certainly the very ability of an individual to acquire ideas implies that he has learned something at some previous time about the specific elements which go into the idea.

*Intratask interference.* Besides meaningfulness of material, the readiness with which material is learned depends also on the amount of interference there is between different parts of the task. A very good example of such intratask interference seems to be the serial position effect that was discussed earlier. Intratask interference can occur in any material regardless of whether or not it is learned in a constant serial order. For example, in learning the Morse code (Keller and Taubman, 1943), the most difficult signals to learn, as we might expect, are those which are most easily confused with other signals. Another experiment on code learning (Plotkin, 1943) shows that, as the similarity between the items to be learned is increased, the degree of confusion is increased.

It is perhaps apparent to you that similarity between items in a body of material to be learned is a principal source of confusion, and hence of increased difficulty, in learning. This principle is generally true, although there are important exceptions. We cannot go into the exceptions here, but it will be well to keep it in mind that the difference between similarity which increases the difficulty in learning and other kinds of similarity which can increase the ease of learning are very important. We shall later examine this matter in some detail, for it makes up an important variable in experimentally produced forgetting, on the one hand, and positive transfer of training, on the other—both topics treated in a later chapter.

As a practical point, however, we can safely conclude that intratask similarity usually produces intratask interference and does not help learning. At least, in most of the examples one meets in everyday learning, this statement is probably true.

*Amount of material.* For most kinds of learning material, as the amount of material is increased, the difficulty of learning *per item* increases. An old experiment by Lyon (1917) remains the best evidence on this point in the experimental literature, though it leaves much to be desired, as Lyon's data did not entirely agree with earlier work. Time to learn material, he found, increases disproportionately as the length of material increases. This finding held for nonsense syllables, for prose material, and for poetry. Subsequent investigators have not been able to confirm Lyon (Hovland, 1951), but they used much smaller amounts of material than did Lyon, and as Hovland remarks, a repetition of Lyon's experiment should be performed. Because he did use an extensive amount of material, Lyon's results are still the most acceptable thus far.

There are many possible reasons why an increase in amount of material should result in a disproportionate increase in time to learn. For one thing, an increase in the amount of material allows more opportunity for intratask interference. This is probably the most important single reason, but other factors such as the distribution of attention and effort, unnecessary repetition of the items learned first, etc., in the aggregate must have considerable influence.

# CHAPTER 9

# RETENTION

Retention was one of the first aspects of human learning to be investigated by laboratory methods; Ebbinghaus (1885) studied it as part of his classical work on rote learning. From Ebbinghaus's day on down to the present, retention—and its converse, forgetting—has been one of the most intensively studied areas in human learning, and we now have a very large body of literature concerning it. A portion of it has been concerned simply with the measurement of retention for various kinds of material and under various conditions. Another portion of it has been in the area of experimentally produced forgetting. The subject of this chapter is the nature of retention; experimentally produced forgetting will be postponed to the next chapter.

Why, you might ask, do we distinguish between retention and forgetting? Is not one simply the opposite of the other? There is no really good excuse for the use of the two terms, for amount forgotten is merely the difference between the amount learned and the amount retained. And, of course, it is always the amount retained which is measured, so of the two terms, perhaps retention is the best one to use. The term "forgetting," however, can be reserved for that body of data obtained from studies in which there is a deliberate attempt to reduce the amount of material individuals will retain or from studies in which forgetting is experimentally produced. There is, therefore, a convenient, although not essential, distinction between retention and forgetting. It is the basis for entitling this chapter "Retention" and the next one "Forgetting."

## THE COURSE OF RETENTION WITH TIME

It is very surprising indeed that no one before Ebbinghaus had thought to measure how much an individual can remember after a period of time has elapsed since learning. Though it is universally appreciated that the retention of most tasks is not complete, Ebbinghaus was the first investigator to give us a picture of the amount of material originally learned that is retained after various intervals of time without practice. Before looking at the results of Ebbinghaus and his successors, it will probably be wise to examine briefly some of the methodological problems in the study of retention.

*Experimental designs.* The measurement of retention brings up some special problems in methodology. One of these concerns the nature of the experimental design used to study retention. It will not do, for example, to use the same subjects repeatedly in the measurement of retention of the same material over varying periods of time, because each succeeding measurement provides a practice session. Also to be avoided are the effects of rehearsal of the learned material between experimental sessions.

The experimental methods that we can use fall into two classes: (1) repeated measurements on the same subjects using different material, and (2) independent measurements on different subjects using the same material. In the first method, the subjects may learn one set of nonsense syllables, be tested for retention after an hour, then learn another set of nonsense syllables that are of equivalent difficulty, be tested after two hours, etc. In the second method, the subjects are divided into several groups, each of which is tested after varying periods of time.

*Method of measurement.* There are three different ways to measure retention; these are not exactly equivalent to one another, so a word of explanation about each is necessary. One method is that of *recall*. In this one, the subject is asked to reproduce, without any external supporting cues, the material which he had learned at an earlier date. In the case of rote verbal learning, this may mean that the subject either must anticipate, as he did in original learning, each item before it appears, or he must reproduce, in any order, the items that he has learned. This is the most conservative of the measures of retention; it always yields lower retention scores than do the other methods.

A second method is that of *recognition*. In this method the subject is presented with the material that he has learned, mixed in with a lot of similar material, and he is asked to pick out that which he has learned. An example of this measure of retention is the multiple-choice objective examination. This method inflates by a factor of "chance" the measurement of what the subject has retained, and this fact makes the method the least useful for experimental purposes.

A third method, that of *savings,* is the measure employed by Ebbinghaus in his original work on learning and memory. In this method, the subject is asked to relearn the material at some later date. The savings is the difference in some measure of learning between original learning and relearning. For example, if the subject originally takes 20 trials to learn the list of nonsense syllables and, after a week's rest, takes 10 trials, there is a savings of 50 per cent. The savings method is the measure of retention that is most widely used because it seems to be most sensitive to experimental variables. It can have negative as well as positive values, it may show some retention when the other methods show none, and it seems to be more stable than the other measures.

*The course of retention.* In his measurements of retention, Ebbinghaus used himself as subject, nonsense syllables as his learning material, and the method of savings as his measure of retention. His results, which are representative of such methods of measurement, are shown in Fig. 38. As you can see, retention falls off very rapidly at first and then more slowly.

Retention, like learning, varies of course with various features of the experimental situation. One important variable is the nature of the material. The results in Fig. 38 are typical of the course of retention when the learning material is disconnected and difficult. The retention curve for meaningful material follows much the same course, but the decline in amount is by no means so steep (McGeoch, 1932). In general, the higher the degree of organization and logic in the material, the slower the rate of fall in retention (Gilliland, 1948). It has been shown, for example, that retention is much better for ideas than for factual material (Briggs and Reed, 1943). Besides the nature of the material, many other factors affect retention curves. Of these, two important ones are the number of repetitions during learning (Ebbinghaus, 1885), and the amount of material learned (Newman, 1939*b*).

*Curves of retention.* We have already seen that there is no *one* curve of learning; neither is there one universal curve of retention. Ebbinghaus's curve, presented in Fig. 38, has often been called "the" curve of retention, but that is probably because it is reproduced so frequently rather than because anyone has the naïveté to assume that it is universal. Occasionally someone attempts to find, by deductive reasoning, a mathematically "ideal" curve of forgetting (London, 1950), but retention varies with such a wide variety of conditions, the method of measurement, ability of the learner, practice, the material learned, etc., that such mathematical expressions probably have little practical value. It is true that most retention curves appear to decline exponentially—the greatest drop is at the beginning—but this fact gives slim grounds for quantitative theorizing.

*Retention of school subjects.* In view of the rather alarming decline in retention with the passage of time that is found in the experimental labora-

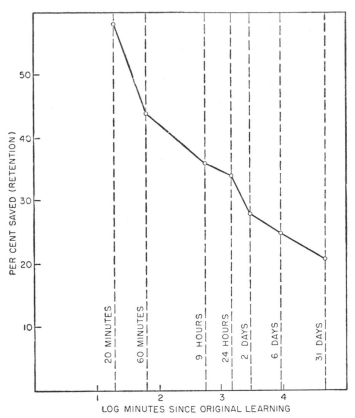

FIG. 38. Savings (retention) as a function of time without practice. This curve was obtained from nonsense material. Notice that the abscissa is plotted on a logarithmic scale. (*Data from Ebbinghaus, 1885.*)

tory, it is reassuring to see that the retention of school subjects fares a little better. Factual material, as one might expect, shows the greatest decline with time. One study showed that university students did about half as well on an examination for factual material after 4 months without additional formal training than they did immediately after learning (Greene, 1931). That is a relatively large loss, considering the fact that the first test provided additional practice. Other studies of retention of factual material, however, have shown somewhat better retention. One with junior high-school students and American history (Brooks and Bassett, 1928) showed a 13 to 23 per cent decline in a period from 3 months to a year after formal instruction ended. Another showed that, while computational skills declined considerably over a summer vacation, the ability to apply the general principles of arithmetic declined very little (Schrepel and Laslett, 1936). In this same study, it is interesting to note, bright students lost less than the less intelligent students.

There have been a whole host of studies concerned with the retention of school subjects. The student will probably agree that little could be gained here by a recitation of these studies. They are of primary interest to those who teach the subjects involved. Foreign language teachers, for example, may be interested in knowing how much is retained after a summer vacation and how much a review of basic grammar will benefit long-term retention. Though studies of the retention of school subjects have considerable implication for educational theories and practice, they do not tell us very much about the processes involved in retention.

*Retention of simple conditioned responses.* Measuring the retention of simple conditioned responses yields some interesting information that has some possible theoretical value. It might be expected that conditioned responses would show the characteristic negatively accelerated decline in strength with the passage of time. That, however, does not seem to be the case. Most conditioned responses are extraordinarily resistant to the effects of a lapse of time. Conditioned flexion responses in sheep have been retained over a period of 2 years (Liddell, James, and Anderson, 1934). Similar long periods of retention have been reported with flexion conditioning in the dog (Wendt, 1937; Kellogg and Wolf, 1939).

Skinner (1950) has provided an especially thorough study of retention of a conditioned operant in the pigeon; it extended over a period of more than 4 years. He obtained extinction curves immediately after learning and, in other animals, after various periods of time. A long time interval, he found, does not abolish the response, but it does decrease the number of responses that an animal makes during the extinction period.

So it seems clear that conditioned responses are better retained than are *single items* of any other kind of learning. The precise explanation for this fact must wait until the next chapter, but in general it can be said that the laboratory conditioned response presents fewer opportunities for interactions between that response and other responses than in any other kind of learning. It so happens that interaction between various learned responses is the most important psychological determiner of what, and how much, is forgotten.

## REMINISCENCE

Some experimental studies of retention show a *rise* rather than a fall in the retention curve. This phenomenon is called "reminiscence." The conditions under which reminiscence has been found in the laboratory fall into two rather distinct classes. The first of these has been called the Ballard-Williams effect, and the second of these types has been called the Ward-Hovland effect.[1] Since the Ballard-Williams effect has some historical precedent, it will be discussed first.

*The Ballard-Williams effect.* Naturally, in order for reminiscence to occur, it is necessary that original learning not be carried to perfection. Otherwise there can be no measured rise in the retention curve. To obtain this effect, the learners are given a test for recall immediately after learning, and then they are given another test for recall at some later time. The number of items recalled on the immediate-recall test is arbitrarily taken at 100 per cent. Any increase that may occur in retention is taken as a percentage of this figure. For example, a later recall may indicate that retention is 150 per cent, which would mean that half again as many items were recalled on the second test as were recalled on the first test.

In the original experiments on this effect, Ballard (1913) had large groups of English school children learn long sections of poetry and nonsense syllables. He asked for an immediate recall and a later recall of what had been learned. For both the poetry and the nonsense syllables, later recall trials showed a rise in the retention curve. This rise reached a peak about 2 to 3 days after original learning. After that the curves of retention followed the usual declining course. These results show that, under certain conditions at least, recalls after the first recall can contain more items than the first recall, even though no intervening learning has been observed to take place.

One possible interpretation of this fact is that the immediate-recall test provides practice in addition to original learning that helps in the later recall test. That this *is* a factor is shown by an experiment by Bunch

---

[1] This division follows McGeoch (1942). Others who have reviewed the problem of reminiscence (Bunch, 1938; Buxton, 1943) have not made use of this classification. It makes sense from an operational point of view, however, and for that reason it is used here.

(1938). He gave a second recall test for some incompletely learned poetry *immediately* after the first recall test. This second recall test, in addition to having all the items that turned up on the first recall test, included some new items. McGeoch (1940), however, has shown that items not present during practice may show up on a recall test. This suggests very strongly that some of the material is actively inhibited, and a second recall test may allow some of these inhibited items to come to the surface.

Another possible factor in reminiscence is that of unobserved practice ("rehearsal") between the immediate-recall tests and the later-recall tests. There is strong evidence, however, that this is not the only factor in the Ballard-Williams type of reminiscence. G. O. McGeoch (1935) has shown that there is no difference in the amount of reminiscence between children who reported reviewing their material between tests and those who did not. Rats show reminiscence in maze learning (Bunch and Magsdick, 1933), and it is not easy to imagine rats rehearsing their paths through a maze between trials. Another point against the possibility of rehearsal as the chief cause of reminiscence is the fact that a variety of psychomotor skills that would be difficult to rehearse away from the specific learning situation show reminiscence (Buxton, 1943). Finally, as we shall see, a number of experiments have controlled against the possibility of rehearsal by forcing the subjects to engage in some activity between successive tests of recall.

*The Ward-Hovland effect.* The Ballard-Williams effect is not easily interpreted. It cannot be *entirely* due to unmeasured rehearsal or to test-retest effects; nevertheless it is difficult to evaluate how much of the reminiscence is due to these factors and how much to other conditions. There is, however, another related body of experimental data that show the reminiscence effect. In these data reminiscence has been called the "Ward-Hovland effect."

There is a very real difference between these two effects and the conditions under which they are obtained. The Ballard-Williams effect takes place over days and may last as long as 5 or 6 days; the Ward-Hovland effect, on the other hand, occurs over a matter of minutes. Ballard and Williams had their subjects do both an immediate- and a later-recall test, but Ward (1937) and Hovland (1938a, 1938b), by comparing the performance of two groups of subjects rather than retesting one group, had only one recall test and this entirely eliminated the effects of an initial test upon a later one. They simply gave recall tests after various periods of time following learning to find out how much of the originally learned material was retained. As in the Ballard-Williams studies, Ward and Hovland usually carried learning to some criterion short of perfection (say to a criterion of 75 per cent correct), though in some experiments they practiced their subjects until they had achieved one perfect repetition of the material. Under these conditions they found a rise in the retention curve for a period of anywhere from 2 to 20 minutes after learning had ended.

Since, in the Ward-Hovland effect, the immediate-recall trial is eliminated, the remaining uncontrolled factor is the possibility of rehearsal between the end of formal practice and the test for retention. To exclude rehearsal, Ward (1937) made his subjects engage in some simple task, such as color association and light reading. Ward obtained reminiscence nevertheless; his subjects showed better retention after a period of time than they did on an immediate-recall test. Subsequent investigators have employed other, more adequate, tasks for preventing rehearsal (see Buxton, 1943), and we may safely conclude that this kind of reminiscence is not due to rehearsal. It should be noted, however, that some kinds of rehearsal-preventing tasks allow more reminiscence to occur than others (Ward, 1937; Shipley, 1939), but even when rehearsal is forced, there is no increase in the amount of reminiscence (Rohrer, 1949).

Despite the fact that there have been a fair number of experiments performed on the Ward-Hovland effect, we are still not very sure under what conditions it occurs and does not occur. There are two conditions which seem to especially favor it; they are massed practice and meaningless material. Hovland (1938b) showed that reminiscence was greater with a faster rate of exposure of the material; the faster rate of exposure produced massed practice. Both Shipley (1939) and McClelland (1942) have confirmed this. More important than the distribution of practice, however, seems to be the nature of the material. Using a list of adjectives rather than nonsense material, Melton and Stone (1942) failed to find the Ward-Hovland effect. A whole host of subsequent experiments have confirmed this; reminiscence occurs with nonsense syllables but does not occur with lists of meaningful words (Buxton, 1948; Buxton and Baken, 1949; Buxton and Ross, 1949; Noble, 1950). Furthermore, E. L. Deese (1938) failed to find the Ward-Hovland effect with the use of poetry as learning material.

*Theories of reminiscence.* The Ward-Hovland effect can be considered to be merely a special case of the distribution of practice problem. In a demonstration of the Ward-Hovland effect, practice is massed followed by a brief rest before a recall or relearning trial. So both the fact of the superiority of distributed practice over massed practice and the Ward-

Hovland effect demonstrate a beneficial influence of a brief rest interval upon learning. The factor of rest therefore seems to be common to both kinds of effects.

Now when we considered massed and distributed practice (p. 152), you may recall that the most acceptable theory to explain their effects upon learning was one of *reactive inhibition*. Each response, or item, in the list being practiced was assumed to build up some inhibition, and this inhibition was assumed to dissipate during a brief period of rest. So the periods of rest that distinguish distributed from massed practice were considered to aid learning and retention because they allowed reactive inhibition to dissipate.

The same theoretical approach can be applied to the phenomenon of reminiscence (Hull *et al.*, 1940). In this case, we can explain the effect in terms of the dissipation of inhibition during the rest period between the last trial of learning and the recall trial. The explanation is supported by the fact that reminiscence takes place after massed practice but not distributed practice, for in massed practice there is little time for inhibition to dissipate until the rest period at the end, while there is in the case of distributed practice. Another source of support for this theory is the fact that reminiscence, like the effects of massed practice, shows up best with items near the middle of the list—in other words, in the serial position effect (Ward, 1937; Hovland, 1938a, 1938b).[2] This effect, you will recall, can be explained by piling up of inhibitory effects in the middle of a series. So an inhibitory theory of reminiscence predicts that it will appear most prominently in connection with both the serial position effect and massed practice.

There seems to be very strong evidence, therefore, that the causes of these three effects—reminiscence, the massed-practice effect, and the serial position effect—are all related. They can be explained by some active inhibitory effect upon performance. The exact nature of this inhibition is unknown, and, as we have seen before (p. 164), it may be that several different orders of inhibition are involved.

In this connection, it is interesting to note that one experimenter has attributed the greater ease of learning meaningful material to the smaller amount of inhibition which is generated with meaningful material (Noble,

[2] Buxton and Ross (1949) have failed to find the serial position effect in connection with reminiscence, but they point out that this may be because their data were unreliable.

1950). This idea accounts for the fact that reminiscence does not seem to occur with meaningful material.

Unfortunately, although inhibition may account for the Ward-Hovland effect, it does little to explain the Ballard-Williams effect. The differences between the Ballard-Williams effect and the Ward-Hovland effect are too great to allow us to account for one in terms of a theory which fits the other. In the first place, the time intervals in the Ballard-Williams effect are too large. In the second place, the Ballard-Williams effect occurs with meaningful material, while the Ward-Hovland effect apparently does not. In all probability the causes of the Ballard-Williams effect are complex; it may be partially due to recovery from inhibition, but there are undoubtedly other factors of considerable importance.

## THE INFLUENCE OF MOTIVATION UPON RETENTION

People have suspected for a long time that retention is not randomly distributed among items that may have the same external characteristics. Retention—or forgetting—seems to be selective in nature. Some people easily remember some things and forget others. Among the factors affecting such selection, we certainly must include the personality characteristics of the individual, and particularly his motivational system. Evidence for this notion has not been very easy to obtain, however. Many experiments have been performed which have shown that there is *selective recall,* but it cannot be clearly established whether or not this selective recall is a matter of how much is learned or how much is retained. A few examples will illustrate this point.

*Ego involvement and selective recall.* An individual is ego-involved in some task when his personal esteem is somehow threatened or called into action by that task. The influence of ego-involvement upon learning and retention has been studied in several different contexts, which range from personality characteristics to social and political attitude formation.

In one experiment (Sharp, 1938), normal and psychoneurotic individuals learned paired associates, the items for which were taken from their personal histories. Some of these items were unacceptable; that is to say, they contained words that referred to painful or unpleasant events in the histories of these individuals. Some of these items were acceptable—they referred to pleasant or painless events—and some of the items were completely neutral. Unacceptable items, the investigator found, took more trials to learn than acceptable items, and they seemed to be less well retained than the others. In interpreting this experiment we should keep it in mind that the three kinds of items might have been different in *difficulty,* as well as acceptability. Since we know, from other experiments, that difficult material is inherently more difficult to remember, the result of this experiment may not necessarily reflect the degree of ego involvement in the items. On the assumption that they do, however, we have evidence in this experiment that unpleasant material is less well retained than pleasant or neutral material. The author of this experiment took the interpretation that the reason these items were less well retained was that they were repressed, in the Freudian sense. This kind of interpretation, however, is not well supported, for to fulfill the requirements of a demonstration of repression, it is necessary to show that, when the source of the threat is removed, the "repressed" items reappear (as in reminiscence). As Zeller (1950*a*) has pointed out, such was not the case in this experiment.

Slightly different approaches to the problem of the influence of selective motivation upon learning and retention are illustrated in two other experiments (Shaw, 1944; Shaw and Spooner, 1945). First, subjects were asked to make personality ratings of themselves and acquaintances. Then they were presented with false ratings (made by the experimenters) of themselves and their friends. At some later time the subjects were asked to recall the false ratings.

The results of the tests of recall showed three factors to be at work: how favorable or unfavorable the ratings were; the degree of agreement between the "true" ratings and the false ratings; and the matter of who was being rated, whether the subjects themselves or their friends. When it was the ratings of the subjects themselves that had to be recalled, they recalled the unfavorable ratings less frequently than the favorable ratings, and they recalled those that disagreed most with the "true" ratings less frequently than those that agreed well. When it was the ratings of the friends that had to be recalled, the subjects recalled both favorable and unfavorable false ratings to about the same extent, but they still recalled the false ratings that agreed best with the "true" ratings better than those that disagreed most with "true" ratings. These results are easily interpreted by assuming that the subjects were ego-involved in the ratings of their friends and in the ratings of themselves, but were not ego-involved in whether their friends were rated favorably or unfavorably. Another somewhat similar study (Wallen, 1942) has come out with comparable results; bogus ratings are frequently altered in memory to make them more compatible with the subjects' own beliefs.

Again, it is not clear in these experiments whether or not the differences reflect different rates of learning or different rates of forgetting for the material, for there is no way, in these experiments, in which learning and retention can be separated. The authors of these experiments have assumed that the experiments demonstrate selective forgetting, but we cannot be altogether certain that this is the correct interpretation.

Another, similar, set of studies (Edwards, 1941, 1942; Levine and Murphy, 1943) shows that items that are favorable to an individual's political viewpoint are better retained than items which are unfavorable. Furthermore, those items which are unfavorable, but which an individual recalls, are those which the individual can rationalize the easiest. Again, it cannot be clearly established that these differences are due entirely to selective forgetting.

Thus, while many studies have shown that the degree of ego involvement that an individual shows for a certain kind of learning material influences how well he recalls that material, it is not clearly established that this influence of ego involvement is entirely upon retention. Perhaps it is an academic question. The important fact is that the attitudes, beliefs, and personal motivations of individuals do influence how well they recall material.

*The recall of completed and incompleted tasks.* A famous experiment (Zeigarnik, 1927) shows that incompleted tasks are recalled more frequently than completed tasks. In this experiment the subjects were given a number of tasks to perform. For some of these tasks, the subjects were interrupted before they could actually finish doing them; for others of the tasks, the subjects were allowed to go on to completion. Sometime later, the subjects were asked to recall as many of the tasks as they could; the subjects remembered better than half again as many incompleted tasks as completed tasks. This experiment has been repeated many times, sometimes with positive results and sometimes with negative results (Martin, 1940; Marrow, 1938; Boguslavsky and Guthrie, 1941).

This disagreement among results has itself become an important problem. One possibility for accounting for it is that it is the success or failure associated with a task that determines whether or not incompleted tasks are remembered better than completed ones. Testing this possibility is an experiment (Marrow, 1938) in which the situation was so arranged that completing a task meant failure and leaving it unfinished meant success. In this experiment, more completed tasks are recalled than incompleted tasks. But unfortunately, the situation is not even this simple; a number of experiments have obtained results that do not confirm Marrow (Rosenzweig, 1933; Alper, 1946a; Glixman, 1949). The difficulty seems to be that success and failure affect different people in different ways. Some people may attempt to repress failure experiences; other people may perseverate, or mull over, failure experiences. Until the reactions of different kinds of people to the success-failure or complete-incomplete situations have been analyzed, nothing very specific can be said about the influence of these conditions upon memory.

It can be remarked, parenthetically, that the problem of incompleted vs. completed tasks is another example of an experimental effect that cannot be clearly attributed either to learning or forgetting. There may be either differential learning or differential forgetting for these kinds of materials.

*Set during learning and retention.* It is hardly necessary to remind college students that a student's method of study is a function of the particular kind of examination to which he is looking forward. An objective examination calls for a different method of study than does an essay examination. This is a reflection of the fact that we develop sets to select out certain aspects of learning material to be practiced. There is a very large difference in retention as a result of the set developed during learning (Peterson, 1916), and as the retention interval increases, this difference between kinds of set increases. For this fact, some selective aspect of motivation seems to be the cause; different motivations select out different aspects of the learning material to be practiced or even to be noticed in the first place. Thus it is that certain aspects of the task are retained better than others.

## QUALITATIVE CHANGES IN RETENTION

So far we have been emphasizing quantitative aspects of retention. Our major concern has been with the question of the amount of material retained after varying periods of time. There are, however, qualitative changes in retention as well. When we return to our home town after 10 years' absence, we are perhaps surprised to discover that things are not quite as we have remembered them. The courthouse is not quite so big as we remembered it, and Elm Street is much wider than we thought. Imagination has done something to memory.

Qualitative changes in retention are not only reflected in what can be called perceptual memory, but also in what we may do about something. I may remember a line from Pope as "Do you good by stealth, and blush to find it fame" and discover that the line is actually, "Do good by stealth, and blush to find it fame." Far from having forgotten the line, I have embellished it with an extra word.

*Gestalt theory and qualitative changes.* The experimental literature on qualitative changes in retention, particularly in perceptual retention, has come, to a very considerable extent, from the gestalt psychologists. They have emphasized changes in remembered perceptual forms as being of fundamental importance to the theory of memory. According to gestalt theory, there is a systematic change in the organization of retained material as a function of time.

Gestalt psychologists have hypothesized that there are "fields of organization" in memory and that these are related to "physiological fields" in the cerebral cortex. Because we are more interested in behavior at the moment than in physiological theories, it will be necessary to ignore the physiological aspects of their theories and stick to those that have a more direct bearing on the phenomena of retention. In doing that, we may do them a certain injustice, but not a grave one.

To get at changes in memory with time, early experimenters compared figures drawn by subjects from memory after varying periods of time with the original figures presented to the subject. In general, the qualitative changes shown by the subjects' reproduced figures seem to be in the direction of loss of detail (Woodworth, 1938). There also seems to be a tendency, when the reproduction of abstract figures is called for, to make the reproductions symmetrical even though the original has not been symmetrical.

On the basis of some of these early observations, the gestalt theorists challenged the idea that the "memory trace" for forms is simply a gradually fading thing. They advanced the notion that the memory trace tends toward a "better" form, and that every form approaches something like an "ideal" in memory. As Koffka (1935, p. 496) remarks: "The change which any pattern undergoes must be determined by the pattern itself. . . . According to the nature of the pattern, lines may gradually become straighter or more curved, longer or shorter."

Experimental results, however, do not always bear out the idea of autonomous changes in memory. Gibson (1929), for example, asked subjects to reproduce, by drawing, some simple figures that he exposed. He did not discover any consistent change in the memory for these figures; instead, different subjects did different things with the figures. Gestalt theory would have predicted a greater consistency in reproduction than he obtained, since according to this theory the major determiner of the change in memory trace is the shape of the form itself. So, in interpreting his results, Gibson emphasized the role of past experience, rather than better form, in the changes that take place in the memory trace with time. He had no direct evidence for such an interpretation, but other data seem to bear him out.

Since Gibson's experiment, there have been many others. Some of them give results in accord with the gestalt interpretation, and some of them do not. The lack of consistent evidence in many experiments (Gurnee, 1940; Hebb and Foord, 1945), coupled with the lack of decisiveness in the theoretical interpretations, has not made the gestalt interpretation a particularly fruitful one. In short, it is not necessary to appeal to "autonomous" changes in the memory trace induced by the configurations of forms to account for the vagaries of perceptual memory.

*Motivation and qualitative changes in retention.* In recent years psychologists have become very much interested in the role of motivation and other characteristics of the individual in determining perception. Many have argued that what we perceive is influenced by what we want to perceive and what we want to avoid. An experiment by Bruner and Postman (1947) will illustrate this point.

Bruner and Postman asked a group of subjects to match the size of a small plastic disk with a light that could be varied in diameter. They did this task fairly accurately. Next, the subjects were asked to push the disk underneath an electrified grill and out the other side. In doing this, they were frequently shocked by contact with the electrified bars. Finally, the subjects were again asked to match the disks with the circle of light. Now the subjects greatly overestimated the size of the disk. This result, the authors believe, indicates the change in perceptual values that can go along with release from tension (the subjects were released from tension because they knew that they were not to be shocked again). At any rate, the experiment does indicate that perceptual judgments may be influenced by conditions extraneous to the perception itself.

It is altogether reasonable to suppose that changes in the *memory* of a perception would be even more striking than they are in the perception itself, if an attempt were made to change the "value" of a perceived object. So Carter and Schooler (1949) did an experiment that tests that possibility. To emphasize differences in motivation, they selected a group of rich children and a group of poor children and had them match circles of light to the size of coins of various denominations. When the children made direct matches, that is, matches with coins in view, the matches of both groups were fairly accurate; there was no effect of motivation on perception (but see Bruner and Goodman, 1947). But when the matches were made from memory without seeing the coins, poor children remembered them as larger than they really are while rich children made reasonably accurate estimates of size. So it appears that the value of objects may influence perceptual memory for those objects.

Certainly the common-sense psychology of everyday life has recognized such effects for a long time, but they are just beginning to be explored experimentally. Laboratory studies, we may hope, will eventually tell us how these effects are brought about. We should like to know, for example, what role deliberate and intentional behavior plays in selective forgetting and in the distortion of memory pictures. We should also like to know to what extent these changes in memory are "unconscious" and unrecognized. At any rate, the notion that motivation has a dynamic effect upon memory is very useful to psychologists concerned with personality problems and psychotherapy.

*Experience and qualitative changes in retention.* Not only motivation but attitudes of an individual may distort his memory picture for specific objects. An experiment by Carmichael, Hogan, and Walter (1932) brings out this point. In their study, subjects were presented with a series of geometrical forms and were told that the figures were to be remembered for later reproduction. Just before each figure was exposed, the subjects were told that "the next figure resembles a ——," giving one of two alternative labels. One figure, for example, was a pair of perfect circles connected in the middle by a straight line. One group of subjects was told that the stimulus resembled eyeglasses; another group of subjects was told that the stimulus resembled a pair of dumbbells. When the series was finished, the subjects were asked to draw all the figures they could remember. The instructions to the subjects influenced how they reproduced the figures. The group which had been told that the stimulus mentioned above resembled eyeglasses reproduced the figure to look like eyeglasses. The group that had been told that the figure resembled dumbbells reproduced a pair of dumbbells. Thus verbal instructions influenced the perceptual memory of these individuals.

*The Aussage experiment.* All the factors that may induce selective changes and distortions in memory operate in the classical *Aussage* experiment. This experiment is probably familiar to most students of introductory psychology. To do the experiment, subjects are presented with a complicated picture or set of events and then asked to report on what they observed. For example, a motion picture of an automobile accident may be presented; then, 5 minutes later, the subjects are asked to write a *deposition* concerning what they have seen. Or they may be questioned about details of the event.

Under these circumstances it always turns out that memory is highly selective and that it undergoes changes in accord with the observer's previous experiences, his motives, and the way in which he tells the story. The inaccuracies of memory, moreover, are not due entirely to a loss of details about what has been observed, but they seem to reflect a systematic change in the perceptual memory for the event. For example, the wording of the questions that are put to the subject may distort his report, and details may be erroneously supplied or eliminated in accordance with what is suggested to him.

Bartlett (1932) has studied in great detail the problems involved in qualitative changes in retention. He showed how memory is altered to fit the attitudes, desires, and experiences of the remembering individual. Unfortunately, however, Bartlett's experimental work and his theories cannot be easily generalized. They are very much embedded in the particular framework of his investigations. His work does show, however, how much memory may be changed by the nature of the individual.

In view of the many psychological causes of qualitative changes in memory, it appears that the autonomous changes in perceptual retention emphasized by the earlier gestalt psychologists must be of very minimal importance in ordinary memory. The richness of experiences and verbal behavior have scarcely been explored as determiners of changes in memory. What we do know about these conditions, however, suggests that they are most potent determiners in changes of the retained material which occur with the passage of time.

# CHAPTER 10

# FORGETTING

The question of what produces forgetting can best be answered by the experimental production of forgetting. It is this deliberate production of forgetting which is the subject matter of this chapter. More specifically, this chapter is concerned with the psychological variables which determine what and how much people forget. This is one of the most fascinating problems in the field of learning, and, as it turns out, it leads us to some fairly clear conclusions.

An assumption frequently made both by psychologists and laymen is that forgetting is simply a matter of the lack of practice. A learned act, it is argued, disintegrates because time passes without any practice. This notion has been dignified by the name *principle of disuse*. The idea is reasonable enough, for in the natural course of events our learning seems to slip away from us with the passing of the years. The schoolteacher who returns to the university for a summer session after 5 years of teaching the sixth grade makes a determined effort to impress her French professor with the fact that she has not looked at French in years and consequently will not remember very much.

One of the first points we can learn from the work on the experimental production of forgetting is that the principle of disuse has very little validity. This, however, has been a difficult point for psychologists to grasp. Indeed, in very recent years, some eminent authorities in the psychology of learning have clung tenaciously to the principle of disuse. Skinner (1938), in his *Behavior of Organisms,* accepts the principle, though he has data that are difficult to reconcile with it (Skinner, 1938, 1950). Thorndike as late as 1943 gave evidence of supporting the principle of disuse (Bregman, Thorndike, and Woodyard, 1943).

*Arguments against the principle of disuse.* The retention curves presented by Ebbinghaus and others are usually taken as evidence of the forgetting that goes with lack of practice. It must be remembered, however, that such curves merely present a quantitative picture of the course of forgetting; they do not allow us to make inferences about the causes of forgetting. It remains for the studies of the experimental production of forgetting to show exactly what conditions are responsible for forgetting.

In a classical paper on the nature of forgetting, McGeoch (1932) pointed out some of the fundamental errors in the assumption that disuse is the reason for forgetting. In the first place, he points out, time, in and of itself, cannot be a sufficient condition because some "forgetting" curves rise instead of fall, *e.g.*, the Ballard-Williams and Ward-Hovland reminiscence effects. Furthermore, some responses—many conditioned responses and some of the behavior of daily life—are not easily forgotten.

A second point that McGeoch made is that disuse does not explain forgetting, if disuse implies only the passage of time, for time in itself does not cause anything. Events happen in time; certain conditions may evolve over time, but these events have their respective causes, not in time, but in the conditions underlying the events. A chemical substance may break down with the course of time, and in the study of physical chemistry we may examine this breakdown as a function of time, but the nature of the substances, their concentrations, temperatures, and so on, determines the breakdown. So the passage of time does not in itself constitute an explanation of the forgetting process. As McGeoch has put it: "Forgetting is found to vary with the character of the events which fill a constant retention interval, and with the conditions obtaining at the time of measuring retention" (1942, p. 455). It is the analysis of these conditions which will lead to an understanding of the nature of the forgetting process itself.

### RETROACTIVE AND PROACTIVE INHIBITION

The type of experiment from which most of our knowledge of forgetting has come is known as the "retroactive-inhibition" experiment. Another kind of experiment, which strictly speaking is not an experiment involving forgetting, is known as the "proactive-inhibition" experiment. The nature of these two kinds of experiments is fundamental to some of the processes involved in forgetting. Consequently, it is very important that the details of how these are done be understood.

## The Retroaction and Proaction Designs

*The retroaction experiment.* In the retroactive-inhibition experiment one measures the impairment of retention that takes place when some activity is interpolated between learning and a later test for retention. Actually facilitation as well as impairment may be produced by interpolated activity, but for the moment we are interested only in the case of retroactive inhibition. To measure either retroactive inhibition or retroactive facilitation we have a rather standard experimental design, and this goes by the name "retroaction experiment."

Two fundamental groups of subjects are used in the retroaction experiment. One group, designated as the experimental group, learns a task (task 1). This group then learns a second task (task 2), which is the interpolated activity. Finally, this group is tested for retention of task 1. A second group, designated as the control group, learns the original task (task 1), but in place of learning task 2, this group rests for a period of time corresponding to the length of time that it takes the experimental group to learn task 2. Finally, the control group is also tested for retention of task 1. As you can see, the principal difference between the two groups is in the presence or absence of the intervening activity. Both groups must learn task 1 to the same degree, and measurement of retention must be under the same conditions. The only variation is in the activity or lack of activity during the intervening period.

Retroactive inhibition is said to have taken place if, in the measurement of the retention of task 1, the experimental group shows evidence of less retention than the control group. This may be indicated in several ways. A free recall of items learned in task 1, for example, may show that the experimental group can recall less than the control. Or the experimental group may take more trials to relearn task 1, thus showing that the interpolated activity reduced savings in relearning.

*The proaction experiment.* Proactive inhibition is the impairment in acquisition or retention of a task as the result of the previous acquisition or performance of another task. Like the retroaction experiment, the experimental design used to study this effect is also useful in the study of any effects of learning one task on the retention or learning of another. Because proactive facilitation is possible, the design is called the "proaction experiment."

There are two basic groups of subjects required for this experiment, a control group and an experimental group. The control group learns task 2, but instead of learning task 1 it rests. The experimental group learns task 1 and then learns task 2. If the experimental group learns task 2 at a slower rate or shows a lower retention for it at a later time than does the control group, proactive inhibition has taken place. As you can see, the proactive-inhibition experiment does not necessarily involve a measure of retention, so it cannot always be said to be an experiment on the production of forgetting. Nevertheless, this experiment is important in understanding the processes involved in forgetting. Especially important are any differences that exist between retroactive inhibition and proactive inhibition.

*The sufficiency of experimentally produced forgetting.* Despite the fact that forgetting can be produced in the retroaction experiment, it is still difficult, not to say impossible, to prevent forgetting from taking place in an experiment. The control group in a retroaction experiment nearly always shows some loss, though the loss may not be so great as that shown by the experimental group. This is another way of saying that we cannot account for all the observed decrement in retention by the conditions varied in some experiment. There is always some forgetting produced by mechanisms beyond our control. The assumption is made, however, that the unaccounted-for decrement in retention is, for the most part, due to the same conditions which produce the experimentally determined forgetting.

It is something like an attempt to verify experimentally Newton's laws of motion. The first law never works in actual earthly experience; a body in motion never travels indefinitely in a straight line. We know, of course, that the law is an ideal principle of inertia, and that when the influence of friction is minimized, the law can be approximated. The ideal experimental investigation of forgetting would demand that we approach, in a control group, conditions such that no decrement in retention would be observed. This is never done in practice. Irion (1948), however, has suggested an addition to the experimental design for retroaction experiments which controls the *set* of the subject. The results of this have been to materially reduce the amount of unaccounted-for decrement (Irion, 1949; Irion and Wham, 1951).

*A summary of the experimental designs.* The basic conditions of the retroaction and proaction experiments may be diagrammed as follows:

PROACTION:

Experimental: Learns task 1 . . . . . learns task 2 . . . . . (recalls task 2)
Control: Rests . . . . . . . . . . . . . learns task 2 . . . . . (recalls task 2)

When the experimental group shows a lower rate of learning or a lower retention on task 2, proactive inhibition has taken place. When the experimental group shows a higher rate of learning on task 2, proactive facilitation has taken place.

RETROACTION:

Experimental: Learns task 1......learns task 2......test on task 1
Control:      Learns task 1..........rests........test on task 1

When the experimental group shows a lower amount of retention on task 1, retroactive inhibition has taken place. When the experimental group shows a higher rate of retention on task 1, retroactive facilitation has taken place.

*Conditions Which Determine Retroactive and Proactive Inhibition*

Under some conditions proactive or retroactive inhibition takes place, while under other conditions facilitation takes place. Which occurs when is a problem that must be postponed for a while, but we can look at some of the conditions under which inhibition occurs. For the moment we shall ignore the problem of facilitation.

*Retroactive inhibition by normal activity.* Perhaps the most general question that can be asked about retroactive inhibition is: Does the activity of everyday life have any inhibitory effect upon retention? This question has been answered in several experiments. The problem was first attacked by Jenkins and Dallenbach (1924). They measured the ability of learners to retain nonsense syllables 1, 2, 4, and 8 hours after learning. There were two conditions in the experiment. In one condition, retention was measured after an interval of sleep had intervened between learning and a test for retention (control). The subjects learned the nonsense syllables to a criterion and then immediately went to sleep for a period corresponding to the retention interval. In the second condition, the subjects learned the nonsense syllables and then went about their ordinary waking activities for a period of time corresponding to the retention interval.

Figure 39 shows the results that Jenkins and Dallenbach obtained. As you can see, recall after sleep is uniformly better than after a period of wakeful activity. Thus it appears that the simple, ordinary activities of daily life do have a detrimental effect upon retention of some material. Results similar to those obtained by Jenkins and Dallenbach have been obtained in experiments by Van Ormer (1932) and Gibb (1941), though the effect is much less pronounced with meaningful material (Newman, 1939a).

All these experiments, however, showed that there was some drop in retention even under conditions of sleep. This drop might seem to support a theory of disuse, for sleep is about as close to nonactivity as one can

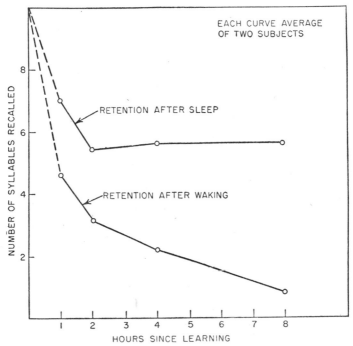

Fig. 39. Retention of nonsense material after sleeping, compared with retention after equal periods of wakeful activity. (*Data from Jenkins and Dallenbach, 1924.*)

obtain with normal human beings. Under the conditions of these experiments, however, there is much opportunity for activity and resulting interference. Some activity occurs between the time the subject learns the material and the time at which he drops off to sleep. Furthermore, there is the possibility that action (*i.e.,* dreaming or muscular activity) during sleep also may inhibit or interfere with retention. Consequently, sleep is only an approach to a vacuum, not the ideal state.

We may note, too, another very important source of disruption for the control subjects in the sleep experiments: the disruption of set (Irion, 1948). The subjects learn the material with a certain set; this set is disrupted by the preparations for sleep. Exactly the same set cannot be reinstated for the test of retention. Since the set of the subject furnishes some of the stimuli that function in learning, its absence or change at the time of test for retention can account for some decrement in retention. In support of this interpretation is an experiment of Irion's (1949) in which he found that a large percentage of forgetting could be eliminated by having the subjects engage in a color-naming task, which made use of the memory drum, before the test for retention.

To get a little closer to a psychological vacuum some investigators have turned to the lower animals that suspend bodily activity when the outside temperature drops. They hoped, for example, that by keeping cockroaches in cold temperatures, thus preventing activity, they could reduce to zero forgetting of a maze habit (Hunter, 1932). It has been found, however, that lowered temperature itself is a variable that contributes to forgetting in such animals (French, 1942). Although such attempts have failed in the past, it is possible that with a different means of producing inactivity more success might be found. Moreover, we have indirect evidence that activity may be important in the forgetting of lower animals in the fact that forcing up the activity of cockroaches definitely retards retention and relearning (Minami and Dallenbach, 1946).

*Retroactive inhibition and amount of interpolated activity.* Retroactive inhibition increases as a function of the amount of interpolated activity— a fact substantiated both with human subjects in rote verbal learning (Twining, 1940; Newman, 1939b) and with rats in maze learning (Marx, 1944). It seems likely, however, that there is a limit to the increase in retroactive inhibition and that each additional unit of interpolated material contributes less and less to forgetting. The sheer amount of intervening activity may not be a very important variable. Rather we should look at the character of the intervening events—what is practiced in the interpolated activity and how much it is practiced.

Let us consider especially the amount of practice that the learner gives to the interpolated material. The solid line in Fig. 45 (p. 206) shows, for example, the effect of increasing the number of trials of interpolated learning upon retroactive inhibition. There you can see that if the degree of original learning is held constant, retroactive inhibition increases with small increases in the amount of practice or number of trials on interpolated learning. With high degrees of practice on the interpolated material, however, there is a slight decline in the amount of retroactive inhibition (Melton and Irwin, 1940; Thune and Underwood, 1943).

These results suggest that there may be an optimum amount of practice of interpolated material to produce the greatest retroactive inhibition. The experimental evidence would seem to indicate that the greatest amount of retroactive inhibition occurs in most situations when both original learning and interpolated learning are carried to about the same degree.

*Retroactive inhibition and time of interpolation.* It is a very surprising fact that the time at which interpolated learning occurs does not make very much difference. In general, the greatest amount of retroactive inhibition is found if interpolated learning occurs soon after original learning or if it occurs just before relearning. It does not seem to matter much if a fairly long time interval elapses between original learning and relearning; the per cent of retroactive inhibition remains about the same (Bunch and McTeer, 1932). One study, in which 16 days elapsed between original learning and relearning, showed that the greatest per cent of retroactive inhibition occurred when interpolated learning was the day after original learning, when it was midway between original learning and relearning, and when it was just before relearning (Postman and Alper, 1946). The surprising fact is, however, that these experiments show very small differences between various interpolation times.

*The warm-up effect.* A factor, already alluded to, that is of considerable importance in both retroactive and proactive inhibition is the warm-up effect. The warm-up effect comes from the disruption of set that occurs during interpolated learning or a rest period before the measure of retention. During the learning of, say, a list of nonsense syllables, the learner acquires a certain set. He assumes a particular posture and gets familiar with the stimuli from the memory drum and surrounding conditions. This set may be disrupted before a test for retention. The learner may get up from his chair and stretch, go out of the room, or even go about his daily activity for a day before the measure of retention. When the learner does begin to relearn or recall the nonsense syllables, it takes him a while to reinstate his set; this is the warm-up effect.

This warm-up effect has been noticed in psychomotor learning as well as verbal learning (Ammons, 1947), and it is important in interpreting the observed decrement in retention frequently observed in both motor skills and verbal skills. Irion (1949) has shown that the set which an individual had during learning can be reinstated after a rest period by having the individual engage in some task similar to the learning task before the test for retention. Thus, exposing color names in the memory drum and asking the subject to read them will reinstate some of the set necessary to relearning the nonsense syllables. After such a pretraining warm-up, subjects re-learn the nonsense syllables much more quickly. The warm-up effect has been demonstrated in a number of situations (Postman and Postman, 1948; C. E. Hamilton, 1950; Irion and Wham, 1951), and we must conclude that it is of considerable importance in accounting for observed decrements in retention.

### Retroaction, Proaction, and Nature of the Material

Perhaps the most important factor in retroactive inhibition and pro-active inhibition is the *kind* of learning material involved. In fact, we can say that the nature of the material learned determines whether inhibition or facilitation will be obtained. Of various possible aspects of the nature of the material, the most important is the relationship between various parts of the material. Specifically, the degree of similarity between original learning (or task 1) and interpolated learning (or task 2) is the most important determinant of the retroaction effect. It is also the most important determinant of the proaction effect.

*Similarity in human learning.* Similarity between items is not an easy concept to define in learning. This is primarily because similarity is basi-cally a psychological concept that must be established by psychological measurements. This is particularly true where no simple physical dimen-sions are involved. To be sure, most human observers can agree upon a scale of similarity for such a simple variable as light from reflected surfaces. Dull grays resemble blacks more than do bright grays. The degree of sim-ilarity bears a simple relationship to the amount of light reflected. In verbal behavior, however, the psychological dimensions of similarity are more complicated; they usually do not have a simple functional relation to a physical dimension, and frequently observers do not agree about similarity between verbal materials. In a rough sort of way, however, you can see what similarity means in verbal behavior in some familiar examples. The words *boat* and *coat* are similar to one another phonetically, though they bear no resemblance in meaning. *Boat* and *ship* are similar in meaning, though not phonetically. These are just two examples, but there are many others. In the experimental work on this point, unfortunately, the variety of types of similarity studied has been rather small. Investigators have at-tempted to discover principles rather than exhaustively study all the pos-sible relationships of similarity. Certainly their work supports the general principle that similarity is critical in the retroactive and proactive effects.

*The Skaggs-Robinson hypothesis.* Robinson (1927) is responsible for the earliest systematic attempt to assess the role of similarity in the production of retroactive inhibition. Robinson's hypothesis has come to be known as the "Skaggs-Robinson hypothesis," which also credits the individual responsible for some of the earlier experimental work. Robinson formulated it as follows: "As similarity between interpolation and original memorization is reduced from near identity, retention falls away to a minimum

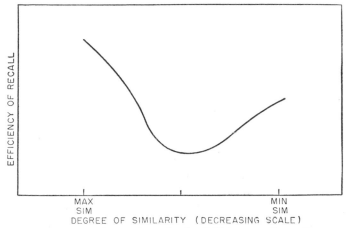

FIG. 40. The Skaggs-Robinson hypothesis. Efficiency of recall, according to this theory, should be at a minimum when the degree of similarity between original learning and interpolated learning is intermediate between identity and dissimilarity. (*From Robinson, 1927.*)

and then rises again, but with decreasing similarity it never reaches the level obtaining with maximum similarity" (Robinson, 1927, pp. 298–299).

For a graphical statement of the principle, turn to Fig. 40. In this illustration, we see that if material identical to the original material is interpolated, recall is maximally efficient, for there is no retroactive inhibition. This is the case in which interpolated learning is simply additional practice on the original material. As the interpolated material becomes less and less similar to the original material, recall decreases in efficiency. It is assumed, however, that retroactive inhibition is a kind of interference caused to some extent by the similarity between original and interpolated material. If that be so, there must be a certain degree of similarity between original and interpolated material that produces a maximum of retroactive inhibition or a minimum in ability to recall. In other words, there must be some point on the similarity continuum where retroactive inhibition is maximal.

*The evidence on the Skaggs-Robinson hypothesis.* In Robinson's (1927) test of the Skaggs-Robinson hypothesis, the design of the usual retroactive-inhibition experiment was modified to use the memory span as the test of retention. The subjects were given a series of eight consonants, of which the first four were designated as original material and the second four as

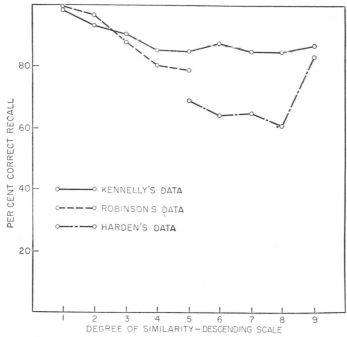

FIG. 41. Empirical tests of the Skaggs-Robinson hypothesis. The first part of the theoretical curve is verified, but there is a question about the second part. (*From Kennelly, 1941.*)

interpolated material. The immediate recall of the first four consonants was measured. The degree of similarity was varied by varying the number of consonants common to the original four. Thus, if D–Q–K–W comprised the original series, D–Q–K–W would be 100 per cent similar in the interpolated series, D–Q–K–Z would be one element different, etc.

This experiment has been repeated in its essential details several times, and Fig. 41 shows the results of all these experiments (Robinson, 1927; Harden, 1929; and Kennelly, 1941). Taken as a rough sort of approximation to the theoretical curve shown in Fig. 40, the relationship appears to be substantiated. McGeoch, however, seemed to think otherwise, as did Kennelly. Thus the matter is not clearly settled.

*A criticism of the Skaggs-Robinson hypothesis.* In the light of present-day interpretations of learning, there is one very serious fault with the Skaggs-Robinson hypothesis. It fails to separate the effects of similarity of stimuli from those of similarity of responses, for it is concerned only with similarity in the learning material. Some basic problems can be solved only by treating stimulus and response dimensions separately. This the Skaggs-Robinson hypothesis cannot do. This failure to deal with stimuli and responses separately has seriously hampered thinking about the role of similarity in retroactive inhibition. It is probably also the basis of the lack of clear-cut, consistent results in verification of the Skaggs-Robinson hypothesis. Because of its failure on this point, the Skaggs-Robinson hypothesis is no longer of fundamental importance; it has been supplanted by notions that are somewhat more complicated but somewhat more justified.

*Osgood's paradigm.* In very recent years, Osgood (1948, 1949) has developed a diagram that shows the effect of similarity upon retroaction when stimuli and responses are considered separately. Osgood's analysis has the advantage of being able to show exactly under what conditions inhibitory effects are to be expected and under what conditions facilitative effects are to be expected.

To formulate his paradigm, Osgood drew upon a large body of data that have been available for some time. One important source was the work with paired associates. Many investigators had made use of the method of paired associates (p. 137) because the method makes it possible to see which items are stimuli and which are responses. You will recall that in the method of paired associates one item serves as a stimulus for the subject to anticipate the next item. Thus, if the subject is given the word *tree,* he will be expected to anticipate the response *elder* before it in turn is exposed to him. Of course, the items in the series are given in a mixed-up order so that the subject cannot learn sequences. Under these conditions the effects of stimulus similarity and response similarity can be assessed.

If responses are held constant between original and interpolated learning and stimuli are varied from identity to dissimilarity, a range of effects from retroactive facilitation to zero retroaction is found (Wylie, 1919; Yum, 1931; McKinney, 1933; Bruce, 1933; R. J. Hamilton, 1943). Thus, if responses are identically the same in original and interpolated learning and stimuli are also identically the same, interpolated learning is simply further practice on original learning; under these conditions, one would expect maximum retroactive facilitation. If, on the other hand, the responses are identical but stimuli are somewhat different, one would still expect retroactive facilitation, but considerably less in amount. This is because interpolated learning gives the individual further practice on the correct *responses,* but the stimuli are not quite the same as those for original learning, so one would expect less facilitation. You can easily see that these examples are simply cases of stimulus generalization (p. 66). As a result, a curve that shows the effects of variations in stimuli when re-

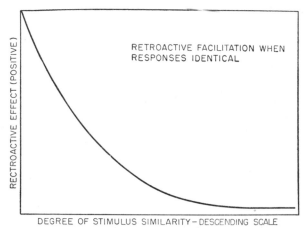

FIG. 42. Retroactive effect as a function of stimulus similarity when responses are identical. Only positive transfer occurs under these conditions. The curve has the same form as a stimulus generalization curve.

sponses are held constant looks very much like one limb of a stimulus generalization curve (Fig. 42).

As Osgood (1949) also points out, it is a well-established fact that when stimuli are the same, but responses different, retroactive inhibition is usually obtained (cf. Bruce, 1933; Gibson, 1940; McGeoch and McGeoch, 1937; Underwood, 1945; Osgood, 1946; Bugelski, 1942). Thus if you are asked to associate the names of states with colors, so that when you are given *Idaho* you respond with *red,* and if you are then given a new set of color names to associate with the same state names, so that when you are given *Idaho* you now respond with *lavender,* you will have difficulty in remembering the original colors associated with the state names. This seems to be because you now have two competing responses to give to the same state name. As the responses required to the same stimuli are made more alike, however, less retroactive inhibition is found, so that finally when the responses are exactly alike, again we are back to retroactive facilitation. If the responses are only slightly different, then retroactive facilitation will occur, but it will be less in magnitude than if the responses are identical (Baker, Wylie, and Gagné, 1950). Thus variation in similarity of responses with stimuli held constant produces effects ranging all the way from maximal retroactive inhibition to maximal retroactive facilitation (see Fig. 43).

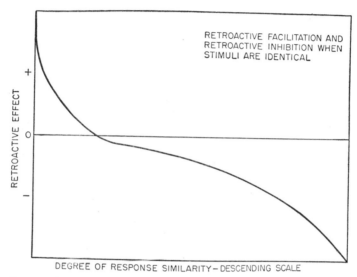

Fig. 43. Retroactive effect as a function of response similarity when stimuli are identical. This curve covers the entire range from maximum positive transfer (simple learning) to maximum negative transfer.

*The retroaction surface.* Finally, Osgood (1949) put all these results together in what he called the "retroaction surface." The retroaction surface is a diagram that requires three dimensions because one dimension must serve for similarity between responses in original and interpolated learning, one dimension for similarity between stimuli, and one dimension for the amount of the retroactive effect. Such a surface is shown in Fig. 44. The part of the figure in the lower left-hand corner is the part where maximum retroactive *inhibition* is found. This part represents the case in which stimuli are identical but responses different. On the other hand, maximum retroactive *facilitation* is found in the upper left-hand corner, where stimuli and responses are both identical. On the opposite side of the diagram, which is the side where stimuli are all unrelated, practically no retroaction at all occurs, because where stimuli and responses are all different and unrelated to one another, there is no chance for interference or facilitation.

We would not expect digging in the garden to have much retroactive effect upon typewriting, because both the stimuli and responses are completely different in the two situations.

In conclusion, three things should be noticed about this diagram. First of all, it entails a minimum of theory; it is just a convenient way of summarizing a lot of investigation which has gone on over the past 40 years.

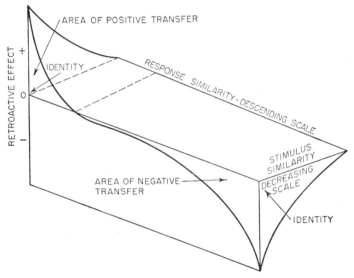

Fig. 44. The transfer surface. This figure shows transfer (retroaction) as a joint function of stimulus similarity and response similarity (see text). (*Redrawn from Osgood, 1949.*)

Secondly, the exact form of the diagram is meaningless, since no one has really quantified similarity relationships, but it is of fundamental importance in human learning since it provides an essential framework upon which to hang much of our knowledge of human learning. Thirdly, it should be emphasized, the diagram applies just as well to proaction as it does to retroaction; as a matter of fact, much of the data upon which the diagram was based were data obtained in proaction experiments.

### THEORIES OF RETROACTIVE INHIBITION AND FORGETTING

Now that we have seen some of the basic facts about retroactive inhibition, it is possible to see how forgetting may be interpreted by means of theories of retroactive inhibition. It has never been claimed that retroactive inhibition provides the model for *all* the observed decrement in retention in human learning, but it is suggested that retroactive inhibition provides us with one of the most important mechanisms of forgetting. So, while we shall examine theories of forgetting not based upon retroactive inhibition, we should regard theories of retroactive inhibition as genuine theories of forgetting.

### Theories of Retroactive Inhibition

*The perseveration theory.* The classical theory of retroactive inhibition is that known as the "perseveration theory." This theory assumes learning takes time to set or gel and then goes on to assume that interpolated learning interferes with the setting-in process of original learning and, in this way, causes retroactive inhibition. Note that the fundamental assumption of this theory is that a learned act or association requires some time to become set in the central nervous system after behavior has stopped. The exact nature of this setting-in process is unimportant at present, and, in fact, it has never been very exactly stated in physiological terms. The important point is that a certain amount of rest is required after performing an act, in order to allow time for that act to become established.

The concept of perseveration has been widely used to explain many effects in learning. For example, it has been advanced to account for the harmful effects of massed practice (p. 152). The notion of perseveration was originally advanced, however, to account for the retroactive inhibition effect. As it happens, however, there are a number of effects studied in retroactive-inhibition experiments that present rather crucial evidence against the perseveration hypothesis.

For one thing, according to the perseveration theory, retroactive inhibition should occur only when the interpolated learning occurs immediately after original learning because this is the time at which interpolated learning should interfere with the setting-in process of original learning. But experimental evidence shows that this is not the case. As you will remember, it has been found that interpolation at various points during long intervals of retention has been shown to have a retroactive effect. Even over a period of weeks, which may intervene between original learning and interpolated learning, retroactive inhibition occurs (Bunch and McTeer, 1932; Bunch, 1941; Postman and Alper, 1946). This is a crucial argument against the perseveration theory.

Also against the theory are a number of effects which it is unable to predict. For example, it cannot predict proactive inhibition upon *retention* of the second task (see proaction design, p. 188); yet proactive inhibition of retention actually does occur (Whitely and Blankenship, 1936; Blankenship and Whitely, 1941; Melton and Von Lackum, 1941; Underwood, 1945, 1948*a*, 1950). Neither can the perseveration theory predict the effect of similarity upon retroactive inhibition. It is also unable to predict retroactive facilitation; indeed the perseveration theory would predict, contrary to fact, that retroactive facilitation could never occur if interpolation occurs immediately after original learning. Largely on these grounds, the theory, as a theory of forgetting, has been all but abandoned in recent years.[1]

There are a few cases, however, where the original notion of a setting-in process does seem to be important. Duncan (1949) was able to show, for instance, that an electro-shock-induced convulsion interfered with the retention of a simple habit in rats, if the shock occurred less than an hour after learning had taken place. This result was interpreted to be favorable to the perseveration hypothesis. Considering, however, the violent nature of the electro-shock-induced convulsions and the differences between them and ordinary types of interpolated activities, it is very questionable whether this experiment bears much upon human verbal learning.

It is known that electro-shock-induced convulsions do have a deleterious effect upon human verbal learning (Worchel and Narciso, 1950). It is not clear, however, that the effects of such convulsions upon human learning and memory are to be attributed to disruption of a setting-in process. Convulsions do seem to do something organic to the individual that alters what he remembers, but such an effect is much too complicated to be explained by the perseveration hypothesis.

*Competition theory.* A purely "psychological" theory that is much more fruitful than the perseveration hypothesis is that of *competition*.[2] This theory has made considerable progress in disentangling the various retro-

---

[1] In an experiment on human maze learning, Bunch (1946) found that interpolated learning 20 minutes after original learning produced retroactive inhibition, while the same interpolated learning performed 120 days after original learning produced retroactive facilitation. This finding could be interpreted as being favorable to the perseveration hypothesis.

[2] McGeoch (1942), its most ardent supporter, has called this the "transfer theory" rather than the "competition theory." The term "transfer" is not used here since it is also used to refer to the simple empirical fact of proaction and retroaction. To avoid confusion between fact and theory, the term "transfer theory" should be abandoned.

active effects, and though there is evidence that it, at least in its simple form, cannot account for all retroactive inhibition, it is probably the most widely supported theory today.

The competition theory of retroactive inhibition suggests that the fundamental condition that produces the decrement in recall is a form of interaction between original and interpolated activities (McGeoch, 1942). Simply stated, the two activities, original and interpolated learning, are confused with one another in such a way that one prevents the recall of the other. More specifically, this theory suggests that the acquisition of the interpolated activity *competes with the original material at the time of the measurement of retention.*

The extent to which the interpolated material will prevent the recall of the original depends chiefly upon the degree of resemblance between the stimuli for the two activities, assuming that the responses are somewhat different. The second or interpolated group of learned responses tends to be performed in the presence of cues which are meant to elicit the first group of learned responses. Thus, the second group of learned responses competes with the first group at the time of recall. This competition makes it more difficult for the original material to be recalled.

There is direct evidence that this competition does take place. Such evidence takes the form of *overt intrusions at the time of recall.* If all the responses the subject makes during relearning or recall are recorded, it is easy to notice that some of these responses come from the interpolated material. These transferred responses take the place of the correct responses; consequently there is a measured decrement in retention. This is simple, direct, negative transfer.

In one experiment in which these overt intrusions of interpolated responses were measured at recall, they were sufficient in number to account for at least 25 per cent of the observed decrement (McKinney and McGeoch, 1935). If there are overt intrusions that come to the surface, it seems to be a reasonable inference to expect that the subjects tend to make many other incorrect responses that they manage to suppress. We might also reason that it takes time to suppress incorrect responses; hence we would expect the latency or reaction time of original responses during recall or relearning to be abnormally long. This is actually the case, for there is a significant increase in reaction time during relearning of the original responses (Postman and Kaplan, 1947). From these long reaction times it is inferred that the correct responses were inhibited for a time by the primary tendency to say the appropriate word for interpolated learning. Everyone has had the experience of not quite being able to recall something, but after a time during which one's "thoughts" were organized, remembering what it is.

*Competition and the retroaction surface.* You have probably recognized by now that the effects of similarity that we considered a few pages ago provide a fundamental mechanism for the competition theory. There is competition because different responses are learned to stimuli which are similar or identical. Thus, the competition theory would say, similarity or identity of stimuli is a *cause* for competition. Therefore, the data on similarity and retroactive inhibition summarized in Osgood's retroaction surface are very much in accord with the competition theory. McGeoch (McGeoch, 1936; McGeoch, McKinney, and Peters, 1937; McGeoch, 1942) devoted much of his attention to the effect of stimulus and response similarity upon competition or "reproductive inhibition," as he sometimes called it. Competition is strongest, he pointed out, when a common item is connected with two different items in succession.

Gibson (1940) has given us a version of the competition theory which is stated directly in terms of stimulus and response similarity. She postulated that competition should occur when there is a low degree of discriminability between stimuli connecting two different responses. Lowest discriminability should occur when the stimuli for original and interpolated learning are identical. In this case, when an individual is asked to recall the material from original learning, the stimuli do not help him to distinguish between original and interpolated learning; the result is intrusion during recall of those responses learned during interpolated practice.

Thus the competition theory is very well able to account for the data on similarity and retroactive inhibition. Since the same similarity relationships hold in proaction as in retroaction, it might be supposed that the competition theory applies equally well to proactive inhibition. And it does. The acquisition of prior responses competes with responses required during learning or recall of a second task. Thus the competition theory is both a theory of retroactive inhibition and a theory of proactive inhibition.

*The two-factor theory.* While the competition theory seems to be correct as far as it goes, some psychologists think that it does not account for all the data of retroactive inhibition (Melton and Irwin, 1940; Melton and Von Lackum, 1941). Consequently they suggest another factor that operates along with negative transfer to produce the retroactive-inhibition effect.

One of the arguments for such a two-factor theory comes from the experiments on intrusions that we considered above. One of the main sources of direct evidence for the competition theory, you will recall, is the fact that there are overt intrusions of interpolated responses at the time of recall. It turns out that there are also overt intrusions of original material at the time of learning the interpolated material. If the stimuli are the same for original and interpolated learning, one certainly can expect that occasionally the learner would give responses appropriate to original learning during interpolated learning. These *overt intrusions at the time of interpolated learning* provide the suggestion for the second factor in the two-factor theory.

According to the two-factor theory, the overt intrusions that occur during interpolated learning do not directly produce retroactive inhibition, but they indirectly cause it by *reducing the strength* of the original responses. Put another way, this means that the subject in a retroactive-inhibition experiment *unlearns* the original responses during interpolated learning (Melton and Irwin, 1940).

Suppose we look at the behavior of an individual in a retroactive inhibition experiment. The experiment has been so designed as to produce the maximal retroactive inhibition effect; that is to say, the stimuli are the same for original and interpolated learning but the responses are different. The subject first masters the original material. He then begins to learn the interpolated material. Occasionally during the learning of the interpolated material, the subject responds with a word or syllable which is appropriate to original learning. These responses are incorrect during interpolated learning, and the subject knows they are incorrect. Therefore he attempts to avoid making these mistakes. As a result these responses are gradually unlearned. Finally, when the subject attempts to relearn the original material, the responses from this material are weaker because of unlearning that has gone on during interpolated learning.

*Evidence for unlearning.* The evidence for unlearning is convincing, although somewhat indirect. First of all, there is the evidence that overt intrusions do occur during interpolated learning. We have already seen that in some detail. Secondly, there is the fact that the amount of retroactive inhibition is not directly correlated with the number of overt intrusions during *relearning* (Melton and Irwin, 1940). This suggests that the competition theory does not account for all the retroactive-inhibition effect. For small amounts of interpolated practice, retroactive inhibition and overt intrusions during relearning both increase, but with larger amounts of interpolated practice, overt intrusions during relearning become practically zero, while the amount of retroactive inhibition is still large.

To see this point in graphical form, refer to Fig. 45. This shows retroactive inhibition plotted against amount of interpolated practice and overt intrusions during relearning also plotted against amount of interpolated practice. The solid line shows the total retroactive inhibition and the lower dotted line the amount of retroactive inhibition attributable to competi-

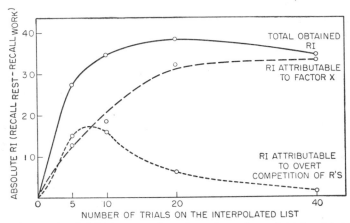

Fig. 45. Retroactive inhibition as a function of number of trials of interpolated learning. The lower dotted curve shows the retroactive inhibition attributable to overt intrusions at recall (X 2). The upper dotted curve is the retroactive inhibition attributable to factor X. (*Melton and Irwin, 1941.*)

tion (two times the number of overt intrusions). The difference between the total retroactive inhibition and that attributable to competition is shown by the higher dotted line. This, presumably, is the retroactive inhibition that is due to unlearning.

There is still a third line of evidence for an unlearning factor in retroactive inhibition. It comes from the fact that retroactive inhibition is greater than proactive inhibition of retention (Melton and Von Lackum, 1941; McGeoch and Underwood, 1943). You will recall that competition works equally well for proaction and retroaction. On the basis of this fact, one would expect that, when proaction was measured by the same technique as that used for retroaction (a measure of retention), the amount of inhibition would be the same. The fact that it is not suggests very strongly the operation of a second factor in retroactive inhibition that does not operate in proactive inhibition. There is no opportunity for unlearning to take place in proactive inhibition.

A number of subsidiary findings seem to be in accord with the two-factor theory. Underwood (1945) finds that increasing the number of interpolated tasks (lists of nonsense syllables) increased the amount of retroactive inhibition, but frequency of overt intrusions during recall remained constant. The implication again is that competition at the time of recall is unable to account for the increase in retroactive inhibition with an increase in the number of lists. Bugelski (1948) has data that show that material which is poorly learned can be unlearned relatively easily, so that subsequent new material can be learned better. Better learning in the new material makes further material more difficult because a greater time is now required for unlearning.

*What is unlearning?* While unlearning is fairly well established as a mechanism in retroactive inhibition, there is by no means clear agreement as to its nature. A deceptively simple interpretation is to say that it is like experimental extinction. Melton suggested this in his original paper on the two-factor theory (Melton and Irwin, 1940). This interpretation is bolstered by a number of incidental facts. Extinction of a conditioned response *can* produce retroactive inhibition of that response (Smith, 1946; Deese, 1950b). Retroactive inhibition in human verbal learning shows "spontaneous recovery" (Underwood, 1948a, 1948b, 1948c), as one might expect if extinction were a factor in retroactive inhibition.

Examples of experimentally produced extinction are rare in human verbal learning (Peak and Deese, 1937). That is apparently because human beings provide their own reinforcement for verbal behavior; verbal behavior does not always demand an externally given reinforcement. There is, however, a famous paradox that has been around in the learning literature for many years that seems to be an example of extinction on the level of human verbal behavior. Dunlap (1932) pointed out that practice does not always improve performance. In fact sometimes practice may be used to eliminate a response, in which case, Dunlap said, it is negative practice. Dunlap's famous example of negative practice was of a typist who consistently made the error of writing "hte" for "the." This error was eliminated from typing by practicing a great number of times the word "hte." Dunlap emphasized the idea that this negative practice had to be done with the correct "mental attitude." The learner must keep in mind that this response is to be eliminated; it is systematically practiced with the idea that it is wrong. Under these conditions the response will be eliminated. It will not be eliminated, however, if the negative practice is not done with the idea of getting rid of the response.

Both negative practice and unlearning seem to be examples of extinction in human verbal learning. Ordinarily we make a distinction between extinction and forgetting (Skinner, 1938), but if we accept unlearning and negative practice as examples of extinction, then we must come to the conclusion that extinction is a factor in what is ordinarily called forgetting.

Something may have been bothering you about this interpretation of unlearning as extinction. You will recall that the nature of extinction is open to dispute and that one of the theories about it is a theory of competition of responses (p. 57). If we accept the competition theory of extinction, and if we say unlearning is extinction, then we must come to the conclusion that the two-factor theory really boils down to a one-factor theory, though that factor operates at two different points in the retroactive inhibition situation. At one point—during interpolated learning—original responses are unlearned because they compete with responses from interpolated learning; at another point—during recall—original responses cannot come out because they compete with the now stronger interpolated responses. This notion has been supported by several investigators (McGeoch, 1942; Bugelski, 1948), and it has the considerable merit of simplicity. It has the disadvantage of assuming an unproved theory of extinction and of being unable to predict the spontaneous recovery effect which occurs in retroactive inhibition and does not seem to occur in proactive inhibition (Underwood, 1948a, 1948b, 1948c). Furthermore, there is evidence that extinction can produce retroactive inhibition of a conditioned response, even when the experimental situation is such that the response acquired during interpolated conditioning cannot directly compete with the response extinguished during interpolated conditioning (Deese, 1950b).

So we must come to the conclusion that the exact nature of the unlearning factor cannot be established. It may be that it is another example of the operation of competition, or it may be that it works through other factors. We cannot even clearly say that it is extinction, because there is no way in human verbal learning to specify exactly the way in which reinforcement is withdrawn; it does, however, bear a close analogy to extinction and to another process in human learning—negative practice—which seems to have extinction as its basis.

*Other Theories of Forgetting*

While retroactive inhibition is of great importance in an interpretation of the phenomena of forgetting, it must not be assumed that all forgetting is accounted for by the mechanisms postulated in retroactive inhibition. Nor can the importance of other sources of forgetting be minimized. There are apparently several mechanisms that can produce a measurable drop in retention, two of which are revealed by the work on retroactive inhibition. The possibility of other mechanisms has led to the postulation of other theories of forgetting. These theories do not supplant the retroactive-inhibition theories; rather they supplement retroactive inhibition with some other cases of forgetting.

*Change in the memory trace.* The influence of various psychological factors upon change in memory has already been mentioned in the preceding chapter. There is good evidence that attitudes, beliefs, desires, and past experience all operate upon the retention of specific responses to change them in certain ways. Strictly speaking, there is no theory of the action of these conditions upon memory. At one time or another, however, they have been postulated as variables which determine loss in retention.

There is the further possibility that some forgetting may involve a simple deterioration in the organic substrate of memory. This is a physiological theory of disuse. Spontaneous changes in the chemical structure of neurons could be responsible for a decay of memory. Unfortunately, because we know nothing of the organic substrate of memory, little more can be said about this possibility. There is little direct evidence which supports the notion. A few scattered studies show that some nonpsychological variables affect memory. Very high $O_2$ pressures, for example, produce a loss of memory (Bean, Wapner, and Siegfried, 1945). The most serious argument in favor of the theory of spontaneous decay of the organic trace is the negative one that we cannot, at present, account for all the observed decrement in retention by the psychological variables we know to be operating. Perhaps when we know a little more about the physiological concomitants of memory we shall be able to be a bit more definite about the possibility of a spontaneous decay of a memory trace.

*The theory of repression.* Another approach to forgetting comes from Freud (1925) and psychoanalysis. To Freud, one of the most important mechanisms whereby organisms resolve conflicts is repression. Because certain instinctive impulses are unpleasant to the ego, *i.e.,* they involve feelings of anxiety, these impulses are repressed. Since Freud's original statement this notion has come to be so generalized that the term "repression" now covers many things besides the instinctive impulses. For example, some assert that ideas that are ego damaging or events that are unpleasant or punishing to the organism may all be repressed.

One of the fundamental aspects of the concept of repression is that anything that is repressed is not lost. It is only submerged below a level where, under ordinary conditions, the individual can voluntarily recall it. If, at another time, the source of the unpleasantness or conflict associated with what is repressed may be removed, the repressed memory may be recovered to voluntary memory. Thus potential recovery of what is repressed is a basic necessity to the theory of repression.

Freud and others have elaborated the psychoanalytic theory of repression at great length. Most of the refinements of the notion are unnecessary to this discussion. Freud's distinction between *primal repression* and *after expulsion,* for example, is unimportant in the present context. The main points are (1) that something can be repressed because it conflicts with the individual's motives or is a source of anxiety to him, and (2) that whatever is repressed is not eliminated from the potential behavioral repertory of that individual but exists in a latent form; it can be reactivated by anything that removes the source of anxiety or conflict in motives.

*Experimental evidence for repression.* Despite the importance of the concept, the experimental evidence for repression is meager. Estes's (1944) experiments on punishment of the lever response in the Skinner box provide an analogy for the process of repression (p. 118). You will recall that Estes found that a response that is rewarded cannot be removed by punishment; it can only be held down for a period of time. It is held down by the anxiety connected with punishment. So it seems to be with many other examples of repressed behavior. The individual who has forgotten his childhood sexual experiences may have done so because of the anxieties connected with sexual activity. A removal of these anxieties may bring back memories of these experiences, just as extinction of the anxiety brought back the lever response in Estes's experiments.

But direct tests of the concept of repression in human learning are few in number. A few studies have reported that pleasant experiences are better recalled than unpleasant experiences (see Zeller, 1950b), and these are suggestive of repression but hardly proof. Some other studies have attempted to produce repression by testing for recall of material known to be painful to certain individuals (Sharp, 1938; Gould, 1942; Heathers and Sears, 1943).

Two recent studies probably come closer to a demonstration of repression than any of the earlier studies. Korner (1950) showed that material that was threatening to an individual was retained less than material that was not threatening, even though both sets of material were learned to the same degree. While Korner's study is perhaps the most adequate of its kind to date, it still does not demonstrate one important property of repression, the property of recovery.

The only experiment that has shown recovery after the source of the anxiety connected with the material has been removed is that of Zeller (1950b). Zeller had subjects learn lists of nonsense syllables. For some of the subjects, failure was associated with the nonsense syllables, and these subjects did not recall the nonsense syllables as well as did the other subjects. After the source of the threat of failure had been removed, these subjects showed a recovery of the ability to recall the nonsense syllables. Zeller very carefully points out that there are other interpretations of his experiment, but it is at least consistent with the notion that repressed material can recover after the source of anxiety connected with its repression is removed.

So, while the evidence for repression is not irrefutable, that which is available gives us some confidence in the hypothesis. There is, of course, much clinical evidence that has been advanced as favorable to the hypothesis of repression. The very fact that some individuals have high anxiety levels has sometimes been suggested as evidence for repression, for the anxiety itself indicates that the individual has not really "forgotten" the source of the anxiety but has only pushed it to a place where it is unavailable to him verbally.

## SOME CONCLUDING REMARKS

The mechanisms that have been suggested in this chapter are probably not the only ones that account for what we call forgetting. Forgetting is a complex phenomenon, and there are undoubtedly many subtle ramifications of it that we have not yet begun to explore. Despite the multiplicity of suggested causes, however, there is a certain satisfaction in the experimental work upon retention and forgetting, particularly that work upon retroactive and proactive inhibition. Some fairly well worked out empirical principles of forgetting have been outlined, and there is good reason to believe that we are on the right track about the theories of forgetting.

Perhaps some remarks about the applications of the principles suggested in this chapter are in order. It may be said that this probably will be a source of disappointment to the student. Our knowledge of experimentally produced forgetting suggests more about what we *cannot* do about increasing the efficiency of remembering than what we *can* do. Nevertheless it is worth while to point out the applications of laboratory studies to everyday life.

*Retroactive inhibition and similarity.* Stimulus similarity and response dissimilarity are probably the most important factors in the production of retroactive inhibition. This is unfortunate, since it is the one major factor about which we can do little. We can do little about it in a practical way, since *what* we learn is more important than the ease with which we learn it. Learning to read German is more important than learning an artificial language designed for the sole purpose of reducing the amount of retroactive inhibition.

An additional unfortunate fact is that the stimulus-response relationships in everyday learning are so complicated that it is not always possible to predict when retroactive inhibition will take place and when retroactive facilitation will take place. There are exceptions. Learning an English-French vocabulary list immediately after learning an English-German vocabulary list will produce retroactive inhibition. This is because the stimuli (English words) are identical, while the responses (French and German words) are different.

*Retroactive inhibition and amount of material.* It should be expected that retroactive inhibition would be greater for material not very well learned than for material well learned. This is the case. Retroactive inhibition varies inversely with the amount of original learning (Shaw, 1942). So one way to minimize retroactive inhibition is to make sure that the material to be retained is well learned.

We have already seen that, in general, more retroactive inhibition results from greater amounts of interpolated learning. This is important in a practical way, too. For example, it has been shown that shorter amounts of advertising material are more effectively recalled than longer amounts (Guest and Brown, 1939); this is because the longer amounts allow for more retroactive inhibition. In another context, Crutchfield (1940) has shown that partial review of material may produce retroactive inhibition. If a student selects a portion of a study assignment for intensive review, this will produce substantial inhibitory effects upon the recall of the un-reviewed portions. In some cases it may produce an actual decrement in the recall for the whole material. Too intensive emphasis upon one part of a material may be harmful; occasional reviews of the unemphasized portions are beneficial.

*Retroactive inhibition and warm-up.* One important way to reduce retro-active inhibition is through a preliminary warm-up. Plunging into an at-tempted recall "cold" is apt to lead to dismaying results. A brief period spent in recapturing the set under which the material was learned should go a long way toward improving the ability to remember. Warm-up, of course, applies to psychomotor behavior as well as to verbal behavior. Athletes, pianists, and others who are required to indulge in difficult psy-chomotor behavior have long recognized the importance of warm-up in improving performance.

*Repression.* If we accept the theory of repression, we must resign our-selves to the possibility that we will deliberately "forget" some things be-cause subconsciously we want to. A man will forget that his wife told him to buy liver at the grocery store because he does not like liver. On a more serious scale, the clinical psychologists and psychiatrists are convinced that an important source of anxieties is in repression of unpleasant or punished ideas. Thus the concept of repression has important applications; these applications are beyond the scope of this book, but they provide a very important part of theories of personality mechanisms and abnormal be-havior.

*Review and memory.* Probably the most important single factor at the control of the individual learner by which he can improve his memory is frequent and well-spaced reviews. Many studies (Spitzer, 1939; Clark, 1940; Sones and Stroud, 1940) testify to the importance of review to good retention. Probably the most important factor about review is the spacing of the reviews. The best retention is obtained when reviews occur soon after learning and at decreasing time intervals thereafter (Tsai, 1927; Sones and Stroud, 1940; Spencer, 1941). In view of the possible inhibiting effects of partial reviews, reviews should probably be complete except when some portion of the material is very much easier than the rest.

# CHAPTER 11

# TRANSFER OF TRAINING

There is no more important topic in the whole of the psychology of learning than that of transfer of training. Practically all educational and training programs are built upon the premise that human beings have the ability to transfer what they have learned in one situation to another. This assumption is evident in everything from the curriculum of the college of classical tradition to the adolescent who is persuaded by his mother to attend dancing school on the fond hope that training in the graces of ballroom dancing will permit him to navigate the length of the house without danger to the less sturdy furniture.

*Importance of transfer of training.* The tremendous degree of dependence that education places upon transfer of training makes us overlook the specific instance. Almost all formal school subjects are taught on the hope that they will transfer. Children are taught to spell in school because society demands that they be able to spell reasonably well outside of school. If a child learns to spell in school, and if he can spell at home, transfer of training has been successful. This example may surprise the reader, since such elementary examples are not ordinarily thought of as being examples of transfer of training. In theory, however, this example is no different from more complicated examples.

The example of children who learn to spell in school and who can use that spelling in writing letters home from summer camp makes it clear that transfer of training is frequently successful. In some other examples, evidence for transfer of training is less easy to obtain. At one time there was a notion in educational circles that one could teach a child to be neat by teaching him to hand in neat papers in arithmetic and spelling. Supposedly, the habits of neat work engendered in school would transfer to other situations. Apparently this program met with a conspicuous lack of success.

On a more serious level is the frequently stated goal of education, particularly higher education, to make people think. The frequently cited example of the scientist with a Ph.D. degree who is a political and moral moron may give us pause to think about the extent of transfer of training in this area. We may seriously ask: Is it possible to teach people to think— just in general? A study of the extent and conditions under which transfer of training takes place may give us an answer to this and similar problems.

Perhaps it is less apparent that transfer of training is a problem of considerable theoretical interest in learning. Since the theory of transfer of training is essential to an intelligent discussion of its applications, it will be necessary to begin with an account of the theory of transfer of training. The theory of transfer of training is simple, and it parallels almost exactly the theory involved in the explanation of experimentally produced forgetting. As a matter of fact, transfer of training and forgetting are but different aspects of the same problem.

*The measurement of transfer of training.* A word needs to be said about the measurement of transfer of training. The experimental designs used to study transfer of training are exactly the same as those used in the study of experimentally produced forgetting (p. 188). Thus the basic designs are as follows:

Transfer group: Test on A . . . . . . Practice on B . . . . . . Retest on A
Control group: Test on A . . . . . . . . . . . . . . . . . . . . . . . . Retest on A

This is the retroaction design. Positive transfer of training takes place if on the retest of A the transfer group shows more improvement than does the control group. In this case, practice on B has transferred to A.

Transfer group: Learns A . . . . . . . . . . . . . . Learns B
Control group: . . . . . . . . . . . . . . . . . . . . Learns B

This is the proaction design. Positive transfer takes place if the transfer group learns B more readily than does the control group. In this case, learning A has transferred to the acquisition of B.

The proaction design, perhaps, has been used more frequently than the retroaction design because it requires less time and effort. The retroaction design allows somewhat better control over extraneous variables, since the control and experimental groups can be matched on the pretest. There are variations to these designs which have been used from time to time (Woodworth, 1938), but these two fundamental designs are the ones which are theoretically important.

There are many ways in which transfer of training may be expressed. One such expression is given by the formula:

$$\frac{(\text{Score, transfer group}) - (\text{score, control group})}{(\text{Total possible score}) - (\text{score, control group})} \times 100$$

When transfer is calculated according to this formula, zero transfer will occur when the score for the transfer group equals that for the control group. Any value by which the transfer score exceeds that for the control group will result in positive transfer. This formula and others are discussed in detail in a paper by Gagné, Foster, and Crowley (1948), which is concerned with the methodology of experiments in transfer of training.

### THE NATURE OF TRANSFER OF TRAINING

Transfer of training means gain or loss on the performance of some task as the result of learning or performance upon some other task. This definition makes it necessary to specify what is meant by "task." A task is any given activity performed under a given set of circumstances. If either the activity or the circumstances under which the activity is performed is changed, the task has been changed. Thus learning to spell in school constitutes one task, while spelling outside of school constitutes another task. The circumstances surrounding the activity of spelling have changed. This may seem to be pushing the notion of transfer of training very far, but there is a continuum from practice on only one task to transfer of training that involves practice and performance on two completely different tasks. Anything may be considered to involve transfer of training that does not involve continued practice upon exactly the same activity performed under exactly the same circumstances.

Transfer may be either negative or positive. Negative transfer occurs when one task interferes with performance on another task; positive transfer occurs when one task facilitates performance on another task. Negative transfer was discussed in the chapter on forgetting. In that chapter a number of variables were considered that determine the amount and kind of negative transfer. Some of the same variables are important to positive transfer as well, and the theory of positive transfer is complementary to the competition theory of retroactive inhibition.

*The major determinants of transfer of training.* In any situation in which transfer of training may occur, the major variable that determines whether positive or negative transfer will be achieved is the nature of the material being learned or practiced. The most important aspect of the material is its degree of similarity. Depending upon the similarity relationships between the two tasks involved in an experiment on transfer of training, negative or positive transfer will be the result.

In order to understand the role of similarity in transfer of training, it is necessary to refer to Osgood's (1949) *retroaction surface,* which was presented in the last chapter. The retroaction surface is a diagram that summarizes the possible effects of degree of similarity between the stimuli for the two tasks and the effects of the degree of similarity of responses required for the two tasks. The example of the schoolboy who learns to spell in school and who can make use of this ability in other circumstances will provide a rough illustration of what is meant by similarity. The responses (spelling certain words) are identical in both situations. The stimuli are different but similar. There is a set to write; ordinary writing materials are provided. The principal differences in the stimuli associated with the task are the differences in the incidental stimulation provided by the school and the home. Another simple example will illustrate the meaning of similarity of responses. I learned to shift automobile gears in an automobile which had the gear shift located on the floor of the car to the driver's right. Shortly after learning to drive, I acquired an automobile in which the gear shift was located on the driving shaft. The essential relations of shifting gears remained, but the direction and extent of movements were different. Thus the responses in this case were similar, though slightly different; the stimuli were also similar, though slightly different between the two situations. It is to be noted, incidentally, that both these are examples of positive transfer.

Osgood's diagram (p. 200) shows under what conditions negative transfer will be achieved and under what conditions positive transfer will be achieved. When both stimuli and responses are the same between the two tasks, obviously the maximum positive effects will be attained. That is because the second task is merely further practice on the first task. As long as there is some degree of similarity between the responses required in the two tasks, there will be some degree of positive transfer. The amount of positive transfer will decrease as the resemblance between the responses decreases. If the responses become dissimilar (do not resemble one another any longer) then the possibility of negative transfer comes up. Negative transfer will be greatest where the responses are dissimilar but the stimuli identical between the two tasks. Consider the example of a secretary faced with a typewriter in which about half of the keys had been mixed up at random. The stimuli associated with typing with this typewriter would be just about the same as those associated with an ordinary typewriter, but the responses learned in connection with an ordinary typewriter would lead to a welter of mistyped letters and a very annoyed secretary. Thus positive transfer occurs when what we have learned in a previous task is appropriate to a current task and negative transfer occurs when what we have learned in a previous task is inappropriate to a current task.

The relationships involved in Osgood's diagram are apparently not easy to grasp, but once the principle is understood, there is little need for confusion as to when positive or negative transfer will take place. The important difference between positive and negative transfer is the similarity of tasks and how that similarity is distributed among stimuli and responses. In general, similarity of stimuli coupled with similarity of responses produces positive transfer. Similarity of stimuli coupled with differences in responses produces negative transfer. In order to understand thoroughly the basis for these generalizations, the student may wish to reread the material in the previous chapter that deals with Osgood's diagram.

*Generalization gradients and positive transfer.* Back in Chap. 4, in connection with conditioning, we considered the phenomenon of stimulus generalization. This term, we saw, applies to the fact that a response conditioned to one stimulus "generalizes" to other physically similar stimuli. Such generalization is one of the aspects of positive transfer. In fact, positive transfer that occurs because stimuli in two situations are similar is merely another name for stimulus generalization. Curves (or gradients) of stimulus generalization (see p. 68), therefore, can be taken as measures of the degree of transfer when stimuli are different and responses are the same. As we shall see later, the concept of response generalization is also useful and is a way of speaking of positive transfer when stimuli may be the same but the responses required are somewhat different though similar.

Investigators have attempted to use stimulus generalization to study transfer in human verbal learning. Although the idea is a good one, they run into some difficulties when they use complex learning materials. Words, for example, do not readily lend themselves to an analysis in terms of some simple continuum within which they may resemble one another. Words may resemble one another in meaning without being alike in their phonetic characteristics (depart and leave, for example). Or they may resemble one another phonetically and be unrelated in meaning (leaf and leave). Thus, difficulty has been encountered in attempts to establish stimulus generalization in human learning.

In two attempts to measure stimulus generalization in human learners (Gibson, 1941; Yum, 1931), subjects learned a list of nonsense syllables as responses to give to a list of geometric forms as stimuli. The learning was by the method of paired associates; that is to say, the subject was presented with one of the geometric forms and was expected to respond with the appropriate syllable. To test generalization, the forms were made slightly different, and the number of times the differing forms elicited the correct response was counted. The result was that the greater the forms resembled those of original learning, the more correct responses were given.

*The complexity of dimensions of similarity in verbal learning.* It is possible for stimuli to resemble one another in other than physical characteristics. Such nonphysical resemblances are the result of *learned* relationships between stimuli and responses. It is possible, for example, that mediating symbols may produce degrees of similarity between otherwise unrelated words (Cofer and Foley, 1942; Foley and Cofer, 1943; Cofer, Janis, and Rowell, 1943). An example would be the tendency to give the same response to *vase* and *earn*. *Earn* is the homophone of *urn,* which is a synonym for vase. Thus the generalization in this case is twice removed from any simple physical resemblance. The relationship between *vase* and *urn* is one of meaning, that between *vase* and *earn* is a mediated relationship brought about by meaning and physical similarity. These mediated generalizations and generalizations due to meaning depend upon previously learned relationships. The complexity of human verbal learning allows for a truly amazing number of such similarity relationships.

There are many ways in which transfer may take place via generalization. Generalization may produce either positive or negative transfer, depending upon the stimulus-response relationships involved. In real life, mediated generalizations may therefore have a variety of effects. The example of mediated generalization given above would most likely lead to negative transfer. If the schoolboy tries to remember a synonym for *vase* and spells it *earn,* he has made a mistake based on the fact that he has allowed a stimulus which has the ability to call out either *earn* or *urn* to call out the wrong response.

Thus, while the theory of transfer of training is quite simple, any specific example may be very complicated, simply because the stimulus—and response—relationships in human learning can be very complicated. This fact accounts for the richness of the possibilities for transfer in human learning.

*Response generalization in conditioning.* So far our discussion has emphasized stimulus generalization. A few words about response generalization are in order. To see how such generalization applies to positive transfer, we can use an example from simple avoidance conditioning. Kellogg and Walker (1938) conditioned dogs to flex their right rear paws to a buzzer by pairing the buzzer with a shock to the right rear leg. The shock was then transferred to the left rear leg. The animals learned this response much faster than they did the original right-leg response—because there is similarity between the responses required in the left and right legs. It is interesting to note, in this connection, that it was easier to recondition the right leg than it was to condition the left leg after original conditioning on the right leg.

In this kind of flexion conditioning there is a rough gradient of response generalization which extends from the right rear foot to the left rear foot, then to the right front foot, and finally to the left front foot (Kellogg and Wolf, 1940). Thus we would expect that the greatest amount of transfer would be to the left rear foot, the next greatest to the right front foot, and the least amount to the left front foot.

*Transfer in human discrimination learning.* For a case of more complex learning that illustrates both stimulus and response generalization in positive transfer, we may turn to some studies of Gagné and his associates (Gagné and Foster, 1949a; Gagné, Baker, and Foster, 1950). The task that their subjects had to learn was a complex, discrimination reaction time. Four lights were on a panel which faced the subjects. A red and green light were together at the top of the panel and another red and green light were together at the bottom of the panel. Each of the reaction switches was connected with one of the lights so that when that particular light came on, the subject was required to throw the correct switch. Thus, there were two measures of learning, the decrease in the time that the correct reaction took and the number of correct reactions that occurred in any group of trials.

This task is especially well suited for the study of transfer of training, since it allows for both stimulus generalization and response generalization. The tendency to respond to any one of the switches can generalize to any of the others. The tendency to respond to a given light can also generalize. Thus, if the upper red light goes on, the subject may respond to it as if it were the lower red light. This generalization along the dimension of color would have led to an incorrect response.

One of the clear conclusions that comes out of these studies is that training which tends to reduce the tendency to generalize any stimulus to incorrect responses benefits the performance of the task as a whole. This is particularly true where only one response is associated with each stimulus. Under these conditions, generalization will always lead to negative transfer. Thus training which reduces generalization will reduce negative transfer. In other tasks, which do not demand such a restricted association of particular responses to particular stimuli, such generalization could be desirable.

A second important point that comes out of these studies concerns the effect of discrimination training upon cues not actually involved in the training. If, for example, learners are trained to make the color discrimination accurately and then trained on the whole task, it is apparent that the color-discrimination training has spread to the position discrimination, so that fewer errors are made in position discrimination. Gagné and his associates seem to think that this is because the color discrimination is more difficult, and training on a more difficult discrimination will help an easier discrimination. Such transfer presumably occurs because there are elements in common between the two sets of responses required in the discrimination.

## LEARNING HOW TO LEARN

Perhaps the most general and important case of positive transfer is learning how to learn. Practice in learning tasks makes it easier to learn new tasks. Subjects in laboratory experiments, for example, learn how to learn nonsense syllables. They will take fewer trials to reach a criterion on the fifth list of nonsense syllables than they did on the first. As a matter of fact, it is general practice to allow subjects in the laboratory to learn several lists of nonsense syllables before an experiment is actually begun.

In showing transfer in this kind of situation, the individual seems to take advantage of the common features of the responses required in learning nonsense syllables. For one thing, he can learn how to read the syllables correctly, which naïve subjects do not always know how to do. He also learns how to pick out the easiest portions of the list and concentrate on these. These and other relationships common to several tasks are what are important in learning how to learn.

*Learning sets.* Harlow (1949) has named another factor in this process of learning how to learn, the formation of *learning sets*. He points out that the formation of learning sets is one of the things that bridges the gap between simple conditioned-response learning and the complex behavior of problem solving and hypothesis formation.

In his study of learning sets, Harlow made use of discrimination learning in monkeys. The monkeys were presented with two stimuli that differed in a number of characteristics; one stimulus, for example, might be a square block of wood painted red, the other might be a blue cylinder. The monkeys were required to choose the rewarded stimulus (which would be shifted in position from trial to trial). After the solution of the first problem, the monkeys were required to solve another problem that involved different stimuli. On the first problem the monkeys took many trials to learn to associate the reward with the correct stimulus. On the second problem, however, they required many fewer trials. On each successive problem, fewer and fewer trials were required, so that after a hundred or so problems the monkeys solved a new problem immediately. Thus the monkeys were able to use what they had learned in earlier problems to solve later problems.

This ability of Harlow's monkeys to learn how to learn is even more striking on discrimination-reversal problems. In these problems the monkeys were first given a number of trials that were just like the simple discrimination problem; then the reward value of the stimuli was reversed for a number of trials. Each monkey was run through a number of discrimination-reversal problems. As with the simple discrimination problems, the monkeys learned to solve these problems very efficiently after they had experience with a number of such problems.

Thus, by a process of transfer of training, the monkeys had progressed all the way from blind trial-and-error behavior in the solution of problems to very intelligent behavior. Not only does the quantitative aspect of learning change as the organism learns how to learn, but the way in which it attacks a problem also changes. Simply to say that Harlow's monkeys could solve problems much more quickly after much experience does not seem to tell the whole story; they seem to engage in hypothesis formation and other indications of intelligent behavior. It should be apparent from these observations that transfer of training is very important in thinking and intelligent behavior, in both animals and men.

*Transfer of verbal training to performance.* Harlow's monkeys had to learn how to learn by doing. They could not be told how to solve problems in advance. They had to learn how to solve problems simply by solving a great many problems, all of which involved the same principle. Human learners, however, can take advantage of the community of verbal behavior available to them in order to find out how to do things beforehand. The resulting verbal practice of an act that is essentially nonverbal in character is generally called "mental practice." Mental practice is quite effective for a number of tasks. It has been shown, for example, that mental practice at dart throwing and basketball shooting in some ways is almost as effective as actual performance at these tasks (Vandell, Davis, and Clugston, 1943).

In an experiment on the acquisition of discrimination reaction time, like those described earlier, the function of verbal practice was analyzed (Baker and Wylie, 1950). In the case of this particular task, the verbal practice had the effect of predifferentiating the stimuli that were signals for the responses. Verbal rehearsal, in this case, prevented negative transfer between the stimuli or incorrect generalizations like those described earlier. The subject could verbally prepare himself so that he would not respond to the top red light as if it were the bottom red light.

These two examples of learning how to learn make the most important point about this kind of transfer. Learning how to learn operates to a very considerable extent through changing the degree of stimulus and response generalization that the learner will show on a task. It reinforces generalization where generalization will result in positive transfer, and it inhibits generalization where generalization will result in negative transfer. The monkeys who had learned how to solve simple discrimination problems on the second trial had learned to generalize a number of things. They had learned, if they chose on the first trial the stimulus that did not get them a reward, to choose on the second trial the opposite stimulus. Conversely, they learned, if they hit the correct stimulus the first trial, to stick with it. Later also, they learned not to generalize on the basis of position cues, but rather to ignore these cues. The human subjects in the discrimination re-action-time experiment learned to tell themselves not to be fooled by color alone, but to watch for both color and position.

## POSITIVE TRANSFER IN SCHOOL LEARNING

Transfer of training has been one of the problems of major concern to the educational psychologist—indeed the problem of transfer of training, in the guise of the "doctrine of formal discipline," is older than the study of learning itself. One does not have to look far to see why transfer of training is so important. In the first place, as we have pointed out before, education assumes transfer, for there is hardly any point in education unless it will transfer out of the educational situation. In the second place, there are a good many practical questions of transfer that arise in education. These problems are not of direct, theoretical interest to the psychology of learning, but they do illustrate the application of psychological principles to problems in education. It is therefore worth our while to consider them.

*Formal discipline.* The basic idea behind "formal discipline" is that mental exercise is good for the mind. The classical curricula in education stem from this notion, and in former days the hapless student studied Greek, algebra, logic, and Latin, not because of their intrinsic interest or value, but because they were supposed to exercise his mind. Learning to conjugate in Latin, presumably, would make a sharper wit as a lawyer. Training in logic would enable the statesman to get to the bottom of an important issue with profound insight.

Despite the apparent prevalence of the practice of formal discipline in traditional kinds of education, the notion never really had the support of thoughtful men (Stroud, 1940). The evils of formal discipline became sort of a straw man in educational circles, however, simply because forty or fifty years ago the educators needed a good lever to pry the traditional curriculum loose from the schools.

Unfortunately, in some minds, the idea of formal discipline has almost become synonymous with the idea of transfer of training. The discerning student should be able to see that nothing is farther from the truth. The notion of formal discipline is an omnibus theory, without any evidence for its far-flung claims. The theory of transfer of training is well grounded in our knowledge of stimulus and response generalization. Given a clear account of the stimulus and response relationships between any two tasks, we ought to be able to predict whether or not positive transfer will occur between them. Formal discipline, on the other hand, says that transfer ought to occur simply because of mental exercise, irrespective of the relations between the tasks involved.

The notion of formal discipline was well accepted in the popular mind, if not in the thinking of such educational pioneers as Locke and Herbart, when experimental psychology came upon the scene. Very soon this young science demonstrated that transfer was a decidedly limited phenomenon, so many people were disturbed. The result was that, for several decades, a great deal of emphasis has been placed on the negative evidence on transfer of training rather than on the positive evidence. For example, a large number of earlier studies showed that the effects of the study of Latin upon the use of English was very slight indeed. Thorndike (1923) showed that there was a slight advantage in the reading of English for students who had previously studied Latin. Similar studies (Thorndike and Ruger, 1923; Wilcox, 1917; Cole, 1924) have shown some very small effects of Latin upon such varied aspects of English as reading, grammar, and spelling, as well as upon the acquisition of modern foreign languages.

The question which was raised by these studies was whether the detailed study of the Latin language in secondary schools and colleges was really worth the time. The findings themselves were used as ammunition against the report of the "Committee of Ten" (National Education Association, 1894) on curriculum practices that had been put out 25 years earlier. But all the issues raised by the disappointing findings on transfer of training from such traditional subjects as Latin and Euclidean geometry are beyond the scope of the present discussion. There are merits to be found on both sides of the argument; the argument itself is one concerning the philosophy of education rather than the psychology of learning. The psychology of learning has simply presented certain facts that must be taken into consideration in any evaluation of the place of discipline subjects in the curriculum. It must be recognized that what is learned does not transfer simply through exercise but transfers through relationships of similarity running through different problems. Consequently the value of disciplinary subjects must be evaluated in terms of the things to which they *can* transfer, and the task of the psychology of learning is to find out what things maximize transfer of training in practice.

*General principles versus specific elements.* The principal mechanism for the operation of transfer of training is generalization. Educators, however, have frequently been concerned with the problem of whether it is the broad aspects of learning that provide the basis for generalization or whether it is the specific elements of some activity. At one time these two suggested modes for transfer of training were thought of as conflicting theories. The more reasonable interpretation, however, is that they are but two aspects of the practical problem of transfer. The mental age of the learner, the nature of the task to be learned, and the nature of the task to which the transfer occurs are all factors that determine which of these two aspects of transfer are most important in any given situation.

Thorndike (1916) is responsible for the notion that specific elements are transferred from one task to another. This notion is very reasonable, when one considers the right kind of examples. Training in addition, for example, benefits performance in multiplication for the simple reason that many of the responses required in addition are the same as those required in multiplication.

Judd (1908), on the other hand, at a very early date emphasized the importance of transfer by general principles, modes of attack, or rationalization. This notion stresses the importance of learning principles or general rules that can be transferred from one activity to another. Supporting this point of view is the fact that (Woodrow, 1927) it is quite possible to increase the ability of people to memorize by teaching them the principles of efficient memorization.

Transfer by general principles appeals to educators because it seems to be a more intelligent kind of process. This is teaching by way of understanding. The importance of specific elements in transfer must never be overlooked as a practical problem, however. The author is willing to guess that a fair number of people who can solve everyday problems in multiplication would not be able to give a very clear account of the relation of multiplication to addition. To the average automobile driver it is much more important that he be able to transfer from one make of auto to another what he has learned by rote about shifting gears than to be able to understand the nature of different variations in transmissions.

Both of these aspects of transfer of training can be subsumed under the general theory of transfer of training by stimulus-response relationships. Understanding a problem means that there is a common aspect to the solution of the problem that runs through several examples mastered by the learner. When a learner has understood a problem he has acquired the ability to solve each of the examples once he recognizes that the general principle can be applied.

This ability to recognize a general principle when it is embodied in a strange situation is an example of transfer which may be an indicator of intelligence. The ability to do this probably depends to a very important extent upon the mental ages of learners. In a study of second-grade children, for example, it was found that simply showing the children that arithmetic procedures could be generalized was more productive of transfer than attempting to teach them rational procedures (Overman, 1930–1931). These children were probably not mature enough to grasp or recognize the general principles involved. They had to be taught, more or less by rote, to apply the rules that they had learned to specific examples. This interpretation is bolstered by the fact that the highest third in mental age of the children in this experiment profited more than the others from the rationalization procedure.

*Training for transfer.* Transfer that occurs in the ordinary course of school learning and that can be measured by any reliable technique is surprisingly small. Consequently educational psychologists have looked for ways to increase the amount of transfer to practical problems that occurs from subject to subject and from school subjects.

One of the troubles with the older studies on the disciplinary values of various parts of the traditional curricula in education is that the methods of instruction usually left the transfer up to the student. More recently (Ulmer, 1939), it has been shown that if the plane geometry of high school is taught with a definite and clear understanding on the part of the students that much of the technique of thinking emphasized in geometry is applicable to many other problems in school and life, there is very much more transfer to other aspects of thinking. With a set to transfer what has been learned in geometry to syllogistic tests of reasoning ability, the general disciplinary value of geometry apparently can be increased.

Perhaps the most important single determinant of the amount of transfer that is possible, and that we can usually do something about, is the knowledge, on the part of the learner, that what he is learning can be transferred. The learner must also be motivated to apply what he has learned to new situations that are similar in character. On the other hand, the teacher can expect little or indifferent transfer when the opportunities for transfer and the need for transfer are not emphasized.

*Training programs and transfer.* An important part of schooling consists of special training programs, examples of which one may find in the public school, government service, or industry. Usually such training programs are designed for some very specific purpose, for example, to produce cash-register salesmen and insurance agents or bombardiers and navigators. The transfer value of such training programs is of paramount importance, because their only justification is that they produce specific and measurable transfer. The transfer that occurs in such situations ought to be relatively easy to evaluate, since the criteria (the activity which is to be benefited by transfer) are readily available and the nature of the training procedures can be controlled and varied.

There were many attempts during the Second World War to evaluate the transfer value of specific training programs, but because of the urgency of military demands most of them were not very adequate experimentally. An example or two, however, will give you an idea of the possibilities of doing routine studies of transfer of training in training programs.

In one such program (Hobbs, 1947), an attempt was made to test the training value of a gadget known as a Firing Error Indicator in flexible gunnery training. This device was designed to give the trainee information about how close the projectile that he fired came to his target. One group of subjects received aerial firing practice using standard gunnery school targets and another group received the same training with immediate knowledge of results given by the Firing Error Indicator. Both groups were given gun camera tests after this training, in which it was possible to score tracking errors quite accurately. The results clearly showed that the use of the Firing Error Indicator contributed nothing additional to proficiency. This was probably because in actual gunnery the operator seldom has "knowledge of results," at least immediately, and the knowledge of results obtained by the Firing Error Indicator in training may have induced the learners to rely on cues that were not available in actual gunnery practice. Thus, in this case, a study of the transfer potentially allowed by a special gadget prevented the Army Air Forces from using a difficult and expensive instrument in training. It is to be noted, however, that the experimenters thought the device to be theoretically sound from the standpoint of learning, and they recommended further study with the use of modifications of this device.

Other studies show more positive results. For example, pilots who received at least part of their basic training on a two-engine plane performed better in advanced two-engine training than those who had received all their basic training on a single-engine plane (Miller, 1947). A less obvious result was obtained with the use of a special kind of optical sight in skeet training. In skeet training, students fire at targets which move through the air. Students trained on the skeet range with a shotgun equipped with the sight, which simulated the sight picture which the trainee would find in air-to-air fixed gunnery, did much better in air-to-air firing than students who had received their skeet training with the usual type of gun.

These experiments are only examples of numerous applied problems in the transfer of training that have been studied in the evaluation of various training procedures and devices. This is one of the important areas for the application of facts and techniques derived from studies in the laboratory. It is apparent that maximum transfer is possible only when the training procedure is exactly like the operational situation. This is frequently impossible to achieve in practice because of expense or inaccessibility. It is then up to the ingenuity of the individuals in charge of the training program to see that the stimulus situation and responses required in training are as much as possible like those in actual operation, so that transfer may be maximized. It is also important that any potential source of negative transfer between training and operational procedure be removed. This may have the effect of increasing the net amount of positive transfer between the two situations.

CHAPTER 12

# EFFICIENCY IN HUMAN LEARNING

Learning is a surprisingly inefficient process. Indeed, we spend great amounts of effort, time, and money learning things of which—by a generous measurement of retention—we may retain only 15 per cent 6 months later. A college senior, for example, who has studied biology as a freshman may have only a hazy concept of the notion of mitosis. Nor can very many people who go through a freshman course in physics put their finger on Young's modulus. Who but a historian will have but a vague glimmer of recognition at the name Wat Tyler?

Or take another aspect of learning. How much of what we learn in formal educational situations can be put to use directly in the everyday business of life? How many college graduates apply to their voting behavior what they have learned in political science courses? How many think of what they learned in Economics 1 when they read an editorial on the national debt?

At another level, many parents spend anxious months wondering why it takes an infant so infernally long to learn the few words necessary to his wants. Or has anyone computed the amount of practice that goes into the memorization of the multiplication tables by the average person?

In some ways learning is inherently inefficient, just as engines of man's devising are inherently inefficient. Some of the reasons for the inefficiency of learning are implied in the earlier chapters. Stimulus generalization permits positive transfer, but it also permits negative transfer. Negative transfer is responsible for much of our confusion about the meaning of words we have learned and mistakes in spelling and addition. The efficiency of learning can be increased by the use of certain techniques, but eventually the limitations of the human learner appear. At the present time we cannot do very much about the human learner or the basic laws of learning, but we do have a few techniques available which can increase somewhat the efficiency of learning.

Some of the procedures that make for more efficient learning have already been discussed in earlier chapters. When we meet those procedures in this chapter, the discussion will be mostly about the basic principles with the experimental evidence omitted. There are other procedures that have not yet been presented because they do not easily fit into our present concepts about the nature of learning, and they will be introduced here. They represent empirical facts for which we have little theoretical basis.

## METHODS OF TUITION

The first problem to be examined is that of the various methods of tuition. Tuition, in its broadest sense, means teaching. So it includes teaching a rat to run a maze by pushing him through with a paddle or teaching students about psychology by lecturing to them. Formally defined, however, tuition is the direct or indirect guidance that one organism may give another in the acquisition of new behavior.

### Guidance in Learning

*Self-initiated behavior and guidance.* Some early experiments on maze learning in the rat show rather clearly that mere guidance through a maze does not always produce efficient learning. Either guiding subjects through the maze manually or blocking off the blind alleys does not always improve rate of learning and sometimes may seriously retard it (Koch, 1923; Tsai, 1930). Other experiments with cats show the same thing. Thorndike (1898) observed that cats which were forced through the movements required for escape from his puzzle boxes did not solve the problem. He had arranged the box in such a way that the cats had to find a loop of string and pull it down with their paws in order to escape. When an animal failed to learn the problem, Thorndike manually guided it through the act in question. In no case did the manually guided animals learn, even after as many as 50 trials.

These observations suggest very strongly that self-initiation of behavior is essential to learning, probably for the same reasons that incidental learning does not seem to be so effective as learning with intent. Under the conditions of forced guidance the organism does not attend to and perceive the aspects of the situation which will lead to success. Indeed the act performed under forced guidance is probably very different from the act performed when the behavior is self-initiated. Guidance may be effective, but the guidance must always allow for the self-initiation of the act in question.

*Imitation as guidance.* The role of imitation in learning has fascinated psychologists for many years. Imitation is, in human learning, an important way in which guidance is administered. Therefore the efficiency of imitative learning is an important topic.

The most fundamental point about imitation is that it is necessary for organisms to *learn to imitate* (Miller and Dollard, 1941). Many early experimenters found it difficult for animals to imitate, and some of them came to the conclusion that imitation was a relatively high-order kind of behavior which may well depend upon the ability to make symbolic representations. Miller and Dollard showed, however, that it is possible to teach even the albino rat to imitate, if you use the right technique. The secret is to reinforce the imitative behavior itself, rather than to reinforce only the result of imitative behavior. In other words, under proper conditions, it is possible to reinforce the act of imitation in itself. Figure 46 (Miller and Dollard, 1941) shows the results of imitative learning in rats. The rats that were taught to imitate were rewarded when they followed a leader rat that had already been trained in a T maze. Another group of rats were taught *not* to imitate by being reinforced for not following the leader rat. In this case the percentage of imitative responses decreased. Miller and Dollard were able to show that by proper training procedures the generalization of imitation could be demonstrated.

Once organisms have learned to imitate, imitation may be used as a form of guidance. The rules for the use of imitation as guidance are fairly simple and mostly involve common sense. The first rule is to use imitation only when it is clearly understood that the teacher's behavior is to be imitated. This is not a difficult rule to follow, since most people learn that imitation is rewarding; indeed, it is sometimes necessary to go to pains to convince them otherwise. Secondly, it is necessary to keep the to-be-imitated behavior pattern short and simple. The span of apprehension is limited in adults and even more so in children and animals. If the teacher's actions are long and complicated, the learner will not remember the beginning of the pattern of behavior after it has been demonstrated. Thirdly, the act must be shown to the learner in such a way that he does not have to change any component of it in order to perform it himself. Never, for example, attempt to illustrate a complicated motor act while standing in front of the learner. Stand to his side, so that he can use the same hand for the same movements you use, for many people are still confused about right and left, despite years of practice.

When these simple rules are followed, imitation becomes one of the most effective tools of guidance, particularly with motor performance. One of the great intellectual differences between the primates and the lower mammals seems to be the degree to which imitation is readily used. While

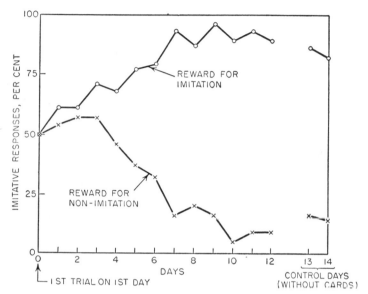

Fig. 46. Learning to imitate. The upper curve is for rats rewarded for imitating a leader. The lower curve is for rats rewarded for not following a leader. (*Miller and Dollard, 1941.*)

imitation is not so important as verbal and symbolic guidance in human learning, it is nevertheless a very potent factor.

*Verbal guidance.* The most important kind of guidance in human learning is verbal guidance. Verbal guidance may be used in many ways. It may be in the form of directional instructions about what to do. Or it may be in the form of information supplied the learner about the adequacy of his performance (p. 245). Some detailed experimental work upon this latter form of verbal guidance will be covered later; at this point it is necessary only to emphasize some general principles about verbal guidance.

Guidance should be in small doses. Anyone who has tried to teach someone else to drive an automobile must realize the drawbacks of massive doses of verbal guidance. By the time the learner has been told how to let the clutch out properly, how far to accelerate in low, how to turn the wheel, etc., he has forgotten the first instructions. Immediate memory span is very limited, even in the brightest of us.

Verbal guidance makes fullest use of our capacity to understand symbolic representation. The use of verbal behavior to give a learner prior information about the consequences of an act is of fundamental importance in the degree of intelligence and insightfulness shown in human learning. If I tell you to avoid eating in Harry's Hamburger Heaven, you have acquired a piece of information which, for a comparable problem, would require even the brightest of animals many trials of discrimination learning. It is verbal guidance that enables us to short-circuit the painfully slow processes of learning that animals require.

One word of caution is in order concerning verbal guidance. The success of verbal guidance depends upon the degree to which the learner is willing to believe what is told him and the extent to which his motivation is on the side of the guidance. We have all learned that not all guidance is beneficial or easy to carry out. As a result we do not always follow advice freely given. We frequently disregard guidance even when we know it to be beneficial, because we lack the proper motivation to follow out the suggested pattern of behavior. It is difficult, for example, to convince the average ten-year-old that a half a pound of popcorn on top of a hamburger and an ice-cream soda will make him acutely uncomfortable. It is easy, however, to convince the average college student about the best way to go about studying, but it is not always easy to get him to carry out the suggestions. So, despite the general usefulness of verbal guidance, there are many situations in which it has little effect upon behavior. This presents tremendous problems to people who manage safety programs, study clinics, etc. The big problem does not always concern the nature of the guidance involved, but concerns ways of getting people to act upon the information received.

*Some general principles about guidance.* It is of primary importance that guidance does not eliminate active participation by the learner. Above all else, doing is important to learning. Guidance should be given in as small doses as possible. Large doses of guidance are difficult to retain, and they may confuse the learner. Guidance is most efficient when given at the outset of learning, since it may prevent the learner from going off in the wrong direction. In this way it is a very efficient substitute for trial-and-error behavior.

*Methods of Formal Instruction*

One of the problems that has occupied the educational psychologists for many years is the attempt to find best ways of instruction for formal teaching. Is there a best way to teach arithmetic or Latin? Is there a best way to teach people how to read or sew? These questions are not concerned with deciding *what* to teach but with *how* to teach, or how to get students to learn what is put to them in the course of the educational process.

Unfortunately there are no simple answers to questions about the best ways of teaching. In the first place, it depends upon what is being taught and what is emphasized as the criterion of having learned. We will all agree that some increase in knowledge or skills is the purpose of education. And we can probably all agree also that different kinds of skills would call for different methods of teaching. But it is probably much less obvious that different *goals* in the teaching of the same skills may call for very different methods of teaching. Thus, if high-school mathematics is taught from the point of view of getting people to know about interest rates charged by banks, the method of instruction may be very different than if the purpose is to have students memorize the formal rules of algebra. The goals or criteria of education are problems for the philosophy of education, not the psychology of learning. Yet a problem in the psychology of learning, the methods of formal instruction, may depend upon what particular goals of education are emphasized.

The situation is further complicated by the fact that particular methods of teaching may have effects other than those upon the specific skills to be acquired. Perhaps "progressive education" represents a much more realistic approach to teaching than the older, more conservative ways. But it has been claimed, perhaps with some justification, that it produces slovenly, heedless children, and parents sometimes complain that progressive education makes children very difficult to live with.

The root of the trouble is, of course, that there are no well-defined criteria of the ends of teaching. Here and there we can decide upon some simple *intermediate* goals which can be measured. Thus we might be satisfied if one method of teaching spelling produces better performance than another method on a test of the Ayres spelling list. Performance on the Ayres spelling list at the end of a semester is only an intermediate goal and is fraught with all the dangers inherent in the use of an intermediate goal. There is an unknown degree of relationship between performance on this test and ability to spell in daily life. What we really want to know, of course, is how well a particular method of spelling produces transfer to the writing problems of ordinary daily life.

The larger, more nebulous problems of education are even more complicated. What about the best ways of teaching good citizenship or desirable modes of personal adjustment? Here the intermediate goals which we may use to test one or more different ways of teaching are even further removed from the ultimate criteria. We could, of course, decide that if one method of handling homerooms in high school produced better scores on a personality inventory than another method, that method was superior. Psychologists do not have very much faith in the ultimate validity of personality inventories, however, and this might be a very dubious procedure.[1]

It will be worth our while, however, to examine some of the accomplishments of the experimental approach to methods of teaching. The examples we shall cover will give us some notions of what can be done by experimental investigation and what the present-day limitations of such investigations are.

*Methods of teaching basic school subjects.* The basic school subjects, reading, spelling, and arithmetic, have received much attention in this matter of teaching methods. The literature is vast and far transcends the experimental problems in learning. Whole books have been written on teaching methods in reading alone. We cannot, of course, examine this whole literature, but we shall look at a few examples of some problems which have been studied experimentally and the major conclusions arising from these studies.

W. A. Brownell (1941, 1947, 1948, 1949) has been concerned with various methods of teaching arithmetic in grade school. Much previous evidence has been gathered that purports to show that children in grades 1 and 2 are not ready for the study of arithmetic (Brownell, 1941). Studies show that the basic abilities for the acquisition of arithmetic are not well developed in children in these grades. Despite the apparent deficiency in basic skills, however, Brownell was able to show that these very young children can learn arithmetic *when the methods of teaching are adjusted to their ability levels.* Further, Brownell gathered evidence which convinced him that children who had the proper kind of instruction in grades 1 and 2 did better in arithmetic later on than did children who did not have the

---

[1] It must not be supposed that educational psychologists are unaware of the problem of criteria of teaching in experiments on methods of teaching. A thoughtful analysis of the problem is presented by Brownell (1948).

proper kind of instruction. He recognizes, however, that the "proper kind of instruction" is not well defined and that probably much depends upon the skill of the individual teacher and the nature of the children doing the learning.

More recently Brownell (1947, 1949) has compared specific methods of teaching subtraction in the grades. He compared the method of "decomposition" with the method of "equal additions." In order to subtract 27 from 83 by the method of decomposition, one would reduce the 83 to 70 by taking away 13, subtract the 7 from 13 to get 6, and then subtract 2 from 7 to get 5. In the method of equal additions, 7 would be subtracted from 13 to get 6, and 3 from 8 to get 5. Previous research had found, without exception, that the equal-additions method was superior. Brownell also found that the equal-additions method was superior *when both methods were taught mechanically.* Decomposition, however, was superior when taught *rationally.* Equal additions is difficult to teach to a level of functional understanding, but decomposition apparently leads to an understanding of the basic processes involved. Thus, even though equal additions produces a higher rate of learning by rote, it is not superior in terms of some other criterion. Brownell also emphasizes the importance of such variables as age of pupil and pupil-teacher differences in the relative value of the two methods. The interactions between methods and kinds of students and/or teachers is of tremendous importance. Brownell points out that it is virtually impossible to come to a general conclusion about the superiority of one or another method. The superiority of the decomposition method in understanding depends on having bright students and able teachers. Whether one or the other method is declared to be superior *in general* depends upon what criteria one adopts. By a criterion of speed and accuracy, equal additions seems to have the edge; by a criterion of ease of rationalization, decomposition clearly has the edge.

The general question of meaningful vs. rote-drill procedures in teaching basic school subjects has achieved much attention. It is surprising to find that one occasionally runs across a study which finds drill on deductive principles superior to meaningful study by inductive procedures (Michael, 1949). One answer seems to be that some children who are below average in intelligence do not profit so much from meaningful teaching; they do better by drill (Anderson, 1949). Or, on the other extreme, it may take a *very* bright child to apply what has been learned by rote to general problems. Thus, while in general teaching for meaning and understanding is superior, it is *not* superior for some children and probably *not* superior when used by some teachers.

There is a truly vast literature on methods of teaching reading. Some of it consists of didactic expositions about the best ways to teach reading that have little or no foundation in experimental fact. Some of it consists of experimental evidence on a comparison of different teaching methods. And some of it consists of an account of the clinical evidence on various methods of *remedial* teaching in reading. The issues involved in the conflict over various methods are confused and clouded. There is no clear understanding about the criteria to be used in the evaluation of various methods of reading; sometimes rate of reading has been used as a criterion, and sometimes comprehension or some other measure of reading ability. There is widespread evidence of large individual differences in the response of learners to one particular method. Some individuals seem to profit greatly from a particular method while others profit hardly at all.[2]

Cronbach, in a recent summary of the literature of educational psychology, has summarized rather well the whole problem of evaluating methods of teaching basic school subjects. Cronbach states (1950, p. 243):

"The foregoing discussions indicate, and several of the current studies prove, that a good deal of previous educational research had led to false or inadequate conclusions. . . . [There is] the need to measure a learning experience in terms of its effect on readiness for subsequent learning (transfer value) and the importance of analyzing individual differences in response to treatments. Unfortunately, all of the suggestions point toward increasing the complexity of educational studies, and no one of the best present studies avoids all of the pitfalls identified above. In view of the limited usefulness of sheerly empirical generalizations, no matter how huge the samples on which they are based, we may look for greater emphasis on intensive studies, perhaps with small samples, which will yield understanding about changes in behavior rather than isolated facts about scores."

*The lecture method in college teaching.* Another question of methods in teaching which has received considerable attention is that of the lecture method in higher education. Many experimental studies have been conducted in an effort to compare the advantages of lecturing with some other

---

[2] The student will find some examples of current, representative studies on methods of teaching reading and spelling in Glock (1949), Freeburne (1949), and Horn (1949).

method of instruction. For example, the difference in retention of the lecture delivered by the instructor and the lecture read privately by the students might be compared. Or the lecture technique might be compared with the use of informal class discussion. The criterion usually employed in these studies is some objective test of what the students have retained. In some studies, however, transfer value and attitudes toward the subject matter have been considered.

Whatever the comparison or the criteria the results are usually equivocal. One experiment (Greene, 1928), which compared reading and lectures, found that the lecture was slightly more effective in producing retention measured by a test given after a period of time. Another such experiment (Corey, 1934), designed to compare the same methods, found a difference in favor of reading. Precisely the same lack of unanimity may be found in comparisons between the lecture technique and the discussion technique. One experiment (Spence, 1928) finds the lecture technique to result in superior achievement, while on the other hand, another experiment (Remmers, 1933) finds the discussion method to lead to superior achievement.

The reason why these studies all achieve different results is that the value of a certain method of instruction will depend entirely upon the specific learning situation. First and foremost, the value of a particular method will depend upon who the learners are and who the teachers are. Obviously, some teachers will do better as lecturers than as discussion leaders. Others, who may be halting in lectures, will have the ability to stimulate the class in an informal discussion. On the other side of the picture, some students will learn better in lecture and others in discussion. There are some students who learn best with no formal tuition at all.

This can all be summed up by saying that the individual differences in teaching and learning produce much greater effects upon any measure of the amount of learning which has gone on than any given comparison of methods of learning. This is especially true where the material learned is complicated and does not involve a simple, mechanical sequence of performance. In some specific training programs comparisons of different teaching techniques may be valuable. But this is true only where the criteria of having learned are well defined and where sufficiently large numbers of learners are involved so that small differences in efficiency may be important in man-hours or money. Such is the case in training in the armed forces, and under these conditions comparisons of various methods of training has resulted in information of value. In nearly all cases, however, the results are purely empirical and apply only to the specific comparisons made; they are of little importance in an understanding of the learning process as a whole.

Thus, methods of instruction must be evaluated in a number of lights. We cannot look to any simple psychological principles to guide us in finding the best ways of teaching people. Sidney Hook (1945) in a popular article on progressive education tells us of the success he had in applying techniques of progressive education to teaching rather tough customers from the sixth grade in the slums of Brooklyn. It is quite possible, however, that another teacher would have achieved equally excellent results by the use of more traditional disciplinarian measures. What the teacher knows and does is far more important than the particular educational method he uses.[3]

*The value of research on methods of teaching.* Despite the pessimistic tone of the past few pages, it can be said that there is some considerable value to research on problems of methods of teaching. An experimental approach to this problem will be most valuable in situations in which the teaching is mechanical and routinized such that the personality characteristics of the teacher have a minimal influence and in situations in which the aims of the educational program are simple and well defined. As we have seen above, a good example is provided by the various training programs for industrial and military jobs. A research program on methods of teaching reception of the international Morse code (Keller, 1943; Keller and Taubman, 1934; Keller, Cristo, and Schonfeld, 1946) led to the discovery of a method that had decided advantages in teaching beginners to recognize the code quickly and accurately. The degree to which such research will be valuable will depend upon the degree to which the method itself is important in how much and how fast the student learns.

In many situations the basic principles of learning can be applied to the evaluation of methods of instruction. We can ask, for example, whether a given method of teaching aircraft recognition will transfer to actual field performance. In many cases, an analysis of the learning situation in terms of its fundamentals will give us some valuable clues about teaching methods.

---

[3] Stephens (1951) has advanced a hypothesis, the hypothesis of spontaneous schooling, to account for the great amount of negative evidence on methods of teaching. In evaluation of this problem, Stephens's hypothesis and its psychological background deserve serious attention.

## METHODS OF STUDY

Problems involved in the evaluation of various methods of study are almost as great as those involved in the evaluation of the various methods of teaching. There seem to be a few more adequate answers, however; this is perhaps because one large source of individual differences is removed. We need be concerned only about individual differences in learners here; there is no problem of an instructor. Also, individual differences in advantages due to study are not so difficult to control and vary. Once we have ruled out intelligence and experience as factors, for example, the advantages gained from various methods of study can be readily evaluated. This seems to be because study implies a much more limited activity than does just learning. Study implies intensive activity in order to learn some very specific thing. We may study in order to learn formulas in organic chemistry or the names of the minor English poets. Because of the highly directive nature of studying, it is possible to make several useful suggestions about methods.

*Reading and recitation in memorizing.* Two classical experiments by Thorndike (1914) and Gates (1917) have thoroughly established the trend of the results obtained in subsequent comparisons of reading and recitation in memorization. These experiments clearly show that periodic recitations or recalls interspersed with reading greatly facilitate retention. This is true for adults as well as for children. It is true for meaningful material and for nonsense material. In one experiment (Gates, 1917) subjects who spent up to four-fifths of the total time in recall rather than reading showed the greatest improvement.

A more recent experiment (Forlano, 1936), with school subjects as the material to be learned, compared the effects of reading and recitation in the actual schoolroom situation. Again, it was clearly established that a very large amount of time devoted to attempted recall rather than to straight reading resulted in reliably greater retention. Another experiment (Skaggs, 1920) has shown that it is better to have one recitation after each reading rather than to have several recitations or readings grouped together.

Various other studies of "implemented recall" induced by oral quizzing, examinations, discussion, etc. (Bridge, 1934; Germane, 1921), have shown that these techniques add much to straight reading, though it is not clear that these techniques are superior to straight recall as the method of recitation.

These experiments all show a rather remarkable degree of agreement, and we must accept the point as well established. It has been pointed out (Stroud, 1940), however, that these studies are limited by the fact that they examined only the process of memorization and that they used relatively small amounts of material to be learned. There is every reason to expect, however, that the same advantages would hold for ideational material and for material of the magnitude, say, of an ordinary college course. Certainly the principle of recitation is a sound one from the point of view of the basic facts of learning.

The reasons for the superiority of reading recitation are many. The most important function is probably to keep the learner active, for activity prevents him from suffering lapses of attention. Reading, for example, is an easy task and recall is not; there is a tendency for some people to read with only "half a mind." While we do not have evidence that directly supports this interpretation, the common experience of anyone who has done intensive studying makes it appear reasonable. McGeoch (1942) suggests as other factors that might operate in favor of recitation: (1) knowledge of results, (2) incentive conditions, (3) principle of effect, (4) early elimination of wrong results, (5) greater efficiency in directing the learner in what to learn.

*Whole and part learning.* A question that bothered psychologists and educators for many years was the question whether it is better to learn material as a whole or by parts. Learning by whole means going through the entire material before going back to any part. Thus, if I were to learn a sonnet by Shakespeare this way, I would read through the entire poem once, attempt to recite, read through it again, attempt to recite again, etc. It is easy to recognize that the typical rote-learning experiment is by the whole method.

The part method is not so simple. There are at least two different types. There is the part progressive method, in which a unit is learned, then a second unit learned, then the two bridged together. In the simple part method no attempt is made to bridge the parts together. It is probable that most people use some form of the part progressive method in actual memorization.

When we compare the part methods with the whole method, no clear-cut results are obtained. One might attempt, however, to find a theoretical solution to the problem by considering the length of time it takes each added increment of material. It has sometimes been found (Lyon, 1914) that the time required to learn a large number of items is greater proportionately than the time necessary to learn a small number of items. In other words, the relationship between time to learn and amount learned is not a linear one. It should follow that the sum of the time required to learn each of the parts of a task separately should be less than the time required to learn the whole task to the same criterion. When the parts are combined, however, additional time is required. It is this additional time which will determine the relative advantage or disadvantage of the whole method. If the time to combine the various parts takes longer than the additional time required to learn a great number of items, the whole method will be superior; if the time to combine the parts is shorter than that required to learn the additional number of items, the part method will be superior. Unfortunately, at the present time, there is no simple way to predict in which direction the advantage will go for a particular condition.

For one thing, it is apparent that most people have to learn to use the whole method. The advantage of the whole method over the part method increases with practice at the whole method (Wylie, 1928; Lakenan, 1913). For another thing, any advantage seems to depend upon the type of material being learned (Jensen and Lemoire, 1937); some materials are easier to learn by the whole method and some by the part method. In many cases there is little difference at all between these two methods of learning (Jensen and Lemoire, 1937).

Probably the relative advantage of whole or part learning also depends upon the degree of similarity between parts of the material to be learned and upon the degree of meaningfulness of the material. These conditions have not been adequately examined experimentally, however. At the present time it does not appear that the difference between whole and part learning is an important one, for the interactions with other variables that determine rate of learning seem to be too large. In other words, the kind of material being learned, the individual doing the learning, and the stage to which learning ability has been advanced seem to be much more important conditions than this particular difference in method of learning. It is probably true, however, that part learning should be called for where the material can be broken down into meaningful units. This is especially true where no particular virtue attaches to the task as a whole. Where a meaningful whole is involved, or where a continuous sequence is called for, the whole method probably has an advantage, since it does not permit the learner to commit the excessive number of errors that have been observed when parts are combined (Pechstein, 1917).

*Massed and distributed practice.* Some of the experimental evidence on the advantage of distributed vs. massed practice was discussed in Chap. 9 (p. 152). It was pointed out that under practically all conditions, for all types of learning, short rest intervals distributed periodically through learning are of great benefit to learning. These rest intervals need be only fairly brief, and a break of only a few seconds will greatly help the learner. There is some evidence that human learners, when working on their own schedule, frequently introduce these short rest intervals more or less automatically. Sometimes, however, highly motivated learners fail to do this. Pianists frequently have the experience, when learning a new composition, of finding that as they repeat a brief passage which is very difficult over and over again, they become progressively worse. A brief rest, or turning to something else for a while, improves performance on this difficult passage.

Retention is helped by distributed practice as well. It is probably important, when studying material to be used at a later time, to break practice into units with fairly long intervals in between. Although there is little evidence to show that the longer rest intervals are intrinsically better than the fairly brief intervals, they simulate the retention interval and as such give the learner practice at recall.

The most important determiner of the relative benefits of distributed practice is the amount of work involved in the task. With difficult work, the rest periods should probably be more frequent, though they need not necessarily be much longer. With very easy work, the natural breaks that occur in the rhythm of work are probably sufficient to prevent deterioration of performance. Thus, when we are learning an especially difficult list of irregular verbs or trying to understand a particularly esoteric passage in our physics text, frequent rests are probably called for. On the other hand, if we are trying to get the "feel" of an Emerson essay, continuous reading is called for.

*Other modes of practice.* There are many other variables which, theoretically at least, could have an influence upon the benefits of practice. The question has been frequently raised as to whether or not there is any advantage in learning through one or another of the sensory modes. Is learning from visual presentation, for example, better than learning from auditory presentation? The answer to this one is that sometimes auditory presentation has been found to be superior to visual presentation (Elliot, 1936; Henmon, 1912) and sometimes visual presentation has been found to be superior to auditory presentation (Koch, 1930; Krawiac, 1946). One thing is clear, however; a combination of both auditory and visual presentation is better than either alone (Henmon, 1912; Koch, 1930; Elliot, 1936). On the other hand, there are most certainly differences in auditory and visual signals as sources of incoming information. Auditory signals have the advantage in capturing attention of being nondirectional; no matter where the individual is placed he can still hear an auditory signal which is in his vicinity, whereas visual signals are apt to be missed if the individual is looking the other way. However, once the individual is attending to the incoming information, probably the differences in rate of learning between auditory and visual presentation are negligible and depend more on the individual doing the learning than on anything else.

Other problems, such as rhythmic grouping of material presented serially or method of presentation of material to the subject, are highly specialized and of little general interest. These problems may turn up in the evaluation of learning a particular task, but they are of little importance to the general problems of learning.

## INFORMATION IN HUMAN LEARNING

There is a famous experiment by Thorndike (1932b) which is a simple demonstration of the important fact that the consequences or aftereffects of an act are important determiners of the subsequent history of that act. If a blindfolded person is requested to draw, with one quick move of a pencil, a line 3 inches long, his accuracy will be poor. If he continues to "practice" without ever being able to see what he is doing, his performance will not materially increase in accuracy. However, if an outsider measures the drawn line and says "right" to the subject if his line is within ⅛ inch of 3 inches and "wrong" if his line deviates by a greater amount, the subject will rapidly show improvement in his ability to approximate the 3-inch criterion.

This little experiment has undoubtedly been the subject of more misinterpretation than anything similar in the field of experimental learning. The experiment was meant to demonstrate the importance of the aftereffects of a response. By implication this is frequently taken to mean that the reward ("right") satisfied the subject's motivation to increase his accuracy and thus eventually free himself from the blindfold. This may well be true, but there is no crucial evidence for or against the generalized principle of effect in learning (p. 27). The line drawing demonstrates only the empirical principle of reinforcement, however, which says that there is a class of stimuli which will increase the strength of a correct response in a learning situation. It does not demonstrate what, in this book, has been called the principle of effect.

Thus, almost any sort of information that leads the human learner to make what the experimenter or teacher defines as the correct response is a reinforcement. Rewards, which are things which an organism exerts effort to achieve, constitute sources of information. Punishment and negative reinforcement likewise are sometimes sources of information and are thus positive reinforcements. The important problem for the psychology of human learning is to study the way in which various sources of information act to change behavior and, perhaps, what are the best kinds of information to use in certain situations.

*Rewards as information.* Information can be of many kinds. Often different kinds of information can be basically analyzed in terms of how much information is supplied the individual; however, for our purposes it is probably best to stick to qualitative classes of information.

In Thorndike's line-drawing experiment the word "right" supplied information to the subject; it is also usually assumed to be a reward. Thus this experiment can be taken as a demonstration of the use of rewards as sources of information. For our purposes at present, it is irrelevant as to whether we consider these rewards to be secondary reinforcements or not. They probably are, but their derivation from sources of primary reinforcement are probably very complicated and obscure. At any rate they certainly seem to be learned rewards.

A comparison of Thorndike's experiment with subsequent, similar experiments shows that rewards are not necessarily the most efficient ways of giving information. If, in the example given above, the outsider had said instead of "right" and "wrong" the actual amount by which the subject's line deviated from the norm, learning would have progressed at a much faster rate (Trowbridge and Cason, 1932). These statements of accuracy are better sources of information than are simple, rewarding statements. It may be argued that these statements are "satisfying" to the subjects, but this argument is not easily testable.

There is no clear-cut evidence which shows that rate or amount of learning is increased by increasing amounts of reward. Thorndike and Forlano (1933) show some evidence in mutiple-choice learning in school children that increasing a monetary reward will increase the rate of learning. However, no such effect has been found by other investigators (Rock, 1935).

It is interesting to note, in this connection, that the promise of a reward is just about as effective as an actual reward (Forlano, 1936).

*Punishment as information.* Some striking results have been obtained on the use of punishment as information. They indicate that punishment sometimes increases the strength of a response (Muenzinger, Bernstone, and Richards, 1938; Muenzinger, 1934; Tolman, Hall, and Bretnall, 1932). In an experiment by Tolman, Hall, and Bretnall, human subjects were shocked for the correct response while learning a maze. This facilitated learning. Presumably this is because the shock added an additional source of information about the nature of the response just made. Electric shock is a powerful kind of stimulus, of course, and it seems to emphasize responses which are contiguous with it. When, in the experiment by Tolman, Hall, and Bretnall, the wrong responses were shocked, learning was slowed down. Apparently, in this case, punishment emphasized the wrong responses. The fact that punishment seems to be in a special category as far as emphasis is concerned is supported by the findings that other, less intense stimuli, such as a nonsense syllable spoken after a response or a light flashed after a response, do not serve to influence learning unless the subjects know the stimuli are to serve as information of a specific sort (Trowbridge and Cason, 1932; Courts, 1937).

A punishing stimulus presumably could be used to code information of a more complicated sort. It would be interesting to see if information given through an electric shock (say, in the form of the Morse code) would have any effect different from those produced by ordinary, less noxious stimuli. Such an experiment would further serve to clarify the "emphasizing" nature of punishment.

*"Spread of effect" and information.* There are a number of well-known experiments upon a phenomenon known as the "spread of effect." These have frequently been used to bolster the notion that certain consequences of responses act by the principle of effect as well as by the informational nature of stimuli. Thorndike, who discovered the spread of effect, thought that it demonstrated beyond any doubt the principle of effect. Operationally stated, however, the spread of effect in Thorndike's (1933) original experiments showed only that the consequences of a response were not specific to the response which it followed. In other words, a reward or punishment affected other responses than that about which information is specifically given. According to Thorndike, the "effect" produced by a reward spread in a more or less blind, mechanical fashion to responses which were temporally adjacent to the particular response rewarded.

The experiment design which Thorndike used was rather unusual, and because of the unique character of the experimental design it became known as the "Thorndikian experiment." Subjects are given a series of items, which may be words on nonsense syllables, to which a number of responses are possible, as in a multiple-choice test. The subjects are instructed to choose a response from those available on each trial. Since the subject has no information about which responses are to be associated with which word, his responses initially should be more or less random. In one experiment, for example, the subject is read a long list of words, one at a time. He is instructed to respond to each word with a number from one to ten. The experimenter answers the subject's number by saying "right," "wrong," or nothing at all. The subject is under the impression that he is taking part in an experiment on learning, and that he must learn to associate the correct number with a particular word. The experimenter, however, has decided beforehand which of the words he will say "correct" to, no matter what number the subject gives. The subject is told that more than one number might be correct, so that there is no way for the subject to know that he is not really in a learning experiment.

The effect Thorndike found was that the statement "correct" not only increased the likelihood of repeating the response that it followed, but it increased the probability of repeating the responses that occurred both before and after the particular response rewarded. This is seen in a typical "spread of effect gradient" in Fig. 47. You can see that the responses on either side of the middle response had no afterconsequences at all. The rewarded response in the middle, however, increased the repetition rate of these responses over that expected by chance.

At the time Thorndike's results were published, they did indeed seem to give strong support to the notion that the consequences of a response operated by the principle of effect as well as by information. In the intervening years, however, a number of complications have been found with this kind of an experiment. Zirkle (1946) showed that it is the response place adjacent to the rewarded item that is affected, not the particular response. By changing the order of the stimulus words on successive trials, Zirkle was still able to demonstrate the spread of effect.

A number of other experiments combine to show almost overwhelmingly that the spread of effect is primarily due to the fact that human beings seldom respond randomly, and it does not at all seem to be related to the principle of effect. More specifically, some of the experiments demonstrate that the guessing habits of the subjects are the important determiners of the spread of effect. When no opportunity for guessing habits is permitted, no spread of effect appears (Jenkins and Sheffield, 1946; Jenkins and Postman, 1948). On the other hand, Sheffield (1949) has shown that pure guessing without any information or reinforcement will result in an aftergradient like that found in the spread of effect. So it seems that the dependent probabilities in human verbal behavior (p. 141) provide the theoretical background for the spread of effect (Smith, 1949).

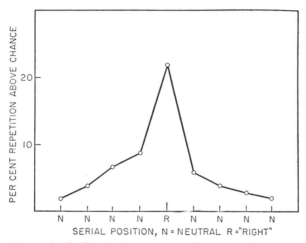

FIG. 47. The "spread of effect" phenomenon. Items contiguous to a rewarded item are raised in strength.

The controversy over the spread of effect has not entirely died down. The fact that the effect varies with the type and intensity of punishment (Stone, 1948b) has been advanced as an argument that the spread cannot entirely be explained on the basis of guessing habits. Marx and Bunch (1951), moreover, find evidence for a somewhat different kind of spread of effect, where no opportunity for guessing habits to bias the results is possible. The gradient they find is one on the errors which the subjects make on trials near in time to a rewarded trial. Errors which occur on the trials immediately before and after a trial which is rewarded tend to be repeated. Marx and Bunch interpret this gradient in terms of interactions between responses based upon gradients of response relationship. If this interpretation is correct, it would seem that this kind of gradient is a rather special case of negative transfer. The principle of effect, again, is not needed to explain these results.

Thus the effects of any kind of information upon the strength of particular responses follows only the rule laid down by the empirical definition of reinforcement. In human learning, for certain purposes, reinforcement and informational aftereffects can be used interchangeably. Thus we may speak of a response as being reinforced when the learner is told that the response was correct or in error by so much, etc. Many kinds of information can be explained well by the principle of effect; most afterconsequences of a response which increase the strength of that response are related to some motivation of the individual. There is no direct proof that the principle of effect is correct, however, and as a consequence the neutral terms "reinforcement" and "information" are more acceptable.

*Ways of giving information.* Finding the best ways to supply individuals with information upon which to act is one of the fundamental engineering problems in psychology. This has been recognized in the field of human engineering, in which field there has been a tremendous amount of experimental work upon the best way to present displays to individuals who operate complicated machines. What is the best way to present to the various members of the crew of an aircraft information necessary to fly the ship? In these cases usually the information is designed such that an individual can make some sort of a decision as to a course of action.

In the case of learning, the problem is only slightly different. The information is designed to tell the individual what he just did so that he can adjust his performance in terms of a criterion set up usually by some outsider, his instructor or the experimenter. Thus, information in learning is nearly always in the form of knowledge of results of previous behavior. Frequently the knowledge of results comes about naturally from the task itself. The piano player knows by his ear whether or not he is performing correctly. In other learning situations, however, it becomes a critical training problem to let the individual get the correct kind of information about his performance.

A good example of the difficulties involved in getting the correct information to the learner is found in flexible gunnery training. In firing guns it is sometimes difficult for the trainee to know if and when he hit the target. During the Second World War various sorts of training devices were developed to give individuals information about their accuracy in firing. One of these, the Waller trainer, was a screen which simulated the sky and against which images of planes were thrown; a simulated gun and sights enabled the trainees to fire at the images. The apparatus was rigged so that it would score a "hit" whenever the individual had the sights lined upon the image of the plane and was pulling the trigger. In addition, there was a tone—a "beep"—which was sounded whenever the individual made a hit. This could be thrown in or out of the circuit so that the effect of this bit of information could be studied. Figure 48 tells the story. You can see that when the tone was sounded for a hit, the subjects did very much better. When the tone was sounded early in practice it resulted in a greater

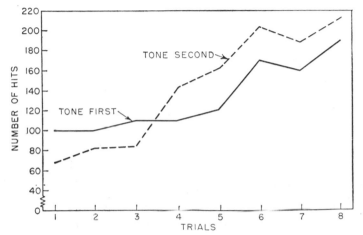

Fig. 48. The effect of knowledge of results upon learning to hit a target. Whenever a hit was made, the tone was sounded. One group had the tone at first and none later. The other group had no tone at first and a tone in the later trials. (*Hobbs, 1947.*)

number of hits. Later, when the tone was withdrawn from this group and given to the second group, the second group immediately increased in number of hits, so that it now surpassed the first group. It is too bad that the investigators in this experiment did not include a third group that was never given the tone.

The same group of studies (Hobbs, 1947) show that where there is little opportunity for knowledge of results, as in the gun camera mounted in the tail of a bomber, relatively little improvement in score took place. This fact ruled out several otherwise excellent, realistic, training devices. A second important point is made by the same studies: sometimes the subject gets the wrong information. Knowledge of results from training with a stationary gunsight and target might be misleading, because in actual practice the gunner must fire at a moving target from a moving plane and must learn to "lead." Thus knowledge of results on a training device could actually lead to negative transfer on the job. While this may not happen very often, it is something which needs to be watched very carefully in any training program.

IMPROVING MEMORY

One of the will-o'-the-wisps most frequently offered to the public by quacks and pseudo psychologists is the offer to improve memory by a training course or by a book, which, needless to say, is for sale by the memory expert. Most of these "memory systems" consist of various rules for increasing the efficiency of learning, rather than suggestions for retaining what has already been learned. Some of the rules which have been offered have some foundation in fact, but others are fairly weird. Most of the memory systems lay heavy emphasis upon such artificial devices as mnemonic aids, etc. Mnemonic aids sometimes can be of some use in reducing intraserial interference effects, but any great use of them is cumbersome and may take more time than it is worth.

There is some sound evidence which shows that ability to memorize can be improved by the proper sort of instruction (Woodrow, 1927). Woodrow studied the effects of instructions upon the proper way to learn for later retention upon the memory for poetry, prose, and factual and ideational material. One group of subjects practiced memorizing large amounts of material without formal instruction in the best way to learn. Another group of subjects practiced memorizing the same material after detailed instruction had been given in the best ways to learn. Both groups were motivated by the information that the practice at memorization would improve the memory in general. On a final test, the group which had been given practice plus instructions showed much greater ability to retain. The group which had been given specific training in methods of memorization averaged about 32 per cent better than did the group which just practiced at memorizing.

Some of the principles that Woodrow used to train his experimental group in his study have already been mentioned in this chapter. Such factors as active recitation, attention to meaning, and mental alertness were emphasized. Unfortunately, Woodrow's study was not analytical, and we cannot tell which of the factors was most important in improving memory. The important point of the study is, however, that training for memory does have a beneficial influence. Such training, however, consists in emphasis upon the basic principles of learning, rather than the elucidation of any "secret" magical key for unlocking memory. Can the retention of what is learned be improved? Is there any way of preventing forgetting? Can interference, unlearning, and repression be minimized, so that the retention of what is already learned will be improved? Most certainly these factors which produce forgetting can be reduced by the appropriate procedures. The unfortunate fact is, however, that they can best be reduced by changing what is learned. It is the nature of the material learned which principally determines at what rate we will forget. Thus, the way to improve memory is to change what is learned. Practically, of course, this is an absurd suggestion. We learn what we learn not because it consists of material which is easy to remember, but because it is important to us for some reason. We cannot ordinarily change the material much in order to avoid retroactive inhibition. In a few cases we can. Mnemonic devices frequently serve this purpose. Organization of material, the use of key cue words, etc., all help out. Basically, however, it is difficult to improve the ease of remembering, since the interfering effects which produce forgetting are inherent in the relations between the various things we learn.

# CHAPTER 13

# THINKING AND PROBLEM SOLVING

We regard thinking and problem solving as the supreme accomplishments of the evolution of mind. That we should feel this way is understandable, for thinking is the sort of thing at which we human beings undeniably excel. Indeed, there is no animal, even among our near relatives, that has anything like the capacity for thinking and problem solving that even a moderately endowed human being has.

Because thinking is so severely limited in the animal species and because it is such a complicated process, we know little about it. Experimental psychologists have avoided the study of thinking and problem solving to a very considerable extent; therefore the richness of the experimental literature upon which we may draw is not nearly so evident here as in the study, say, of the distribution of practice. With the limitations of the available data in mind, we shall attempt to examine some of the basic processes involved in thinking and problem solving and how they are related to learning.

## SYMBOLIC BEHAVIOR

One of the basic components of the ability to solve problems and to think is the ability to behave symbolically. Symbols are stimuli which stand for or lead to other stimuli. The relation of symbols to the stimuli for which they stand is an artificial one that comes about through learning. Symbols have meaning as the result of learning. Thus, learning is of fundamental importance to symbolic behavior.

We can distinguish at least three different kinds of symbolic behavior. (1) The most primitive kind is exemplified by the Pavlovian conditioned response. (2) A second kind of symbolic behavior is that in which the symbolic cues are not directly in the environment but either exist within the organism or are mediated by cues which the organism has learned. Thus, in this kind of symbolic behavior the organism appears, to the observer, to be responding in the absence of cues. (3) A third kind of symbolic behavior is that in which organisms make use of a learned, communicative language. By the use of words, the tools of language, organisms are able to manipulate their environment symbolically and thus indulge in the most highly developed form of vicarious trial-and-error behavior. It hardly need be said that as far as we know at present this variety of symbolic behavior is limited to human beings.

Correlated with these three varieties of symbolic behavior are functions which they serve in the life of the organism. Simple, conditioned symbolic behavior serves to lead the organism from place to place. The formation of symbolic representation in this sense is nothing more than learning in its most basic aspect. The second function of symbolic behavior is to bridge a gap in the absence of external stimulation. This we can call the representational function of symbols. The higher animals can produce their own representational symbols that will enable them to respond appropriately even after the external stimulus has been removed. This function is well correlated with the intellectual status of the animal. The rat is limited to very brief delays, while the primates can respond appropriately long after the external stimulus has been removed. The third function, which we can call the linguistic function, enables the organism to *manipulate* his environment symbolically. Some experiments will illustrate some of the important points about these symbolic functions.

*Delayed-reaction experiments.* W. S. Hunter was one of the psychologists who realized at an early date the importance of symbolic behavior in ideational and thinking processes (Hunter, 1924). Hunter was especially interested in those kinds of tests that would force the organism to react to a stimulus in its absence, since, he believed, this was the really important characteristic of symbolic behavior.

One of the tests that Hunter used is known as the "delayed-reaction test." The basic technique in the delayed-reaction test is to present the organism with an incentive while it cannot respond. The incentive is then hidden, so that the animal must make the reaction appropriate to obtaining the incentive after it has disappeared. For example, a monkey may be presented with two cups; while the monkey is restrained, another experimenter places some raisins under one of the cups. The monkey is held for a period of time and then is allowed to choose one of the cups. Thus the animal is forced to react to some substitute for the incentive, since he cannot see the incentive at the time he is free to react. Hence the importance of the delayed-reaction test in the study of symbolic behavior; in this test the organism must have some way of symbolically "remembering" where the incentive is.

In his original studies of the delayed reaction, Hunter (1912) found that rats could delay a maximum of about 10 seconds. Subsequent experiments (Honzik, 1931; McCord, 1939) were able to extend the maximum delay for the rat by making the problem easier. McCord (1939), by giving the rat more cues upon which to build secondary reinforcements, was able to bring the rat's successful delay period up to several minutes.

Other animals show longer delays. In his original experiment, Hunter (1912) found that, under conditions comparable to those used with the rat, the dog could delay about 5 minutes, while young children could delay almost half an hour. Subsequent investigations have established very long delay periods with higher animals. In a series of studies of primates, Harlow and his associates (Harlow, Uehling, and Maslow, 1932; Harlow and Israel, 1932; Maslow and Harlow, 1932; Harlow, 1932) found that the anthropoid apes could delay longer than monkeys but that subnormal humans (adults with mentals ages of about two) did only about as well as the apes.

Hunter originally made the observation that the rats and dogs he tested had to keep the same bodily posture and orientation throughout the delay period in order to make the correct choice, while some raccoons and children he tested did not have to remain stationary during the delay period in order to complete the test successfully. Thus it appeared as though the rats and dogs used kinesthetic cues to bridge the delay while raccoons and children did not. Subsequent investigators (Loucks, 1931; Honzik, 1931; McCord, 1939) have shown that it is not necessary for the rat to maintain its bodily posture if the delayed-reaction test is set up properly. The fact that simple kinesthetic cues alone are not necessarily responsible for the ability to delay led investigators to look for other internal cues that animals might use in bridging the gap.

Seward (1949), in an analysis of the experimental literature, came to the conclusion that the "symbols" animals use in solving delayed-response problems are not self-initiated signs of external cues. Rather, suggests Seward, most experiments on delayed reaction represent rather complicated cases of secondary-reinforcement learning. This probably gets to the crux of the problem. The ability to solve the typical delayed-reaction test means that organisms have some capacity—either direct as in the case of kinesthetic cues or indirect as in the case of learned, secondary cues—to mediate delay periods through some stimulus present either in the environment or in the animal. The delayed-reaction test *does not* indicate that animals have the capacity to manipulate symbols (to self-initiate and maintain them) in order to bridge the delay period. In other words, there is no evidence that any animal solves the delay problem, as an adult human being would, by telling himself that the incentive is under the left cup, for example. If there are cues that are associated with the incentives and that

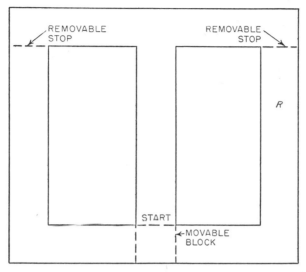

FIG. 49. A floor plan of a temporal maze. In the double-alternation problem the animal is required to run around twice in one direction and then twice in the other direction before being rewarded.

are present when the incentive is hidden, the animal can bridge the gap. In many delayed-reaction experiments these cues must come from the animal itself. In other experiments they may come from the animal's environment.

*Alternation problems.* One of the best indicators of the ability to solve problems that are almost wholly dependent upon self-initiated symbolic processes seems to be provided by the alternation tests. In the *double-alternation* maze problem (Hunter, 1928), an animal is presented with a simple maze consisting of two alternative pathways, each of which is square and brings the animal back to the starting point. An example of such a "temporal maze" is shown in Fig. 49. The animal is required to learn a sequence of running the alleys. For example, the double-alternation problem requires the animal to go twice to the right and then twice to the left in order to receive a reward.

The rat finds this problem all but impossible to solve unless it is laid out spatially, as in an ordinary maze (Hunter and Hull, 1941). Raccoons (Hunter, 1928), cats (Karn, 1938), and monkeys (Gellerman, 1931a) have all been shown to be able to solve the double-alternation problem after prolonged training. Furthermore, Schlosberg and Katz (1943) have been able to show that rats can master double alternation in lever pressing, a fact of considerable importance in the theoretical interpretation of double alternation. Finally, an important finding about double alternation is that while preverbal children find it difficult to solve, children who can verbalize learn the problem quite easily (Gellerman, 1931b; Hunter and Bartlett, 1948).

It seems to be apparent that, in order to solve the double-alternation problem, the animal must have some central mechanism that can tell him where he is in the sequence. The central mechanism needed is of a fairly low order, considered from the human point of view, since it only involves the ability to "count" to two. The double-alternation problem, however, seems to be a more clear-cut case of symbolic behavior in the absence of secondary supporting cues than does the delayed-reaction problem, since it is almost impossible to find grounds for external cues that can help the animal solve the double-alternation problem. As Hunter points out, even kinesthetic cues must be ruled out, since the kinesthetic cues cannot tell the difference between going around to the right twice and going around to the right only once. In other words, the kinesthetic cues cannot provide the mechanism for counting. We are left with the almost inescapable conclusion that the double-alternation problem involves some central symbolic process. The double-alternation problem, then, is one of the best examples of the second order of symbolic behavior.

It is only fair to say, however, that there is not universal agreement about this conclusion. "Peripheral" theorists have stoutly maintained that somehow the animals must be responding to cues (either internal or external) in order to solve the double-alternation problem. They point as evidence to the fact that double-alternation lever pressing is much easier than double-alternation maze learning. This is because, they would argue, the kinesthetic cues in the double-alternation lever pressing make a shorter, neater pattern. The sequence, two pushes to the right followed by two pushes to the left, takes only a brief period of time and it might be learned as a unit. Schlosberg and Katz (1943) have argued, however, that such reasoning overlooks the point that it is still difficult to imagine how the organism differentiates between the first and second push in the same direction. In other words, how does the organism know when two pushes are up? There are hypothetical answers to this question in terms of peripheral stimuli, but these answers push the refinement of kinesthetic discrimination very far.

The great ease with which children who can use language solve the double-alternation problem is testimony to the greater freedom the addition of linguistic ability gives to symbolic behavior. Children who can talk can manipulate the situation verbally. They can verbally rehearse the correct pattern and then use the cues employed in the verbal rehearsal to organize actual performance in the maze into its proper sequence. Verbal behavior is so important to symbolic behavior that some psychologists have argued that it is impossible to have symbolic behavior without something akin to verbal representation.

*A summary of symbolic functions.* One function of symbols is to lead the organism from place to place. This is the simplest function. The formation of symbolic representation in this sense is nothing more than learning in its most basic aspect. The rat is almost entirely limited to this kind of symbolic representation. A second function of symbolization is to bridge a gap in the absence of stimulation. This we may call the representational function of symbols. The higher animals apparently can produce their own substitute symbols which will last for relatively long periods of time. A third function of symbolization is in verbalization, which serves to lay the problem out as a whole. The entire double-alternation problem can be grasped in a few seconds by an adult human being simply by the use of the symbols RRLL. Human beings have a considerable, though eventually limited, ability to completely disentangle problems by symbolic representation. Verbal symbols also provide a convenient storehouse from which we can immediately bring past experience to bear on the problem at hand. This function of symbols is almost entirely limited to the human organism. Animals can "remember," but almost entirely only when they are faced with the appropriate conditioned stimuli. Humans, however, can draw upon a large number of linguistic symbols, which, in the last analysis, are the most important things that contribute to their high ability to solve problems.

### TRANSFER OF TRAINING

Another factor of paramount importance in the ability to solve problems and think is that of transfer of training. Transfer of training is fundamental to the ability to solve problems *intelligently* and, by thinking, to discover *general* solutions to families or types of problems. Therefore, the reader should understand thoroughly the nature of transfer of training before reading this section.

You will remember that transfer of training is mediated by stimulus generalization and response generalization. Both stimulus and response generalization can occur by way of simple, physical resemblances or by way of learned, secondary resemblances. Positive transfer of training occurs when the response transferred is appropriate to the solution of a new problem, and negative transfer of training occurs when the response transferred is inappropriate or incorrect for the solution of a new problem.

*Insightful problem solving.* The ability to transfer what has been learned leads to intelligent and seemingly purposeful solutions of problems. This is the kind of problem solving that has been called "insightful." We shall see how insightful problem solving is but a special case of the role of transfer of training in problem solving.

This view has been made most explicit by the data obtained by Harlow (1949) on the formation of *learning sets.* You will recall that Harlow trained monkeys on a large number of discrimination problems. At first it took the monkeys a long time to master a problem. After the monkeys had learned several problems, however, a new problem was easier for them. Eventually they could solve a new problem almost immediately. The important point about Harlow's data is that they show that monkeys can learn to solve problems by "insight" after they have had much experience with that type of problem.

In order to see how insightful problem solving arose as a special category, it is necessary to go back and look at some older data. Some years ago, Köhler (1925), an important leader among the gestalt psychologists, made some observations upon the learning of primates that led him to the belief that animals were not entirely victims of past associations and accidents of the environment. Köhler observed the way in which apes solved relatively complicated problems.

Typical examples of the problems that Köhler studied were the box problem and the stick problem. In the box problem, some incentive (usually a banana) was suspended by a string from the ceiling of the chimpanzee's cage. It was out of reach. A series of boxes of various sizes were placed in the cages with the chimpanzees. One particularly bright animal learned to use one of the boxes as a platform from which to jump to the food. This was a very difficult problem, since it forced the animal to be diverted from the primary incentive and to look somewhere else for a means to solve the problem. An even more difficult problem is made by an arrangement of the situation so that the ape must stack two boxes on top of each other before the banana can be reached. In Köhler's account of the behavior of the apes in this situation, he pointed out that they could reason through or "have insight into" the one-box-on-top-of-another problem, but they did not have insight into the gravitational problem of building a stable structure, and the solution to this problem came about largely by trial and error.

The stick problem is even more interesting. A banana is placed outside of the cage beyond the reach of the ape. The animal must learn to rake in the banana with a stick which is provided in the cage. This proved to be a difficult problem in itself, but some apes gave indication of seeing the proper relationship between the stick and the banana.

More striking still, Köhler found one ape, the brightest of the lot, which was able to solve a still more complicated problem. The banana was removed to a point beyond which it could not be reached by only one stick. Two sticks were placed in the cage with the ape; the two sticks were of such a size that one could fit inside of the other, which made a longer stick. After a long time, this particularly bright ape learned to solve this problem.

Köhler described the problem-solving behavior of his apes as intelligent and directional. According to Köhler, the animals showed much more intelligent behavior than is implied in the term "trial and error." Köhler emphasized the ability of the apes to survey the problem situation, to take account of the relationships present, and to organize their behavior in such a way as to solve a problem in a systematic manner. This ability to organize relationships in order to solve a problem is what has been called "insight" by the gestalt psychologists.

Harlow (1951a) points out, however, that data obtained subsequent to Köhler's have not borne out his interpretation in terms of a special concept of insight. Several investigators (Jackson, 1942; Birch, 1945; Schiller, 1949) have found that chimpanzees either do not solve Köhler's problems at all or they solve them only after much *previous experience* with the tools of solution. Harlow points out that there is no evidence that primates solve problems suddenly; with experience gained from many problems they may master new problems with few or no errors, but only as a result of that experience. As has frequently been pointed out, Köhler's original data cannot be cited to the contrary since Köhler knew little or nothing of the previous learning history of his subjects.

There are all sorts of gradations between apparently intelligent insight and random, blind trial and error. "Partial insights" have been recognized for many years (Hartmann, 1933; Wheeler, 1940), and, as Kellogg (1938) points out, the existence of a continuum from insight to trial and error argues strongly against any special category of insightful problem solving. The major determiner of the rate of problem solving, with the ability of the animal held constant, is the amount of positive transfer the animal can bring to bear on that particular problem.

Thus, while insight is recognized as a descriptive term to apply to certain kinds of behavior, it is important to remember that the degree of insight shown depends to a very considerable extent upon the history of learning in the animal in question. The amount of positive transfer which can be brought to bear on a particular problem may itself vary with the organism doing the learning. The nature of individual differences in transfer of training is almost an unexplored field, and some systematic data should go a long way toward helping us analyze some of the phylogenetic differences in ability to learn and solve problems.

*Direction and transfer of training.* One of the concepts that has come out of the experimental work on problem solving in human subjects is that of *direction* or *Einstellung*. The notion is a very simple one; it says that the direction or set given to the subject determines to a very large extent how rapidly and successfully he will solve the problem. For example, Maier (1930, 1931), in some of his experiments on human problem solving, showed that even if subjects are given explicit information about the use of tools and parts in the solution of problems, they did not solve the problems very rapidly or very well unless they were also given a set or direction that told them in what direction to work.

The major function that direction serves is to allow the subject to pick out the appropriate cues from the many that are before him. Some of Duncker's (1945) observations show this. A piece of cork was an essential tool for the solution of the problem in one of his experiments; the problem was much more quickly solved when the cork was sitting loose with the other materials than when it was used as the stopper for an ink bottle also sitting with the other materials. As a stopper for the ink bottle, the subject was given the wrong set about the use of this particular tool.

Direction or set can come about, in an experiment, from the instructions of an experimenter. More than likely, however, in everyday life direction comes about by way of transfer of training. The learner applies what he has previously learned to the solution of the new problem. If the application is correct, positive transfer will result; if the application is incorrect, negative transfer will occur.

The role of transfer of training in direction is illustrated by some experiments of Luchins (1942). Luchins had a group of subjects solve a number of problems such as this one: Given a jar containing 3 quarts, one containing 21 quarts, and one containing 127 quarts, how would you measure out exactly 100 quarts? The solution is to subtract 21 quarts from the 127 quarts, which makes 106 quarts, and then to subtract 3 quarts twice. These problems always required the use of all three jars. After solving these problems, the subjects were given a number of problems in which three jars were specified but only two needed for solution. Most of the subjects attempted to solve the problem by the use of all three jars. Thus, they were applying, incorrectly, what they had learned in a previous problem to a new problem. When the subjects were warned beforehand by the statement, "don't be blind," a much smaller number persisted in an attempt to use all three jars on the second group of problems. So we see that instruction modified the transfer which the subjects brought to bear.

Thus direction can have both a positive and negative effect, and the application of a direction to a new problem can come about through transfer of training. When other factors besides transfer are considered, it appears that the direction is at the mercy of a number of fortuitous things such as the instructions of the experimenter (or teacher) or the arrangement of stimuli in the individual's field. Probably the active use of transfer of training itself in establishing direction comes about through experience. This would be some justification for the old belief that the best way to have people learn how to grapple with new problems is to give them a lot of experience in solving problems unaided by instruction.

## SOME EXAMPLES OF PROBLEM SOLVING

A few of the prerequisites for intelligent problem-solving behavior have been outlined. The ability to manipulate symbols in the absence of external supporting cues is one of these. A background of previous experience from which to draw transfer of training is another. These aspects of behavior set the stage for problem solving. In the next few pages we shall consider some special problems in problem solving by looking at some examples.

*Problem solving in the rat.* The rat, it seems, can solve problems of apparent complexity when conditions are right. One of the best examples of the ability of the rat to solve relatively complex problems is found in Maier's tests (1929), in which the rat is required to put together two previously acquired responses in order to solve a new one.

In one of Maier's problems, a rat is allowed to explore three tables connected by small runways. It is fed on one of these tables and then placed on a second table. Later, the other tables are hidden from view so that the rat must select the way to get to the correct table by putting together the fact that it has been fed on one table with the general pattern of the maze which was previously learned. In another of Maier's problems, the direct pathway to the goal is blocked so that the rat must use an indirect pathway that has never been learned as such but only explored incidental to the solution of another problem in order to get to the goal.

Hull (1935b) has analyzed these problems of Maier's into a relatively simple combination of habits or conditioned responses in varying degrees of strength. It is not necessary to follow Hull's analysis in detail, but by the notion of the *fractional anticipatory goal response* (p. 130), Hull is able to show that the correct solution, on the part of the rat, of Maier's problem, could merely represent the superior strength of one simple habit over another. The important feature about Hull's analysis is that it does not require the rat to react to stimuli in their absence. In other words, Hull's analysis minimizes the role of symbolic representation.

Harlow (1951a) points out that no one has ever really analyzed the cues the rat makes use of in Maier's problems, so that there are no grounds for deciding whether Maier is right in attributing "reasoning" to rats or whether Hull is right in reducing the whole performance to simple habits. Harlow himself points to the importance of the one rewarded trail in Maier's studies, and he suggests that the Maier tests merely represent the effects of one trial learning.

*Problem solving in carnivores.* There is a tremendous literature on problem solving in various subprimate mammals, mostly in cats and dogs. Thorndike's original work (1898) required that cats learn how to escape from puzzle boxes by manipulating a string. Many investigators have followed variants of this puzzle-box technique. Sometimes more than one device must be manipulated so that escape from the box depends upon the performance of a serial act in its correct order. A double-platform puzzle box is shown in Fig. 50.

While many of the studies on problem boxes and other devices were fruitful material for a controversy concerning insight vs. trial and error, they have little significance for us. Unfortunately, while many investigators did approach their studies analytically, very few of them controlled for amount and variety of previous experience. Since previous experience is so critical to an interpretation of the ability to solve problems, these studies do not add very much to our understanding of problem solving. About all that can be said is that the carnivores seem to be somewhere in between the rat and the primates in their ability to solve problems.

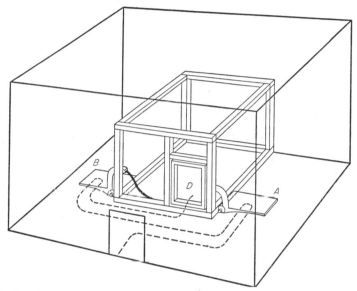

FIG. 50. The double-platform box. When the two pedals are pushed successively the door opens. (*Lashley, 1929.*)

*Problem solving in primates.* As in the case of the carnivores, the literature on problem solving in monkeys and apes is tremendous. One simple example, together with a few critical comments, will serve to make the necessary points about problem solving in primates.

In one of his numerous experiments on primates, Yerkes (1943) placed an ape in a room with an oblong wooden box that was open at both ends. The box was about 170 centimeters long and very narrow. There was a small door in the top of the box at the middle. This door could be opened by the experimenter, and a banana could be locked inside while the ape watched. A pole was also placed in the room; the pole was just the length of the box. Thus, the only way the ape could get the banana which was placed in the middle of the box was to push it out one end with the stick. Initially, the ape exerted much effort in an attempt to pry open the latch of the compartment where the banana was placed. Gradually the ape lost interest in this endeavor, and it exhibited signs of frustration. The ape even attempted to induce the experimenter to obtain the banana for it. In one case this pattern of behavior continued for twelve 15-minute experimental periods which were administered on twelve successive days.

For the particular animal in question, however, the solution came fairly quickly. Yerkes describes the solution as follows: The ape (a chimpanzee in this case) had begun to play with the pole, rolling it about the room. The pole rolled into position alongside the box. The ape reached into the box with its arm in a vain attempt to reach the banana. The ape then ran to the opposite end of the box, where it again looked in. Then, to quote Yerkes (1943, pp. 135–136): "Her next move was to go directly to the pole and grasp it with every evidence of definiteness of purpose. Our notes record: 'At that very instant, and before she had approached the open end of the box with the pole, it was clear to the observer that the problem had been solved.' " The ape instantly pushed the pole through the box and then ran around to the other side to obtain the banana.

The solution was thus sudden and complete, which meets the requirements of insightful behavior. Did the ape suddenly perceive the relationship between the box and stick? Yerkes thought so, and he even gave credit to the ape for symbolically trying out the stick before it grasped it for an actual try. On the other hand, there is the possibility that the solution was a chance one depending upon the random behavior of the ape. After all, it did take the ape quite a while before it was able to grasp the problem.

While we cannot be sure just how the solution to this problem came about, there are some data from Harlow (1951b) that show that the comparatively unintellectual cebus monkey can solve this kind of problem, given enough practice at instrumental problems. Harlow stresses the role of experience in insightful solutions that demand the use of tools. Yerkes does not mention the past history of his animals, but if this particular ape was like those studied by Harlow and others, it probably required a considerable background of instrumental problem solving in order to solve this particular problem.

*Problem solving in human beings.* Problem solving in preverbal children seems to be on a level comparable with that found in anthropoid apes. Kellogg and Kellogg (1933) made a number of comparisons between the problem-solving ability of a young chimpanzee and a young human child who were raised together. The Kelloggs were impressed with the amount of experience necessary for either the ape or the child to solve what appeared to be very obvious problems. It was only when the child began to make use of verbal behavior that he clearly outstripped the chimpanzee in his ability to solve problems. In part, the early similarity between the ape and the child may be due to a slower rate of maturation in the child; nevertheless, it is clear that there is a dramatic change in the ability to solve problems that comes with the use of language.

In adult human beings problem solving reaches its highest levels. Despite this fact, there are still ways in which problem solving in human adults resembles that found in animals. Despite the fact that human beings make use of the manipulatory symbolic function of language to make systematic analyses of problems they are asked to solve, they still indulge in a good deal of blind, trial-and-error behavior (Ruger, 1910).

There is an important methodological difference between studies of problem solving in human beings and in animals. This is dependent upon the use of language. In the first place, the experimenter can give verbal instruction to the human subject that replaces long and tedious training in animals. In the second place, and more important, human subjects can give verbal reports to the experimenter of the particular method that they used in solving a problem at hand. These additional data supply much information that is lacking in studies of animals and young children. We must be careful, however, in interpreting the data obtained by verbal report. There is good reason for believing that people do not always solve problems in the way in which they think they do. Many studies (Hull, 1920; Smoke, 1932; Heidbreder, Bensley, and Ivy, 1948; Bouthilet, 1948) show that some people can solve problems without being aware of the fact. They cannot always tell you how they solved the problems, and they may actually be ignorant of the fact that they have solved them.

If we keep in mind the limitations of verbal reports as data, it is a little easier to interpret the studies that show insightful solutions of problems by human beings. The criterion of insight in human adult problem solving is that the subject reports a sudden flash of experience which tells him how to solve the problem. Because these dramatic solutions to problems do not always occur in laboratory experiments, insight has come to mean almost any solution which is arrived at by deliberate, conscious analysis of the problem (Duncker, 1945).

As in problem solving in lower organisms, rapid and successful solution of a problem depends upon previous experience. It is interesting to note in this connection that sudden experiences of insight into the solution of a problem occur more frequently after past experience with similar problems.

Durkin (1937) had two groups of subjects solve a problem which consisted of an abstract kind of jigsaw puzzle. One group had experience putting together parts of the puzzle, while the other group did not. When asked to put together the whole puzzle, individuals in the group which had had experience putting together parts experienced sudden "flashes" of insight into the fact that they could use what they had already learned. The group which had not been given experience with the parts showed no sudden insight into the solution of the whole.

There are many factors which operate to help or hinder the rate at which human beings solve problems. These are factors that operate generally in learning. One curious exception turns up in data on problem solving, however. Several experiments (Cook, 1934; Ericksen, 1942) show that massed practice is at least as good as and perhaps superior to distributed practice in problem solving. This is very puzzling since practically all other kinds of learning show an advantage of distributed practice. There are probably several reasons for this anomaly. For one thing, the rest periods in these experiments were very long. In Cook's (1934) experiment they were 24 hours in length, and in Ericksen's (1942) experiment they were 48 hours in length. It is very possible for these tasks that the optimal time interval for distribution had passed. The length of these intervals is long enough to allow some forgetting to take place. It is also to be noted that in both of these experiments the biggest advantage of massed practice occurred early in the learning process. Therefore, it may have been that brief practice periods with long rests did not allow the subjects enough time to grasp the relationships involved in the problems, or it may have held them too rigidly to a given *set* or direction.

## THINKING

One of the criticisms frequently put to the experimental psychologist is that he does not pay enough attention to such really important problems as thinking. In a sense the criticism is justified, since the amount of work done upon the problem of thinking is small in comparison with the amount of work done on some less important problems.

In another sense, however, the criticism is not justified. In order to understand clearly what conditions contribute to the nature of thinking, it is necessary to understand fully the more elementary phenomena of behavior. Our knowledge of the basic problems in behavior and learning is still very hazy. Another reason why there has not been too much investigation of problems in thinking is that nobody seems to know very well what thinking is. There is a very serious problem of definition involved in the study of the thinking processes. People mean different things by the word "thinking." In order to be consistent it will be necessary to outline a rather arbitrary definition for future discussion.

Thinking is a special case of problem solving. When we do some "thinking" it is because we have a problem on our hands that bothers us. The thinking process is directed toward the solution of that problem. The difference between thinking and any other type of problem solving is in the use of language. To be sure, in almost all problem solving done by adult human beings, language is used in the solution. In thinking, however, language comes to predominate. Here we are dealing with the formation of concepts that are embedded in language. It is *by* language that the human learner forms concepts. Animals can form concepts, but only in a very limited sense, since language is almost necessary for anything but the most rudimentary manipulation of concepts.

Thinking, then, is linguistic problem solving. It is most frequently implicit problem solving. That is to say, the human being usually thinks without any activity being apparent to the outside observer. Thus there is a lot of mental activity that is not overtly available to the experimenter. This is a fundamental reason why thinking is so difficult to study; much of the actual process of thinking is unavailable for study. It is not surprising that many investigators have preferred to study problem solving in animals rather than human subjects, for much more of the process of problem solving is immediately available in the case of animal behavior than it is in human behavior.

Despite the many difficulties, however, some progress has been made in an understanding of the process of thinking. Much of the experimental work has been concerned with how concepts develop and the role of experience in the direction which thinking takes. Practically no work at all has been done on creative thinking, and in this area we must be content with only the most meager of suggestions.

*Concept formation.* One of the most fundamental conditions in the ability to engage in complicated thinking is the ability to form concepts. There has been a very considerable amount of study of concept formation; consequently there is much which can be said about this kind of thinking.

Leeper (1951) has classified concept formation into three categories: (1) inductive concept formation, (2) deductive concept formation, and (3) inventive concept formation. Most experimental work upon concept formation has been done on inductive concept formation. This consists of the process of classing together objects on the basis of some common characteristic or characteristics. In inductive concept formation the individual abstracts some quality of the object under consideration and then classes that object on the basis of that quality. Thus inductive concept formation requires that the individual recognize the common attribute among several objects and then supply it a name. For example, I may develop a concept of "scholar" by noting that my colleagues apply the term only to full professors over fifty years of age who are a bit eccentric. That the concept does not agree with the more socially accepted version of a scholar is irrelevant. I have acquired a concept and presumably will use it in accord with the qualities I have abstracted.

In deductive concept formation, objects are assumed to belong to a class that has a certain quality in common. The common quality is assumed beforehand rather than discovered. Thus, I may state that all Orientals are untrustworthy. Untrustworthiness in Orientals is not a concept discovered through my personal experience with Orientals, but is a "postulate" which may fit in with my preconceived attitudes toward foreigners.

Inventive concept formation is a lot like inductive concept formation. In inventive concept formation, however, the individual actively tries a number of solutions on the basis of his experience and knowledge before the solution to a problem is finally completed. Thus, in a sense, inventive concept formation is a judicious mixture of deductive concept formation with inductive concept formation. In inventive concept formation the individual forms "hypotheses," but then he tests these hypotheses against his experience.

*Experimental work on concept formation.* A famous experiment by Hull (1920) is illustrative of the experimental work which has been done on inductive concept formation. Hull had subjects engage in a paired-associate learning problem. Chinese characters were paired with English words. Chinese characters, as it happens, are compounded of certain elements, called "radicals," which may vary in position and size within the character. The radicals are sort of analogous to syllables in English. The words "experimental" and "perimeter," for instance, have the syllable "per" in common, though in different locations. In Hull's experiment, whenever a certain radical occurred it was always combined with a certain English word, so that while the English word would be combined with a different character each time, it would always accompany the same radical. The subjects' problem then was to recognize and associate the radical with the appropriate English word.

Most of the time the subjects consciously recognized the appropriate radical and learned to associate it with the proper English word. There were, however, many cases in which the subjects obviously had learned to associate the proper English word with the proper radical, but could not recognize the radical. Thus the subjects were recognizing something that they could not verbalize. Inductive concepts can be formed, then, without direct recognition of the fact on the part of the individual.

Other experimenters (Smoke, 1932; Heidbreder, 1924) have studied the role of hypothesis formation in the discovery of concepts. Smoke (1932) reports that his subjects systematically tested and rejected a number of hypotheses—thus making use of transfer—until they finally came upon one which gave them enough correct responses to be satisfying. Heidbreder (1924), however, emphasizes the fact that the learner does not always have to be actively engaged in hypothesis formation in order to arrive at a solution to the problem. In especially difficult problems, some subjects engaged in what Heidbreder called "spectator behavior"; these subjects would resign themselves to responses which were more or less random, and they would spend their time in passive observation of the material presented to them. Under these conditions, subjects eventually solved the problems. Thus, a period of quiescent observation may be just as valuable as a period of active hypothesis formation.

Another series of studies (Long and Welch, 1942; Welch and Long, 1943) are concerned with the influence of level of abstraction on ability to form concepts. A number of children were presented with four different problems in reasoning, all of which involved the same principle. Two of the problems were placed in a very concrete context, while the other two were presented in a very abstract manner. When the children had learned the principle through experience with a test involving the lower level of abstractness, they could generalize to another version of the problem on the same level of abstraction, but not very well to a higher level of abstraction. Those children who readily discovered the principle concerned in the test involving a lower level of abstraction could generalize to the higher order of abstraction better than those children who needed hints and promptings to discover the principle.

*Deductive thinking.* In deductive thinking it is not necessary for the individual to learn the nature of the concept through experience. A concept is presented to the individual, and he is expected to manipulate it in certain ways. The ways in which concepts are supposed to be manipulated have been studied and codified by the logicians. Because the nature of logic is so intimately connected with thinking, it has frequently been assumed that the rules of logic are the psychological principles of thinking. Nothing could be further from the truth. The rules of logic are exactly like the rules of mathematics or the rules of chess. They are principles for manipulating things; in the case of chess the rules are for the manipulation of men on a chessboard; in the case of logic the rules are for the manipulation of ideas or concepts. Presumably the rules of logic which are propounded and argued by logicians have been arrived at by experience. They are rules which enable us to deal with our external world in a way which achieves workable results.

Thinking, on the other hand, is a psychological process. We learn the rules of logic, which is to say that we learn to adjust our thinking processes to certain rules that have been established by logicians. Psychologically these rules are quite arbitrary; they are only meaningful in the context of logic. The relationship between the psychology of thinking and formal logic has been admirably propounded by J. R. Kantor (1945, 1950).

The important problem posed by a distinction between thinking and logic is that thinking by the rules of logic is not always psychologically easy. People are governed by emotional attitudes and prejudice. College students, for example, who have learned the rules of syllogistic thinking, and who can use these rules when placed in abstract examples, make mistakes when the concepts to be manipulated have an emotional toning for them.

This last point is demonstrated in an experiment by Morton which is presented by Underwood (1949). Morton compared the ability of college students to solve two sets of syllogisms that were identical logically. One set was presented in symbolic $(x, y)$ terms; the other set was presented in concrete terms with the use of materials from current events. These subjects solved the two sets of syllogisms completely differently. The set that was couched in terms of examples from current events most frequently showed conclusions which reflected the prevailing opinions of newspapers and radio commentators. A conclusion which conformed to public opinion was more likely to be accepted than one which conformed to the rules of logic. A further demonstration of this point is provided by an experiment by Thistlethwaite (1950), who found that college students made many more "mistakes" in solving syllogisms when they involved racial issues than when they involved neutral material.

Some earlier studies established the importance of the *atmosphere effect* in deductive thinking (Woodworth and Sells, 1935; Sells, 1936; Sells and Koob, 1937). These studies show that the verbal context of the syllogism is an important determiner of the conclusion which will be accepted as valid. If the premises are stated in the affirmative, there will be a tendency to accept an affirmative conclusion even though it may not be correct. Woodworth (1938) points out that the atmosphere effect is not confined to syllogistic reasoning, but occurs in many situations involving complicated verbal responses. Woodworth reminds us that in writing, a frequent error is to make the verb agree with the singular or plural atmosphere of the subject phrase rather than the noun which is the grammatical subject.

*Creative thinking.* Very few experimental psychologists have had the bravery to attack the problem of creative thinking. Woodworth (1938), in his textbook on *Experimental Psychology,* devoted a few pages to the topic, but these pages consisted almost entirely of a discussion of the subjective reports of famous creative scientists, artists, and writers about how they went about their creative activities. There is no experimental evidence on creative thinking at all. So there is very little concrete information we can discuss about the relationship between creative thinking and learning.

There is one strong suggestion which turns up in practically all the protocols obtained from creative scientists and artists. This suggestion concerns the important role of unconscious development in the creative processes. Nearly everyone has had the experience of trying in vain to solve a difficult problem, and, after a brief period of rest, of suddenly coming upon the solution. These kinds of experiences have been interpreted as "unconscious cerebration"—thinking without awareness. Whether this interpretation is correct or not we cannot say, but it certainly is a reasonable notion.

No one has made very specific suggestions about how the unconscious development of ideas works. One notion, however, is that unconscious thinking must be very much like conscious thinking, the only difference being that we are not ourselves aware of the thinking process during unconscious thinking. Another notion is that the unconscious process is not really thinking at all, but merely a recovery process, whereby competing ideas, inhibition from work, and bad directions or *Einstellungen* are dissipated. This is probably the more acceptable interpretation, but the lack of evidence on the subject makes any interpretation hazardous.

Certainly creative thinking must involve at least two aspects: (1) a thorough mastery of the information or techniques to be manipulated in the situation, and (2) the ability to organize and reorganize the material in novel combinations. The first of these aspects implies the highest level of acquisition of information before creative thinking can be undertaken. Today's mathematician cannot "create" without knowing much about the nature of mathematics. "Natural" geniuses occasionally turn up who are able to create new ideas without a complete knowledge of their field. There are several examples in the history of mathematics and many in the history of music. But these individuals usually happen along at a time when some completely new field is being developed so that only the barest essentials of knowledge are necessary to create. This does not happen very often, however, and we can state almost unequivocally that knowledge is fundamental to creativity.

The second of these factors is the intangible element. We do not know what the basic ability is, and how much of it is a true ability of the individual or how much a matter of the circumstances of the moment. Various psychologists interested in problems of intelligence have offered theories about this ability, but none of these is very satisfactory. Perhaps a major part of the ability is acquired. If this is true, a major problem for the psychology of learning is opened up. Certainly, one of the most exciting things to investigate about learning would be the acquisition of the ability to manipulate ideas in original ways. We must not put out too much hope for this, however, for the psychology of learning is a long way from the understanding of the fundamentals which would be necessary before such a program could be profitably undertaken.

# CHAPTER 14

# LEARNING AND THE NATURE
# OF THE LEARNER

All living organisms have the ability to maintain themselves by internal chemical regulations, to reproduce themselves, and to respond to external stimuli. One might add that all living animals have the ability to learn. This may not be quite true, but the ability to learn has been demonstrated in simple one-celled organisms, in degenerate parasitic organisms, and in highly organized multicellular animals. So certainly the ability to learn is as widely distributed as the animal species themselves.

Animals show great differences in their abilities to learn, however. The kind of learning of which an earthworm or water snail is capable is of quite a different order from that of which a chimpanzee is capable. These differences in ability to learn occur between species, in which case they are clearly inherited differences, and they also occur between different individuals that are closely related. In the latter case the differences in ability to learn may be produced by environmental as well as by hereditary mechanisms.

In this chapter we shall briefly survey the differences in learning ability between animals of different species, and, in addition, examine the differences in ability to learn which occur between human beings of different groups and classes. In this survey, three factors will be emphasized: (1) the relation of learning ability to the necessity for adaptability forced on the organism by its environment, (2) the relation of learning ability to what is called and measured as intelligence in human beings, and (3) the relation of learning ability to other differences, principally in the anatomy of the nervous system.

## THE PHYLOGENY OF LEARNING

First of all we shall examine the available evidence on learning ability throughout the animal kingdom. Actually there is a tremendous amount of

275

data available—far more than would be possible to cover in a single, short chapter—so the studies we shall examine will be highly selected studies which are intended to establish the main trend of findings in the comparative literature.

*Limitations.* Some words of caution are needed concerning studies in comparative psychology. Many of the older studies consisted in qualitative observation of animals under natural conditions. The data obtained from these observations are anecdotal in character and very unreliable. We cannot take much stock in them. Consequently, we shall be limited to the data obtained in experimental studies, even though these probably give us a conservative picture of the learning ability of animals.

Another important shortcoming of comparative psychology concerns the extent to which we may actually compare the learning ability of different animals. Studies of animal behavior are conducted by different investigators at different times using different techniques. This makes it difficult to compare the ability of one animal or group of animals with another. We can only arrive at some rough estimates of the relative ability of different kinds of animals to learn; a more refined comparison must await more precise, standardized methods.

*Classification.* All organisms are divided into two major groups—plants and animals—and each of these is further subdivided into a number of major subgroups. These are called "phyla." Each phylum in the animal kingdom consists of a group of animals all of which have some fundamental characteristics in common. The phylum Porifera, for example, consists of multicellular animals organized in loose, semicolonial forms. The animals in this phylum have no specialized organs, but they do have specialized cells. The principal feature of the Porifera is a canal system through which water is circulated as a means of bringing nutriments and oxygen to the cells.

Some of these phyla include many animals and some include only a few. Some of them are more important in an evolutionary sense than others. We cannot review learning ability in all of the phyla now recognized by zoologists, and consequently we shall pick out for discussion a few important ones with many members. Because each of these phyla will include many different kinds of animals we cannot be exhaustive in our treatment of the phylogeny of learning. We shall select representative members of each of the phyla, and for the more important phyla we shall select representative members of each of the important classes and orders of these phyla.

Our account of the phylogeny of learning will be in a rough approximation to the evolutionary order—from simple to complex—of the animal kingdom, but because no two zoologists agree exactly in this evolutionary order, this cannot be a very precise treatment. In all cases, intelligence and learning ability do not follow the more frequently accepted evolutionary orders. Many animals that are lower on the evolutionary scale appear to be more intelligent or have a higher ability to learn than many animals higher on the scale. In order to help the student who is unfamiliar with the classification of animals, Table II, which lists the phyla and major classes of the phyla with typical examples of each, is given.

TABLE II

*The Important Animal Phyla and Major Classes of Each*

| Phylum | Classes | Examples |
|---|---|---|
| Protozoa | Mastigophora | *Euglena* |
| | Rhizopoda | *Amoeba* |
| | Sporozoa | *Plasmodium* |
| | Ciliata | *Paramecium* |
| Porifera | Calcarea | Sponges with spicules of lime |
| | Noncalcarea | Sponges with spicules of silica |
| Coelenterata | Hydrozoa | *Hydra* |
| | Scyphozoa | Jellyfish |
| | Anthozoa | Sea anemones |
| Platyhelminthes | Turbellaria | *Planaria* |
| | Trematoda | Liver flukes |
| | Cestoda | Tapeworms |
| Echinodermata | Asteroidea | Starfish |
| | Echinoidea | Sea urchin |
| Annelida | Polychaeta | *Nereis* |
| | Oligochaeta | Earthworm |
| Arthropoda | Crustacea | Lobster, crab, sow bug |
| | Chilopoda | Centipede |
| | Insecta | Cockroach, ant, wasp, beetle, etc. |
| | Arachnida | Spiders |
| Mullusca | Gastropoda | Snail |
| | Cephalopoda | Octopus |
| | Pelecypoda | Oysters, clams, etc. |
| Chordata | Superclass Pisces | Fish, lampreys, sharks |
| (Subphylum | Superclass Tetrapoda | Amphibians, reptiles, birds, and |
| Vertebrata) | | mammals |

## The Lower Organisms

All the groups below the vertebrates—which are members of the phylum Chordata—and those vertebrates below the birds will be considered as "lower organisms." This somewhat arbitrarily delimited group includes by far the greater portion of animals numerically speaking, but it is certainly the weaker half of the phylogenetic scale, intellectually speaking.

*Unicellular animals.* All unicellular animals belong to the phylum Protozoa. Despite the fact that each animal consists of only one cell, the members of this group are surprisingly complex. As a matter of fact, the cells in the Protozoa are far more complicated than the cells of the Metazoa or multicellular organisms. These unicellular animals are also surprisingly capable of adaptive behavior.

Many investigators have looked for evidence of learning in various members of the Protozoa. And there is certainly abundant evidence that these animals change their behavior—at least for short periods—as the result of "experience." Whether these changes in behavior are truly learning is another matter. It does not matter what we call it, as long as we recognize that the modifiability of these organisms is of a very primitive and simple variety. A few examples will make this clear.

Two early experiments (Smith, 1908; Day and Bentley, 1911) were performed on *Paramecium*. *Paramecium* is a little cigar-shaped animal covered with cilia, or hairlike processes (Fig. 51). One important characteristic of *Paramecium* is its avoidance reaction. When it encounters certain stimuli it will back away rapidly at an angle and then, by means of the action of its cilia, swim off in the opposite direction. Smith (1908) conceived the idea of putting paramecia in a capillary tube so that when they reached the surface film at the end of the tube they could not back away at an angle and go off in another direction as they usually do. Initially, the animals tried to do this. They would back away from the surface film, but they could not progress forward again without bumping into the film again. After bumping into the film a few times they would finally double up and turn around. The interesting fact is that on successive trials the animals would spend less and less time bumping into the surface film before turning around. Day and Bentley (1911) concluded that the animals had truly learned to turn around.

Another even more simple example of the same kind of modification of behavior in the Protozoa comes from Mast and Pusch (1924). They worked with *Amoeba,* which is negatively photosensitive—it tends to avoid light. They placed a beam of light in the path of the moving amoeba; it would bump into the beam and then back away. They found that the number of bumps per trial would decrease with each trial. They thought

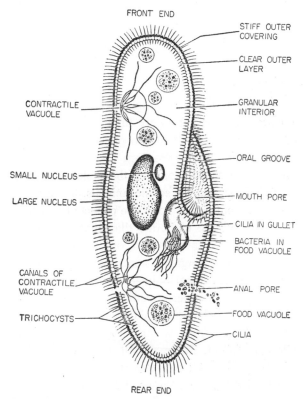

FRONT END

STIFF OUTER COVERING

CLEAR OUTER LAYER

CONTRACTILE VACUOLE

GRANULAR INTERIOR

ORAL GROOVE

SMALL NUCLEUS

LARGE NUCLEUS

MOUTH PORE

CILIA IN GULLET

BACTERIA IN FOOD VACUOLE

CANALS OF CONTRACTILE VACUOLE

ANAL PORE

TRICHOCYSTS

FOOD VACUOLE

CILIA

REAR END

FIG. 51. *Paramecium caudatum.* Despite the fact that this is a one-celled organism, it has a very complicated structure. The animal locomotes by beating its cilia and rotating in a forward spiral movement. (*Buchsbaum, 1948.*)

this effect might be fatigue, but they tested for retention and found that the animal had retained the habit of immobility after a rest period.

Both of these examples represent just about the simplest cases of modification of behavior. The second example—the case of the *Amoeba*—is an example of what G. Humphrey (1933) has called "habituation." Habituation is learning *not* to respond to stimuli which should be ignored or avoided if the organism is to survive. Humphrey believes that habituation is the simplest of all the categories of learning. It is even more fundamental than the basic associative process in the Pavlovian conditioned response. It may well be that this kind of modification is just about the limit to which the learning ability of the Protozoa can go.

A much higher level of apparent learned behavior in a Protozoan is presented by French (1940). French showed that paramecia could learn to escape from a glass tube that permitted free swimming. The manner in which the paramecia accomplished this is strikingly reminiscent of Thorndike's trial-and-error learning experiments with mammals. As a matter of fact, French called his experiment an example of trial-and-error learning in *Paramecium*. If French's observations can be repeated and extended, we may have evidence that a much higher kind of learning is possible in unicellular animals than was heretofore thought.

*Simple multicellular animals.* The two phyla which follow the Protozoa in the evolutionary scale are the Porifera and the Coelenterata. The Porifera (the familiar household sponge is the skeleton of one of these animals) are very primitive, usually sessile animals. They have no organized organ systems; consequently, it is not to be expected that the behavior they exhibit would be much more elaborate than that of the single-celled animals. The coelenterates are much more complicated and active creatures. They possess well-organized organ systems, including a rudimentary nervous and sensory system. Typical animals of this phylum are the jellyfish and the little hydra of fresh-water streams.

As you might expect, behavior in the Porifera is very simple. The osculum or mouth, which admits water, opens and closes in response to stimulation (Parker, 1919), but each cell acts individually. Coordination is only due to the fact that all cells are stimulated at once. It is not surprising that these animals have no more detectable ability to learn than do the Protozoa.

The coelenterates have a specialized system for the conduction of impulses from receptors to effectors. It is to be expected, then, that these animals would show a much higher level of adaptive behavior. The kind of modifiability which Humphrey called habituation has been definitely established in the sea anemone (Fleure and Walton, 1907).

It is curious that a considerable portion of the effector system of these animals is without nervous control. These animals can eject small barbs, which are toxic, into their immediate environment. They do this on proper stimulation, but each cell operates on its own; it is not controlled by the nervous system. One would expect, then, that this reaction would not be easy, or even possible, to condition.

Thus, despite the greater capability of the coelenterates for adaptive behavior, there is no evidence which shows that they can *learn* any better than the simple one-celled animals or the primitive Porifera.

In terms of structure, a considerable advance is made in the phylum Platyhelminthes, which includes the flatworms. Many of the animals of this phylum are degenerative parasites which spend most of their lives inside of a host organism. One would expect that the capacity for adaptive behavior in the parasitic worms would be very low, since they have found anatomical and ecological ways of adapting to their environments.

The free-living flatworms, however, present a considerable advance over the early phyla in terms of structure. The flatworms are bilaterally symmetrical animals; that is, each side of the body is a mirror image of the other. They exhibit a metabolic gradient in the cephalocaudal direction; the metabolism is highest in the head region. Finally, the nervous system is rather well organized. It has two trunks which go down each side of the body and two enlargements, or ganglia, in the head end of the animal. Thus the nervous system is under the domination of a plexus of nerve cells in the anterior region. This is the beginning of a brain.

Many of the flatworms exhibit elaborate patterns of behavior. The little *Planaria,* which may be found in fresh water, is a very interesting creature to watch under the dissecting microscope (Fig. 52). It has several complex swimming and feeding reactions. Its behavior varies with its motive state, *i.e.,* it is inactive when it is full and active when it is hungry.

Evidence of learning ability in the flatworms is scant, however. Hovey (1929) managed to get something which looks very much like learning out of the marine flatworm *Leptoplana.* This animal is excited to movement in the presence of light. When it is touched on the anterior end, however, movement ceases. Hovey brought a dark-adapted leptoplana into the light, whereupon it began to creep; he touched it on the head, and it stopped. Thereafter, whenever the animal began to crawl in the light, Hovey would stop it by touching it. Finally the animal came to be entirely motionless in the light, so that it was not necessary to "reinforce" the animal by a contact. This inhibition was retained for a considerable period.

*Echinoderms, mollusks, and annelids.* The animals we have mentioned thus far are all animals which depend very little on adaptive, modifiable behavior for survival. Some of these animals behave little more than do some plants. Even the most active of these creatures generally rely on relatively stereotyped behavior.

Gradually, however, through the phylogenetic series, plasticity in behavior becomes more important. Animals higher in the series are more frequently faced with situations in which an instinctive or reflexive mode of behavior will not be adaptive. This plasticity develops very slowly, but the next few phyla which we shall review will show definite advances in the ability to learn.

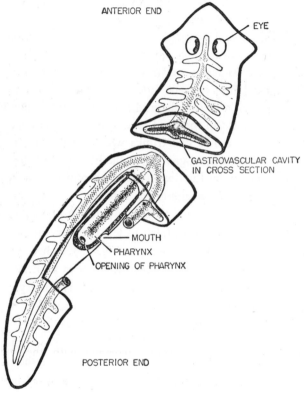

Fɪɢ. 52. *Planeria.* A free-living flatworm. Body structure, including nervous system, is bilaterally symmetrical. (*Buchsbaum, 1948.*)

The phylum Echinodermata in some ways is lower on the evolutionary scale than the flatworm. The animals in this phylum are radially symmetrical rather than bilaterally symmetrical. There is no dominant gradient of metabolism or dominant neural ganglion. The nervous system is organized into a radial net. Perhaps the most familiar example of an echinoderm is the starfish.

Jennings (1907) and Ven (1921) have both reported something which looks very much like learning in the starfish. Maier and Schneirla (1935), however, present fairly conclusive evidence that Jennings and Ven had not really demonstrated learning. The inherent limiting capacity of the echinoderms does not seem to be the nervous system, since there are ganglion cells to be found in the nervous system, but rather seems to be body form itself, which precludes a cooperation between the parts of the body based upon the control of a dominant part. The echinoderm is then doomed to be clumsy in its actions. And, because the body does not have a dominant region of nervous activity, probably it can never learn as a whole, though it may be possible that the separate parts (such as the rays of a starfish) can be habituated in Humphrey's sense. Thus, while the zoologist generally places the echinoderms higher on the evolutionary scale than the flatworms, behaviorally the echinoderms appear to be inferior to the flatworms.

A really great advance, both physically and behaviorally, is found in the segmented worms, the annelids. The annelids are bilaterally symmetrical animals whose bodies are divided up into separate segments. In the annelids there is a nerve trunk which runs the length of the body. In each segment there is a local enlargement of this trunk, with lateral fibers running out to the body. In the foremost segments of the worm there is a very large ganglion which is the "brain" of the animal. It is the organ which asserts the dominance of the anterior region of the body in behavior. Despite this dominance, the annelid still has sufficient freedom from complete control by this ganglion so that when it is removed, it is very difficult for the casual observer to detect a difference in behavior.

In the annelids we have the first clear-cut evidence of learning of a relatively high order. Copeland (1930), working with the marine worm, *Nereis,* paired a light stimulus with clam juice diffused through water for a number of trials. The clam juice would attract the worms. After a number of trials, the animals learned to appear when the light alone appeared. This is good evidence for the Pavlovian conditioned response at this low a level in the phylogenetic scale.

A famous experiment by Yerkes (1912) definitely established that the earthworm, also an annelid, could learn a simple T maze. Light was used to make the animals move through the maze (earthworms are negatively phototropic and will thus move to avoid light). One alley of the maze was wired so that the animal would receive an electric shock; also sandpaper and a salt bed were placed in this alley. In the other alley, the worm was brought in contact with warm, moist earth. Yerkes's worm learned to go to the alley with the warm earth in about 100 trials. A repetition of the experiment by Heck (1920), using many animals, confirmed Yerkes's results.

One of the most striking results obtained by Yerkes and by Heck was that the animals could still perform the learned response after the cephalic ganglion had been removed. Furthermore, removal of the cephalic ganglion did not prevent new animals from learning the problem. Thus, whatever changes learning brought about in the nervous system were not limited to the cephalic ganglion. Perhaps this is not surprising in view of the fact that the cephalic ganglion is not entirely necessary for coordinated behavior in the earthworm.

The phylum Mollusca consists of a group of animals which are fundamentally bilaterally symmetrical, though many of them depart from strict symmetry. Most of the mollusks are quite active, though, of course, in the adult stage the familiar bivalves (oysters, clams, etc.) are sessile. One class of the mollusks, which includes the squid and octopus, represents one of the most complex and highly developed of the invertebrates. Certainly these animals are the largest invertebrates. They possess well-developed nervous systems, and sensory systems.

Thompson (1917) found it possible to establish a true conditioned response in the fresh-water snail. He paired a tap to the muscular foot of the snail with the presentation of lettuce to the mouth parts. Normally, when food is presented to the hungry snail, chewing movements will result. Also, under normal conditions, extraneous stimulation, such as a tap to the foot, will result in no mouth movements. After a large number of trials, however, a tap to the foot came to elicit chewing movements, even when the tap was not accompanied by food. The most remarkable fact about this particular demonstration of learning is that the foot is controlled by a ganglion (pedal ganglion) separate from that which controls activity of the mouth parts (cephalic ganglion). Apparently the ganglion which controls the foot gained some degree of functional control over the ganglion which controls the mouth parts.

In the case of the higher mollusks—the octopus and the squid, for example—the cephalic ganglion exerts a very considerable controlling influence over the rest of the nervous system. It becomes the main center of integration for the input from the sense organs.

These mollusks, with their highly developed nervous systems, are capable of learning behavior that we would ordinarily think of only in connection with the higher vertebrates. Some experiments by Boycott and Young

(1950) show that the octopus is capable of very rapid discrimination learning. They trained their animals to pick up a crab when it was presented alone, but to avoid the crab when it was presented with a white square. The crab was dropped into the octopus's tank. Ordinarily, the animals would rush toward the crab and pick it up. Some of the times, however, the octopus was shocked when it picked up the crab. This was always when the crab was presented on the white square. In a very few trials, the animals learned to avoid the crab when it was presented with the white square and to pick it up when it was presented alone.

*Arthropods.* One of the most successful groups of animals, from the evolutionary point of view, is the phylum Arthropoda. This phylum includes the insects and their near relatives as well as a number of marine and fresh-water forms, such as the lobster and the crayfish. These animals are segmented, and perhaps their most characteristic feature is the hard, chitinous exoskeleton. The nervous system of the arthropods is typically of the "ladder type." That is to say, there is a pair of ganglia in every body segment, with the ganglion pairs connecting both lengthwise and across. There is a cephalic ganglion which exerts dominance over the others and which is primarily responsible for the integration of behavior.

In the insects, which comprise a class of the arthropods, the nervous system is very highly developed. And it is in these animals, primarily the social insects, that the ability to learn is most highly developed. Other arthropods can learn simple discrimination habits and conditioned responses (Yerkes and Huggins, 1903; Schwartz and Safir, 1915), but in the insects we come upon some remarkable instances of adaptive behavior which can hardly be surpassed anywhere below the primates.

Perhaps the most striking examples of adaptive behavior in the insects comes from Von Frisch's famous observations upon bees (1950). Von Frisch has spent a lifetime experimenting upon the vision of bees and their very remarkable ability to communicate with one another. In one of his early experiments he showed that bees could learn to discriminate between a blue and a gray. He placed a number of watch glasses full of water on top of a series of gray papers. In addition, there was one watch glass full of sugar water placed on top of a piece of blue paper. The bees could easily learn to pick out the blue paper and ignore the gray papers, no matter how they were arranged.

There has been much attention given to Von Frisch's work upon communication in bees. By a series of brilliantly executed experiments he has clearly established that bees can communicate, by an elaborate series of movements, such things as location and distance of a food supply. It is not altogether certain whether or not this ability is learned; Von Frisch himself avoids comment on the matter, but Thorpe (1950) takes it almost as established fact that the ability to communicate must be learned. It is indeed difficult to see how it could be otherwise, but the possibility exists that it is not. Therefore, we cannot conclude that it is certain that communication in bees is learned.

Schneirla (1929, 1933) has clearly shown that ants can learn very easily some rather complicated mazes. Furthermore, if the maze is changed so that a former blind alley becomes a true pathway, the ant readily adjusts to this change. There is little of the blind persistence in old modes of adjustment one sees in other invertebrates.

Maier and Schneirla (1935), in their book on comparative psychology, summarize the results of many naturalistic studies of insect behavior which suggest very strongly that the daily life of the insects—social insects in particular—probably depends to a large extent upon learned behavior. It certainly seems to be well established that flying insects such as wasps and bees learn a great deal about the environment immediately around their nests. Such learning seems to be at a much higher level than anything similar in other invertebrates. The terrestrial insects are not far behind the flying insects in their ability to find their way about familiar territory. Despite the strong dependence upon instinctive modes of behavior in the insects, it is apparent that these animals have developed the ability to learn to a high degree. Indeed, this group appears to be an exception to the general rule that where instinctive behavior is highly developed, the ability to learn is not.

*Lower vertebrates.* The most important group of animals in the phylum Chordata (animals that have a stiff tube and nerve cord running the length of the body) is the vertebrates. These animals, characterized by a chain of cartilages or bones running lengthwise (the vertebrae) and a cephalic enlargement containing the brain, have reached the highest level of evolution behaviorally. Some of the animals in this group appear to have less learning ability than some of the insects, but the highest levels of learning ability are also reached in this group.

The lower vertebrates include the cyclostomes, the sharks, the true fish, the amphibians, and the reptiles. This group of animals includes a tremendous range of different types. Behaviorally, these animals differ from one another almost as much as the arthropods differ from the vertebrates. One important characteristic, however, which these animals possess in common is a very highly developed central nervous system. The nervous system is much more completely organized in these animals than it is in any of the invertebrates. Another feature of the development of the nervous system in these animals is the development of a very large ganglion under the influence of the sensory systems in the dominant anterior portion of the body.

A relatively high order of learning ability has been clearly established in the fish. Reeves (1919) was able to teach several different kinds of fish to discriminate colors. One color would be associated with food, while another was not. After a large number of trials, the fish would learn to swim to the compartment that was illuminated by the color associated with food.

In another experiment, Haralson and Bitterman (1950) rigged up a Skinner box for fish. They taught fish to strike at a small target with the nose by reinforcing them with small amounts of food. The animals learned to do this quite readily, and as far as could be determined from the preliminary experiments, fish do not differ too greatly from rats in simple, operant behavior.

There is but little evidence to show that the amphibia have any greater capacity for learning than do the fish. Maier and Schneirla (1935) suggest that the amphibia may learn to improve feeding responses and other basic activities through practice. It is characteristic of the lower organisms in general that such behavior is "instinctive" and does not improve much with practice. Thus, while in general the amphibian seems to possess a lower ability to learn than, say, the social insects, the *kind* of learning in which it engages under natural conditions may be more characteristic of the higher organisms.

It should be noted in passing that several investigators (Yerkes, 1903; Burnett, 1912) have found that the frog can learn simple maze problems. The limit of the ability of the frog to learn mazes seems to be considerably below that of the ant, but then, the maze does not represent nearly so well the kind of activity that the frog engages in while under natural conditions as it does for the ant.

The reptiles show the first indication of fairly well developed forebrains. The forebrains are small, but their appearance is of considerable significance. Of interest in this connection is a comparison between the learning ability of an amphibian, the newt, and a reptile, the terrapin (Seidman, 1949). The terrapin possesses a cortex that is something besides an accessory to the sense of smell, while the newt does not. These two animals were tested on their relative ability to reverse a direction habit set up in a simple T maze. The terrapins used in the experiment were able to reverse the learned habit much more readily than were the newts. The terrapins showed a much greater "plasticity" in their behavior. This experiment is one of the few direct comparisons of learning ability between two animals which differ in some important neurological characteristic. The comparative study of learning needs many more such studies.

While the behavior of reptiles seems to be much more readily modifiable than that of lower animals, they still have not achieved a very high degree of "intelligence." Apparently they can solve only very simple problems. Kellogg and Pomeroy (1936) experienced great difficulty in training water snakes to negotiate a very simple maze. Yerkes (1901) trained a turtle in a kind of problem box. While Yerkes points out that the turtle is better than the frog at this sort of thing, it still takes a very large number of trials for the animal to learn the relatively simple habit involved. The reptiles are more adaptable than the lower vertebrates, but they are still a long way from the intelligence of the higher birds and mammals.

*The Higher Organisms*

To the biologist, it is not very sensible to draw a line between reptiles and birds to separate lower from higher animals. For the psychologist, however, it seems to be the most logical place to make the division. Modifiability of behavior is a very conspicuous feature of mammalian and bird behavior. There are examples of very high orders of intelligence both among the birds and the mammals. Certainly there is no other group of vertebrates that can approach these two groups in this respect.

*Birds.* Birds possess a large repertory both of stereotyped, "instinctive" behavior and of modifiable behavior. They are active creatures with well-developed senses, particularly in vision and hearing. The central nervous system is both large (in comparison to body weight and size) and well developed. Especially are their cerebral hemispheres and cerebellums highly organized.

The experimental studies of learning ability in birds are too numerous to cover. There are many examples, well known to everyone, of the adaptability of bird behavior. Homing, migration, feeding of young, song patterning are all cases of well-organized adaptive behavior.

There is no doubt that some of these instances involve considerable amounts of learning. Homing is a good case in point. Homing ability can be greatly improved by training (Warden, Jenkins, and Warner, 1936). While homing behavior cannot entirely be the result of learning, the evidence is strong that the learning of landmarks plays a considerable role.

Another interesting case of highly organized behavior on the part of some birds is the ability to "talk." Strangely enough, this fascinating ability has been much neglected by comparative psychologists. Mowrer (1950) has made a beginning of the study of how birds learn to talk, but about all that can be said at present is that they have a surprising talent for it. Mowrer reports that birds will sometimes spontaneously repeat phrases that they could only have heard months previously. Mowrer is of the opinion that birds use their ability to talk in order to keep their keeper (a secondary reinforcement!) near them. Mowrer also cites Lashley, who thinks that the ability to talk may be sexual in origin and tied up with courtship behavior.

Skinner (1950) has studied learning in the pigeon in great detail. His experiments are too elaborate for us to review in any detail; suffice it to say that by appropriate techniques of reinforcement he has trained pigeons to "match from samples" and perform very complicated discriminations. In popular publications, Skinner has reported his success in training pigeons to play a toy piano and to "cooperate" in playing ping pong and in many other clever demonstrations.

There is no way to compare directly the learning ability of birds with that of the higher mammals. Few experiments allow us to make even a rough comparison. Skinner, however, has paralleled almost completely his experimental work on rats (1938) with that on the pigeon (1950), and the remarkable fact is that the differences which exist between these two species in operant behavior seem to be primarily differences in such things as absolute magnitude of rate of responding, etc. Skinner's experimental situations, however, were not designed to explore the limits of intelligence in these animals, so it is not quite fair to conclude that the pigeon is about comparable to the rat in learning ability.

*Mammals below the primates.* The student of psychology should be well aware of the great variety of learned acts which have been studied in mammals. Mazes, problem boxes, Skinner boxes, and discrimination boxes have all provided abundant data on the learning ability of mammals. The comparative literature shows that there are some differences in the ability to learn certain specific problems. These differences appear to be related to the kind of environment to which the animal has become adapted. The rat, for example, seems to learn the maze better than most lower mammals and about as well as the higher mammals, including man. This seems to be because the maze represents the sort of learning problem that the rat has become adapted to; it could be that natural selection has especially fitted the rat for maze learning.

The curious fact is that there is little difference in the *rate* of learning of simple problems among the mammals. The rat learns to operate a lever in the Skinner box just about as fast as does the dog. The ant, as a matter of fact, learns mazes almost as well as the rat and is perilously close to the human in this ability. The real feature which seems to differentiate the higher animals from the lower is the *difficulty* of the problem to be learned. We have already seen (p. 255) that the delayed-reaction test and the double-alternation test seem to show the intellectual differences between various species. Rats do very badly on the double-alternation test, but monkeys can learn to solve the problem quite easily.

Maier and Schneirla (1935) have gathered together all the data obtained on the delayed-reaction test prior to 1935 and have constructed a table which shows roughly the comparative ability of different mammals on this task. Rats are at the bottom of the list of the animals tested. Raccoons probably come next, with cats following along closely behind. Dogs, lemurs, monkeys, and the anthropoid apes follow along in that order.

A good example of a test of learning ability which seems to discriminate between mammals of various species is Hamilton's (1911, 1916) multiple-choice test. In this test, an animal is presented with four doors, one of which is open. The only thing that the animals can learn from trial to trial in escaping from this box is that the door which was open on the previous trial will not be open on the next trial. Hamilton tested this device on rats, gophers, cats, dogs, one horse, and humans. The gophers were the poorest in performance on this device. Apparently they could not learn to avoid the door which had been open on the previous trial. The rats were next in line, with the horse following close behind. The cats were definitely superior and the dogs even better. Of course, none of these animals came anywhere near Hamilton's human subjects.

Many other examples, which show approximately the same order of ability through the mammals, could be cited. These behavioral studies show that the intellectual capacity of mammals roughly follows the same order as the degree of development of the cortex. In the rat the cortex is smooth, without the convolutions which so materially increase the surface area of the cortex in the higher species. Most of the rat's cerebral cortex is taken up with direct sensory or motor projection areas. Relatively little of the rat's brain is "silent." Since it is usually assumed that the silent areas of the brain are the "association" areas, the common conclusion has been that the rat's brain lacks extensive association areas. In cats and dogs the convolutions increase in number and the *relative* amount of area devoted to direct projection seems to decrease. Particularly prominent in this respect is the development of a relatively large silent area in the frontal lobe. As a matter of fact, the conspicuous development of the frontal area of the cortex is one of the most striking features of the brain of the higher mammals.

It seems to be clear, then, that the development of the capacity to learn and retain complicated problems is accompanied by an increase in the complexity and dominance of the cerebral cortex. The increased capacity to solve problems is also accompanied by an elaboration of the frontal areas of the brain. The exact significance of this last fact eludes us; we do not know precisely what function the frontal areas have in the higher mammals. We can only point to the apparent relationship between anatomy and behavior with the hope that the intervening link in terms of function will someday be found.

*Primates.* It is in the primates that the highest level of intellectual capacity is reached. In accord with the general pattern throughout the animal world, this increased capacity for modifiable behavior is accompanied by a decrease in the importance of stereotyped and instinctive behavior. It is also characteristic that the high level of intellectual capacity in the primates is accompanied by the greatest elaboration of the cerebral cortex.

Psychologists have studied the behavior of the primates in great detail. The number and variety of problems which have been devised for monkeys and apes to solve is tremendous. It would be pointless, however, to review each of these problems in this discussion. In Chap. 13 (p. 265), some examples of problem solving in apes were discussed in detail. It is only necessary to add that, on practically all the problems studied, the primates do far better than any of the lower mammals. And it should be remarked that the anthropoid apes are, in general, much better than the monkeys. One gets the impression, from reading the writings of those who have worked with apes, that the chimpanzees are the most intelligent of the apes. This may be an illusion, however, based on the fact that the chimpanzee is much more tractable than his cousins; then, too, the chimpanzee resembles the human being much more in temperamental factors than do other apes; consequently, we may have a "halo effect" in judging the intelligence of chimpanzees.

Perhaps the most interesting thing about the learning ability of the primates is its limitations. Kellogg and Kellogg (1933), in their study of the behavior of an infant chimpanzee and a child reared in the same home for a year, found that the chimpanzee kept up in its intellectual development with the child until the child began to use words. After this the chimpanzee began to drop behind the child. Apparently an important limitation to the ability of the ape is its inability to speak.

This inability to speak in itself is a major puzzle in the psychology of the apes. Apparently the ape has all the vocal apparatus necessary for speech. The chimpanzee can make all the vowel and consonant sounds in human speech. Several investigators in the past (see Warden, Jenkins, and Warner, 1936) have attempted to teach apes to speak. Only meager success was achieved. Nearly all observers report that the apes attempt to inspire when speaking. Thus, the best that can be achieved is a kind of whispered "mama" or "cup."

More recently, Hayes (1950) has made a serious and determined effort to make chimpanzees talk. After much effort, Hayes finally managed to get one of his subjects to whisper three words, "papa," "mama," and "cup." With intensive training, this chimpanzee got to the point of using these words appropriately; that is, it would say "cup" when it was thirsty. However, this was about the limit of its talking ability. Hayes had reared this chimpanzee in his own household, and it cannot be said that the chimpanzee did not have every opportunity to learn to talk. Hayes thinks that the chimpanzee's inability to talk is not due to a lack of intelligence but rather seems to be a kind of aphasia. There seems to be something missing in the nervous system which makes symbolic speech possible.

This inability to talk, probably as much as anything else, is responsible for the gulf in learning ability that exists between the chimpanzee and the human being. Nowhere else in the phylogenetic series is there such a gap in intellectual ability as there seems to be between the average ability of the anthropoid apes and that of the human being. The exact reasons for this gap remain one of the great unsolved problems of comparative psychology. Perhaps Hayes's hypothesis of aphasia in the apes may serve as a useful clue in the solution of this problem.

## INDIVIDUAL DIFFERENCES IN HUMAN LEARNING

There are a few pathologically deficient human beings who do not appear to have an ability to learn much above that of the anthropoid apes. As a matter of fact, there are occasional cases of human beings who seem to be below the level of the lower mammals (Fuller, 1949). On the other side of the picture, of course, learning ability in human beings far exceeds anything in the animals. Thus it is apparent that the range in ability to learn within the human species is almost as great as that over the entire phylogenetic range below man. We shall examine some of these individual differences in learning ability in man and how they are related to intelligence and age in particular.

### Intelligence and Learning Ability

One of the most common assumptions in psychology is that there *should* be a high relationship between ability to learn and intelligence as measured by intelligence tests. As a matter of fact, intelligence is very frequently defined in terms of the ability to learn. The surprising fact is, though, that no one has been able to establish a very high relationship between intelligence tests and ability to learn in laboratory tests of learning. Indeed, as we shall see, practically all varieties of data on learning and intelligence show very low relationships between the two. This fact obviously needs some explanation, but perhaps we had better defer the explanations until we have examined some of the data.

*Rate of learning and intelligence.* Woodrow (1940), in a very large-scale study, correlated the *rate* of gain on several different tasks with intelligence test scores. The average correlation between rate of gain and intelligence was .085. This figure means that there was practically no relationship at all between intelligence and rate of gain. The conclusion needs to be tempered by several facts, however. The tests of learning were very simple, involving such things as addition and code substitution. With more complex tasks a higher relationship between rate of learning and intelligence may have been found. The second fact is that only college students were used as subjects. This means that there was a severe restriction in the "range of talent." Students of statistics will remember that restriction of range of talent has the effect of reducing correlations. It could well have been that with a larger range of intelligence, a higher correlation may have been found.

*Memory of learned material and intelligence.* It would certainly be expected that there would be a higher relationship between verbal memory and intelligence than that found by Woodrow between rate of learning and intelligence. Such is the case, though the correlations are still surprisingly low. Garrett (1928) correlated intelligence test scores (Thorndike's test) and a number of different rote and logical memory tasks. All the memory tests were positively related to intelligence, but the largest correlation was only .39. This was a correlation between memory of a Turkish-English vocabulary and the intelligence test. Some of the other correlations were practically zero. None of the correlations was of sufficient magnitude to assure us that the intelligence test and the tests of memory were measuring very many of the same things.

Even lower relationships are found between gains in school learning and intelligence. Dysinger and Gregory (1941) find that the correlation between the difference in scores on an objective examination given before and after a course in psychology and the Army Alpha Intelligence Test was to all intents and purposes zero. The same result was found in the case of gains in biology (Drake, 1940).

These correlations are very perplexing, since intelligence tests themselves are composed of items which the individual must have "learned" sometime in his past. Apparently there is little or no relation between what an individual learns incidental to his daily activities and what he may learn at a specific time in a test of learning. Woodrow (1946) has put it one way by saying that there is no general "improvement" or "gain" factor.

Woodrow (1946) has attempted to show why these rather peculiar results are really to be expected. He takes as his starting point the two-factor theory of intelligence—the theory which says that there are two groups of factors which make up intelligence, a general factor and factors specific to any one test. Under the assumptions of this theory, Woodrow points out, it is quite possible for the correlation between a general intelligence factor and gain to be zero. Therefore, it is not surprising that intelligence-test scores (which are heavily weighted with the general factor) should show negligible correlations with gains from practice. There are factors peculiar to any situation which determine the rate of learning in that situation; it is these specific factors which reduce the correlation between gains and intelligence. Thus, argues Woodrow, there is nothing really paradoxical about the low correlations between learning ability and intelligence. Ability to achieve in any specific situation may not be largely a matter of intelligence, though intelligence will correlate highly with achievement in general. The correlations between the general factors in any specific learning situation and intelligence will remain essentially the same from the beginning of practice to mastery, but the correlations between the specific factors may change. To illustrate: If motivation is a specific factor, and if two individuals have two different levels of motivation, then their performance on the last trial of a nonsense-syllable learning experiment may be very different while their performance on the first trial may be about the same. Their initial scores were about the same because they had the same ability (general factor). One was more motivated than the other; consequently, he had a higher score at the end. That part of his score at the end which was different from the other individual represented the contribution of motivation. The contribution of ability to the final score was about the same, but this is obscured by the difference in motivation. Such a hypothetical situation would produce a low correlation between intelligence and gains.

## Age and Learning Ability

It is very obvious that there are large differences in ability to learn in individuals of different age groups. This fact is recognized in the educational psychologist's concept of *readiness,* which is concerned with the right mental and chronological age with which to begin some school subject, and it is recognized by many familiar adages, such as "You can't teach an old dog new tricks." This source of individual differences in ability to learn has been studied intensively in the last half century, and we shall attempt to review a few of the more important findings from this work.

*Learning ability in children.* Unfortunately there is not very much experimental work which enables us to compare the ability to learn in very young children with that in older children. There are a few isolated studies on very young children, but the results of these are not always consistent.

Mateer (1918) studied the ease of conditioning in a group of children ranging in age from one to seven years. She placed a blindfold over the child's eyes as a conditioned stimulus. The unconditioned stimulus was a piece of chocolate placed in the mouth. The conditioned responses were swallowing and chewing movements elicited by the blindfold. The correlation between number of trials to a criterion and chronological age was .571, which indicates that there was a fair-sized relationship between ease of conditioning and age. Other studies (Osipova, 1926; Dernowa-Yarmolenko, 1933) have shown an *inverse* correlation between ease of avoidance conditioning and chronological age in older children, but this may be because the avoidance-conditioning problem is too "easy" for older children, and they may misinterpret the nature of the experiment.

A critical point in the learning history of the individual is the point at which he begins to use words. The transition from learning which is preverbal to learning which is verbal has not been very well studied, but there is one study (Kuenne, 1946) which is suggestive of some possibilities. This was a study in transposition (p. 71) or ability to respond to relational properties of stimuli. It turned out that the children who were too young to have highly developed verbal skills behaved in the same way as animals do in this situation (p. 73); they were unable to master "far-transposition" problems, whereas the older children found the "far-transposition" problems quite easy. Older, verbal children spontaneously verbalized the principle necessary to the solution of the problem, while the younger children did not.

Another example of a problem which, while it can be solved by intelligent animals, would be much easier to solve with the use of words, is the double-alternation problem (Hunter and Bartlett, 1948). Again, ability to solve this problem shows a high correlation with chronological age (between two and six years) and mental age. The older children, who solved the problem most easily, could verbalize the solution, while the younger children could not.

Practically the only studies on verbal learning per se in very young children are concerned with the immediate-memory span. Numerous investigations have plotted the course of the increase in immediate-memory span with an increase in chronological age (see Bayley, 1926; Hurlock and Newmark, 1931). Immediate-memory span shows a high correlation with chronogical age; consequently the measurement of it has found its way into the standardized intelligence tests.

The literature on the relative learning ability of school-age children is tremendous. It would be fruitless to review all or even a large part of the studies in this area. Instead, we shall attempt to outline briefly the principal findings, with a few representative studies as examples.

As far as simple perceptual-motor skills are concerned, there is little evidence that ability to learn increases with age (McGinnis, 1929; Hicks, 1931; Langhorne, 1933). Munn (1946) points out that older children usually show a higher level on *initial* performance, but the total *amount* and percentage of improvement on any task is about the same for the younger children as it is for the older children. Munn suggests that the higher initial level of performance usually found can best be accounted for in terms of maturation.

The ability to memorize nonsense syllables as well as connected material is correlated with chronological age (Stroud and Maul, 1933). When the correlations are corrected for *mental ages,* however, they practically become zero. It is largely on this evidence that it has been concluded that memorizing ability is related to intelligence in children.

The data on learning ability in children are summarized by Munn (1946). After an examination of the available data, Munn came to the conclusion that there was very little difference in learning ability per se between children of various ages. The differences which do show up in various studies are usually in retention and in problem solving. Munn suggests that these differences probably are the result of differences in motivation and amount of previous transfer, rather than differences in the ability to learn. The differences which exist between very young children and older children in perceptual-motor learning, Munn thinks, are largely due to differences in maturation. Munn admits that he cannot support these conclusions directly with data. The fact that Munn and others cannot support their hypotheses with any data means that much of the research of the relative learning ability of children has been beside the point. Certainly there is very little novel or new information which comes out of this research. Perhaps the next few years may see a revival in interest in this field, with an emphasis upon the *causes* of individual differences with age rather than the simple measurement of such individual differences.

*Learning ability in adults.* The available data on learning ability in adolescents and adults are considerably more interesting, for they settle some problems which have been with us for a long time. It has been long assumed that older people do not learn so well as adolescents and people in the years of early maturity. Common folklore, in fact, has it that the period of adolescence is the period of greatest learning ability. The experimental data do not quite support these beliefs, and it will be interesting to compare what has been assumed about learning ability and age and what has actually been found to be the case.

The most extensive study of learning in adults is that of Thorndike *et al.* (1928), and we shall draw very heavily upon Thorndike's data. Thorndike measured the ability to learn in adults of various ages with a truly amazing variety of tests. These included learning to draw lines while blindfolded, learning to write with the wrong hand, learning codes, learning new languages, and learning various school subjects. As the result of the examination of all these data, Thorndike suggests the curve shown in Fig. 53 as the best approximation to the true curve of the relationship between learning ability and age. You will notice that the curve rises rather steeply

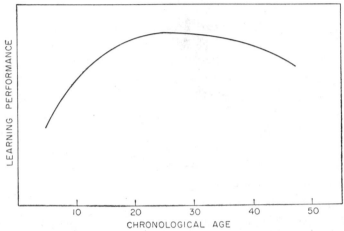

FIG. 53. "Ideal" curve for learning ability as a function of age. Thorndike drew this curve after testing people of different chronological ages on many learning tasks. (*Thorndike et al., 1928.*)

through the years of adolescence and reaches a peak somewhere in the mid-twenties. Thereafter the curve shows a slow decline. The general relationship portrayed in this curve must be modified by a number of particular conditions, however. The last limb of the curve declines less steeply, for example, for individuals who have more education. The curve also declines less steeply for meaningful tasks than it does for meaningless tasks. This last fact was interpreted by Thorndike to mean that in more complex tasks, older individuals can compensate by increased motivation and experience for a decline in "sheer modifiability."

From Thorndike's data it is apparent that the commonly held beliefs about age and learning should be modified in two ways. (1) The maximum ability to learn appears to be reached in the mid-twenties rather than in the teens. (2) The decline in ability to learn in older people, while present, is not nearly so severe as we have been led to believe. To be sure, in the years beyond fifty there seems to be a much steeper decline than that indicated by Thorndike's curve (Miles, 1933a, 1933b, 1935).

It is interesting to note that the ability to learn, as measured by Thorndike and Miles, as well as in Ruch's (1934) experiments, appears to decline *less* severely with age than do intelligence-test scores (Miles and Miles, 1932; Jones and Kaplan, 1945). Furthermore, the decline of intelligence-test scores appears to set in a few years earlier than does decline in learning ability.

## HEREDITY AND INDIVIDUAL DIFFERENCES IN LEARNING ABILITY

How much of individual differences in learning ability can be attributed to differences in genetic make-up? This is a fundamental question, to which, I am afraid, there is no answer. The data on the phylogeny of learning suggest that there must be very profound differences in learning ability that are attributable to the genetic limitations of the organisms in question. There are very few data, however, that compare the learning ability of animals of the same species which differ in known, genetic constitution. What little data there are supply some very provocative results, and we shall briefly review some of them.

Tryon (1940a, 1942), in a famous experiment, demonstrated that maze-learning ability in the rat is inherited to a very considerable degree. He began his experiment in 1927 with an unselected population of 142 rats. These rats were trained on a 17-choice point maze for a total of 19 trials. The score for each rat was the total number of entrances into blind alleys (number of errors). He then mated together the rats which showed the fewest number of errors (the "brightest rats") and those which showed the largest number of errors (the "dullest rats"). The same procedure was followed for the next generation. The brightest offspring from the original bright group were mated together, and the dullest offspring from the original dull group were mated together. This procedure was continued for 18 generations.

The results of Tryon's experiment are shown in Fig. 54. The graphs in Fig. 54 show the distribution curves for errors in each successive generation. Note that in the original group the ability was approximately normally distributed. In the second generation the distributions hardly changed, but by the third generation ($F_2$), the dull and bright groups began to separate from one another. By the eighth ($F_7$) generation, the distribution of scores for the two groups hardly overlapped at all. Tryon's experiment

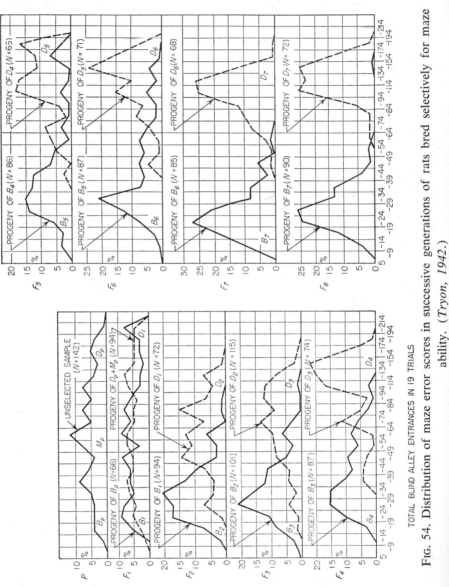

FIG. 54. Distribution of maze error scores in successive generations of rats bred selectively for maze ability. (*Tryon, 1942.*)

was a very well controlled one, and there seems to be no doubt at all that he had selectively bred two groups of rats with different abilities at maze learning. Tryon's experiment has been repeated (Heron, 1935), and today there are many psychological laboratories in America that keep separate stocks of maze-dull and maze-bright rats for experimental purposes.

Maze-learning ability is not a unitary trait. There are many factors that contribute to a rat's ability to learn mazes (Tryon, 1940b). Consequently, Searle (1949) has attempted to discover what factors are responsible for the differences in maze-bright and maze-dull rats. First of all, Searle found that the maze-learning ability was not general to all learning problems. On some learning tests the dull rats did as well as the bright rats. Secondly, Searle compared the two groups of rats on a number of other psychological characteristics. He found that the bright rats were more emotional, they were more highly motivated for food under standard conditions, and they were not timid of apparatus and strange things. The dull rats, on the other hand, were not highly motivated for food, were timid of apparatus and strange things but were relatively bold in free open spaces. Searle came to the conclusion that the differences in the maze-dull and maze-bright rats were not primarily intellectual ones but were motivational and emotional ones. The bright rats showed better performance in mazes because they were more highly motivated and less afraid of the maze.

Thus, it may be argued, Tryon did not demonstrate a genetic difference in learning ability per se. However, the differences he did demonstrate were genuine enough. Searle's conclusions suggest that the frequently observed differences in learning ability between animals of different species may not be intellectual but rather may be differences due to higher activity levels, less timidity, etc. It is certainly most probable that differences in learning ability reflect a number of different basic factors rather than a unitary trait of sheer ability to learn. Woodrow's (1946) inability to find a general "learning factor" in human subjects bolsters this belief. Probably individual differences in human learning are due to a number of factors, both inherited and acquired. Some of these factors may be very specific to some particular kinds of learning problems and others may be more general, running through several problems or groups of problems. Certainly a vast amount of work needs to be done before we can begin to see what the factors are which contribute to learning ability in animals and humans. This is one area of research where the application of factor-analysis techniques seems to be very promising.

# CHAPTER 15

# EMOTION AND CONFLICT

It is apparent to everyone that learning has a considerable role in emotional and affective behavior. Most of our likes and dislikes, for example, are acquired. All students of elementary psychology know that fear of snakes and mice is not necessarily native. Many if not most of our fears are the result of experience. Clinical psychologists and psychiatrists place much emphasis upon the role of experience in the development of disturbances of personality. Thus, learned emotional reactions are of great importance in the development of personality.

So it is easy to see why many investigators have concerned themselves with the role of learning in the development of emotionally disturbed behavior. A problem which is perhaps equally important, but one which has received much less attention, is that of the role of emotional behavior in learning. We shall have occasion to examine these questions briefly in the course of this chapter, as well as some questions about behavior under conflict. Fundamentally, then, this chapter is concerned with the interaction between emotion and learning.

## CONDITIONED EMOTIONS

*Emotional conditioning in infants.* One of the most famous of all conditioning studies is that of the conditioning of emotional reactions by Watson and Raynor (1920). They were interested in the possibility of teaching an infant to fear. All sorts of stimuli were tried as fear-producing stimuli—white rats, dogs, masks, burning newspapers—none of which produced an emotional response. One stimulus which definitely produced a startle reaction followed by crying was a loud sound. Watson and Raynor then conditioned the sight of a white rat to this fear reaction by pairing the presentation of the rat with the sound. After a very few pairings the rat came to elicit the reaction originally specific to the sound. This conditioned fear generalized to other animals and to furry objects, such as a wad of cotton.

This experiment attracted a great deal of interest. Watson and Raynor thought that it showed how the complex and irrational fears of daily life could arise, and they placed much emphasis upon the importance of conditioned emotional reactions in the development of the personality of the child. But perhaps the most striking feature of the experiment itself is the remarkable ease with which the fear was conditioned.

Unfortunately Watson and Raynor's results have not always been easy to duplicate (Bregman, 1934), though H. E. Jones (1931) finds that fear of electric shock is easy to condition in infants. Jones (1930a, 1930b) also conditioned the galvanic skin response in infants. The galvanic skin response is a result of activity of the sympathetic division of the autonomic nervous system, and it is this division which is so prominent in the physiological activity of emotion.

These studies show that emotionally disturbed states can be and probably frequently are conditioned to neutral stimuli during the early life of the infant. It is a hazardous jump to say that *all* emotional responses except those to a few unconditioned stimuli are acquired by a process of conditioning, but it is probably safe to say that emotional conditioning is an important factor in the early development of human and animal behavior.

Nothing has been said thus far about emotional responses other than fear, but child psychologists have long recognized the importance of conditioning in the development of affection and love in the child. Child-guidance manuals emphasize the importance of feeding the infant in pleasant and cheerful surroundings and the importance of a relaxed and enjoyable attitude on the part of the mother. This advice is probably justified, since it is known that the eating activities of the infant can be either conditioned or inhibited by simple conditioning procedures (Munn, 1946).

*The nature of emotional conditioning.* Skinner (1935, 1937) has made a strong case for two different kinds of conditioned responses. One of these, limited to responses mediated by the autonomic nervous system, is based upon the principle of contiguity or association; the other, limited to the skeletal muscles, is based upon the principle of effect. Thus, Skinner would argue, many of the autonomic responses which have been called emotional responses—sweating, increase in pulse rate, dilation of pupils, etc.—are conditioned by the simple process of association. If a stimulus (such as an electric shock or the firing of a pistol) that elicits these responses is paired with a neutral stimulus, the neutral stimulus will come to have the power to elicit these responses.

These autonomic responses, however, are *not* what Skinner calls emotion. Emotion, according to Skinner, is a "state" like drive; it is reflected in the change of strength of operant behavior. Emotion causes people to raise their voices and speak rapidly, or it causes them to speak haltingly and softly. It changes the measurable characteristics of all kinds of operant behavior. While Skinner does not emphasize the role of autonomic activity, it must be apparent that the disruptive changes in operant behavior are usually accompanied by autonomic activity of the sort that has usually been identified as emotional.

Mowrer (1947) suggests that the state of emotion which causes a disruption in operant behavior is the result of autonomic activity. This seems to be a very reasonable interpretation, and it is reminiscent of the old James-Lange theory of the consciousness of emotions. According to Mowrer, the conditioning of emotions would be a twofold process; first of all, conditioning of autonomic responses occurs by the principle of association. The conditioned stimulus which sets off these autonomic responses then indirectly becomes a cause for a state of emotion, since the emotional state results directly from these visceral responses. While this interpretation is not foolproof, it is a remarkably consistent and adaptable notion of the nature of conditioned emotions.

Mowrer carries this analysis one step further in the case of conditioned fears and anxieties. He agrees with Skinner that operant behavior (skeletal responses) must be conditioned by the principle of effect. He goes further and says specifically that they must be conditioned by need reduction. He then uses this interpretation to account for punishment and avoidance learning.

An example of avoidance learning will show how Mowrer's notion works. A rat is placed in a small box divided into two compartments by a low barrier. The floor of both compartments is electrified so that the rat can be shocked. The rat is placed in one of the compartments and a buzzer is sounded. A few seconds later the electric shock is turned on. Both the buzzer and the shock are kept on until the rat jumps over the barrier into the next compartment. When it gets into the next compartment it is allowed to rest for a few minutes. Soon, however, the buzzer sounds again, followed by shock. The rat soon learns to avoid the shock by jumping into the other compartment when the buzzer sounds. When the rat jumps to the buzzer it is turned off.

Because the buzzer is contiguous with the shock, says Mowrer, it comes to elicit a lot of emotional (autonomic) reactions that are unpleasant to the rat; jumping over the barrier terminates the buzzer and thus the emotional response is relieved. This constitutes need reduction, which in turn is reinforcing for the response of jumping over the barrier. So really, one might say, the rat jumps over the barrier because jumping terminates the unpleasant emotional activity conditioned to the buzzer. Such behavior has the appearance of *anticipatory* behavior—and Mowrer believes that he has solved the problem of anticipatory behavior—which has always been something of a stumbling block to reinforcement theory.

Mowrer has some incidental evidence to bolster this view. He shows that anxiety reduction is correlated with rate of learning (Mowrer, 1940). He has, furthermore, been able to show that rate of learning of the jumping response is highest when the buzzer is terminated coincidental with the response rather than before or after it (Mowrer and Lamoreaux, 1942). While Mowrer cannot offer direct proof of the dual nature of learning involving emotional activity (particularly fear), his analysis is a useful one in both learning theory and personality theory.

We need not necessarily accept the distinction between contiguity conditioning of autonomic responses and need-reduction conditioning of operant responses, but we can accept the notion that disturbance of operant behavior as the result of an emotional conditioned stimulus has autonomic activity as its intermediary mechanism. It is probably the autonomic activity that is conditioned first (the experimental evidence shows overwhelmingly that autonomic responses are easier to condition than skeletal responses), and the operant activity is cued by the autonomic response.

## EXPERIMENTAL NEUROSES

One of the most striking contributions of the study of learning to an analysis of the problems of emotion and personality mechanisms comes from some observations made in Pavlov's laboratory. These observations have become the basis of what has been called "experimental neurosis." The experimental neuroses since Pavlov's time have been investigated in a wide variety of conditions and situations, but because of their priority we shall begin with Pavlov's observations.

*Pavlov's experiments.* In the course of many studies on the conditioned salivary response, workers in Pavlov's laboratory noticed that animals sometimes developed long-standing disturbances of normal behavior.

Pavlov began to study these disturbances seriously after an experiment in which he attempted to condition salivation to an electric shock. The electric shock worked all right as a conditioned stimulus for a while, but after an attempt at the study of generalization, the conditioned salivation was replaced by a violent struggle (defensive reaction).

A subsequent experiment led Pavlov to an intensive study of disturbances of behavior. This experiment started out as an attempt to test the limits of form discrimination in the dog. An animal was trained to salivate to the presentation of a luminous circle on a screen. Then an attempt was made to get the animal to discriminate between a circle which was reinforced and an ellipse which was not reinforced. The ellipse was gradually changed over the course of the experiment so that it came to look more and more like the circle. For a while, the animal continued to discriminate, but then as the two stimuli became more and more alike, discrimination suddenly became poor. In addition, the whole character of the animal's behavior changed. The dog, which had been trained to stand quietly in the stock, began to struggle and squeal. Eventually the animal became quite violent and resisted being taken to the experimental room. This behavior is what Pavlov called an experimentally produced neurosis.

Pavlov continued the study of experimental neurosis in dogs with great zeal, though with the idea of investigating individual differences between dogs rather than in studying the course of the phenomenon. Consequently, for the study of the mechanisms involved in experimental neurosis, we shall do better to turn to the studies from other laboratories.

*Subsequent studies of experimental neurosis.* Since the original investigations in Pavlov's laboratory, experimental neurosis has been produced in many different kinds of animals in different laboratories. In the United States, W. H. Gantt has closely followed Pavlov's work and has been able to confirm Pavlov's observations on experimental neurosis in the dog produced by difficult discrimination (Gantt, 1936).

Liddell and his coworkers at the Cornell Behavior Farm have studied for many years the production of experimental neurosis. Liddell has not limited his observations to dogs, but he has studied sheep, goats, and pigs. Liddell (1944) has summarized many of his observations in a chapter on experimental neurosis, and it is from this chapter that we shall draw our description of the experiments in his laboratory.

In Liddell's laboratory the conditioned flexion response has been used rather than the conditioned salivary response. In flexion conditioning a buzzer serves as a signal for an electric shock to the animal's forelimb.

Using this conditioning technique, Liddell and his associates have produced many different varieties of experimental neuroses by many different methods. In sheep, for example, experimental neurosis was produced by forcing the animals to discriminate between a signal associated with shock and one not associated with shock. The result was a state of agitation similar to that observed by Pavlov in dogs. Liddell noticed, in addition, that the disturbance spread to behavior outside of the experimental room. In other cases, Liddell has produced experimental neuroses by making too long a delay between the conditioned stimulus and the shock.

Liddell has observed several kinds of disturbed behavior. Some animals, instead of developing agitated states, go into conditions of rigidity and inhibition of behavior. These too persist outside of the laboratory. Actually Liddell and his associates have recorded a great variety of different kinds of disturbances. Some of these have been psychosomatic in character—disturbances in heart rate, gastrointestinal functioning, etc.—while others have been purely behavioral.

In all the experiments from this laboratory, the role of restraint imposed upon the animals during the course of the experiments has been emphasized. The animals, of course, must be domesticated before experimentation can begin. This means that their normal behavior must be restrained. They are harnessed into the conditioning stock at the beginning of experiments, and this is a further restraint. The monotonous repetition of the stimuli used in the experiments furthers the strain under which the animals are placed.

Gantt (1944) has given us a complete case history of a neurotic dog. Unfortunately this account suffers from the defects of all case histories. We are not sure what caused the disturbed behavior in the dog, since it was subjected to so many different treatments—electric shock, difficult discrimination, delay, etc.—and we are not sure how much of the disturbed behavior was due to the nature of the particular dog studied. At any rate, there is no doubt that this dog was seriously disturbed in its behavior and that this disturbance persisted for many years.

Some of the most interesting observations of experimentally produced disturbances of behavior come from Masserman (1943). Rather than use the classical salivary or flexion-conditioning techniques, Masserman set up an operant situation in which cats were trained to open a small food box after a conditioned stimulus had been presented. The techniques that were used to produce abnormal behavior were frustration, conflict, and punishment. Suffice it to say at present that by these techniques Masserman was able to produce markedly deviant behavior in his cats. Some cats became "phobic" toward the box, particularly after punishment. Other cats went into semicataleptic states, refusing to move or eat for long periods of time. Masserman attempted a wide variety of therapeutic devices to relieve the neuroses after they had been established. Rest was about the most effective means of alleviating the animals' symptoms. Other things such as reducing the hunger drive through force feeding outside of the experimental room, "reassurance," and social imitation of other, nonneurotic cats were also effective.

*Behavioral disturbances in rats.* One very special case in the story of experimentally induced disturbances of behavior concerns experiments with rats. The rat is the standard animal of the psychological laboratory, and it is not surprising that workers eventually turned to it for the production of experimental neurosis. Cook (1939) reported experimental neurosis in the rat in a situation which was much like that of Pavlov's or Liddell's. The animals were restrained, a factor which Cook believed to be important, and secondly a conflict was set up between punishment (electric shock) and reward (food) to the same response. The results were much like those achieved in other animals by other investigators. Bijou (1942, 1943), in experiments much like Cook's, has reported essentially similar results.

Some dramatically different results were reported by N. R. F. Maier about the same time as Cook's. Maier (1939) made use of the discrimination response required on the Lashley jumping stand. The Lashley jumping stand, which is shown in Fig. 55, consists of a platform upon which the animals are placed and a wall with two openings in it which is about 8½ inches away from the stand. The rats are trained to jump to one of these two openings. Usually light pieces of cardboard are placed in front of the opening with different symbols on them; one, for example, might have a triangle on it and the other might have a square. One of the cards will fall back as the rat hits it, allowing the rat to enter the opening, while the other will remain firmly in place when the rat hits it so that the rat will fall into a net below. Rats usually learn quickly to discriminate between the stimuli on the cards and to jump with a high degree of accuracy to the correct door. In Maier's experiment, however, sometimes, during training of the rats, they resisted jumping, and when this happened, Maier stimulated them with a blast of compressed air or electric shock.

During this procedure some of Maier's rats apparently become violently disturbed. This disturbed behavior was striking indeed. Suddenly, at one trial, an animal would jump off the stand for a great distance and begin to run about the room wildly. After a few minutes the animal would stop and go into a convulsive fit and after violent clonic and tonic spasms would become comatose.

In these experiments, the situation was set up so that the rats could not solve the problem. No matter what the rats did, only about half the time

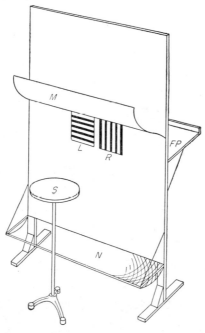

FIG. 55. The Lashley jumping stand. The rat jumps from the stand to one or the other of the doors. If the choice is correct the stimulus card gives way; if the choice is wrong the rat falls to the net below. (*Lashley, 1935.*)

would the jump from the platform toward one of the cards lead to a successful response. The stimuli were randomly associated with the reinforcement. Maier believed that it was the conflict set up by this impossible discrimination that led to the abnormal behavior.

It soon became apparent to other investigators, however, that something else might well account for the bizarre behavior that Maier found. It was found that this same kind of behavior could be produced in untrained rats simply by auditory stimulation (Morgan and Morgan, 1939). It turned out that in Maier's original experiments, no rat showed the abnormal pattern of behavior unless the air blast was used. The air blast itself produced a sound which was just about at the right frequencies and intensity to produce the largest number of audiogenic seizures, as the behavioral disturbance produced in this situation came to be called.

There has been more than a decade of controversy concerned with whether or not the behavioral disturbances observed in Maier's experiments can occur without auditory stimulation. Finger (1944), in his review of the subject, definitely took the stand that all the observed disturbances of behavior produced in Maier's experiments and others like them were due to the presence of auditory stimulation. Maier has defended the idea that at least in part the observed disturbances of behavior are due to psychological conditions. We must, however, defer Maier's discussion of this problem for a bit.

### Theories of Experimental Neurosis

As you can see by now the data on experimental neurosis are not very systematic. About the only general feature of all the experiments which have been reported is that some form of disturbed behavior has been claimed in all of them. The deviant behavior has differed greatly in kind. Some of the things reported have been catalepsy, somnambulance, refusal to eat, aggressiveness, resistance, hyperactivity, and change of behavior toward cagemates and humans. These disturbances of behavior have been produced by a wide variety of conditions, including excessively fine discrimination, restraint, prolonged delay periods, conflict between rewards and punishment, frustration of high motivation, etc. It is not surprising, then, that the theories of experimental neurosis have been numerous and contradictory. We shall review these theories, not so much from the standpoint of pitting them against each other as from an attempt to see how each can account for certain kinds of data.

*Pavlov's theory.* Pavlov framed his theory of experimental neurosis within the outline of his general theory of cerebral physiology. Pavlov believed that the primary cause of the experimental neurosis was a conflict in the cerebral cortex between opposed forces of excitation and inhibition. The excitation is produced by reinforcement and the inhibition by extinction. Both conditioning and extinction occur in discrimination, and when the stimuli get close to one another, the conflict between the opposing forces of excitation and inhibition gets strong enough to disturb the whole cerebral physiology.

Pavlov's theories about cerebral physiology have more or less fallen into disrepute, though the interpretation of experimental neurosis in terms of conflict has not. If we were to rephrase Pavlov's theory in more contemporary language, we might say that experimental neurosis occurs because of the inability of the animal to tell when to respond and when not to. This conflict could be the result of a discrimination that is too difficult for the animal. It should be noted in passing, however, that such a conflict can arise from causes other than difficult discrimination. If the animal must delay a conditioned response too long after the presentation of the conditioned stimulus there will again be a conflict between the tendency to respond and the tendency to inhibit that response.

In an evaluation of Pavlov's theory, it should be remarked that Pavlov's experimental results were obtained by very "mild" treatments compared with the treatments other investigators have given their animals. It is probable that the disturbances Pavlov observed were not very serious, though it is difficult to evaluate this statement because of the lack of useful criteria in judging the extent of such disturbances. There is no reason to doubt, however, that under the conditions of Pavlov's experiment the animals did change their behavior.

*The Liddell-Anderson theory.* The results of the experiments from Liddell's laboratory have been interpreted in papers by Anderson and Liddell (1935) and Liddell (1944). Liddell and Anderson have been much more willing to remain at the level of description of the phenomena involved in experimental neurosis than has Pavlov. They emphasize the tension under which the organism is placed during the experimental sessions. The restraint under which the animal is placed increases the tension already inherent in the difficulty of the discrimination required. Other factors contribute to the tension, according to Liddell; such things as the relationship of the experimenter to the subject and the monotonous repetition of stimuli in the experimental situation all help produce the breakdown.

Thus the approach of Liddell and Anderson is much more clinical and psychological than Pavlov's. They look for a number of factors in the environment of the experimental animals which might lead to the production of tension. Apparently, however, Liddell and Anderson have not systematically explored the factors which they believe to be important for experimental neurosis. At any rate, there is no direct evidence of a test of each of the factors separately and in combination.

*Masserman's theory.* Masserman, like Pavlov, emphasizes the role of conflict. In Masserman's case, however, the conflict is taken to be a conflict of motives rather than a conflict of excitation and inhibition. Masserman's account of experimental neurosis is much more like the notions of the causes of human neurosis than are the ideas of Pavlov. He emphasizes the role of anxiety in the production of phobic reactions and fixations. Conflict between the motive to get food and anxiety associated with punishment of the food-getting responses, Masserman believes, is primarily responsible for the neurosis in his experimental animals. The animals in Masserman's experiments are presented with an impasse; they cannot eat without getting punished, and yet they are hungry. The conflict finds expression in a wide variety of deviant behavior; the particular form exhibited by any one animal will depend upon the situation and past history of the animal.

The stimulus-response analysis of conflict, which we shall examine shortly, is closely related to Masserman's notions. This analysis of conflict is not concerned with the problem of abnormal behavior per se, but it provides a background for the understanding of the mechanisms whereby the abnormal behavior can come into being. Thus, Masserman's theories are much closer to the current theories of punishment, anxiety, and conflict than are the other theories of experimental neurosis.

*Maier's theory.* A few pages back we saw that there is some reason to doubt that the deviant behavior produced in Maier's experiments on rats is strictly due to an abnormal psychological condition. The abnormalities of behavior which he has observed can be produced, it has since been discovered, by simple auditory stimulation. Nevertheless, Maier has stoutly maintained that at least in part the seizure states observed in his animals are due to psychological conditions. He argues this for the following reasons: seizures are sometimes produced by electric shock (Griffiths, 1942), especially when the animals can make no other choice but make the wrong response; mild auditory stimulation plus conflict produces about as many seizures as intensive auditory stimulation alone (Maier and Longhurst, 1947). Maier (1949) also summarizes much evidence that seems to show an increase in frequency of seizures as the psychological tensions become greater.

The debate as to whether or not the seizures are entirely produced by auditory stimulation has not died down, but Maier and Longhurst's evidence would seem to indicate that the seizures can at least be facilitated by a conflict situation. It is important to note, however, that the seizures themselves are not the only kind of abnormal behavior which Maier noticed in his experiments, and it will be worth while to examine some of Maier's other data as well as his theory.

You will recall that, in Maier's experiments, the rats are required to discriminate between two cards. The cards are rewarded and punished in a random manner so that there is no solution to the problem. Animals soon refuse to choose in this situation, even though they are very hungry and are rewarded with food for their correct choice, and it is necessary to "drive" them with electric shock or an air blast. Usually the rats when forced to make a choice fixate on a particular response—jumping to the left card or jumping squarely at the middle, missing both cards. Once the animal becomes fixated it never deviates from this pattern of behavior. This Maier has called an "abnormal fixation."

These animals, Maier says, are frustrated, and frustration is responsible for the fixation. Animals, he finds, that have developed a fixation refuse to jump to an open window in which food is clearly displayed, in contrast to normal animals that readily modify their behavior. Maier believes, moreover, that his experiments show that behavior elicited during a state of frustration has certain unique properties. Frustrated behavior is not motivated behavior in the usual sense; it solves no problems and has no goals. Aggression, regression, and fixation are all characteristics of behavior under frustration. Behavioral disturbances can be described in terms of aggression, regression, and fixation, so, Maier believes, a major portion of the disturbances in behavior which have been reported in experiments on experimental neurosis are due to frustration.

*A summary of research on experimental neurosis.* You can see that there are many different notions about how the deviant behavior known as experimental neurosis arises. The picture is not so discouraging as it seems, however, since it is probable that abnormal behavior can be produced by many different factors. A few of these factors are important, and these we shall discuss.

Nearly everyone agrees that extreme emotion is disorganizing to behavior. Even those psychologists who go to great lengths to point out the motivational character of emotion (Leeper, 1948a) agree that when emotions become very strong they are disruptive to behavior. Strong emotions have been produced in human subjects in the laboratory, and it has been shown that such strong emotions do indeed disrupt skilled behavior (McKinley, 1933; Patrick, 1934). However, the disruption of behavior produced in these situations cannot be called abnormal or neurotic; the disturbance is situational and represents, more or less, the typical response of human beings in this situation.

In many studies of experimental neurosis in animal behavior, disruption of behavior has been produced by stimuli which elicit strong emotional responses. These disturbances, as well as the emotional behavior, are situational in character, however. The animals are disturbed in the laboratory but not in other situations. As in the case of emotional disruption in human behavior, it is doubtful whether we gain anything by calling this behavior neurotic. It is normal to be disturbed by emotion-eliciting stimuli; some animals are more disturbed than others, but even extreme disturbance can hardly be called neurotic.

Perhaps the condition most frequently mentioned as a source of disturbed behavior in the experiments on animal neurosis is conflict. Pavlov emphasized conflict between inhibition and excitation, while Masserman has emphasized conflict between motives. Conflict does not necessarily produce an *abnormal* disturbance of behavior, though it usually does produce some kind of disturbance, as we shall see shortly.

Like the presence of an emotion-producing stimulus, conflict—which also produces an emotional state—does not always result in disturbances of behavior that generalize to all of the organism's activities. More frequently, animals are disturbed in the experimental situation but show no change in behavior outside of the experimental situation. This may well reflect the inferiority of animals in dealing with the kind of symbolic behavior which requires response to a stimulus in its absence. To get around this, Hunt and Schlosberg (1950) subjected rats to continual conflict. They did this by electrifying the water supply, thus setting up a continuous conflict between thirst and shock avoidance. They managed to confirm many of the observations of behavior under conflict (p. 317) in this experiment, but indications of neurotic or abnormal behavior as a result of the experimental treatment were not great. Some of the animals developed "tantrums," during which they would run about the cage, throwing food pellets about, etc. Also some of the animals continued to behave as if they were being shocked when drinking long after the current had been turned off. The authors do not suggest any indications of permanent disturbances of behavior which might be comparable to human neurosis.

In summary, then, it might be said that many examples of experimental neurosis are merely examples of disturbances of behavior due to the presence of emotion-producing stimuli or conflicts that are purely situational in nature. They are examples of abnormal behavior only in the sense that they are situations in which organisms do not always act adaptively or can act adaptively. On the other hand, some investigators have reported examples of abnormal behavior that are *not* purely situational but that occur in activity outside of the experiment itself. These examples seem to come principally from the carnivores and higher mammals. Like human neuroses, these generalized disturbances of behavior seem to respond to therapeutic treatment (Masserman, 1943; Lichtenstein, 1950*b*).

Perhaps the main conclusion we should draw from the study of experimental neurosis is that disturbances of behavior can be learned, and this disturbed behavior can spread by stimulus and response generalization to many different aspects of the organism's life. The animal in the experiments on neurosis, for example, may generalize the anxiety produced by punishment through the mediation of elements common in the experimental situation and other aspects of life. In Lichtenstein's experiment (1950*a*) a fear of food produced by shock while eating in the experimental room was generalized to eating in the home cage. Some animals would refuse to eat pellets of food in their home cage after being shocked for eating those pellets in the experimental room. The same pellets ground up and made into a gruel were readily eaten, however.

Probably the major stumbling block to a direct analogy of the disturbances of behavior produced in animals in the laboratory and the disturbed behavior of human neurosis is in the low capacity animals have for engaging in symbolic and linguistic behavior. Human beings can much more readily generalize and extend their fears and conflicts because they can symbolically face themselves with the fear of punishment or with the conflict even when the objective situation does not demand it. In brief, human beings "worry" about their problems; animals apparently do not. Thus while it is possible to see the origins of disturbed behavior in animal studies, it is probably not too fruitful to regard these studies as directly analogous to neurosis in human beings.

## CONFLICT

The importance of conflict in disturbances of behavior makes it necessary for us to examine this problem in greater detail. Actually a fair beginning has been made in the study of conflict behavior, particularly that kind of conflict which involves different motivations. We are not directly concerned here with the role of conflict in the production of disturbances of behavior, but rather with the general principles that govern behavior under conflict.

Lewin (1931, 1935) has been responsible for a very interesting analysis of conflict behavior from the standpoint of the field of psychological forces that exist in the individual's life space at any one moment. From Lewin's analysis comes a distinction between three different types of conflict situations. These are (1) approach-avoidance conflict, (2) approach-approach conflict, and (3) avoidance-avoidance conflict. Approach-avoidance conflict occurs when the same stimulus object is both desirable and unpleasant. An example of such conflict is seen in the thirsty rats in the Hunt and Schlosberg experiment, which were shocked for drinking. In approach-approach conflict, the organism is faced with the necessity of making a choice between two equally desirable goal objects. I can spend my savings for a new car or for a vacation. Finally, in avoidance-avoidance conflict, the organism is faced with stimuli which are to be only avoided. I can go to the dentist and suffer in the chair or I can avoid the dentist and endure a toothache.

N. E. Miller (1944) has given us a very complete summary of the work on conflict. We shall draw upon Miller's analysis almost entirely. First of all, Miller points out, there are four principles that are fundamental to an understanding of conflict behavior. These are:

1. A tendency to approach a goal is stronger the nearer the organism is to the goal.

2. The tendency to avoid an unpleasant stimulus is stronger the nearer the subject is to the stimulus.

3. The tendency to avoid increases more rapidly with nearness to the unpleasant stimulus than does the tendency to approach with nearness to a goal.

4. These *gradients* of approach and avoidance are dependent upon the strength of drive upon which they are based. With stronger drives, the tendency to approach goals or avoid unpleasant stimuli are much stronger.

Brown (1948) was able to demonstrate that these principles do apply to behavior in simple situations. Brown trained a group of rats to run down a straight alley to food that was associated with the presence of a light. The animals wore a harness which could be attached to a calibrated spring, so that if the animals were momentarily restrained, the strength of pull could be measured at any point in the alley. In the experiments which followed, Brown measured the strength of pull at two different points in the alley, at one point near the goal and at one point far from the goal. For a study of the avoidance gradient, the animals were shocked in the goal box and then the strength of the tendency to avoid the goal box was measured at two different points in the alley.

The results of Brown's studies are shown in Fig. 56. You can see that the avoidance gradient is steeper than the approach gradient, and you can

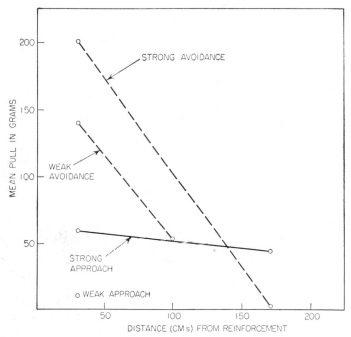

FIG. 56. Interaction of approach-avoidance gradients. Conflict appears at intersections of approach and avoidance gradients. (*From Miller, 1944; data from J. S. Brown.*)

also see that increasing the drive, either by making the animals more hungry or by increasing the shock, raises the level of both the approach and avoidance gradients.

*Approach-avoidance conflict.* If the same goal were made both attractive and unpleasant, one would expect from the results found by Brown that the animals would approach part way, then stop and vacillate. This is what happened. Miller, Brown, and Lipofsky (1943) trained animals to run to the goal box in order to get fed and then shocked the animals while they ate. Thus, both an approach-gradient and an avoidance-gradient were set up. The results showed that if the shock were very strong the animals would run only a little way down the alley and then hesitate; if the shock were weak they would run almost the full length of the alley before they stopped. Thus the principles tested by Brown are almost completely verified in this experiment.

*Avoidance-avoidance conflict.* The avoidance-avoidance conflict situation is one of the most interesting of the cases. This is the kind of conflict in which vacillation is maintained the longest. In approach-avoidance conflict, for example, the vacillation will not be maintained very long. The rat, after it has passed the place of momentary conflict, will continue to go down the alley and eventually eat the food. When it eats the food in this case the approach gradient is strengthened while avoidance gradient is weakened through extinction, since the rat is not shocked. Thus on the next trial the conflict may entirely disappear.

This is not the case with avoidance-avoidance conflict, however. In this case the organism must choose between two undesirable alternatives. It will move away from one of the alternatives, but this brings it closer to the other one, which in turn causes the organism to move in the opposite direction until, again, it is too close to the first alternative. Thus avoidance-avoidance conflict sets up what Miller has called a "stable equilibrium." Two experiments (Klebanoff, 1939; Hunt, 1943) demonstrate very clearly the tendency toward vacillation as well as a tendency to leave the field in avoidance-avoidance conflict.

*Approach-approach conflict.* As Miller pointed out, approach-approach conflict should produce little or no vacillation. Miller makes the analogy to the unstable equilibrium of a pencil balanced on its point; once it starts to fall, it falls all the way. This is true of the approach-approach situation. Once the conflict is resolved and the organism tends to approach one goal, a decision is made and it goes on to that goal with unimpeded progress. In Klebanoff's (1939) experiment, reported by Miller (1944), animals always chose the nearer goal, and when they were placed midway between two goals, they always made a decision with a minimum of vacillation.

Godbeer (1940), however, reports considerable vacillation in an approach-approach conflict situation in children. Williams (1943) attributes this to the child's ability to anticipate symbolically the frustration of losing one of the goals, something a rat cannot do. Williams points out that many supposed cases of pure approach-approach conflict also involve an element of avoidance of some sort, so that it is not always to be expected that approach-approach situations will produce no vacillation.

Miller (1944) recognizes this, and he suggests that approach-approach situations sometimes involve another kind of conflict, which he calls "double approach-avoidance conflict," that is, when one goal is approached an avoidance builds up *not* to relinquish the other goal. The net result is an approach tendency that may become weaker as the organism approaches the goal. The distant goal may seem more attractive, and the organism may turn back to it.

*The spatial analogy in approach and avoidance conflict.* Most of the experiments cited thus far on conflict have been experiments in which spatial distance from a goal is a variable. The space in these cases is real, three-dimensional space. However, from Lewin (1935, 1938) has come the notion that conflict, as well as other variables, can be conceived within the framework of *forces within a psychological space.* The analysis of conflict presented here, which comes largely from Miller, is heavily influenced by this notion. For example, when we speak of avoiding the dentist or avoiding the toothache as examples of the sort of conflict dealt with in the experiments reviewed above, we are more or less implicitly conceptualizing these situations in an imaginary psychological space. We conceive of the individual as a point in space, surrounded by barriers and buffeted by two opposing forces. The unfortunate difficulty about this way of thinking is that no one has made even a beginning at getting this psychological space down to the point where we can measure distances in it. It is a nonmetrical space. There are ways of dealing mathematically with such nonmetric spaces, but unfortunately these techniques have not proved useful in handling actual research problems. The psychological space, as a result, remains a convenient explanatory device rather than the powerful tool for research it could be. A major step forward in the theory of behavior would be achieved if we could find some way of making measurements in this conceptual psychological space.

*Conflict and anxiety.* As Miller (1944) and Williams (1943) point out, nearly all situations in which conflict is strong and persistent are situations in which an avoidance tendency exists. An avoidance tendency is nearly always accompanied by a conditioned anxiety state. As a matter of fact, according to Mowrer, the avoidance tendency depends upon the conditioned anxiety. At any rate, any situation in which a severe conflict exists is a fruitful situation for the presence of anxiety. It may well be that the disturbances of behavior in experimental neurosis where conflict is present may be due to anxiety. The spread of anxiety via stimulus generalization could then account for the existence of the disturbed behavior outside of the laboratory.

## THE EFFECTS OF EMOTION ON LEARNING

Thus far in this chapter we have dealt with problems of the acquisition of emotional behavior. The relationship between emotion and learning is two-edged, however. There is also an influence of aroused emotional activity upon rate of learning. This is an important problem which has practical as well as theoretical significance.

Leeper (1948*a*) has made out a strong case for emotions as a case of motivation. He has reiterated the old notions that emotional activity— especially the autonomic components—is really adaptive; the visceral activity is organized during emotion to meet the crisis with which the organism is faced. Behavior, says Leeper, is organized to meet the motivations of fear or anger. Thus, the pianist who shows stage fright and is disorganized in his performance is really organized in his behavior to flee the platform; the apparent disorganization occurs because the motivation to do this is in conflict with other motives that lead to remaining on the platform.

Actually, there is much justification for Leeper's arguments. What are usually called emotional reactions are usually accompanied by motivations to achieve specific goals. Organisms that are afraid flee to points of safety. Organisms that are angry attack other organisms or objects. Achievement of the goal usually reduces the emotional reaction. Once the rat in Mowrer's "shuttle box" (p. 304), for example, reaches the safe compartment, its heart rate goes down and other signs of emotional disturbance disappear. Overt aggression, clinical psychologists tell us, reduces the tension of anger.

There are, however, many facts that Leeper ignores but which need to be considered. Behavior is usually disorganized when the motivation to escape or attack or love conflicts with other motives. The rats in Hunt and Schlosberg's experiment that were shocked for drinking showed signs of "tantrums" and other disorganized activity. What is usually identified as an emotional response arises out of the conflict between motives or frustration of a motive. Thus, a rat that is both hungry and thirsty may show emotional behavior when faced with the necessity of choosing *either* water or food but not both. Or a rat that is frustrated in the attainment of a goal may show emotional behavior. Skinner (1938) points out that rats when not reinforced after having learned lever pressing show great irregularity in rate of responding, and this meets the criterion of disorganized behavior.

Thus there is something that can be called "emotional disorganization." It seems to occur when there is a conflict of motives or frustration of a motive. Furthermore, painful stimulation per se seems to produce emotional disorganization. It is possible, in addition, that the ordinary appetitive drives may likewise produce emotional disturbance when they get too strong. The irritability of the hungry baby is something everyone is acquainted with. Therefore, while emotions seem to be intimately connected with motives, it would be a mistake to abandon the notion of emotional disorganization as a concept. Further, the need for a concept of emotion becomes even more apparent when the characteristics of conscious experience are considered. While this is not a problem for discussion here, nevertheless it reinforces our belief in the necessity for a special concept of emotion. For our purposes here, emotion can be defined by a disturbance of motivated behavior.

*The influence of emotion on learning in animals.* There is a famous old principle in psychology, known as the Yerkes-Dodson principle, that illustrates the role of intensive painful stimulation in producing effects upon learning. Yerkes and Dodson (Yerkes and Dodson, 1908; Dodson, 1915) studied discrimination learning in mice and kittens. They were concerned with two variables: (1) the difficulty of discrimination and (2) the intensity of electric shock used in teaching the animals to avoid one of two stimuli. The animals were allowed to enter one of two compartments that were lighted to different degrees of brightness. If they entered the wrong compartment they were shocked; if they entered the right compartment they were returned to their home cage. The difficulty of discrimination was varied by changing the difference in illumination between the two compartments. The easiest discrimination was one in which one compartment was black and the other was white. Two other discriminations were successively made more difficult by reducing the difference in brightness.

The results of the study on mice are shown in Fig. 57. This figure shows the number of trials required for the three discriminations as a function of the intensity of the shock. As you can see, for the easiest discrimination the strongest shock resulted in the fastest learning. This was not true, however, for the other, more difficult discriminations. For the medium discrimination a shock of moderate intensity produced the most rapid learning, while for the difficult discrimination a shock of low intensity produced the most rapid learning.

On the basis of these experiments, Yerkes and Dodson formulated the principle that the optimum intensity of shock (which they conceived as punishment) varied inversely with the difficulty of discrimination. Very intense painful stimulation produced emotional disorganization that was detrimental to learning. This was especially true with the more difficult discriminations.

A more direct determination of the role of emotion on learning is provided by an experiment of Higginson's (1930). This investigator attempted (1) to induce fear in rats before running them in a maze by placing them inside a cage with a cat, or (2) to induce anger by pinching their tails and

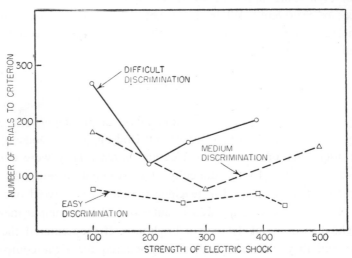

FIG. 57. The effect of shock intensity on discrimination problems of different degrees of difficulty. (*From Yerkes and Dodson, 1908.*)

brushing their noses. The result of this treatment was to increase the number of trials required to learn the maze. Behavior in the maze was much less organized for these rats than for control rats.

*The influence of emotion on learning in humans.* Several studies indicate that emotional stress induced by an experience of threat of failure has a detrimental effect upon rate of learning. For example, McClelland and Apicella (1947) found that emotional stress induced by false failure scores resulted in more trials to reach a criterion on card sorting. Lazarus and Deese (1951), however, find that the situation is not a simple one. In an experiment upon the effects of failure-induced stress upon the learning of a target-pursuit task, they found some evidence which led them to believe that emotional stress induced early in the learning process, before skills have been well organized, produced a detrimental effect upon learning, while stress induced later in learning produced a slightly facilitating effect.

These situations in which emotion is induced during learning in human subjects are complicated. They probably involve a drastic change in motivation of the subjects as well as the introduction of emotional disorganization. In the experiment by Lazarus and Deese, for example, the threat of failure may have caused some subjects to want to quit working at the learning task and to leave the examining room. This motivation is not consistent with the production of the best of performance, and it is conceivable that the lowered effectiveness of performance observed when the emotional stress was induced early in learning was due in part to this desire to escape an unpleasant situation. There are, of course, many possible reasons for the decrement in performance observed at this point, just as there are many reasons for the rise in performance observed when the emotional stress was introduced later in performance.

It must be apparent to the reader that our current notions about emotion and motivation are much too primitive to account very well for the numerous experimental findings. Psychologists have spilled many words on the subject of emotion, but no one seems yet to have come up with a solution to the problem of definition. This is one of the areas in psychology which is most in need of a systematic reevaluation, and, until we have such a reevaluation, we admit only to the vaguest of understanding of the nature of emotion and its relation to the learning process. We have many experiments which purport to deal with learning and emotion, but since psychologists cannot even agree upon the definition of emotion, these experiments are erected upon shifting sands. Operationally speaking, psychologists have studied the effects of threat of failure, electric shock, etc., upon learning. These things, it has been loosely agreed, produce emotion, but until we can decide what else besides emotion they produce and what kinds and how much emotion they produce, we are not in a very good position to evaluate the experimental literature.

# CHAPTER 16

# PHYSIOLOGICAL PROBLEMS
# IN LEARNING

One of the most fundamental problems of physiological psychology concerns the nature of changes in the nervous system that accompany learning. It is a fundamental postulate—almost, but not quite, self-evident—that the changes in behavior called learning are in the last analysis reflections of changes in the nervous system. It is not surprising, then, that there has been a great deal of experimental work on the relationship between the nervous system and learning. That work, however, has not solved the basic problem. As a matter of fact, it has done little more than show us how complicated the problem is. The reader, however, should find this chapter one of the most rewarding and interesting in the whole of learning.

The experimental information we have shows some of the relationships between the gross structure of the nervous system and the ability to learn. Most of it comes from studying learning or retention after various portions of the nervous system have been removed. This technique has been supplemented by some studies of drugs and learning as well as by some few studies that make use of direct electrical stimulation of the nervous system. The comparative crudity of both the physiological techniques and our methods of measuring learning ability leaves us a long way from an answer to the questions of what and where changes take place in the nervous system during learning. But we do have a number of answers about the role of various systems, centers, and pathways of the nervous system in learning, and these we shall examine.

## CONDITIONING

The conditioned response is about the simplest kind of learning that has been studied in the higher animals. Because conditioning is so simple and relatively unambiguous, it is a favorite method with investigators who study neural mechanisms in learning. Some of them have used the classical salivary conditioned response, but most of them have employed the conditioned flexion response. A few others have made use of other, more typical operant responses such as lever pressing.

## Pathways in Conditioning

Most conditioning studies make use of two stimuli that are paired together. One, the unconditioned stimulus, elicits a response without prior learning. The other, the conditioned stimulus, comes to elicit the response as the result of pairing with the unconditioned stimulus. Thus there are at least three peripheral pathways involved, the sensory pathways for the conditioned and unconditioned stimuli and the motor pathway for the response. Whether or not the conditioned response and unconditioned response are *exactly* alike in character is not important for the moment; somewhere along the line they follow a *final common path* to the effectors.

*The pathway for the response.* There are some interesting observations that tell us that somewhere prior to the final common path the conditioned response and unconditioned response must occupy different pathways. Harlow (1937) showed that adaptation of the unconditioned response left the conditioned response intact. What Harlow did was condition a startle response in monkeys to the presentation of the bell. The stimuli that were originally used to elicit the startle response were repeatedly presented until the animals no longer startled to these stimuli; the conditioned stimuli were then presented, and despite the fact that the *unconditioned* startle response had been adaped out, the *conditioned* startle response was still present.

A study by Kellogg (1941) illustrates the same functional separation of the conditioned and unconditioned responses. In this case, however, Kellogg showed that a typical conditioned flexion response disappeared under Nembutal but that the same response to the unconditioned stimulus (an electric shock) was left intact. Likewise, if during the course of an experiment the animals dozed off to sleep, the conditioned response disappeared but the unconditioned response remained. As in the case of Harlow's experiment, these results suggest that the conditioned response and the unconditioned response are functionally distinct from one another somewhere in the central nervous system.

A number of studies combine to show that elicitation of the unconditioned response itself is not necessary for conditioning to take place. Two studies (Light and Gantt, 1936; Kellogg *et al.*, 1940) show that when the motor nerves are made inoperative so that the unconditioned response cannot be made, dogs still learn to avoid a shock by responding to a conditioned stimulus. In these studies, the animals were trained in flexion conditioning when the motor nerves for the appropriate paw were not functioning; later, after the nerves had recovered, the conditioned response could be elicited. Kellogg (Kellogg *et al.*, 1940) suggests that this is a result of response generalization and he reasons that, since the other limbs could respond, the animals simply generalized the conditioned response to the inoperative leg after it recovered.

Two other studies (Crisler, 1930; Finch, 1938) present even more clearcut evidence that the unconditioned response is unnecessary for learning. In these experiments the salivary response was used. During training, in which some neutral stimulus was paired with a stimulus—such as morphine or acid—that elicits salivation, the unconditioned response was blocked by atropine. When tests were made after the atropine had worn off it was apparent that the salivary response had been conditioned. On the basis of these studies we can definitely rule out the unconditioned response as a necessary factor in conditioning.

*The pathway for the unconditioned stimulus.* Having ruled out the motor response as a necessary component for conditioning we can turn to the unconditioned stimulus. The evidence here rather clearly indicates that the effect of the unconditioned stimulus must go *through* the central nervous system. To study this point, Loucks (1935) attempted to condition the flexion response in dogs by direct stimulation of the motor cortex. When the motor regions of the cortex are stimulated by an electrical current various movements can be elicited. The location of the stimulation will determine what movements will be elicited. Loucks found the location which, when stimulated, gave rise to a flexion response in one of the dog's limbs—thus he short-circuited the sensory and association pathways that the unconditioned stimulus would have to go through—and applied stimuli directly to the motor side. Despite a great number of trials, Loucks was unable to obtain conditioning under these conditions, and from that fact we probably must conclude that the unconditioned stimulus must go through the central nervous system.

In substantiation of this view are two experiments (Tracy, 1927; Hilgard and Allen, 1938) that show that elicitation of the unconditioned response by direct stimulation of the motor nerve does not result in conditioning. In the experiment by Hilgard and Allen the finger-withdrawal response in human subjects was employed. The response of the finger was elicited by electrical stimulation of the motor nerve on a place on the arm. This was paired with a conditioned stimulus. Again, despite a great many trials, no evidence of conditioning was obtained.

*The pathway for the conditioned stimulus.* In Loucks's (1935) study of stimulation of the motor cortex, he discovered that such stimulation could serve as a conditioned stimulus even though it could not serve as an unconditioned stimulus. One interpretation of this result would be that the stimulus to the cortex produces a movement; this movement in turn produces kinesthetic stimulation in the limb, and such kinesthetic stimulation could serve as a conditioned stimulus for a flexion response in some other limb. Loucks, however, eliminated this possibility by narcotizing the hind limbs so that they could not move. He still got conditioning using stimulation of the motor cortex as a conditioned stimulus. Anatomists now tell us, however, that there are projections from the cutaneous senses in the motor region of the cortex, and it apparently was these that Loucks was stimulating.

Such an interpretation is borne out by a finding that direct stimulation of a sensory region of the cortex can result in conditioning (Loucks, 1938). Thus, while it appears that the sensory fibers themselves can be eliminated as conditioned stimuli, the effect of the conditioned stimulus apparently must go through the central nervous system. The fact that the peripheral pathways and the direct sensory and motor components of the central nervous system have been so thoroughly eliminated as loci for conditioning makes us now turn to the heart of the central nervous system itself.

## The Central Nervous System

One of the first questions we might ask about the neural mechanisms of conditioning concerns the larger structures of the nervous system. Is conditioning limited to one structure or several structures of the nervous system? The first and most obvious place one might look for the locus of conditioning is to the most recent phylogenetically and most highly developed part of the nervous system, namely, the cerebral cortex.

*The cortex and conditioning.* Pavlov's theory of conditioning led him to the belief that conditioning must be limited to the cerebral cortex. He thought that if the cortex were entirely removed, conditioning would be impossible. A great number of investigations (Poltyrew and Zeliony, 1930; Lebedinskaia and Rosenthal, 1935; Ten Cate, 1934; Culler and Mettler, 1934; Girden *et al.,* 1936; Bromiley, 1948; etc.) have shown, however, that it is possible to set up conditioned responses after complete removal of the cerebral hemispheres. The earlier reports from American laboratories of decorticate conditioning stressed the diffuse and unadaptive nature of the conditioned responses. Instead of a neat avoidance response, about all that could be conditioned was a generalized struggle to the conditioned stimulus. Bromiley (1948), however, was able to obtain isolated adaptive flexion responses in the limb stimulated after complete removal of the cortex.[1]

Removal of parts of the cerebral cortex tells essentially the same story. A conditioned response established to light as the conditioned stimulus can both be learned and retained after the primary visual area of the cortex has been removed (Wing and Smith, 1942; Wing, 1946, 1947). In the case of a conditioned response to the sound, the removal of the auditory area of the cortex in cats causes the conditioned response to be completely abolished, but retraining after the removal of the auditory area reestablishes the response (Raab and Ades, 1946). One might interpret these findings to indicate that, in the case of light-intensity discrimination, the conditioned response is established both at the cortical level and the subcortical level, while in the case of the sound-intensity discrimination, the conditioned response is normally established only at the cortical level but *can* be established at the subcortical level.

One further group of data shows that simple conditioned responses can be established in the absence of critical cortical tissue. It has been known for some time that conditioned responses can be established under the influence of the drug curare (Girden and Culler, 1937). The conditioned response under curare does not carry over to the normal state, though it may carry over to a subsequent drug state (Girden, 1947), and responses established without the drug do not carry over to the drug state. The effects of curare are many. Among them is a *depression* of cortical excitability and a *facilitation* of spinal excitability (Culler *et al.,* 1939). Because curare depresses the cortex, Morgan (1951) has pointed out, conditioning under curare is subcortical, but when the cortex is functioning the subcortical conditioning is depressed. Morgan points out that this interpretation is borne out by some data of Girden's (1940). Girden removed

---

[1] Bromiley offers several hypotheses to account for the differences between his results and those of the earlier investigators. One possibility is that in the earlier studies extensive damage to *subcortical* centers occurred. Another possibility lies in the fact that the type of unconditioned stimulus used in the earlier studies elicited a rage response, characteristic of the decorticate dog.

the auditory cortex of dogs and then conditioned the animals to a bell while they were under curare. Under these conditions the conditioned response occurred *both* in the curarized state and in the normal state. This was because there was no auditory cortex to inhibit the subcortical conditioning; consequently when the curare was removed the conditioned response could appear.

Thus it has been rather clearly established that conditioning can occur at subcortical levels, though conditioning normally involves only the cortex. Thus while the cortex may be more adapted to whatever is involved in learning, subcortical tissue may serve the same function.

*Spinal conditioning.* Having established that the cortex is not necessary for conditioning, we can turn to the lowest level of the central nervous system, the spinal cord. Can conditioning occur in the spinal cord? Shurrager and Culler (1938, 1940) say "yes"; they report that they could obtain conditioned responses from the isolated spinal cord of the dog. These responses were of a rather special nature, however, and it will be necessary for us to examine their technique in detail in order to evaluate the results. The dogs were placed under heavy ether anesthesia, the spinal cord was severed, and the semitendinosus muscles of the rear legs were exposed. Since the investigators were working with the isolated posterior portion of the animal, they could not put the conditioned stimulus in through the usual sensory channels. They used, then, electrical and cutaneous stimulation of the tail as a conditioned stimulus. They began to condition the semitendinosus muscle in one leg by pairing a shock to the muscle with a shock or touch to the tail after the anesthetic had worn off somewhat. In this manner they were able to obtain both conditioning and extinction. The conditioned response was a minute response, usually near the insertional end, of the semitendinosus muscle.

By the use of a different technique, Kellogg and Deese (Kellogg *et al.,* 1947; Deese and Kellogg, 1946, 1949) attempted to repeat these observations. Kellogg and Deese severed the spinal cord at about the same place as in the Shurrager and Culler experiments, but they left the limbs intact and waited awhile, with the idea of working with the animals after the operative shock had worn off. In one experiment (Kellogg *et al.,* 1947) they used stimulation to the other leg as a conditioned stimulus, and in another experiment (Deese and Kellogg, 1949) they used stimulation to the tail as had Shurrager and Culler. Under these conditions they could obtain responses, which if taken by themselves looked like conditioned responses; that is to say, the responses occurred to the conditioned stimulus in the absence of the unconditioned stimulus. These responses, however, did not follow the usual course of conditioning and extinction, and finally it was discovered that they were part of a "mass reflex" that occurs to any stimulation to the posterior portion of the spinal animal. Therefore, these responses were not conditioned responses. Kellogg and Deese admitted the possibility that the presence of the *unconditioned stimulus* to the leg could *sensitize* the existing leg reflex to tail stimulation, and they suggested that this sensitization could be an intermediate between pure conditioning and pure reflex behavior.

It must be understood, however, that the observations of Kellogg and Deese were not the same as those of Shurrager and Culler, and therefore it is quite possible that a true conditioned response was observed in the Shurrager and Culler experiments. This possibility is lessened, however, by the discovery of possible sources of artifacts and the careful repetition of the Shurrager and Culler experiments by Pinto and Bromiley (1950) with negative results.

Thus we do not know whether or not spinal conditioning can occur. Pinto and Bromiley (1950), despite the exhaustive nature of their work, still hold out for the possibility. They carefully point out the possible sources of artifacts in spinal conditioning experiments, and this suggests that further experiments controlling these conditions should be carried out.

### COMPLEX LEARNING

Nearly everyone agrees that any kind of learning more complicated than simple conditioning or very simple discrimination requires the presence of some cortical tissue. Exactly what tissue and in what amount, however, is a question that is still pretty much a mystery. An examination of some experimental data will show what progress has been made in the discovery of the relationship between the structure of cortex and learning ability.

*Maze learning in rats.* To K. S. Lashley, more than any other single individual, we owe our present understanding of the relationship of the anatomy of the nervous system to learning. Among the various things that Lashley has studied is maze learning in rats after various amounts of the rats' cortex have been removed. The data obtained from these studies have been perhaps the most influential data in the development of our present-day concepts of brain function in learning.

In one experiment, Lashley (1929) made use of three different mazes of three degrees of difficulty. The floor plan of these mazes is shown in

FIG. 58. The rats in Lashley's study were first subjected to a variety of brain lesions of various sizes and locations. Then they were run on a series of problems, which included the three mazes, and compared on these problems with normal animals. The most important conclusions to come out of the study were (1) the greater the extent of the lesion, the greater

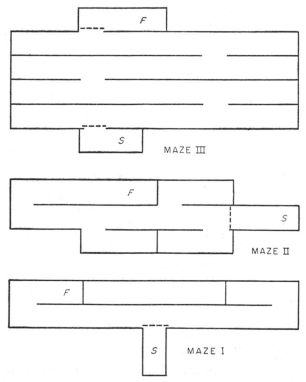

FIG. 58. The floor plan of the three mazes used by Lashley in his study of brain damage and learning in rats. (*Lashley, 1929.*)

the impairment of learning ability; (2) the more difficult the maze, the more effective a lesion of a given size; (3) there is no relationship between location of lesion and impairment of learning ability. The first two of these points are illustrated in Fig. 59, which shows the relationship between errors made during learning and the size of lesion and the difficulty of the maze.

*Problem solving in rats.* Lashley (1920) in an early study found that there was no impairment of performance on a double-platform puzzle box with lesions of up to 50 per cent of the cortex. This problem, however, was a relatively simple one that required little manipulatory skill on the part of the rat. All the rat had to learn was a simple sequence of movements much like those required for an easy maze. With the use of certain other kinds of puzzle boxes, however, Lashley (1935) found a relationship between learning ability and cortical destruction much like that found for the

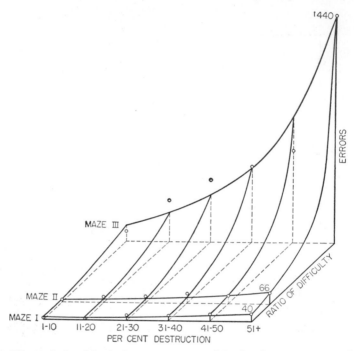

FIG. 59. The relationship between amount of brain damage, maze difficulty, and errors in learning. The greatest effect of brain damage is on the most difficult maze. (*Lashley, 1929.*)

three mazes. Lashley came to the conclusion that adaptive, manipulative abilities were most affected by cerebral lesions; simple habits involving running and climbing movements were scarcely affected at all.

Maier (1932*a*, 1932*b*) finds results with his "reasoning" problem in rats that are in accord with Lashley's findings. You will recall that in Maier's problems the rats are made familiar with separate parts of a maze and then are required to demonstrate, by performance, that they are familiar with the relations between the separate parts. Maier finds that very small lesions (10 to 20 per cent of the cortical tissue) are sufficient to disrupt the ability to solve these problems. As in Lashley's studies, the location of the lesions does not matter very much, though Maier finds a slight tendency for lesions in the extreme front and back parts of the cortex to be more serious.

*The concept of mass action.* Two facts about the effects of cortical damage on learning and problem solving in rats led Lashley to formulate a special concept. These facts are: the correlation between amount of damage and amount of decrement in learning and retention, and the finding that it does not seem to matter much where the lesions are placed. The concept that Lashley formulated is known as "mass action." This notion states that whatever function the cortex has in learning, it functions as a whole.

Morgan (Morgan and Stellar, 1950) has discussed three possible interpretations of mass action. First of all there is the possiblity that the cortex really does act as a whole; this Morgan calls a "general mass factor." Secondly there is the possibility that really specific parts of the cortex work in any given learned act, but that these are dispersed over the cortex; this Morgan calls a "dispersed specific factor." The third possibility is that there are really "well-localized specific factors" in learning but that so many of these are involved in the performance of any single act that the effects of brain lesions give the appearance of mass action. Unfortunately, Morgan points out, there are no data that enable us to pick any one of these possible interpretations as being more correct than the others. We do not know, in a word, whether mass action reflects primarily the organization of the rat's cortex or whether it reflects the fact that learning involves a multiplicity of sensory media and motor pathways.

*Complex learning in primates.* In the primates, investigators have looked for more localized cerebral correlates of learning and memory. Particularly have they looked at the portion of the forepart of the brain known as the "prefrontal areas." Consequently, we have no principle of mass action that applies to the primate brain but rather some suggestions about localization of function.

Some of the earliest experiments on memory and the function of the prefrontal areas are those of Jacobsen (1935). Jacobsen studied the ability of monkeys to solve the delayed-response problem (p. 255) after removal of the prefrontal areas. You will recall that normally the monkey can choose the correct stimulus after a fairly long delay period. Jacobsen found that following removal of the prefrontal areas the monkeys could not solve the delayed-response problem if the delay were any more than a few seconds in length. Control studies (Jacobsen and Haslerud, 1936; Jacobsen and Elder, 1936) showed that damage to other regions of the cortex had no such effect upon the delayed response.

In Jacobsen's original study he reported that while the delayed response was seriously affected by prefrontal lesions, simple discrimination learning was but little affected. Finan (1939) in a subsequent investigation attempted to establish what was unique about the delayed-response situation that made it so vulnerable to frontal lesions. He studied the behavior of monkeys in three situations: (1) a temporal maze in which the shorter pathway was the correct one, (2) a shuttle box that required the monkeys to make a response within a fixed interval of time, and (3) a delayed-response test. In agreement with the earlier studies, Finan found no effect on the tests of *unilateral* lesions of the prefrontal areas. *Bilateral* lesions, however, produced an impairment in the ability to perform the delayed-response test but had no effect upon the other two tests.

In another experiment Finan (1942) was able to eliminate the effect of frontal lesions upon the delayed-response problem. He did this by feeding the animals *before* the delay period. Under these conditions monkeys with prefrontal lesions could solve the delayed-response problem as well as normal monkeys. Finan thought that perhaps the prefrontal areas were important in establishing secondary or derived reinforcement, so that in their absence the animals could not bridge the delay by secondary cues (p. 256).

Other interpretations of these facts exist, however. One such interpretation is in terms of attention. Animals with prefrontal lesions may suffer from wandering attention; the notion here is that they cannot "concentrate" on one stimulus for as long a time as normal animals. Therefore the animals with prefrontal lesions would not always notice the food being placed under the cup in the delayed-response tests. Prefeeding them with the food, however, would make them a little more attentive to what was going under the food cup.

This interpretation is supported by some other data. Wade (1947) was able to get monkeys to solve the delayed-response problem after prefrontal lesions by placing them under a light sedative. This cut down on their activity and seemed to make them more attentive to what the experimenter was doing. Furthermore, Malmo (1942) has shown that disturbing stimuli disorganize the performance of monkeys in the delayed-response situation and prolong learning or relearning after removal of prefrontal tissue. Prefrontal animals can solve the delayed-response test if the delay period is made in the dark. Thus it is very possible that the serious defects in performing delayed response that Jacobsen observed in his prefrontal monkeys may have been due to a change in the ability of animals to be attentive or keep going on what they are doing.

Harlow and his associates have studied the effects of removal of the prefrontal areas on a number of different learning problems. While removal of the bilateral frontal areas does produce a deficit in the learning of discrimination and discrimination-reversal problems, the differences between operated animals and normal animals are not large (Harlow and Dagnon, 1943). Subsequent studies (Spaet and Harlow, 1943; Harlow and Johnson, 1943) led Harlow to believe that whatever the effects of prefrontal removal, they are not simple. Data from Harlow's laboratory support the notion of loss of attention, but other factors are important, too. The postoperative performance of monkeys is influenced by a number of things, including previous test history, length of recovery period, conditions of testing, etc. (Campbell and Harlow, 1945).

One additional paper from Harlow's laboratory suggests an additional mechanism to account for differences in learning and retention between prefrontal and normal animals. Harlow and his associates agree that the delayed-reaction test is one of the most difficult for the animal with prefrontal lesions to solve. They suggest that the reason for this is that on successive trials the same stimulus is not always the correct one. On one trial, for example, the right cup may have the raisin hidden under it, while on the next trial the left one may be correct. The only way the monkey can solve the problem is by watching where the raisin goes; there are no stimulus cues that are associated with the correct response on every trial. The confusion brought about by the necessity of contradictory reactions to the same stimuli seems to be uniquely difficult for the prefrontal animal.

In the experimental test of this notion (Settlage, Zable, and Harlow, 1948), contradictory reactions to similar and identical stimuli were required. The discrimination tests taken individually were very easy for the operated animals. Indeed, on the individual discrimination problems, operated monkeys do only a little worse than normal monkeys (Harlow and Dagnon, 1943). But when tests are juxtaposed that require contradictory reactions, the operated monkeys do very much more poorly than normal animals. Thus the effect of removal of the prefrontal areas seems to involve an impairment of the ability to relinquish previously adaptive reactions. In other words, animals with prefrontal lesions are more *perseverative* in their behavior than are normal animals.

*A summary.* This brief review makes it apparent that we have much to learn about the relationship of the anatomical structure of the nervous system to the ability to learn. The data on complex learning and brain lesions in primates are most interesting because they indicate both that there is some specificity in the function of the cortex and that not yet have we hit on the right combination of functions and areas. It is probable that the fault lies with both neurophysiology and psychology. On the neurophysiological and anatomical side we are still not altogether clear about the structure of the cortex. New techniques of electrical recording in the past few years have given us a much improved picture of the sensory projection areas of the cortex, but there is still much to learn. On the psychological side, we still cannot be sure that we are looking at the right abilities. We are not sure that we are setting up our tests of learning in order to get out the kinds of functions that might be well localized.

The lack of clarity in the data has led to a great deal of speculation. This speculation has ranged all the way from extreme localization of function in the cortex to a denial of *any* special psychological functions being localized in the cortex (Kantor, 1947). The truth probably lies somewhere in between. There is some logic to the notion that psychological functions cannot be *localized* somewhere in the cortex or some other part of the brain because after all the cortex or brain is only one of many biological systems that participate in any given behavior. On the other hand, it is reasonable to look for *crucial* structures in behavior. Learning must be accompanied by some physical changes within the organism and the best place to look for those changes is in the higher structures of the central nervous system. The data, at the moment, indicate that some kinds of learning functions are localized within the cortex of the higher mammals, but we are not sure exactly what they are. The fact, for example, that the prefrontal areas are of more importance than other areas to the delayed-reaction test indicates that there is some localization. On the other hand, we have not been able to pin down exactly what it is about the delayed-reaction test that makes it so vulnerable to prefrontal lesions.

## NEUROPHYSIOLOGICAL THEORIES OF LEARNING

At one time psychology abounded with neurophysiological theories of learning. Not much was known about neurophysiology and less about learning, so that there was ample room for the wildest sort of speculation. Nearly everyone was convinced that the solution to the problem of the relationship of learning to the functions of the nervous system was just around the corner. All that needed to be done was a lot of experimentation and eventually one of the theories would be proved to be correct.

Today we have no such illusions. For many years now, theorists (Tolman, 1932; Skinner, 1938; Kantor, 1947) have deplored the fruitlessness of neurophysiological theorizing. They have claimed that the really important task for psychologists is to establish a science of behavior. After we begin to thoroughly understand behavior, perhaps we shall be in a better position to understand the relationships between behavior and physiology. Speculative theory is a waste of time, they say, and is potentially dangerous because it may lead us to believe that we have "explained" something when we have only translated it into words about some hypothetical events within the nervous system.

There is much to be said for this argument. Neurophysiological theories have not been very useful. And certainly a study of behavior in its own right needs no justification as a kind of adjunct to physiology. On the other hand, the argument may have gone too far. Both neurophysiology and psychology are in better condition than they were a few years ago. It is very possible that speculation of a sort could lead to some new experimental findings that in turn may be an opening wedge into the problem of the neurophysiology of learning. For this reason it will be worth our while to examine some of the contemporary theories about physiological mechanisms in learning.

*Recurrent nerve circuits.* A few years ago, Lorente de Nó (1938), by histological and physiological studies, discovered that there are closed loops of activity in the central nervous system; that is to say, there are cases in which once a neuron is fired the impulse will travel through some collateral neurons back to the original neuron reactivating it (Fig. 60). Once this recurrent firing gets going, if conditions are right, it could go on forever.

It was immediately obvious to physiological psychologists that this recurrent nerve circuit theoretically could provide a basis for memory. Learning would set up recurrent circuits that would go on indefinitely; when the time came for a measure of retention of the learned act, external stimuli (presumably conditioned stimuli) would summate with the recurrent circuit to produce performance of the learned act.

It was also almost immediately apparent that there were several difficulties with this argument. In the first place, though theoretically recurrent nerve circuits could go on indefinitely, in practice the vast majority of them must be limited to time intervals of the order of seconds. The comparatively enormous time intervals that learned acts can survive without practice make recurrent circuits a poor basis for memory. In the second place, it has been argued, any change in the general excitability level of the central nervous system ought to change activity in many recurrent circuits. Anesthetics, for example, ought to eliminate many recurrent circuits because they depress the excitability of the central nervous system. Therefore, anesthetics should result in a loss of retention of many learned acts. No such effect has ever been reported.

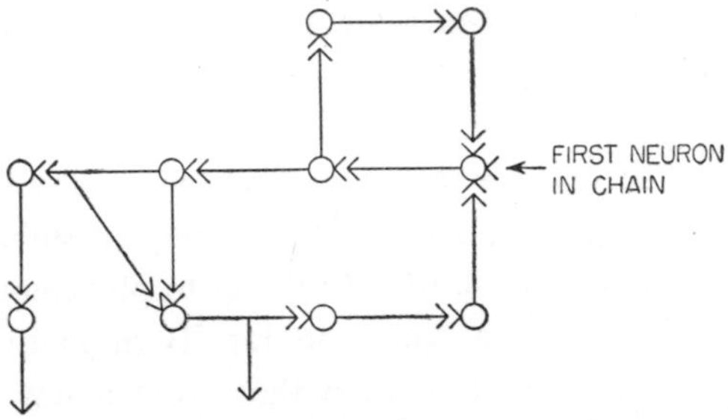

FIG. 60. Schematic diagram of a recurrent nerve circuit.

Recently there has been a revival of interest in recurrent nerve circuits as the basis of memory, since they bear a strong analogy to the "memory" circuits of electronic computers. But reasoning from analogy is always dangerous unless the analogy is regarded only as a springboard from which to find something testable. We still can regard recurrent nerve circuits as an important possibility in the chain of physiological events responsible for learning and memory, but it is probably not useful to regard them as the essential mechanism.

*Hebb's theory.* Hebb (1949) has put forward one of the most completely worked out neurophysiological theories of learning to appear in recent years. Because it is new, we are not in a position to evaluate the ultimate value of Hebb's position, but it is an interesting one and certainly worth an examination.

Hebb begins by pointing out that we must have some way of reconciling the seemingly incompatible demands of perception and learning. Learning apparently demands that *specific* cells be excited in order for a specific response or perception to be remembered. Perception, on the other hand, seems to demand that patterns of excitation, rather than specific cells, be involved in the physiological basis of psychological events. We know, for example, that a square always looks like the same square no matter from what direction it is regarded or what portion of the retina is stimulated.

He solves this dilemma by making learning basic to perception. He suggests, for example, that we must *learn* to perceive the square as a square no matter how it is viewed. The problem then remains to postulate the manner in which specific cells become the basis for memory. Hebb does this by suggesting a dual trace mechanism. There are two factors in the development of the memory of a specific response. One factor is something like the recurrent nerve circuit. The recurrent nerve circuit can act briefly to preserve a particular pattern of excitation for a while until some secondary, permanent change has time to develop. The secondary change, the one really responsible for everything but immediate memory span, Hebb hypothesizes to be the result of growth of nerve fibers toward one another at the synapses or junction of neurons involved in the pattern of excitation.

The growth of fiber endings at synapses is an old idea, and it has frequently been applied to learning. Various objections have been made to the idea from time to time, and consequently Hebb apologizes a bit for reviving it. There are, however, enough plausible physical possibilities about how this growth activity could come about that it is not altogether unreasonable. Hebb specifically suggests that one cell acts upon another to form knoblike growths that make easier the transmission of impulses. It might be mentioned that very recently some neurophysiologists have advanced a similar hypothesis to account for a reflex sensitization phenomenon known as "potentiation" (Eccles and Rall, 1951).

Hebb unfortunately does not suggest any direct way in which this dual trace theory might be tested. He believes that it is not inconsistent with modern data in neurophysiology and anatomy, and he believes it helps solve the paradox of the generalization of perception and the stability of learning. The theory makes use of both the dynamic properties of recurrent nerve circuits and the stability of structural changes. In this way the theory just about exhausts the broad possibilities of the physiology of learning.

*The Katz and Halstead theory.* Most theories of the neurophysiology of learning have assumed that the change that occurs during learning is a change in some aspect of the juncture between neurons, the synapse. Katz and Halstead (1950), however, have assumed that the change is in the *membrane* of the neuron. The nerve membrane, you will recall, is the structure that neurophysiologists find to be responsible for the potential difference between the inside and outside of a neuron. The physical make-up of this membrane is in some doubt, but Katz and Halstead propose that its most important feature is an organization of protein molecules. This is not a notion widely accepted among neurophysiologists, but there is little or nothing basically wrong with the idea.

The important point about the possible protein structure of the nerve membrane is that Katz and Halstead make the *organization* of the protein structure the basis for memory. An initial protein molecule in a neuron becomes organized in a certain way, and this is responsible for a template that produces replicas all along the neural membrane in much the same way that a gene is supposed to act as a template to produce identical molecules in the cytoplasm of cells. The important point is that the protein molecules in a nerve membrane must become oriented in a certain way before that nerve can become a functioning member of a neural network. The way in which this works can best be illustrated in a quotation from Katz and Halstead (1950, p. 25):

"We visualize the initiation of a memory trace broadly as follows: An impulse arrives at a neuron not yet physiologically operative in a receptor area of the cortex. We assume that neurons of the cortex possess a large number of different protein molecules which have random configurations. The effect of the first stimulus is to cause one of these randomly oriented molecules to assume a specific configuration. Thus, an act of orientation occurs as a result of the impulse. . . . By whatever mechanism, a new template molecule arises in the neuron and protein replicas are synthesized; these become part of the neural membrane. When organization of the membrane is complete, the neuron is capable of conducting an impulse."

At the present time there seems to be no way to test the theory directly, but at least it is a step in the right direction. It is a chemical theory, and we may anticipate that shortly the biochemists will present us with enough information about the specific chemical effect of various narcotics, stimulants, and poisons upon the nervous system so that we may test this or possibly similar theories by seeing if appropriate chemicals have the predicted effect upon learning or retention.

*The present status of neurophysiological theories.* As you can see, we are a long way from really knowing very much about the neurophysiology of learning. We have examined three theories that are representative of contemporary theories, and it is possible that from one of these sources a really useful theory may spring. It is possible, on the other hand, that real advances may not come from theory at all. Another possibility is that the border lines of neurophysiology and psychology may be extended toward one another until we can see the basis for behavior directly from experimental findings.

This last suggestion may not be so remote as it seems. For a long time physiologists have been studying facilitating effects of "conditioning" stimuli upon subsequent reflexes (Fulton, 1949). The facilitating effects they have observed have been of very brief duration—in the order of milliseconds—and therefore cannot be said to be prototypes of learning. Recently, however, facilitating effects have been observed that last for several minutes (Lloyd, 1950; Eccles and Rall, 1951). On the logarithmic time scale that such events seem to work, this is a long way toward the relatively permanent "facilitation" of responses to conditioned stimuli that pairing with unconditioned stimuli seems to produce. Of course, any such notion at this stage is pure speculation and cannot be said to be very significant. One other interesting point in this connection that deserves to be mentioned, however, is that Eccles and Rall (1951) advance very much the same hypothesis to account for reflex potentiation (facilitation) that Hebb does to account for learning. They suggest that swelling of end knobs at synaptic junctions might be responsible. They are aware that similar hypotheses have been advanced to account for learning and they briefly discuss the possibility of a relationship between learning and potentiation.

Some really useful information ought to come from the knowledge of the chemistry of the nervous system and its relation to functioning of the nervous system. This should be particularly true in the case of narcotics and poisons. Unfortunately, however, the theory of narcosis is in almost as bad a situation as the theory of learning. Consequently to hope for very much from chemical hypotheses at this stage is to hope for the blind to lead the blind. It is not even very clear whether some narcotics work primarily by inhibiting nerve metabolism or whether they work directly upon some mechanism in nerve discharge. Probably most narcotics affect both. In the near future, however, we may sufficiently understand upon what systems various narcotics work and how they work to be able to use them as tools of research upon learning.

Thus, while we are not very much better off in establishing a particular hypothesis about the neurophysiology of learning than we were 20 years ago, several avenues of approach give hope of future progress. This much could not have been said 20 years ago, and such a change may be predictive of great advances.

# CHAPTER 17

# CURRENT THEORETICAL PROBLEMS

One of the major aims of contemporary psychologists is to construct a general theory of learning that will serve both to integrate the experimental facts in the field of learning and to predict new, as yet undiscovered, facts. The development of general theories of learning involves many problems, however. In this chapter we shall review very briefly some of the more important problems in the construction of theories of learning as well as the general problem of the place of theory in the psychology of learning.

*A definition of learning.* You may recall that in the first chapter it was decided to postpone a definition of learning until we had examined the data of learning. We have looked at these data and now should be able to understand the nature of a definition of learning.

A little reflection will let you see that learning is really not so much a *phenomenon* as it is a *construct* designed to help explain and order a set of phenomena. Learning, like some other concepts in psychology, such as fatigue or motivation, has confused people for a long time. The earlier investigators thought that learning—as well as fatigue and motivation— were psychological events to be investigated. Over the years, however, it has become clear that the things psychologists investigate are *changes in behavior;* concepts like learning and fatigue are designed to describe the relationship between behavior and certain variables that are related to the changes.

It follows that a definition of learning must deal on the one hand with a change of behavior and, on the other hand, with a particular set of operations. Both parts of the definition are important. It is necessary to specify the operations as well as the nature of the change in behavior. With this in mind then, we shall define learning as *an increase in the strength of a response that comes about through repetitions of that response or repetitions of stimulus situations appropriate to the emission of that response.*

It will be useful to examine just what this definition covers and what it does not cover. First of all, it should be apparent, it is complementary to the definition of reinforcement given in Chap. 2 (p. 12). A reinforcement is said to be present any time an increase in the strength of response occurs. Therefore, by definition, reinforcement is basic to learning. Reinforcement, however, is not further defined by these pairs of definitions; reinforcement is stated only in terms of a change in response strength.

The second point about the definition of learning given above concerns the *indicants* (Stevens, 1951) used to measure a change in response strength. Three of these were specified in Chap. 2 (p. 14) and a fourth was added in Chap. 3 (p. 44). By now it should be very apparent to you that there are many more such indicants or measures. Most of them were discussed somewhere in this book. In many cases the change in strength of a response measured is difficult to see because of the problems involved in picking out some one indicant in complicated behavior. In the studies of problem solving, for example, experimenters are frequently content to describe the change of behavior with experience rather than give us some quantitative index of it.

Finally, let it be said, this definition of learning is far from satisfactory as it stands. The worst leak in the definition concerns the use of the expression, "an increase in the strength of a response." We use the term to cover many measures of behavior, yet knowing full well that two different measures of behavior in the same situation may not be correlated. In a little bit we shall attempt to improve this situation by considering the ways in which we may specify a change in strength.

## CURRENT PROBLEMS IN LEARNING THEORIES

Rather than examine each of the current theories of learning by itself— a task already done very adequately by Hilgard (1948)—we shall look at certain problems that various theories have faced and attempt to see how adequately they have solved these problems. The particular problems that we shall examine are either basic ones or ones that are interesting to people who would like to apply theories of learning to various psychological problems.

Certain of the fundamental problems in the theory of learning have already been discussed. It would be unnecessary at this point, for example, to spend very much time looking at the problem of the nature of reinforcement, for that problem was discussed in Chap. 2. Some of the important theoretical problems we have not yet touched, however, and it will be these that we shall examine here.

## The Problem of Quantification

Two of the great tools that have advanced the physical sciences so much are (1) carefully controlled experiments that yield highly quantified data and (2) the use of mathematics in the development of theory. Experimental psychologists have, wherever possible, attempted to imitate the physical sciences both in doing carefully quantified experiments and in trying to develop mathematical theories. Unfortunately this imitation has not always been so successful. In learning, for example, the basic data are so variable (with a few notable exceptions) that the application of the exact classical mathematical methods leaves much to be desired. To be sure, one may fit an equation to a learning curve, but the amount of variation around the mean fitted points is so great as to lead to serious misinterpretations if one takes the "fit" too literally. Recently, however, there has been a growing appreciation of the role of the mathematics of probability in biological and social sciences, and the application of probability theory to the data of learning may leave us a little more satisfied.

With this much background, then, we can turn to some of the current problems in the quantification of variables and theory in the psychology of learning. Because the theorists are many and prolific, we can do little more than sample some of the current views.

*Hull's approach.* The quantitative theory of learning that comes closest to deserving the adjective "classical" is that of Hull (1935a, 1943, 1950, etc.). Hull's method has been to make a number of postulates and then to see what theorems he can derive from the postulates. The postulates are fundamental statements that are not directly tested experimentally. The theorems are derived from the postulates by the rules of logic, and the theorems should be experimentally testable. Thus one of Hull's postulates concerns a stimulus trace or afterdischarge as the result of stimulation. This stimulus trace cannot be directly measured. In conjunction with some other postulates, however, the stimulus trace leads to some predictions about the form of the relationship between ease of conditioning and time intervals between stimuli. This relationship can be tested.

The value of the theory, according to Hull, lies in the excellence of the agreement between experimental fact and the theorems. The agreement of theorems and facts reflects on the excellence of the postulates. Any failure of agreement between theorems and facts should lead to a revision of the postulates. And, let it be said, Hull has scrupulously followed failures of his theory with revisions of his postulates.

Hull's theory is quantitative, however, only in the sense that the postulates are given exact mathematical expression. This in itself is admirable, but the mathematical expressions used point up a serious defect in Hull's postulates. Hull's postulates are in the form of quite complicated mathematical functions, and in view of the almost limitless possibilities one might have in the selection of such functions for any one postulate, his choices appear quite arbitrary.

For example, let us take the equation for response strength as a function of number of reinforcements introduced in Chap. 2 (p. 19). Hull writes this equation in the following way:

$$sHr = M - Me^{-kN}$$

He has chosen this particular equation as a postulate to represent the growth of habit strength (as he calls it) just because it is about the simplest kind of equation that represents growth properties. There is no other rationale to it. And so it is with all Hull's equations; they are complicated and somewhat arbitrary. While logic in this matter is on Hull's side—he has fulfilled the letter of the hypothetical-deductive method in logic—as a practical working matter it does not appear to be very fruitful.

If we examine the way in which Hull fits his equations to data, we see another drawback to the theory. Hull finds, as we found in Chap. 2, that the equation for habit strength given above will fit many different varieties of curves relating response strength to number of reinforcements. This is scarcely remarkable, however, since the parameters of the equation, $k$ and $M$, are allowed to be determined by the data. In other words, the constants are empirical, derived from the data and not from theory. If Hull had some way of independently *predicting* the value of these constants, and then could find that his equations fitted a number of different curves, it would indeed be a noteworthy accomplishment.

Thus we can summarize Hull's contribution by saying that he has taken all the fundamental relationships discussed in the earlier part of this book, put them in the form of postulates, and given them some arbitrary quantitative expression. In other words, he has specified number of reinforcements, delay of reinforcement, amount of reinforcement, motivation, etc., as determiners of the strength of response at any one moment and made a guess as to the mathematical relationships between these variables and strength of response. Hull's contribution is an important one, for it is difficult to find any other theory in psychology that has resulted directly in so much experimental work.

The great limiting feature of the approach of Hull and his associates has been, however, the essentially arbitrary mathematical functions used. As a way of developing a quantitative theory of behavior, Hull's procedure has little to recommend it over the purely empirical procedure of fitting data, more or less at random, to likely looking equations.

*The approach of mathematical biophysics.* A group of workers under the leadership of N. Rashevsky at the University of Chicago has spent many years applying mathematical analysis to problems of biology, especially those involving the central nervous system (Rashevsky, 1938, 1940; Householder and Landahl, 1945). These workers have postulated certain properties as belonging to the central nervous system. In general these postulates are based upon experimental fact in so far as possible, but in view of the paucity of fact concerning the particular points the mathematical biophysicists have been interested in, most of their postulates represent only likely possibilities. However, taking these postulates, the mathematical biophysicists have derived rather complex equations that express the growth of a habit with trials or reinforcements.

Two criticisms apply to the work of mathematical biophysics. The first criticism is similar to one of those applied to Hull's work. This concerns the nature of the constants or parameters used in the fitting of equations to learning curves. They must, as in the case of Hull's equations, be derived from the data. To be sure, the parameters may be defined in terms of some hypothetical property of the nervous system, such as number of "inhibiting neurons." Their exact values, however, must be obtained from the data fitted to the curves. Actually Householder and Landahl (1945) make some improvement in the technique of testing a theory when they apply the values obtained in one set of experiments to another set to see if they fit the new data.

The second criticism of the work of the mathematical biophysicists is one that does not apply to the work of Hull and his associates. This is the lack of interest they seem to have in generating new data. Householder and Landahl (1945) have made a few suggestions about some possible experiments arising out of their theory of discrimination learning, but the number of such suggestions nowhere near approaches the richness of Hull's theory in this respect. This is an important point, since one of the principal values of a theory lies in its ability to generate experimental tests. It is only from data obtained in experiments that the frontiers of our knowledge are really advanced, and if a theory suggests no new way of obtaining data about the events at hand it is not a very useful theory.

*Estes's approach.* Very recently Estes (1950) has presented a theory that in approach is somewhere between Hull and the mathematical biophysicists. He sticks pretty much to a behavioral level and avoids setting up his postulates in terms of the nervous system, as does Hull. On the other hand, he starts by generating his learning curves out of simple assumptions, as do the mathematical biophysicists.

Estes's fundamental assumption is that from an available pool of stimuli, each trial or repetition will condition a certain number of new stimuli. His application of this assumption to simple or classical conditioning is so straightforward that it will be worth while for us to examine it.

In classical conditioning, the conditioned stimulus always occurs contiguously with the response. This is because the unconditioned stimulus always elicits the response and the conditioned stimulus and unconditioned stimulus overlap in time. Estes assumes that each time the conditioned stimulus is paired with the response, a certain number of elements, $x$, of the conditioned stimulus are conditioned to the response. Since elements already conditioned cannot be conditioned again, this gives a decreasing pool of available elements from which to condition. This available pool of elements, at any one moment, is given by

$$(S_c - x)$$

$S_c$ is the total of the elements and $x$ the number conditioned already. Thus the *increment* in elements conditioned at any trial is given by the equation

$$\Delta x = k \frac{(S_c - x)}{S_c}$$

The constant, $k$, reflects the number of the total elements of the conditioned stimulus that affect the organism at any one trial. Estes assumes a continuous process and is thus able to write from the above equation a differential equation showing the rate of change of $x$, the number of elements conditioned at any one trial with respect to number of trials, $T$,

$$\frac{dx}{dT} = k \frac{(S_c - x)}{S_c}$$

In order to arrive at the *amount* of conditioning, *x*, that has gone on up to a given number of trials, we must integrate or add up the momentary rates given in the differential equation. This yields

$$x = S_c - (S_c - x_0)^{-qT}$$

This equation is very much like that presented by Hull, and if you break down (differentiate) Hull's equation you come out with some assumptions that are not too unlike Estes's. The difference is that Estes started with the assumptions.

Now that you have seen how psychologists can go about developing an equation, let us see what it will do. A fundamental difficulty with Estes's equations, as with others, is that they can be tested only by evaluating the constants from learning data. No one has yet come up with a theory that predicts the value of constants independently. This is for many reasons. For one thing, there is a certain arbitrary value that depends upon the selection of some one indicant to measure response strength. For another and more fundamental reason, we simply do not have the basic information to enter fixed values of parameters into equations of learning curves. Presumably this will come about only when we thoroughly understand enough of the nature of the neurophysiology underlying learning to make such terms as "number of elements" have physical meaning with definite and fixed values.

## The Problem of What to Measure

Another fundamental problem that has concerned learning theorists is *what* to measure. More specifically this is the question of what to choose as an indicant or indicants of the strength of response. This question is very closely allied to the problems of quantification and definition. As a matter of fact, a solution to this problem is basic to both a satisfactory definition of learning and a worth-while attempt to quantify it. So again we shall examine a few of the contemporary approaches to an important problem.

*Skinner's approach.* Skinner has made what is perhaps the most radical approach to this problem. He has stated that there is only one fundamental measure of the strength of response in the case of operant behavior. Since, within Skinner's framework, operant activity is of far greater importance than respondent activity to psychology, this means that in the more important cases there is only one measure of the strength of response. This measure is the *probability of occurrence of a response* (Skinner, 1950).

Skinner takes as the fundamental task of psychology the prediction and control of behavior. The one measure that satisfies the requirements of the prediction of behavior is the probability of occurrence of a particular act. The best measure of the probability of occurrence in a free, operant situation, such as lever pressing, is the rate of response or the number of responses per unit time. Thus in all Skinner's experimental work he relies only on this one measure, the rate of response.

It might be argued that there are other measures of the probability of occurrence. If, for example, we present an organism with a stimulus, we may ask: What is the probability that a response will occur to that stimulus? Skinner apparently ignores the kind of measure that would lead to an answer to this question, however. Skinner certainly does not admit measures of magnitude of response or measures of latency of response as indicants of strength of response. These measures do not at all fulfill the requirement of giving a measure of the probability of occurrence (Skinner, 1950).

*Hull's approach.* Hull's approach has been just about opposite from Skinner's. He has suggested at least four different measures of strength of response. Apparently any measure that shows a systematic improvement as a function of practice would be allowable by Hull as a measure of the strength of response. Hull has assumed that any such measure is simply an external indicator of the change in some hypothetical internal property. Thus, what Hull calls habit strength (and in part what we have called response strength) is related to a number of external indicants. The trick is to find the nature of the relationship between the external indicants and the hypothetical internal property.

One solution that Hull has attempted is to use one of the familiar psychological scaling techniques, the method of paired comparisons (Hull et al., 1947). The method of paired comparisons theoretically allows one to convert a series of measurements with unknown properties into a fundamental linear scale. The scale which Hull comes out with by using the method of paired comparisons on some measure of response strength he suggests as an operational definition of $sEr$ (what we have called response strength). So, one could argue, if two different indicants of response strength were taken in the same experiment and then, by the method of paired comparisons, converted to a fundamental scale of response strength, the resulting scale ought to be identical for both measures. Zeaman (1949) has actually done this experiment. He has compared running time and latency in a simple runway as indicants of response strength. The results of his calculations, by the method of paired comparisons, are shown in Fig. 61. As you can see, the two measurements differ somewhat from one another. The reasons for the failure of these two measures of response strength to agree are many. Zeaman suggests that they may be measures of two different habits. If this were so, Zeaman's test would not necessarily mean that the theory relating a number of different measures to the same thing had failed, but it would mean that a great deal of care must be exercised in setting up equivalent measures of the same habit.

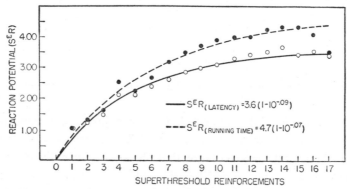

FIG. 61. Reaction potential as measured through latency and running time. The values for reaction potential derived by paired comparisons are not the same for these two indexes. (*Zeaman, 1948.*)

Thus it cannot be said that Hull's simple assumption that various indicants are all related to the same underlying change is met. There is some parallel between the different measures, but assuming the method of paired comparisons to be valid, they do not square up to each other exactly. While this failure is not a serious one at the moment, it must be emphasized that any further progress in quantitative theory demands a clear and unambiguous measure of the strength of response.

*A solution.* You are probably confused at this point. There seems to be no firm stone that one can grasp. We have rejected Skinner's attempt to set up a single measure of response strength, and we have found, in the last analysis, Hull's admission of several measures of response strength not to stand up to an experimental test. Consequently, we are left in a quandary as to *what* to measure as learning. This is tantamount to admitting that we are in a quandary also about a definition of learning, since what we measure specifies the general definition presented earlier.

There is a solution, however, though the solution is down a pathway that has not appealed to many learning theorists. The important thing about the change in behavior during learning is that it is always in the direction of some criterion. It is the criterion that defines what we measure and in what direction that change in behavior of the learner goes. This usually means that the organism achieves some goal defined by an experimenter or teacher with a decrease in the expenditure of time and energy. Thus the experimenter in the rat laboratory defines an errorless run through the maze as the criterion of learning, and the end of the maze is the goal (it is irrelevant whether or not the goal contains food; the definition is purely in terms of what the experimenter sets up as a goal).

An increase in response strength is always specified by some criterion. The criterion is predetermined, usually by an independent observer, and by one means or another, the organism is made to meet the criterion. The criterion may be a vague one, such as running the maze in "less time" or typing "with fewer errors," or the criterion may be an exact one, as running the maze "twice consecutively without errors."

The really important feature about the decision to allow a criterion to determine what we measure is that it does not always demand a one-to-one correspondence between different measures of response strength. Thus latency and probability of occurrence of a response may be positively correlated in one instance and negatively in another. An example will help. In the case of buzz-shock conditioning, if the conditioned stimulus comes on a few seconds before the shock, the organism, with practice, will come to delay the conditioned response for longer and longer periods, while at the same time the probability of occurrence of a conditioned response will increase. More usually, as you know, latency *decreases* with an increase in the number of reinforcements.

Thus, what is measured as an increase in response strength will depend upon the criterion set up by an independent observer, or, in the case of human learning, sometimes by the learner himself. The thing that you may not like about this notion of learning is that it places too much burden on the experimenter or the teacher. Yet, if you stop to think about it, this is the only practical way we have to define learning. Learning cannot be defined without a criterion. The criterion supplies the *direction* that the change of behavior is going to take. Thus the ultimate definition of learning must say that *learning is a change of behavior (increase in response strength) as a function of experience and in the direction of a predetermined criterion.*

This definition of learning almost precludes a general theory of learning. Rather we may have rather specific theories about changes of certain kinds and the variables that control them. Skinner, for example, has concerned himself with the variables that control the rate of emission of responses. This is a legitimate and worth-while enterprise within the framework of the notion of learning that has been implied in this chapter. Hull's notion, on the other hand, hardly fits the definition and analysis of learning that we have given. Hull, you will recall, attempts to relate a number of *different* kinds of changes in behavior to a set of common intervening variables. This implies that the common processes governing the changes in the measures specified must result in invariant relationships between the measures. We have seen that these measures are not necessarily always related in the same way.

An admission that learning must vary with the criteria chosen to evaluate it must mean that we cannot find any common set of changes that *always* must occur during learning. To the extent that learning theorists have not recognized this, theoretical issues in learning are confused and clouded. Let us take the example of the influence of work upon rate of learning. You will recall (p. 157) that the theory about work and rate of learning most widely accepted today involves an assumption of inhibition. The accumulation of inhibition during the performance of any response is supposed to temporarily weaken that response. A number of different experiments, each of which involved different learning situations with different criteria and different ways of measuring behavior, were taken as showing the effect of work upon behavior. What was not recognized at the time we took up this problem, however, is that learning may or may not show a decrement during continuous work (massed practice or greater force required for a response), depending upon the measure of response strength chosen.

Thus, instead of defining learning in terms of change of some hypothetical state, we define learning by a set of operations and a change in behavior. Confusion between changes in behavior called learning and those attributed to motivation and fatigue are eliminated if we remember that the definition of learning specifies a change in a certain direction as a function of the repetitions of responses or situations suitable for that response. If the repetitions of the situation occur, but the organism does not change in the direction of the criterion, learning has not taken place.

This definition further eliminates confusion between negative and positive transfer. Negative transfer hinders learning where the criteria are incompatible with the subject's attempt to use previously learned responses. Positive transfer helps learning where the criteria are compatible with the subject's attempt to use previously learned responses.

Definitional problems are never real problems, and it is easy enough for someone to quarrel with the present notion of learning simply by setting up some other definition. The advantage of this definition is that it enables us to talk about a large amount of data without fear of being self-contradictory. Individual theorists may be concerned with special problems in what we have called learning, and they may, as a consequence, redefine terms to suit their special problems. However, the present definition enables us to examine a wide variety of problems of functional relationships between variables without concern to whether or not we are investigating the "right" variables.

## THE APPLICATION OF LEARNING THEORY

One important topic that we must treat briefly is the application of learning theory to problems in human behavior. Many of those who have worked at the theoretical problems in learning have had in mind an eventual application to human behavior. As a matter of fact, some psychologists have maintained that theory is only useful in so far as it aids in the process of the prediction and control of behavior. Just exactly how the various theories of learning and the experimental evidence obtained in the psychological laboratory can aid in the prediction and control of behavior is an interesting point.

Sometimes people mean the principles and laws obtained from laboratory investigation when they speak of learning theory. We may speak of applying learning theory, for example, when we apply the principles governing partial reinforcement to a situation. In a sense this usage is correct, though it may lead to confusion. The theory is involved in the generality of the events investigated in the laboratory. We may say, for example, that the persistence with which a spoiled child badgers his mother for candy is due to the fact that his mother, in desperation, has occasionally reinforced the behavior of whining and begging. We do not know, of course, whether or not this is the case, but in light of the laboratory experiments, this is what we should expect partial reinforcement to lead to.

At other times people speak of applying learning theory when they mean applying a particular *theory* about some aspect of learning to a problem at hand. For example, we may apply the theory of need reduction to a clinical behavioral problem. In this case we are applying a theory about behavior to events of everyday life. The principle of need reduction has not been demonstrated to apply without question to well-controlled events in the laboratory, much less to the casual events of everyday life. The application of theory in this sense, as you might expect, is much more hazardous than the application of experimentally derived principles of learning.

With this distinction in mind, then, we can see some of the areas of human behavior where the application of principles from the study of learning can be of importance.

*Application to personality problems.* In recent years there have been several attempts to apply basic data and theories of learning to personality problems. Perhaps the earliest such attempt is that of Guthrie (1938). One of the more recent and more successful is that of Dollard and Miller (1950). They have taken the fundamentals of learning, as well as some special theories such as need reduction, and applied them to the development of personality. A few examples of how they apply these principles will show us in an interesting way the value of learning theory for problems in personality.

Very early in their book, Dollard and Miller show how the theory of need reduction could account for one basis of fear of being left alone in children. If a baby is left to get very hungry when it is alone, so that it may cry and fret while the hunger drive increases, when the child is finally fed there will be a large-scale need reduction involving cessation of the crying activity, etc. These responses of crying, fearfulness, etc., then get reinforced and thus this becomes the characteristic response of the child when left alone.

The above example involves a lot of "ifs," but that is the way one must proceed in dealing with human personalities. The real test of the theory of learning at this level is in how it works. For example, if the child is fed before it gets to struggling and crying when alone, according to the theory, the child should learn to accept being alone. If this is true, then the theory has some additional advantage.

Dollard and Miller apply the same sort of reasoning to problems in the readjustment of maladjusted people. They give a detailed account of the case history of one woman who was very disturbed in her personal life. They carefully followed the course of psychotherapy in the case and pointed out how each aspect of psychotherapy worked in terms of learning theory. They showed, for example, how talking out a problem to a psychotherapist could be interpreted as the extinction of anxiety responses connected with events in the individual's life that aroused anxiety. In great detail they interpreted transference as a special case of stimulus generalization and showed how discrimination learning helps the patient to distinguish between behavior that is appropriate to various life situations and that which is inappropriate.

Thus the principal contribution of learning theory to problems of personality is in the understanding of how certain personalistic reactions may arise. Of course, there are many other things, such as heredity and socioeconomic circumstances, that must be considered in the development of personality. But the place of learning is an important one, and when we see, as Dollard and Miller have, some of the problems of personality in the light of learning, some of the mystery of the development of personality clears up.

*Application to training and education.* At the beginning of the twentieth century there was much hope that the experimental study of learning would lead, in a fairly short time, to a *scientific* analysis of the problems of teaching and training. Many of the early books on learning were greatly concerned with the application of such facts as there were to problems in education. And, in a very real sense, some valuable contributions were made in this way. The early studies of transfer of training, particularly that of Thorndike and Woodworth (1901), were influential in the decline of the notion of formal discipline. But, all in all, the experimental study of learning did not live up to the hopes for application that it aroused. By 1930 workers in the experimental study of learning disclaimed any attempt to achieve results that would have immediate application. This was accompanied by a greatly increased interest in learning theory. More recently, however, there have been some signs of a return to the problems of application, though on a more modest scale. There are now many laboratories that are concerned with the application of basic principles of learning to particular problems in training.

The influence of E. L. Thorndike sat heavily upon educational psychology for many years. In recent years, however, educational psychologists have expressed interest in a wide variety of theories about learning. Several recent symposia on problems of learning in education (Swenson, Anderson, and Stacey, 1949; Henry, 1950) show an increasing awareness of the ways in which some problems of education can be looked at in terms of more recent learning theory. The educational psychologists, of course, have been somewhat critical of learning theory for its preoccupation with animal behavior and the highly artificial kind of human learning characteristic of the laboratory. On the other hand, educational psychology has just begun to tap the possibilities of modern learning theory, and it may well turn out that psychology's concern for carefully controlled experiments may be of greater benefit to education in the long run than the same amount of effort devoted to problems of immediate practical importance.

At the present time it seems likely that the educator will find the greatest use for learning theory in the same methods as those used by Dollard and Miller in the application of learning theory to problems of personality. The educator should find the contemporary notions of punishment and anxiety, retroactive inhibition and positive transfer, etc., valuable as frames of reference within which to view the processes of classroom learning. He will find that learning theory does not tell him what to do in so many steps, but he will find an appreciation of what to expect in the classroom. An analysis, for example, of the experimental findings on punishment should lead to a more adequate understanding of the problems of adjustment and social behavior in the early grades.

One notion that needs to be eliminated is that the psychology of learning is solely responsible for the basic contributions to the understanding of the processes of classroom learning. Social psychology and the psychology of personality have fundamental contributions to make. The psychology of learning can give some fundamental principles, but the understanding of individual variability and differences in the application of these principles can come only through the understanding of the social processes and individual processes in the learning situation. Thus an application of learning theory to the larger problems in education can be made only in conjunction with the application of social theory and theories of personality and development.

## SOME CONCLUDING REMARKS

In this short book we have followed a somewhat devious and tortuous path through the experimental literature on learning. One thing disturbs the author very much, and that is that the student may fail to see the forest for the trees. To make matters a little worse, the author may have been guilty of producing some misconceptions.

This is the place where the author relieves his mind of a few of the doubts that he has had concerning what has been accomplished in this book. If you do not remember a single experiment after you close this book at the end of the semester, the author will not feel too badly. If, however, you do not come away from this book with an understanding of the aims of the study of learning, the author will be disappointed. The way in which organisms learn is much like the way in which organisms breathe, move, or digest. It is an important function of organic life, and one that obeys lawful, natural principles, albeit complicated ones. Psychologists do not yet fully understand the nature of the principles underlying learning, but they do understand enough to see the rough outlines of the natural laws governing different kinds of learning. If you appreciate this, you have gained much from this book.

The author has been guilty of occasional oversimplification and somewhat summary treatment of controversial issues. This has been for a good reason. An attempt has been made to avoid burdening the student's mind with the occasional disputatious quarreling one sees among learning psychologists. But in doing this, the author may have laid the groundwork for some misconceptions on the part of students.

For one thing, there has been too much emphasis on the stimulus and response in this book. The idea could be obtained that rats and men are "stimulus-bound"—that they never react except when faced with an external stimulus. Or the idea may be grasped that all behavior is a rigid sequence of stimuli and responses. Nothing could be further from the truth, and, while at one time learning psychologists thought this way, pure stimulus-response analysis is almost a thing of the past. Skinner's (1938) emphasis upon emitted behavior, for example, is testimony to this. The characteristic of the operant is that it comes from the organism with little in the way of supporting external stimuli. Supposedly the origin of the operant is central in nature. Hebb (1949) has emphasized the process of *set* or *determining tendency* as autonomous central events that organize and direct behavior.

The importance of motivation in performance, first emphasized by Tolman, is another source of testimony to the freedom of the organism from momentary external stimuli. The internal drive state, it is now almost universally recognized, keeps behavior going in organized patterns in the absence of external stimuli.

There has been a growing awareness in recent years that learning may be described in many ways, depending upon what has been learned. Tolman, long an advocate of this kind of thinking, has written a paper in which he outlines a number of ways of describing learning (Tolman, 1949). Certainly, if we accept the notion that learning can be defined only in terms of the criteria of an external observer, then there must be many ways of describing learning, depending upon what those criteria are. The learning of responses to external stimuli is only one of these ways. Relationships between stimuli may also be learned; this relationship can then be used by the organism in directing patterns of responses.

Note very carefully, however, that all this is not to say that stimulus-response analysis is not important. For even many purely "central" events may be analyzed into stimulus and response components. How does creative thinking get started, for example? One evening while driving home in my car and while thinking about some problems in partial reinforcement, I came across the solution of how to treat some work-decrement curves that had been bothering me. There is not much in common between partial reinforcement and work-decrement curves, but somewhere in the chain of thoughts about partial reinforcement there was a stimulus to the correct responses of how to treat the work-decrement curves.

While the traffic engineer will probably be a little alarmed at my lack of intellectual contact with external stimuli at this point, there is no doubt that the chain of events in the thinking process in this situation was internally governed. They did, however, go in a *serial* sequence that for purposes of analysis can be treated in terms of stimulus and response.

Thus in the application of the paradigm of stimulus and response analysis to the problem of transfer, do not be too literal in your interpretation of "stimuli" and "responses." The paradigm itself seems to hold very well for thinking processes, when these processes are analyzed out into their serial components. We have dealt with negative and positive transfer in laboratory examples in which everything is explicitly out in the open, but the value of the concepts derived from laboratory studies is in their usefulness when applied to the complex problems of behavior in nature.

# REFERENCES

ALBERTS, E., and EHRENFREUND, D. (1951) Transposition in children as a function of age. *J. exp. Psychol.*, 41, 30–38.

ALLPORT, G. W. (1937) *Personality*. New York: Holt.

ALPER, T. G. (1946a) Memory for completed and incompleted tasks as a function of personality: An analysis of group data. *J. abnorm. soc. Psychol.*, 41, 403–420.

ALPER, T. G. (1946b) Task-orientation vs. ego-orientation in learning and retention. *Amer. J. Psychol.*, 59, 236–248.

AMMONS, R. B. (1947) Acquisition of motor skill: I. Quantitative analysis and theoretical formulation. *Psychol. Rev.*, 54, 263–281.

ANDERSON, E. E. (1941a) The externalization of drives: I. Theoretical considerations. *Psychol. Rev.*, 48, 204–224.

ANDERSON, E. E. (1941b) The externalization of drives: III. Maze learning by non-rewarded and satiated rats. *J. genet. Psychol.*, 59, 397–426.

ANDERSON, G. L. (1949) Quantitative thinking as developed connectionist and field theories of learning. In E. J. Swensen *et al., Learning Theory in School Situations*. Minneapolis: University of Minnesota Press.

ANDERSON, O. D., and LIDDELL, H. S. (1935) Observations on experimental neurosis in sheep. *Arch. Neurol. Psychiat., Chicago,* 34, 330–354.

AUSTIN, S. D. M. (1921) A study in logical memory. *Amer. J. Psychol.*, 32, 370–403.

BAKER, K. E., and WYLIE, R. C. (1950) Transfer of verbal training to a motor task. *J. exp. Psychol.*, 40, 632–638.

BAKER, K. E., WYLIE, R. C., and GAGNÉ, R. M. (1950) Transfer of training to a motor skill as a function of variation in rate of response. *J. exp. Psychol.*, 40, 721–732.

BALLARD, P. B. (1913) Oblivescence and reminiscence. *Brit. J. Psychol. Monogr. Suppl.*, 1, No. 2.

BARTLETT, F. C. (1932) *Remembering*. London: Cambridge.

BAYLEY, N. (1926) Performance tests for three, four and five year old children. *Ped. Sem.*, 33, 435–454.

BEAN, J. W., WAPNER, S., and SIEGFRIED, E. C. (1945) Residual disturbances in the higher functions of the C.N.S. induced by oxygen at high pressure. *Amer. J. Physiol.*, 143, 206–213.

BERNARD, J. (1942) The specificity of the effect of shock on the acquisition and retention of motor and verbal habits. *J. exp. Psychol.*, 31, 69–78.

BIEL, W. C., and FORCE, R. C. (1943) Retention of nonsense syllables in intentional and incidental learning. *J. exp. Psychol.*, 32, 52–63.

BIJOU, S. W. (1942) The development of a conditioning methodology for studying experimental neurosis in the rat. *J. comp. Psychol.*, 44, 91–106.

BIJOU, S. W. (1943) A study of "experimental neurosis" in the rat by the conditioned response technique. *J. comp. Psychol.,* 36, 1–20.

BILLS, A. G. (1931) Blocking: A new principle of mental fatigue. *Amer. J. Psychol.,* 43, 230–245.

BIRCH, H. G. (1945) The relation of previous experience to insightful problem-solving. *J. comp. Psychol.,* 38, 367–383.

BLANKENSHIP, A. B., and WHITELY, P. L. (1941) Proactive inhibition in the recall of advertising material. *J. soc. Psychol.,* 13, 311–322.

BLODGETT, H. C. (1929) The effect of the introduction of reward upon maze behavior of rats. *Univ. Calif. Publ. Psychol.,* 4, 113–134.

BLODGETT, H. C., and McCUTCHAN, K. (1947) Place vs. response learning in the simple T-maze. *J. exp. Psychol.,* 37, 412–422.

BLODGETT, H. C., McCUTCHAN, K., and MATHEWS, R. (1949) Spatial learning in the T-maze: The influence of direction, turn, and food location. *J. exp. Psychol.,* 39, 800–809.

BLUM, R. A., and BLUM, J. S. (1949) Factual issues in the "continuity" controversy. *Psychol. Rev.,* 56, 33–50.

BOGUSLAVSKY, G. W., and GUTHRIE, E. R. (1941) The recall of completed and interrupted activities: An investigation of Zeigarnik's experiment. *Psychol. Bull.,* 38, 575–576.

BOOK, W. F. (1925) *Learning to typewrite.* New York: Gregg.

BORING, E. G. (1945) The use of operational definitions in science. *Psychol. Rev.,* 52, 243–245.

BOUTHILET, L. (1948) *The measurement of intuitive thinking.* Ph.D. dissertation, University of Chicago.

BOYCOTT, B. B., and YOUNG, J. Z. (1950) The comparative study of learning. In *Symposia of the Society for Experimental Biology.* London: Cambridge. Vol. IV.

BREGMAN, E. O. (1934) An attempt to modify the emotional attitudes of infants by the conditioned response technique. *J. genet. Psychol.,* 45, 169–198.

BREGMAN, E. O., THORNDIKE, E. L., and WOODYARD, E. (1943) The retention of the ability to draw lines of a given length blindfolded. *J. exp. Psychol.,* 33, 78–80.

BRENNER, B. (1934) Effect of immediate and delayed praise and blame upon learning and recall. *Teach. Coll. Contr. Educ.,* No. 620.

BRIDGE, M. (1934) The effect on retention of different methods of revision. *Australian Council on Education Research Series,* No. 28. Melbourne: University Press.

BRIGGS, L. J., and REED, H. B. (1943) The curve of retention for substance material. *J. exp. Psychol.,* 32, 513–517.

BROGDEN, W. J. (1939) Sensory pre-conditioning. *J. exp. Psychol.,* 25, 323–332.

BROGDEN, W. J. (1947) Sensory pre-conditioning of human subjects. *J. exp. Psychol.,* 37, 527–540.

BROGDEN, W. J., LIPMAN, E. A., and CULLER, E. A. (1938) The role of incentive in conditioning and extinction. *Amer. J. Psychol.,* 51, 109–117.

BROMILEY, R. B. (1948) Conditioned responses in a dog after removal of neocortex. *J. comp. physiol. Psychol.,* 41, 102–110.

BROOKS, F. D., and BASSETT, S. J. (1928) The retention of American history in the junior high school. *J. educ. Res.,* 18, 195–202.

BROWN, J. S. (1948) Gradients of approach and avoidance responses and their relation to motivation. *J. comp. physiol. Psychol.,* 41, 450–465.

BROWNELL, W. A. (1941) *Arithmetic in grades I and II.* Durham, N.C.: Duke University Press.

BROWNELL, W. A. (1947) An experiment on "borrowing" in third-grade arithmetic. *J. educ. Res.,* 41, 161–171.

BROWNELL, W. A. (1948) Criteria of learning in educational research. *J. educ. Psychol.,* 39, 170–182.

BROWNELL, W. A. (1949) *Meaningful vs. mechanical learning.* Durham, N.C.: Duke University Press.

BRUCE, R. W. (1933) Conditions of transfer of training. *J. exp. Psychol.,* 16, 343–361.

BRUNER, J. S., and GOODMAN, C. C. (1947) Value and need as organizing factors in perception. *J. abnorm. soc. Psychol.,* 42, 33–44.

BRUNER, J. S., and POSTMAN, L. (1947) Tension and tension release as organizing factors in perception. *J. Pers.,* 15, 300–308.

BRYAN, W. L., and HARTER, N. (1897) Studies in the physiology and psychology of the telegraphic language. *Psychol. Rev.,* 4, 27–53.

BRYAN, W. L., and HARTER, N. (1899) Studies on the telegraphic language. The acquisition of a hierarchy of habits. *Psychol. Rev.,* 6, 345–375.

BUCHSBAUM, R. (1948) *Animals without backbones* (2d Ed.). Chicago: University of Chicago Press.

BUGELSKI, B. R. (1942) Interference with recall of original responses after learning new responses to old stimuli. *J. exp. Psychol.,* 30, 368–379.

BUGELSKI, B. R. (1948) An attempt to reconcile unlearning and reproductive inhibition explanations of proactive inhibition. *J. exp. Psychol.,* 38, 670–682.

BUGELSKI, B. R. (1950) A remote association explanation of the relative difficulty of learning nonsense syllables in a serial list. *J. exp. Psychol.,* 40, 336–348.

BUNCH, M. E. (1935) Certain effects of electric shock in learning a stylus maze. *J. comp. Psychol.,* 20, 211–242.

BUNCH, M. E. (1938) The measurement of reminiscence. *Psychol. Rev.,* 45, 525–531.

BUNCH, M. E. (1941) A comparison of retention and transfer of training from similar material after relatively long intervals of time. *J. comp. Psychol.,* 32, 217–231.

BUNCH, M. E. (1946) Retroactive inhibition or facilitation from interpolated learning as a function of time. *J. comp. Psychol.,* 39, 287–291.

BUNCH, M. E., and McTEER, F. D. (1932) The influence of punishment during learning upon retroactive inhibition. *J. exp. Psychol.,* 15, 473–495.

BUNCH, M. E., and MAGSDICK, W. K. (1933) The retention in rats of an incompletely learned maze solution for short intervals of time. *J. comp. Psychol.,* 16, 385–409.

BURNETT, T. C. (1912) Some observations on decerebrate frogs with special reference to the formation of associations. *Amer. J. Psychol.,* 30, 80–87.

BUXTON, C. E. (1940) Latent learning and the goal gradient hypothesis. *Contr. psychol. Theor.,* 2, No. 6.

BUXTON, C. E. (1943) The status of research in reminiscence. *Psychol. Bull.,* 40, 313–340.

BUXTON, C. E. (1948) Interaction of meaningfulness and length of rest interval as factors in measured reminiscence. *Amer. Psychologist,* 3, 235–236.

BUXTON, C. E., and BAKEN, M. B. (1949) Correction vs. non-correction learning techniques as related to reminiscence in serial anticipation learning. *J. exp. Psychol.,* 39, 338–341.

BUXTON, C. E., and ROSS, H. V. (1949) Relationship between reminiscence and type of learning technique in serial anticipation learning. *J. exp. Psychol.,* 39, 41–46.

CAMPBELL, R. J., and HARLOW, H. F. (1945) Problem solution by monkeys following bilateral removal of the prefrontal areas: V. Spatial delayed reactions. *J. exp. Psychol.,* 35, 110–126.

CARMICHAEL, L., HOGAN, H. P., and WALTER, A. A. (1932) An experimental study of the effect of language on the reproduction of visually perceived form. *J. exp. Psychol.,* 15, 73–86.

CARR, H. A. (1919) Distribution of effort. *Psychol. Bull.,* 16, 26–28.

CARR, H. A. (1925) *Psychology.* New York: Longmans.

CARR, H. A., and WATSON, J. B. (1908) Orientation in the white rat. *J. comp. Neurol.,* 18, 27–44.

CARTER, L. F., and SCHOOLER, K. (1949) Value, need and other factors in perception. *Psychol. Rev.,* 56, 200–207.

CLARK, K. B. (1940) Some factors influencing the remembering of prose material. *Arch. Psychol.,* N.Y., 35, No. 253.

COFER, C. N., and FOLEY, J. P., JR. (1942) Mediated generalization and the interpretation of verbal behavior: I. Prolegomena. *Psychol. Rev.,* 49, 513–540.

COFER, C. N., JANIS, M., and ROWELL, M. M. (1943) Mediated generalization and the interpretation of verbal behavior: III. Experimental study of antonym gradients. *J. exp. Psychol.,* 32, 266–269.

COLE, L. E. (1924) Latin as a preparation ∙for French and Spanish. *Sch. & Soc.,* 19, 618–622.

COOK, B. S., and HILGARD, E. R. (1949) Distributed practice in motor learning: Progressively increasing and decreasing rests. *J. exp. Psychol.,* 39, 169–172.

COOK, S. W. (1939) The production of "experimental neurosis" in the white rat. *Psychosom. Med.,* 1, 293–308.

COOK, T. W. (1934) Massed and distributed practice in puzzle solving. *Psychol. Rev.,* 41, 330–355.

COPELAND, M. (1930) An apparent conditioned response in *Nereis virens. J. comp. Psychol.,* 10, 339–354.

COREY, S. M. (1934) Learning from lectures vs. learning from readings. *J. educ. Psychol.,* 25, 459–470.

COURTS, F. A. (1937) The alleged retroactive effect of visual stimuli subsequent to a given response. *J. exp. Psychol.,* 20, 144–154.

COWLES, J. T. (1937) Food tokens as incentives for learning by chimpanzees. *Comp. Psychol. Monogr.,* 14, No. 7.

CRESPI, L. P. (1942) Quantitative variation of incentive and performance in the white rat. *Amer. J. Psychol.,* 55, 467–517.

CRESPI, L. P. (1944) Amount of reinforcement and level of performance. *Psychol. Rev.,* 51, 341–357.

CRISLER, G. (1930) Salivation is unnecessary for the establishment of the salivary conditioned reflex induced by morphine. *Amer. J. Physiol.,* 94, 553–556.

CRONBACH, L. J. (1950) Educational Psychology. *Annu. Rev. Psychol.,* 1, 235–254.

CRUTCHFIELD, R. S. (1940) Inhibitory effects in partial review. *Psychol. Bull.,* 37, 489.

CULLER, E. A. (1928) Nature of the learning curve. *Psychol. Bull.,* 25, 143–144.

CULLER, E. A., COAKLEY, J. D., SHURRAGER, P. S., and ADES, H. W. (1939) Differential effects of curare upon higher and lower levels of the central nervous system. *Amer. J. Psychol.,* 52, 266–273.

CULLER, E. A., and METTLER, F. A. (1934) Conditioned behavior in a decorticate dog. *J. comp. Psychol.,* 18, 291–303.

DAY, L., and BENTLEY, M. (1911) A note on learning in Paramecium. *J. Anim. Behav.,* 1, 67–73.

DEESE, E. L. (1938) *A study of the retention of meaningful verbal material at short time intervals.* M.A. dissertation, Yale University. Cited in Noble (1950).

DEESE, J. (1948) *The retroactive inhibition of a conditioned response as a function of extinction during interpolated conditioning.* Ph.D. dissertation, Indiana University.

DEESE, J. (1950a) A quantitative derivation of latent learning. *Psychol. Rev.,* 57, 291–294.

DEESE, J. (1950b) The effect of extinction upon rate of reconditioning. *J. exp. Psychol.,* 40, 488–493.

DEESE, J. (1951) The extinction of a discrimination without performance of the choice response. *J. comp. physiol. Psychol.,* 44, 362–366.

DEESE, J., and BOWEN, H. M. (1950) Unpublished data, The Johns Hopkins University.

DEESE, J., and CARPENTER, J. A. (1951) Drive-level and reinforcement. *J. exp. Psychol.,* 42, 236–238.

DEESE, J., and KELLOGG, W. N. (1946) Modification of reflex behavior in spinal dogs. *Proc. Ind. Acad. Sci.,* 55, 171–177.

DEESE, J., and KELLOGG, W. N. (1949) Some new data on the nature of 'spinal conditioning.' *J. comp. physiol. Psychol.,* 42, 157–160.

DENNY, M. R. (1946) The role of secondary reinforcement in a partial reinforcement learning situation. *J. exp. Psychol.,* 36, 373–389.

DERNOWA-YARMOLENKO, A. A. (1933) The fundamentals of a method of investigating the function of the nervous system as revealed in overt behavior. *J. genet. Psychol.,* 42, 319–338.

DODSON, J. D. (1915) The relation of strength of stimulus to rapidity of habit-formation. *J. Anim. Behav.,* 5, 330–336.

DOLLARD, J., and MILLER, N. E. (1950) *Personality and psychotherapy.* New York: McGraw-Hill.

DORÉ, L. R., and HILGARD, E. R. (1938) Spaced practice as a test of Snoddy's two processes in mental growth. *J. exp. Psychol.,* 23, 359–374.

DRAKE, C. S. (1940) The iota function. *J. educ. Res.,* 34, 190–198.

DUNCAN, C. P. (1949) The retroactive effect of electroshock on learning. *J. comp. physiol. Psychol.,* 42, 32–44.

DUNCKER, K. (1945) On problem solving (trans. from 1935 original). *Psychol. Monogr.,* 58, No. 270.

DUNLAP, K. (1932) *Habits.* New York: Liveright.

DURKIN, H. E. (1937) Trial-and-error gradual analysis, and sudden reorganization: An experimental study of problem solving. *Arch. Psychol.,* N.Y., 30, No. 210.

DYSINGER, D. W., and GREGORY, W. S. (1941) A preliminary study of some factors related to student achievement and grades in the beginning course in psychology. *J. gen. Psychol.,* 24, 195–209.

EBBINGHAUS, H. (1885) *Uber das . . . Gedachtnis: Untersuchungen zur experimentelen Psychologie.* Leipzig: Duncker and Humblot.

ECCLES, J. C., and RALL, W. (1951) Effects induced in a monosynaptic path by its activation. *J. Neurophysiol.,* 14, 353–376.

EDWARDS, A. L. (1941) Political frames of reference as a factor influencing recognition. *J. abnorm. soc. Psychol.,* 36, 34–50.

EDWARDS, A. L. (1942) The retention of affective experiences; a criticism and restatement of the problem. *Psychol. Rev.,* 49, 43–53.

EHRENFREUND, D. (1948) An experimental test of the continuity theory of discrimination learning with pattern vision. *J. comp. physiol. Psychol.,* 41, 408–422.

ELLIOT, F. R. (1936) Memory for visual, auditory and visual-auditory material. *Arch. Psychol.,* N.Y., No. 199.

ELLSON, D. G. (1938) Quantitative studies of the interaction of simple habits: I. Recovery from specific and generalized effects of extinction. *J. exp. Psychol.,* 23, 339–358.

ELLSON, D. G. (1939) The concept of the reflex reserve. *Psychol. Rev.,* 46, 566–575.

EPSTEIN, B. (1949) Immediate and retention effects of interpolated rest periods on learning performance. *Teach. Coll. Contr. Educ.,* No. 949.

ERICKSEN, S. C. (1942) Variability of attack in massed and distributed practice. *J. exp. Psychol.,* 31, 339–358.

ESTES, W. K. (1944) An experimental study of punishment. *Psychol. Monogr.,* 57, No. 263.

ESTES, W. K. (1949a) Generalization of secondary reinforcement from the primary drive. *J. comp. physiol. Psychol.,* 42, 286–295.

ESTES, W. K. (1949b) A study of the motivating conditions necessary for secondary reinforcement. *J. exp. Psychol.,* 39, 306–310.

ESTES, W. K. (1950) Towards a statistical theory of learning. *Psychol. Rev.,* 57, 94–107.

ESTES, W. K., and SKINNER, B. F. (1941) Some quantitative properties of anxiety. *J. exp. Psychol.,* 29, 390–400.

FINAN, J. L. (1939) Effects of frontal lobe lesions on temporally organized behavior in monkeys. *J. Neurophysiol.,* 2, 208–226.

FINAN, J. L. (1940) Quantitative studies in motivation: I. Strength of conditioning in rats under various degrees of hunger. *J. comp. Psychol.,* 29, 119–124.

FINAN, J. L. (1942) Delayed response with pre-delay reinforcement in monkeys after the removal of the frontal lobes. *Amer. J. Psychol.,* 55, 202–214.

FINCH, G. (1938) Salivary conditioning in atropinized dogs. *Amer. J. Physiol.,* 124, 136–141.

FINGER, F. W. (1944) Experimental behavior disorders in the rat. In J. McV. Hunt (Ed.), *Personality and the behavior disorders.* New York: Ronald.

FINGER, F. W. (1949) Hunger drive and general activity in the rat. *Amer. Psychologist,* 4, 223–224.

FLEURE, H., and WALTON, C. (1907) Notes on the habits of some sea anemones. *Zool. Anz.,* 31, 212–220.

FOLEY, J. P., JR., and COFER, C. N. (1943) Mediated generalization and the interpretation of verbal behavior: II. Experimental study of certain homophone and synonym gradients. *J. exp. Psychol.,* 32, 168–175.

FORLANO, G. (1936) School learning with various methods of practice and rewards. *Teach. Coll. Contr. Educ.,* No. 688.

FRANK, L. B., and DEESE, J. (1949) Latent learning under conditions of high motivation: B. with reinforcement. *Amer. Psychologist,* 4, 359.

FREEBURNE, C. M. (1949) The influence of training in perceptual span and perceptual speed upon reading ability. *J. educ. Psychol.,* 40, 321–352.

FRENCH, J. W. (1940) Trial and error learning in Paramecium. *J. exp. Psychol.,* 26, 609–613.

FRENCH, J. W. (1942) The effect of temperature on the retention of a maze habit in fish. *J. exp. Psychol.,* 31, 79–87.

FREUD, S. (1925) *Collected Papers,* Vol. 4. London: Hogarth.

FULLER, P. R. (1949) Operant conditioning of a vegetative human organism. *Amer. J. Psychol.,* 62, 587–589.

FULTON, J. F. (1949) *Physiology of the nervous system* (3d Ed.). New York: Oxford University Press.

GAGNÉ, R. M. (1941) The effect of spacing of trials on the acquisition and extinction of a conditioned operant response. *J. exp. Psychol.,* 29, 201–216.

GAGNÉ, R. M., BAKER, K., and FOSTER, H. (1950) Transfer of discrimination training to a motor task. *J. exp. Psychol.,* 40, 314–328.

GAGNÉ, R. M., and FOSTER, H. (1949a) Transfer of training from practice on components in a motor skill. *J. exp. Psychol.,* 39, 47–68.

GAGNÉ, R. M., and FOSTER, H. (1949b)

Transfer to a motor skill from practice on a pictured representation. *J. exp. Psychol.,* 39, 342–354.

GAGNÉ, R. M., FOSTER, H., and CROWLEY, M. E. (1948) The measurement of transfer of training. *Psychol. Bull.,* 45, 97–130.

GANTT, W. H. (1936) An experimental approach to psychiatry. *Amer. J. Psychiat.,* 92, 1007–1021.

GANTT, W. H. (1938) The nervous secretion of saliva: The relation of the conditioned reflex to the intensity of the unconditioned stimulus. *Proc. Amer. Physiol. Soc., Amer. J. Physiol.,* 123, 74.

GANTT, W. H. (1944) *Experimental basis for neurotic behavior.* New York: Hoeber.

GARRETT, H. E. (1928) The relation of tests of memory and learning to each other and to general intelligence in a highly selected adult group. *J. educ. Psychol.,* 19, 601–613.

GATES, A. I. (1917) Recitation as a factor in memorizing. *Arch. Psychol.,* N.Y., 6, No. 40.

GELLERMAN, L. W. (1931*a*) The double alternation problem: I. The behavior of monkeys in a double alternation temporal maze. *J. genet. Psychol.,* 39, 50–72.

GELLERMAN, L. W. (1931*b*) The double alternation problem: II. The behavior of children and human adults in a double alternation temporal maze. *J. genet. Psychol.,* 39, 197–226.

GERMANE, C. E. (1921) The value of the written paragraph summary. *J. educ. Res.,* 3, 116–123.

GIBB, J. R. (1941) The relative effects of sleeping and waking upon the retention of nonsense syllables. *Psychol. Bull.,* 38, 734.

GIBSON, E. J. (1940) A systematic application of the concepts of generalization and differentiation to verbal learning. *Psychol. Rev.,* 47, 196–229.

GIBSON, E. J. (1941) Retroactive inhibition as a function of degree of generalization between tasks. *J. exp. Psychol.,* 28, 93–115.

GIBSON, J. J. (1929) The reproduction of visually perceived forms. *J. exp. Psychol.,* 12, 1–39.

GILLILAND, A. R. (1948) The rate of forgetting. *J. educ. Psychol.,* 39, 19–26.

GIRDEN, E. (1940) Cerebral mechanisms in conditioning under curare. *Amer. J. Psychol.,* 53, 397–406.

GIRDEN, E. (1947) Conditioned responses in *curarized* monkeys. *Amer. J. Psychol.,* 60, 571–587.

GIRDEN, E., and CULLER, E. A. (1937) Conditioned responses in curarized striate muscle in dogs. *J. comp. Psychol.,* 23, 261–274.

GIRDEN, E., METTLER, F. A., FINCH, G., and CULLER, E. A. (1936) Conditioned responses in a decorticate dog to acoustic, thermal, and tactile stimulation. *J. comp. Psychol.,* 21, 367–385.

GLAZE, J. A. (1928) The association value of nonsense syllables. *J. genet. Psychol.,* 35, 255–267.

GLIXMAN, A. F. (1949) Recall of completed and incompleted activities under varying degrees of stress. *J. exp. Psychol.,* 39, 281–295.

GLOCK, M. D. (1949) The effect upon eye-movements and reading rate at the college level of three methods of training. *J. educ. Psychol.,* 40, 93–106.

GODBEER, E. (1940) *Factors inducing conflict in the choice behavior of children.* Dissertation, Yale University. Cited in S. B. Williams (1943).

GORDON, K. (1925) Class results with spaced and unspaced memorizing. *J. exp. Psychol.,* 8, 337–343.

GOULD, R. (1942) Repression experimentally analyzed. *Character & Pers.,* 10, 259–288.

GRAHAM, C. H., and GAGNÉ, R. M. (1940) The acquisition, extinction and spontaneous recovery of a conditioned operant response. *J. exp. Psychol.*, 26, 251–280.

GRANT, D. A., and HAKE, H. W. (1949) Acquisition and extinction of the Humphreys' verbal response with different percentages of "reinforcement." *Amer. Psychologist*, 4, 226.

GREENE, E. B. (1928) The relative effectiveness of lecture and individual reading as methods of college teaching. *Genet. Psychol. Monogr.*, 4, 457–563.

GREENE, E. B. (1931) The retention of information learned in college courses. *J. educ. Res.*, 24, 262–273.

GRICE, G. R. (1948) An experimental test of the expectation theory of learning. *J. comp. physiol. Psychol.*, 41, 137–143.

GRICE, G. R. (1951) The acquisition of a visual discrimination habit following extinction of response to one stimulus. *J. comp. physiol. Psychol.*, 44, 149–153.

GRIFFITHS, W. J. (1942) The production of convulsion in the white rat. *Comp. Psychol. Monogr.*, 17, No. 8.

GRINDLEY, G. C. (1929–1930) Experiments on the influence of the amount of reward on learning in young chickens. *Brit. J. Psychol.*, 20, 173–180.

GUEST, L. P., and BROWN, R. H. (1939) A study of the recall of radio advertising material. *J. Psychol.*, 8, 381–387.

GULLIKSEN, H. (1932) Studies of transfer of response: I. Relative vs. absolute factors in the discrimination of size by the white rat. *J. genet. Psychol.*, 40, 37–51.

GURNEE, H. (1940) Comparative retention of open and closed visual patterns. *Psychol. Bull.*, 37, 568.

GUTHRIE, E. R. (1930) Conditioning as a principle of learning. *Psychol. Rev.*, 37, 412–428.

GUTHRIE, E. R. (1934) Pavlov's theory of conditioning. *Psychol. Rev.*, 41, 199–206.

GUTHRIE, E. R. (1935) *The psychology of learning.* New York: Harper.

GUTHRIE, E. R. (1938) *The psychology of human conflict.* New York: Harper.

HAKE, H. W., GRANT, D. A., and HORNSETH, J. P. (1948) Generalization and discrimination in the conditioned eyelid response to sound stimuli. *Amer. Psychol.*, 3, 361.

HAMILTON, C. E. (1950) The relationship between length of interval separating two learning tasks and performance on the second task. *J. exp. Psychol.*, 40, 613–621.

HAMILTON, G. V. (1911) A study of trial and error behavior in mammals. *J. Anim. Behav.*, 1, 33–66.

HAMILTON, G. V. (1916) A study of perseverance reactions in primates and rodents. *Behav. Monogr.*, 3, No. 2.

HAMILTON, R. J. (1943) Retroactive facilitation as a function of degree of generalization between tasks. *J. exp. Psychol.*, 32, 363–376.

HARALSON, J. V., and BITTERMAN, M. E. (1950) A lever-depression apparatus for the study of learning in fish. *Amer. J. Psychol.*, 63, 250–256.

HARDEN, L. M. (1929) A quantitative study of the similarity factor in retroactive inhibition. *J. gen. Psychol.*, 2, 421–430.

HARLOW, H. F. (1932) Comparative behavior of primates: III. Complicated delayed reaction tests on primates. *J. comp. Psychol.*, 14, 241–252.

HARLOW, H. F. (1937) Experimental analysis of the role of the original stimulus in conditioned responses in monkeys. *Psychol. Rec.*, 1, 62–68.

HARLOW, H. F. (1949) The formation of learning sets. *Psychol. Rev.*, 56, 51–65.

HARLOW, H. F. (1951a) Thinking. In H. Helson (Ed.), *Theoretical foundations of psychology.* New York: Van Nostrand.

HARLOW, H. F. (1951b) Primate learning. In C. P. Stone (Ed.), *Compara-*

*tive psychology* (3d Ed.). New York: Prentice-Hall.

HARLOW, H. F., and DAGNON, J. (1943) Problem solution by monkeys following bilateral removal of the prefrontal areas: I. The discrimination and discrimination reversal problems. *J. exp. Psychol.*, 32, 351–356.

HARLOW, H. F., and ISRAEL, R. H. (1932) Comparative behavior of primates: IV. Delayed reaction tests on subnormal humans. *J. comp. Psychol.*, 14, 253–262.

HARLOW, H. F., and JOHNSON, T. (1943) Problem solution by monkeys following bilateral removal of the prefrontal areas: III. Test of initiation of behavior. *J. exp. Psychol.*, 32, 495–500.

HARLOW, H. F., and SPAET, T. (1943) Problem solution by monkeys following bilateral removal of the prefrontal areas: IV. Responses to stimuli having multiple sign values. *J. exp. Psychol.*, 33, 500–507.

HARLOW, H. F., UEHLING, H., and MASLOW, A. H. (1932) Comparative behavior of primates: I. Delayed reaction tests on primates from the lemur to the orang-outan. *J. comp. Psychol.*, 13, 313–344.

HARTMANN, G. W. (1933) Insight vs. trial-and-error in the solution of problems. *Amer. J. Psychol.*, 45, 663–677.

HAYES, K. J. (1950) Vocalization and speech in chimpanzees. *Amer. Psychologist*, 5, 275–276.

HEATHERS, L. B., and SEARS, R. R. (1943) Unpublished data. Cited in Sears (1944).

HEBB, D. O. (1949) *The organization of behavior.* New York: Wiley.

HEBB, D. O., and FOORD, E. N. (1945) Errors of visual recognition and the nature of the trace. *J. exp. Psychol.*, 35, 335–348.

HECK, L. (1920) Über die Bildung einer Assoziation beim Regenwurm auf Grund von Dressurversuchen. *Lotos Naturwiss Zeit.*, 68, 168–189.

HEIDBREDER, E. (1924) An experimental study of thinking. *Arch. Psychol.*, N.Y., 11, No. 73.

HEIDBREDER, E., BENSLEY, M. L., and IVY, M. (1948) The attainment of concepts: IV. Regularities and levels. *J. Psychol.*, 25, 299–329.

HENMON, V. A. C. (1912) The relation between mode of presentation and retention. *Psychol. Rev.*, 19, 79–96.

HENRY, N. B. (Ed.) (1950) Learning and instruction. *49th Yearb. Nat. Soc. Stud. Educ.*, Part I. Chicago: University of Chicago Press.

HERON, W. T. (1935) The inheritance of maze learning ability in rats. *J. comp. Psychol.*, 19, 77–89.

HICKS, J. A. (1931) The acquisition of motor skill in young children: An experimental study of the effect of practice in throwing at a moving target. *Univ. Ia. Stud. Child Welf.*, 4, No. 5.

HICKS, V. C., and CARR, H. A. (1912) Human reactions in a maze. *J. Anim. Behav.*, 2, 98–125.

HIGGINSON, G. D. (1930) The aftereffects of certain emotional situations upon maze learning among white rats. *J. comp. Psychol.*, 10, 1–10.

HILGARD, E. R. (1948) *Theories of learning.* New York: Appleton-Century-Crofts.

HILGARD, E. R., and ALLEN, M. K. (1938) An attempt to condition finger reactions based on motor point stimulation. *J. gen. Psychol.*, 18, 203–207.

HILGARD, E. R., and MARQUIS, D. M. (1940) *Conditioning and learning.* New York: Appleton-Century-Crofts.

HILL, C. J. (1939) Goal-gradient, anticipation, and perseveration in compound trial-and-error learning. *J. exp. Psychol.*, 25, 566–585.

HOBBS, N. (1947) Psychological research on flexible gunnery training. *Army Air Force Aviation Psychology Program Research Report,* No. 11. Washington, D.C.: Government Printing Office.

HOBHOUSE, L. T. (1901) *Mind in evolution.* New York: Macmillan.

HONZIK, C. H. (1931) Delayed reaction in rats. *Univ. Calif. Publ. Psychol.,* 4, 307–318.

HONZIK, C. H., and TOLMAN, E. C. (1936) The perception of spatial relations by the rat: A type of response not easily explained by conditioning. *J. comp. Psychol.,* 22, 287–318.

HOOK, S. (1945) The case for progressive education. *Saturday Evening Post,* 217, June 30, 1945, pp. 28–29.

HORN, T. D. (1949) Learning to spell as affected by syllabic presentation of words. *Elem. Sch. J.,* 49, 263–272.

HOUSEHOLDER, A. S., and LANDAHL, H. (1945) *Mathematical biophysics of the central nervous system.* Bloomington, Ind.: The Principia Press.

HOVEY, H. B. (1929) Associative hysteresis in flatworms. *Physiol. Zool.,* 2, 322–333.

HOVLAND, C. I. (1936) "Inhibition of reinforcement" and phenomena of experimental extinction. *Proc. nat. Acad. Sci., Wash.,* 22, 430–433.

HOVLAND, C. I. (1937*a*) The generalization of conditioned responses: I. The sensory generalization of conditioned responses with varying frequencies of tone. *J. gen. Psychol.,* 17, 125–148.

HOVLAND, C. I. (1937*b*) The generalization of conditioned responses: II. The sensory generalization of conditioned responses with varying intensities of tone. *J. genet. Psychol.,* 51, 279–291.

HOVLAND, C. I. (1937*c*) The generalization of conditioned responses: IV. The effects of varying amounts of reinforcement upon the degree of generalization of conditioned responses. *J. exp. Psychol.,* 21, 261–276.

HOVLAND, C. I. (1938*a*) Experimental studies in rote-learning theory: I. Reminiscence following learning by massed and distributed practice. *J. exp. Psychol.,* 22, 201–224.

HOVLAND, C. I. (1938*b*) Experimental studies in rote-learning theory: II.

Reminiscence with varying speeds of syllable presentation. *J. exp. Psychol.,* 22, 338–353.

HOVLAND, C. I. (1938*c*) Experimental studies in rote-learning theory: III. Distribution of practice with varying speeds of syllable presentation. *J. exp. Psychol.,* 23, 172–190.

HOVLAND, C. I. (1940*a*) Experimental studies in rote-learning theory: VI. Comparison of retention following learning to some criterion by massed and distributed practice. *J. exp. Psychol.,* 26, 568–587.

HOVLAND, C. I. (1940*b*) Experimental studies in rote-learning theory: VII. Distribution of practice with varying lengths of list. *J. exp. Psychol.,* 27, 271–284.

HOVLAND, C. I. (1951) Human learning and retention. In S. S. Stevens (Ed.), *Handbook of experimental psychology.* New York: Wiley.

HULL, C. L. (1920) Quantitative aspects of the evolution of concepts: An experimental study. *Psychol. Monogr.,* 28, No. 123.

HULL, C. L. (1930) Knowledge and purpose as habit mechanisms. *Psychol. Rev.,* 37, 511–525.

HULL, C. L. (1931) Goal attraction and directing ideas conceived as habit phenomena. *Psychol. Rev.,* 38, 487–506.

HULL, C. L. (1932) The goal gradient hypothesis and maze learning. *Psychol. Rev.,* 39, 25–43.

HULL, C. L. (1933) The meaningfulness of 320 selected nonsense syllables. *Amer. J. Psychol.,* 45, 730–734.

HULL, C. L. (1935*a*) The conflicting psychologies of learning—a way out. *Psychol. Rev.,* 42, 491–516.

HULL, C. L. (1935*b*) The mechanism of the assembly of behavior segments in novel combinations suitable for problem solution. *Psychol. Rev.,* 42, 219–245.

HULL, C. L. (1943) *The principles of behavior.* New York: Appleton-Century-Crofts.

HULL, C. L. (1947) Reactively hetero-geneous compound trial-and-error learning with distributed trials and terminal reinforcement. *J. exp. Psychol.*, 37, 118–135.

HULL, C. L. (1950) Behavior postulates and corollaries—1949. *Psychol. Rev.*, 57, 173–180.

HULL, C. L., FELSINGER, J. M., GLADSTONE, A. I., and YAMAGUCHI, H. G. (1947) A proposed quantification of habit strength. *Psychol. Rev.*, 54, 237–254.

HULL, C. L., HOVLAND, C. I., ROSS, R. T., HALL, M., PERKINS, D. T., and FITCH, F. B. (1940) *Mathematico-deductive theory of rote learning. A study in scientific methodology.* New Haven: Yale University Press.

HUMPHREY, G. (1933) *The nature of learning in its relation to the living system.* New York: Harcourt, Brace.

HUMPHREYS, L. G. (1939) The effect of random alternation of reinforcement on the acquisition and extinction of conditioned eyelid reactions. *J. exp. Psychol.*, 25, 141–158.

HUNT, J. McV. (1943) Motor behavior of rats in a conflict situation. Cited in N. E. Miller (1944).

HUNT, J. McV., and SCHLOSBERG, H. (1950) Behavior of rats in continuous conflict. *J. comp. physiol. Psychol.*, 43, 351–357.

HUNTER, W. S. (1912) The delayed reaction in animals and children. *Behav. Monogr.*, 2, No. 1.

HUNTER, W. S. (1924) The symbolic process. *Psychol. Rev.*, 31, 478–497.

HUNTER, W. S. (1928) The behavior of raccoons in a double alternation temporal maze. *J. genet. Psychol.*, 35, 374–388.

HUNTER, W. S. (1932) The effect of inactivity produced by cold upon learning and retention in the cockroach, *Blatella germanica. J. genet. Psychol.*, 41, 253–266.

HUNTER, W. S., and BARTLETT, S. C. (1948) Double alternation behavior in young children. *J. exp. Psychol.*, 38, 558–567.

HUNTER, W. S., and HULL, B. E. (1941) Double alternation behavior of the white rat in a spatial maze. *J. comp. Psychol.*, 32, 253–266.

HURLOCK, E. B. (1924) The value of praise and reproof as incentives for children. *Arch. Psychol., N.Y.*, 11, No. 71.

HURLOCK, E. B., and NEWMARK, E. D. (1931) The memory span of pre-school children. *J. genet. Psychol.*, 39, 157–173.

IRION, A. L. (1948) The relation of set to retention. *Psychol. Rev.*, 55, 336–341.

IRION, A. L. (1949) Retention and warming-up effects in paired associate learning. *J. exp. Psychol.*, 39, 669–675.

IRION, A. L., and WHAM, D. S. (1951) Recovery from retention loss as a function of amount of pre-recall warm-up. *J. exp. Psychol.*, 41, 242–246.

JACKSON, T. A. (1942) Use of the stick as a tool by young chimpanzees. *J. comp. Psychol.*, 34, 223–235.

JACOBSEN, C. F. (1935) Functions of the frontal association areas in primates. *Arch. Neurol. Psychiat., Chicago,* 33, 558–569.

JACOBSEN, C. F., and ELDER, J. H. (1936) Studies of cerebral function in primates: II. The effect of temporal lobe lesions on delayed response in monkeys. *Comp. Psychol. Monogr.*, 13, No. 63, 61–65.

JACOBSEN, C. F., and HASLERUD, G. M. (1936) Studies of cerebral functions in primates: III. The effect of motor and premotor area lesions on delayed response in monkeys. *Comp. Psychol. Monogr.*, 13, No. 63, 66–68.

JENKINS, J. G. (1933) Instruction as a factor in "incidental" learning. *Amer. J. Psychol.*, 45, 471–477.

JENKINS, J. G., and DALLENBACH, K. M. (1924) Oblivescence during sleep and waking. *Amer. J. Psychol.*, 35, 605–612.

JENKINS, R. L. (1945) The constructive use of punishment. *Ment. Hyg., N.Y.*, 29, 561–574.

JENKINS, W. O., McFANN, H., and CLAYTON, F. L. (1950) A methodological study of extinction following aperiodic and continuous reinforcement. *J. comp. physiol. Psychol.*, 43, 155–167.

JENKINS, W. O., and POSTMAN, L. (1948) Isolation and "spread of effect" in serial learning. *Amer. J. Psychol.*, 61, 214–221.

JENKINS, W. O., and SHEFFIELD, F. D. (1946) Rehearsal and guessing habits as sources of the "spread of effect." *J. exp. Psychol.*, 36, 316–330.

JENKINS, W. O., and STANLEY, J. C. (1950) Partial reinforcement: A review and critique. *Psychol. Bull.*, 47, 193–234.

JENNINGS, H. S. (1907) Behavior of the starfish, *Asterias forreri De Loriol. Univ. Calif. Publ. Zool.*, 4, 53–185.

JENSEN, M. B., and LEMOIRE, A. (1937) Ten experiments on whole and part learning. *J. educ. Psychol.*, 28, 37–54.

JONES, H. E. (1930a) The galvanic skin reflex. *Child Develpm.*, 7, 106–110.

JONES, H. E. (1930b) The retention of conditioned emotional reactions in infancy. *J. genet. Psychol.*, 37, 485–498.

JONES, H. E. (1931) The conditioning of overt emotional responses. *J. educ. Psychol.*, 22, 127–130.

JONES, H. E., and KAPLAN, O. J. (1945) Psychological aspects of mental disorder in later life. In O. J. Kaplan (Ed.), *Mental disorders in later life*. Stanford University, Calif.: Stanford University Press.

JOST, A. (1897) Die Assoziationfestigkeit in ihrer Abhangigkeit von der Verteilung der Wiederholungen. *Z. Psychol.*, 14, 436–472.

JUDD, C. H. (1908) The relation of special training to general intelligence. *Educ. Rev.*, 36, 28–42.

KANTOR, J. R. (1945) *Psychology and Logic*, Vol. I. Bloomington, Ind.: The Principia Press.

KANTOR, J. R. (1947) *Problems of physiological psychology*. Bloomington, Ind.: The Principia Press.

KANTOR, J. R. (1950) *Psychology and Logic*, Vol. II. Bloomington, Ind.: The Principia Press.

KARN, H. W. (1938) The behavior of cats in a double alternation problem in the temporal maze. *J. comp. Psychol.*, 26, 201–208.

KATZ, J. J., and HALSTEAD, W. C. (1950) Protein organization and mental function. *Comp. Psychol. Monogr.*, 20, No. 1, 1–38.

KELLER, F. S. (1943) Studies in international Morse code: I. A new method of teaching code reception. *J. appl. Psychol.*, 27, 407–415.

KELLER, F. S., CRISTO, I. J., and SCHONFELD, W. N. (1946) Studies in international Morse code: V. The effect of the "phonetic equivalent." *J. appl. Psychol.*, 30, 265–270.

KELLER, F. S., and TAUBMAN, R. E. (1943) Studies in international Morse code: II. Errors made in code reception. *J. appl. Psychol.*, 27, 504–509.

KELLOGG, W. N. (1938) An eclectic view of some theories of learning. *Psychol. Rev.*, 45, 165–184.

KELLOGG, W. N. (1941) Experimental data on different neural mechanisms for learned and unlearned responses. *J. exp. Psychol.*, 29, 334–341.

KELLOGG, W. N., DEESE, J., PRONKO, N. H., and FEINBERG, M. (1947) An attempt to condition the chronic spinal dog. *J. exp. Psychol.*, 37, 99–117.

KELLOGG, W. N., and KELLOGG, L. A. (1933) *The ape and the child*. New York: McGraw-Hill.

KELLOGG, W. N., and POMEROY, W. B. (1936) Maze learning in water snakes. *J. comp. Psychol.*, 21, 275–295.

KELLOGG, W. N., SCOTT, V. B., DAVIS, R. C., and WOLF, I. S. (1940) Is movement necessary for learning? An experimental test of the motor theory of conditioning. *J. comp. Psychol.*, 29, 43–74.

KELLOGG, W. N., and WALKER, E. L. (1938) "Ambiguous conditioning," a phenomenon of bilateral transfer. *J. comp. Psychol.*, 26, 63–77.

KELLOGG, W. N., and WOLF, I. S. (1939) The nature of the response retained after several varieties of conditioning in the same subject. *J. exp. Psychol.*, 24, 366–383.

KELLOGG, W. N., and WOLF, I. S. (1940) "Hypothesis" and "random activity" during the conditioning of dogs. *J. exp. Psychol.*, 26, 588–601.

KENDLER, H. H. (1945) Drive interaction: II. Experimental analysis of the role of drive in learning theory. *J. exp. Psychol.*, 35, 188–198.

KENDLER, H. H. (1947) An investigation of latent learning in a T-maze. *J. comp. physiol. Psychol.*, 40, 265–270.

KENDLER, H. H., and GASSER, W. P. (1948) Variables in spatial learning: I. Number of reinforcements during training. *J. comp. physiol. Psychol.*, 41, 178–187.

KENDLER, H. H., and MENCHER, H. C. (1948) The ability of rats to learn the location of food when thirst motivated. *J. exp. Psychol.*, 38, 82–88.

KENDLER, H. H., and MENCHER, H. C. (1949) Variables in spatial learning: II. Degree of motivation during training and test trials. *J. comp. physiol. Psychol.*, 42, 493–501.

KENNELLY, T. W. (1941) The role of similarity in retroactive inhibition. *Arch. Psychol., N.Y.*, 37, No. 260.

KIENTZLE, M. J. (1946) Properties of learning curves under varied distribution of practice. *J. exp. Psychol.*, 36, 187–211.

KIMBLE, G. A. (1947) Conditioning as a function of the time between condi-tioned and unconditioned stimuli. *J. exp. Psychol.*, 37, 1–15.

KIMBLE, G. A. (1949) Performance and reminiscence in motor learning as a function of the degree of distribution of practice. *J. exp. Psychol.*, 39, 500–510.

KIMBLE, G. A., and BILODEAU, E. A. (1949) Work and rest as variables in cyclical motor learning. *J. exp. Psychol.*, 39, 150–157.

KITSON, H. O. (1922) A study of the output of workers under a particular wage incentive. *Univ. J. Bus.*, 1, 54–68.

KLEBANOFF, S. G. (1939) *An experimental analysis of approach-approach and avoidance-avoidance conflict.* Dissertation, Yale University. Cited in N. E. Miller (1944).

KLÜVER, H. (1933) *Behavior mechanisms in monkeys.* Chicago: University of Chicago Press.

KOCH, H. L. (1923) The influence of mechanical guidance upon maze learning. *Psychol. Monogr.*, 32, No. 5.

KOCH, H. L. (1930) Some factors affecting the relative efficiency of certain modes of presenting material for memorizing. *Amer. J. Psychol.*, 42, 370–388.

KOFFKA, K. (1935) *Principles of Gestalt psychology.* New York: Harcourt, Brace.

KÖHLER, W. (1925) *The mentality of apes.* New York: Harcourt, Brace.

KONORSKI, J. (1950) Mechanisms of learning. In *Symposia of the Society for Exp. Biol.* London: Cambridge. Vol. IV.

KORNER, I. N. (1950) Experimental investigation of some aspects of the problem of repression: Repressive forgetting. *Teach. Coll. Contr. Educ.*, No. 970.

KRAWIAC, T. S. (1946) A comprison of learning and retention of materials presented visually and auditorially. *J. gen. Psychol.*, 34, 179–197.

KRECHEVSKY, I. (1932) "Hypothesis" vs. "chance" in the pre-solution period in sensory discrimination-learning. *Univ. Calif. Publ. Psychol.,* 6, 27–44.

KRECHEVSKY, I. (1935) Brain mechanisms and "hypotheses." *J. comp. Psychol.,* 19, 425–468.

KRECHEVSKY, I. (1938) An experimental investigation of the principle of proximity in the visual perception of the rat. *J. exp. Psychol.,* 22, 497–523.

KUENNE, M. R. (1946) Experimental investigation of the relation of language to transposition behavior in young children. *J. exp. Psychol.,* 36, 471–490.

LAKENAN, M. E. (1913) The whole and part methods of memorizing poetry and prose. *J. educ. Psychol.,* 4, 189–198.

LANGHORNE, M. C. (1933) Age and sex differences in the acquisition of one type of skilled movement. *J. exp. Educ.,* 2, 101–108.

LASHLEY, K. S. (1920) Studies of cerebral function in learning. *Psychobiology,* 2, 55–135.

LASHLEY, K. S. (1929) *Brain mechanisms and intelligence.* Chicago: University of Chicago Press.

LASHLEY, K. S. (1935) Studies of cerebral function in learning: XI. The behavior of the rat in latch-box situations. *Comp. Psychol. Monogr.,* 11, No. 52.

LASHLEY, K. S. (1942) An examination of the "continuity theory" as applied to discriminative learning. *J. gen. Psychol.,* 26, 241–265.

LASHLEY, K. S., and WADE, M. (1946) The Pavlovian theory of generalization. *Psychol. Rev.,* 53, 72–87.

LAZARUS, R. S., and DEESE, J. (1951) The effects of psychological stress on psychomotor performance. *Amer. Psychologist,* 6, 262–263.

LEBEDINSKAIA, S. I., and ROSENTHAL, J. S. (1935) Reactions of a dog after removal of the cerebral hemispheres. *Brain,* 58, 412–419.

LEEPER, R. W. (1948a) A motivational theory of emotion to replace "emotion as a disorganized response." *Psychol. Rev.,* 55, 5–21.

LEEPER, R. W. (1948b) The experiments by Spence and Lippitt and by Kendler on the sign-Gestalt theory of learning. *J. exp. Psychol.,* 38, 102–106.

LEEPER, R. W. (1951) Cognitive processes. In S. S. Stevens (Ed.), *Handbook of experimental psychology.* New York: Wiley.

LEPLEY, W. M. (1934) Serial reactions considered as conditioned reactions. *Psychol. Monogr.,* 46, No. 205.

LEPLEY, W. M. (1935) A gradient in incidental learning. *J. exp. Psychol.,* 18, 195–201.

LEUBA, C. J. (1930–1931) A preliminary experiment to quantify an incentive and its effects. *J. abnorm. soc. Psychol.,* 25, 275–288.

LEVINE, J. M., and MURPHY, G. (1943) The learning and forgetting of controversial material. *J. abnorm. soc. Psychol.,* 38, 507–517.

LEWIN, K. (1931) Environmental forces in child behavior and development. In C. Murchison (Ed.), *A handbook of child psychology.* Worcester, Mass.: Clark University Press.

LEWIN, K. (1935) *A dynamic theory of personality.* New York: McGraw-Hill.

LEWIN, K. (1938) The conceptual representation and measurement of psychological forces. *Contr. psychol. Theor.,* 1, No. 4.

LICHTENSTEIN, P. E. (1950a) Studies of anxiety: I. The production of feeding inhibition in dogs. *J. comp. physiol. Psychol.,* 43, 16–29.

LICHTENSTEIN, P. E. (1950b) Studies of anxiety: II. The effects of lobotomy on a feeding inhibition in dogs. *J. comp. physiol. Psychol.,* 43, 419–427.

LIDDELL, H. S. (1944) Conditioned reflex method and experimental neurosis. In J. McV. Hunt (Ed.), *Personality and the behavior disorders,* Vol. I. New York: Ronald.

LIDDELL, H. S., JAMES, W. T., and ANDERSON, O. D. (1934) The comparative physiology of the conditioned motor reflex based on experiments with the pig, dog, sheep, goat and rabbit. *Comp. Psychol. Monogr.,* 11, No. 51.

LIGHT, J. S., and GANTT, W. H. (1936) Essential part of a reflex arc for establishment of conditioned reflex. Formation of conditioned reflex after exclusion of motor peripheral end. *J. comp. Psychol.,* 21, 19–36.

LITTMAN, R. A. (1949) Conditioned generalization of the galvanic skin reaction to tones. *J. exp. Psychol.,* 39, 868–882.

LLOYD, D. P. C. (1950) Post-tetanic potentiation of response in monosynaptic reflex pathways of the spinal cord. *J. gen. Physiol.,* 33, 147–170.

LONDON, I. D. (1950) An ideal equation derived for a class of forgetting curves. *Psychol. Rev.,* 57, 295–302.

LONG, L., and WELCH, L. (1942) Influence of levels of abstractness on reasoning ability. *J. Psychol.,* 13, 41–59.

LORENTE DE NÓ, R. (1938) Analysis of the activity of the chains of internuncial neurons. *J. Neurophysiol.,* 1, 207–244.

LORGE, I. (1930) Influence of regularly interpolated time intervals upon subsequent learning. *Teach. Coll. Contr. Educ.,* No. 438.

LORGE, I., and THORNDIKE, E. L. (1933) The comparative strengthening of a connection by one or more occurrences of it in cases where the connection was punished and was neither punished nor rewarded. *J. exp. Psychol.,* 16, 374–382.

LOUCKS, R. B. (1931) Efficacy of the rat's motor cortex in delayed alternation. *J. comp. Neurol.,* 53, 511–567.

LOUCKS, R. B. (1935) The experimental delimitation of neural structures essential for learning: The attempt to condition striped muscle responses with faradization of the sigmoid gyri. *J. Psychol.,* 1, 5–44.

LOUCKS, R. B. (1938) Studies of neural structures essential for learning: II. The conditioning of salivary and striped muscle responses to faradization of cortical sensory elements, and the action of sleep upon such mechanisms. *J. comp. Psychol.,* 25, 315–332.

LUCHINS, A. S. (1942) Mechanization in problem solving. The effect of Einstellung. *Psychol. Monogr.,* 54, No. 248.

LYON, D. O. (1914) The relation of length of material to time taken for learning and the optimum distribution of time. *J. educ. Psychol.,* 5, 1–9, 85–91, 155–163.

LYON, D. O. (1917) *Memory and the learning process.* Baltimore: Warwick and York.

McCLEARY, R. A. (1950) The nature of the galvanic skin response. *Psychol. Bull.,* 47, 97–117.

McCLELLAND, D. C. (1942) Studies in serial verbal discrimination learning: I. Reminiscence with two speeds of pair presentation. *J. exp. Psychol.,* 31, 44–56.

McCLELLAND, D. C., and APICELLA, F. S. (1947) Reminiscence following experimentally induced failure. *J. exp. Psychol.,* 37, 159–169.

McCORD, F. (1939) The delayed reaction and memory in rats: I. Length of delay. *J. comp. Psychol.,* 27, 1–37.

MACCORQUODALE, K., and MEEHL, P. E. (1948) On the distinction between hypothetical constructs and intervening variables. *Psychol. Rev.,* 55, 95–107.

McCULLOCH, T. L., and PRATT, J. G. (1934) A study of the pre-solution period in weight discrimination by white rats. *J. comp. Psychol.,* 18, 271–290.

MACE, C. A. (1935) Incentives: Some experimental studies. *Industr. Hlth. Res. Bd. Rep.,* No. 72.

MACFARLANE, F. A. (1930) The role of kinesthesis in maze learning. *Univ. Calif. Publ. Psychol.*, 4, 277–305.

MCGEOCH, G. O. (1935) The conditions of reminiscence. *Amer. J. Psychol.*, 47, 65–89.

MCGEOCH, J. A. (1932) Forgetting and the law of disuse. *Psychol. Rev.*, 39, 352–370.

MCGEOCH, J. A. (1936) The direction and extent of intra-serial associations at recall. *Amer. J. Psychol*, 48, 221–245.

MCGEOCH, J. A. (1940) Recall without overt learning. *Psychol. Bull.*, 37, 493.

MCGEOCH, J. A. (1942) *The psychology of human learning.* New York: Longmans.

MCGEOCH, J. A., and MCGEOCH, G. O. (1937) Studies in retroactive inhibition: X. The influence of similarity of meaning between lists of paired associates. *J. exp. Psychol.*, 21, 320–329.

MCGEOCH, J. A., MCKINNEY, F., and PETERS, H. N. (1937) Studies in retroactive inhibition: IX. Retroactive inhibition, reproductive inhibition and reminiscence. *J. exp. Psychol.*, 20, 131–143.

MCGEOCH, J. A., and UNDERWOOD, B. J. (1943) Tests of the two-factor theory of retroactive inhibition. *J. exp. Psychol.*, 32, 1–16.

MCGINNIS, E. (1929) The acquisition and interference of motor-habits in young children. *Genet. Psychol. Monogr.*, 6, 209–311.

MCKINLEY, F. (1933) Certain emotional factors in learning and efficiency. *J. gen. Psychol.*, 9, 101–116.

MCKINNEY, F. (1933) Quantitative and qualitative essential elements of transfer. *J. exp. Psychol.*, 16, 854–864.

MCKINNEY, F., and MCGEOCH, J. A. (1935) The character and extent of transfer in retroactive inhibition: Disparate serial lists. *Amer. J. Psychol.*, 47, 409–423.

MACKWORTH, N. H. (1948) The break-down of vigilance during prolonged visual search. *Quart. J. exp. Psychol.*, 1, 6–21.

MAIER, N. R. F. (1929) Reasoning in white rats. *Comp. Psychol. Monogr.*, 6, No. 29.

MAIER, N. R. F. (1930) Reasoning in humans: I. On direction. *J. comp. Psychol.*, 10, 115–143.

MAIER, N. R. F. (1931) Reasoning in humans: II. The solution of a problem and its appearance in consciousness. *J. comp. Psychol.*, 12, 181–194.

MAIER, N. R. F. (1932a) The effect of cerebral destruction on reasoning and learning in rats. *J. comp. Neurol.*, 54, 45–75.

MAIER, N. R. F. (1932b) Cortical destruction of the posterior part of the brain and its effect on reasoning in rats. *J. comp. Neurol.*, 56, 179–214.

MAIER, N. R. F. (1939) Qualitative differences in the learning of rats in a discrimination situation. *J. comp. Psychol.*, 27, 289–332.

MAIER, N. R. F. (1949) *Frustration.* New York: McGraw-Hill.

MAIER, N. R. F., and LONGHURST, J. U. (1947) Studies of abnormal behavior in the rat: XXI. Conflict and "audiogenic" seizures. *J. comp. Psychol.*, 40, 397–412.

MAIER, N. R. F., and SCHNEIRLA, T. C. (1935) *Principles of animal psychology.* New York: McGraw-Hill.

MALMO, R. B. (1942) Interference factors in delayed response in monkeys after removal of the frontal lobes. *J. Neurophysiol.*, 5, 295–308.

MARROW, A. J. (1938) Goal tension and recall. I. *J. gen. Psychol.*, 19, 3–35.

MARTIN, J. R. (1940) Reminiscence and gestalt theory. *Psychol. Monogr.*, 52, No. 235.

MARX, M. H. (1944) The effects of cumulative training upon retroactive inhibition and transfer. *Comp. Psychol. Monogr.*, 18, No. 2.

MARX, M. H., and BUNCH, M. E. (1951) New gradients of error reinforcement in multiple-choice human learning. *J. exp. Psychol.,* 41, 93–104.

MASLOW, A. H., and HARLOW, H. F. (1932) Comparative behavior of primates: II. Delayed reaction tests on primates at Bronx Park Zoo. *J. comp. Psychol.,* 14, 97–108.

MASSERMAN, J. H. (1943) *Behavior and neurosis.* Chicago: University of Chicago Press.

MAST, S. O., and PUSCH, L. (1924) Modification of response in Amoeba. *Biol. Bull.,* 46, 55–59.

MATEER, F. (1918) *Child behavior.* Boston: Badger.

MEEHL, P. E., and MACCORQUODALE, K. (1948) A further study of latent learning in the T-maze. *J. comp. physiol. Psychol.,* 41, 372–396.

MEEHL, P. E., and MACCORQUODALE, K. (1949) "Cognitive" learning in the absence of repetition of stimuli. *J. comp. physiol. Psychol.,* 42, 383–390.

MEEHL, P. E., and MACCORQUODALE, K. (1951) A failure to find the Blodgett Effect and some secondary observations on drive conditioning. *J. comp. physiol. Psychol.,* 44, 178–183.

MELTON, A. W. (1936) The methodology of experimental studies of human learning and retention: I. The functions of a methodology and the available criteria for evaluating different experimental methods. *Psychol. Bull.,* 33, 305–394.

MELTON, A. W., and IRWIN, J. McQ. (1940) The influence of degree of interpolated learning on retroactive inhibition and the overt transfer of specific responses. *Amer. J. Psychol.,* 53, 173–203.

MELTON, A. W., and STONE, G. R. (1942) The retention of serial lists of adjectives over short time intervals with varying rates of presentation. *J. exp. Psychol.,* 30, 295–310.

MELTON, A. W., and VON LACKUM, W. J. (1941) Retroactive and proactive inhibition in retention: Evidence for a two factor theory of retroactive inhibition. *Amer. J. Psychol.,* 54, 157–173.

MICHAEL, R. E. (1949) Relative effectiveness of two methods of teaching certain topics in ninth grade algebra. *Math. Teach.,* 42, 83–87.

MILES, C. C., and MILES, W. R. (1932) The correlation of intelligence scores and chronological age from early to late maturity. *Amer. J. Psychol.,* 44, 44–78.

MILES, W. R. (1933a) Abilities of older men. *Person. J.,* 11, 352–357.

MILES, W. R. (1933b) Age and human ability. *Psychol. Rev.,* 40, 99–123.

MILES, W. R. (1935) Training, practice and mental longevity. *Science,* 81, 79–87.

MILLER, G. A. (1951) Speech and language. In S. S. Stevens (Ed.), *Handbook of experimental psychology.* New York: Wiley.

MILLER, G. A., and FRICK, F. C. (1949) Statistical behavioristics and sequences of responses. *Psychol. Rev.,* 56, 311–324.

MILLER, G. A., and SELFRIDGE, J. A. (1950) Verbal context and the recall of meaningful material. *Amer. J. Psychol.,* 63, 176–185.

MILLER, N. E. (1944) Experimental studies of conflict. In J. McV. Hunt (Ed.), *Personality and the behavior disorders.* New York: Ronald.

MILLER, N. E. (1946) The resistance to experimental extinction of anxiety as an acquired drive. *Amer. Psychologist,* 1, 290.

MILLER, N. E. (1947) Psychological research on pilot training. *Army Air Force Aviation Psychology Program Research Report,* No. 8. Washington, D.C.: Government Printing Office.

MILLER, N. E. (1948) Studies of fear as an acquirable drive: I. Fear as motivation and fear-reduction as reinforcement in the learning of new responses. *J. exp. Psychol.,* 38, 89–101.

MILLER, N. E. (1951) Learnable drives and rewards. In S. S. Stevens (Ed.), *Handbook of experimental psychology*. New York: Wiley.

MILLER, N. E., BROWN, J. S., and LIPOFSKY, H. (1943) Unpublished data. Cited in Miller (1944).

MILLER, N. E., and DOLLARD, J. (1941) *Social learning and imitation*. New Haven: Yale University Press.

MINAMI, H., and DALLENBACH, K. M. (1946) The effect of activity upon learning and retention in the cockroach, *Periplaneta americana*. *Amer. J. Psychol.*, 59, 1–58.

MITRANO, A. J. (1939) Principles of conditioning in human goal behavior. *Psychol. Monogr.*, 51, No. 4.

MORGAN, C. T. (1951) The psychophysiology of learning. In S. S. Stevens (Ed.), *Handbook of experimental psychology*. New York: Wiley.

MORGAN, C. T., and MORGAN, J. D. (1939) Auditory induction of an abnormal pattern of behavior in rats. *J. comp. Psychol.*, 27, 505–508.

MORGAN, C. T., and STELLAR, E. (1950) *Physiological psychology* (2d Ed.). New York: McGraw-Hill.

MOWRER, O. H. (1939) A stimulus-response analysis of anxiety and its role as a reinforcing agent. *Psychol. Rev.*, 46, 553–566.

MOWRER, O. H. (1940) Anxiety reduction and learning. *J. exp. Psychol.*, 27, 497–516.

MOWRER, O. H. (1947) On the dual nature of learning: A reinterpretation of "conditioning" and "problem solving." *Harv. educ. Rev.*, 17, 102–148.

MOWRER, O. H. (1950) *Learning theory and personality dynamics*. New York: Ronald.

MOWRER, O. H., and JONES, H. M. (1943) Extinction and behavior variability as functions of effortfulness of task. *J. exp. Psychol.*, 33, 369–386.

MOWRER, O. H., and JONES, H. M. (1945) Habit strength as a function of the pattern of reinforcement. *J. exp. Psychol.*, 35, 293–311.

MOWRER, O. H., and LAMOREAUX, R. R. (1942) Avoidance conditioning and signal duration: A study of secondary motivation and reward. *Psychol. Monogr.*, 54, No. 5.

MUENZINGER, K. F. (1934) Motivation in learning: I. Electric shock for correct responses in the visual discrimination habit. *J. comp. Psychol.*, 17, 267–277.

MUENZINGER, K. F. (1948) Concerning the effect of shock for right responses in visual discrimination learning. *J. exp. Psychol.*, 38, 201–203.

MUENZINGER, K. F., BERNSTONE, A. H., and RICHARDS, L. (1938) Motivation in learning: VIII. Equivalent amounts of electric shock for right and wrong responses in a visual discrimination habit. *J. comp. Psychol.*, 26, 177–185.

MUNN, N. L. (1946) Learning in children. In L. Carmichael (Ed.), *Manual of child psychology*. New York: Wiley.

NATIONAL EDUCATION ASSOCIATION. (1894) *Report of the Committee of Ten on secondary school studies*. New York: American Book.

NEWMAN, E. B. (1939a) Forgetting of meaningful material during sleep and waking. *Amer. J. Psychol.*, 52, 65–71.

NEWMAN, E. B. (1939b) The effect of crowding of material on curves of forgetting. *Amer. J. Psychol.*, 52, 601–609.

NOBLE, C. E. (1950) Absence of reminiscence in the serial rote learning of nonsense syllables. *J. exp. Psychol.*, 40, 622–631.

OSGOOD, C. E. (1946) Meaningful similarity and interference in learning. *J. exp. Psychol.*, 36, 277–301.

OSGOOD, C. E. (1948) An investigation into the causes of retroactive interference. *J. exp. Psychol.*, 38, 132–154.

OSGOOD, C. E. (1949) The similarity

paradox in human learning: A resolution. *Psychol. Rev.*, 56, 132–143.

OSIPOVA, V. N. (1926) The speed of formation of association reflexes in children of school age. *Nov. refl. fiziol. nerv. Sist.*, 2, 218–234. Cited in Razran (1933).

OVERMAN, J. R. (1930–1931) An experimental study of the effect of the method of instruction on transfer in arithmetic. *Elem. Sch. J.*, 31, 183–190.

PARKER, G. H. (1919) *The elementary nervous system.* Philadelphia: Lippincott.

PATRICK, J. R. (1934) Studies in rational behavior and emotional excitement: II. The effect of emotional excitement on rational behavior of human subjects. *J. comp. Psychol.*, 18, 153–195.

PAVLOV, I. P. (1927) *Conditioned reflexes* (trans. by G. V. Anrep). London: Oxford.

PEAK, H., and DEESE, L. (1937) Experimental extinction of verbal material. *J. exp. Psychol.*, 20, 244–261.

PECHSTEIN, L. A. (1917) Whole vs. part methods in motor learning. A comparative study. *Psychol. Monogr.*, 23, No. 99.

PERIN, C. T. (1942) Behavior potentiality as a joint function of the amount of training and the degree of hunger at the time of extinction. *J. exp. Psychol.*, 30, 93–113.

PERIN, C. T. (1943) The effect of delayed reinforcement upon the differentiation of bar responses in white rats. *J. exp. Psychol.*, 32, 95–109.

PERKINS, C. C. (1947) The relation of secondary reward to gradients of reinforcement. *J. exp. Psychol.*, 37, 377–392.

PETERSON, J. (1916) The effect of attitude on immediate and delayed reproduction: A class experiment. *J. educ. Psychol.*, 7, 523–532.

PINTO, T., and BROMILEY, R. B. (1950) A search for 'spinal conditioning' and

for evidence that it can become a reflex. *J. exp. Psychol.*, 40, 121–130.

PLOTKIN, L. (1943) Stimulus generalization in Morse code. *Arch. Psychol.*, N.Y., 40, No. 287.

POLTYREW, S., and ZELIONY, G. P. (1930) Grosshirnrinde und Assoziationfunktion. *Z. Biol.*, 90, 157–160.

POSTMAN, L. (1947) The history and present status of the law of effect. *Psychol. Bull.*, 44, 489–563.

POSTMAN, L., and ALPER, T. G. (1946) Retroactive inhibition as a function of time of interpolation of the inhibitor between learning and recall. *Amer. J. Psychol.*, 59, 439–449.

POSTMAN, L., and KAPLAN, H. L. (1947) Reaction time as a measure of retroactive inhibition. *J. exp. Psychol.*, 37, 136–145.

POSTMAN, L., and POSTMAN, D. L. (1948) Change in set as a determinant of retroactive inhibition. *Amer. J. Psychol.*, 61, 236–242.

RAAB, D. H., and ADES, H. W. (1946) Cortical and midbrain mediation of a conditioned discrimination of acoustic intensities. *Amer. J. Psychol.*, 59, 59–83.

RASHEVSKY, N. (1938) *Mathematical biophysics.* Chicago: University of Chicago Press.

RASHEVSKY, N. (1940) *Advances and application of mathematical biology.* Chicago: University of Chicago Press.

RAZRAN, G. H. S. (1933) Conditioned responses in animals other than dogs. *Psychol. Bull.*, 30, 261–324.

REED, H. B. (1924) Repetition and association in learning. *Ped. Sem.*, 31, 147–155.

REED, H. B. (1938) Meaning as a factor in learning. *J. educ. Psychol.*, 29, 419–430.

REEVES, C. D. (1919) Discrimination of lights of different wave-lengths by fish. *Behav. Monogr.*, 4, No. 3.

REMMERS, H. H. (1933) Learning, effort, and attitudes as affected by three methods of instruction in elementary psychology. *Purdue Univ. Stud. Higher Educ.*, 21, Series 33, No. 6.

RENSHAW, S., and SCHWARZBECK, W. C. (1938) The dependence of the form of the pursuit meter learning function on the length of the inter-practice rests: I. Experimental. *J. gen. Psychol.*, 18, 3–16.

REYNOLDS, B. (1945a) The acquisition of a trace conditioned response as a function of the magnitude of the stimulus trace. *J. exp. Psychol.*, 35, 15–30.

REYNOLDS, B. (1945b) Extinction of a trace conditioned response as a function of the spacing of trials during the acquisition and extinction series. *J. exp. Psychol.*, 35, 81–91.

REYNOLDS, B. (1945c) A repetition of the Blodgett experiment on "latent" learning. *J. exp. Psychol.*, 35, 504–516.

REYNOLDS, B. (1949) The relationship between strength of habit and the degree of drive present during acquisition. *J. exp. Psychol.*, 39, 296–305.

RICHTER, C. P. (1927) Animal behavior and internal drives. *Quart. Rev. Biol.*, 2, 307–343.

RITCHIE, B. F., EBELING, E., and ROTH, W. (1950) Evidence for continuity in the discrimination of vertical and horizontal patterns. *J. comp. physiol. Psychol.*, 43, 168–180.

ROBINSON, E. S. (1921) The relative efficiencies of distributed and concentrated study in memorizing. *J. exp. Psychol.*, 4, 327–343.

ROBINSON, E. S. (1927) The "similarity" factor in retroaction. *Amer. J. Psychol.*, 39, 297–312.

ROBINSON, E. S., and BILLS, A. G. (1926) Two factors in the work decrement. *J. exp. Psychol.*, 9, 415–443.

ROCK, R. T., JR. (1935) The influence upon learning of the quantitative variation of after-effects. *Teach. Coll. Contr. Educ.*, No. 650.

ROHRER, J. H. (1947) Experimental extinction as a function of the distribution of extinction trials and response strength. *J. exp. Psychol.*, 37, 473–493.

ROHRER, J. H. (1949) Factors influencing the occurrence of reminiscence: Attempted formal rehearsal during the interpolated period. *J. exp. Psychol.*, 39, 484–491.

ROSENZWEIG, S. (1933) The recall of finished and unfinished tasks as affected by the purpose with which they were performed. *Psychol. Bull.*, 30, 698.

RUCH, F. L. (1934) The differentiative effects of age upon human learning. *J. gen. Psychol.*, 11, 261–285.

RUGER, H. A. (1910) The psychology of efficiency: An experimental study of the processes involved in the solution of mechanical puzzles and in the acquisition of skill in their manipulation. *Arch. Psychol., N.Y.*, 2, No. 15.

SALTZMAN, I. J. (1949) Maze learning in the absence of primary reinforcement: A study of secondary reinforcement. *J. comp. physiol. Psychol.*, 42, 161–173.

SALTZMAN, I. J. (1951) The relative efficiency of incidental and intentional learning. *Amer. Psychologist*, 6, 266.

SALTZMAN, I. J., and KOCH, S. (1948) The effect of low intensities of hunger on the behavior mediated by a habit of maximum strength. *J. exp. Psychol.*, 38, 347–370.

SCHILLER, P. H. (1949) Innate constituents of complex responses in primates. Personal communication. Cited in Harlow (1951b).

SCHLOSBERG, H. (1937) The relationship between success and the laws of conditioning. *Psychol. Rev.*, 44, 379–394.

SCHLOSBERG, H., and KATZ, A. (1943) Double alternation lever-pressing in the white rat. *Amer. J. Psychol.*, 56, 274–282.

SCHLOSBERG, H., and SOLOMON, R. L. (1943) Latency of response in a choice discrimination. *J. exp. Psychol.*, 33, 22–29.

SCHMIDT, H. O. (1941) The effects of praise and blame as incentives to learning. *Psychol. Monogr.*, 53, No. 240.

SCHNEIRLA, T. C. (1929) Learning and orientation in ants. *Comp. Psychol. Monogr.*, 6, No. 30.

SCHNEIRLA, T. C. (1933) Motivation and efficiency in ant learning. *J. comp. Psychol.*, 15, 243–266.

SCHREPEL, M., and LASLETT, H. R. (1936) On the loss of knowledge by junior high-school pupils over the summer vacation. *J. educ. Psychol.*, 27, 299–303.

SCHWARTZ, B., and SAFIR, S. R. (1915) Habit formation in the fiddler crab. *J. Anim. Behav.*, 5, 226–239.

SEARLE, L. V. (1949) The organization of hereditary maze-brightness and maze-dullness. *Genet. Psychol. Monogr.*, 39, 279–375.

SEARS, R. R. (1944) Experimental analysis of psychoanalytic phenomena. In J. McV. Hunt (Ed.), *Personality and the behavior disorders.* New York: Ronald.

SEIDMAN, E. (1949) Relative ability of the newt and the terrapin to reverse a direction habit. *J. comp. physiol. Psychol.*, 42, 320–327.

SELLS, S. B. (1936) The atmosphere effect. *Arch. Psychol., N.Y.*, 29, No. 200.

SELLS, S. B., and KOOB, H. F. (1937) A classroom demonstration of "atmosphere effect" in reasoning. *J. educ. Psychol.*, 28, 514–518.

SETTLAGE, P., ZABLE, M., and HARLOW, H. F. (1948) Problem solution by monkeys following bilateral removal of the prefrontal areas: VI. Performance on tests requiring contradictory reactions to similar and to identical stimuli. *J. exp. Psychol.*, 38, 50–65.

SEWARD, J. P. (1942) An experimental study of Guthrie's theory of reinforcement. *J. exp. Psychol.*, 30, 247–256.

SEWARD, J. P. (1943) Reinforcement in terms of association. *Psychol. Rev.*, 50, 187–202.

SEWARD, J. P. (1949) An experimental analysis of latent learning. *J. exp. Psychol.*, 39, 177–186.

SEWARD, J. P. (1951) Experimental evidence for the motivating function of reward. *Psychol. Bull.*, 48, 130–149.

SEWARD, J. P., and LEVY, N. (1949) Sign learning as a factor in extinction. *J. exp. Psychol.*, 39, 660–668.

SHARP, A. A. (1938) An experimental test of Freud's doctrine of the relation of hedonic tone to memory revival. *J. exp. Psychol.*, 22, 395–418.

SHAW, F. J. (1942) Influence of degree of original learning upon associative and reproductive inhibition. *Proc. Ia. Acad. Sci.*, 49, 413–417.

SHAW, F. J. (1944) Two determinants of selective forgetting. *J. abnorm. soc. Psychol.*, 39, 434–445.

SHAW, F. J., and SPOONER, A. (1945) Selective forgetting when the subject is not "ego involved." *J. exp. Psychol.*, 35, 242–247.

SHEFFIELD, F. D. (1948) Avoidance training and the contiguity principle. *J. comp. physiol. Psychol.*, 41, 165–177.

SHEFFIELD, F. D. (1949) "Spread of effect" without reward or learning. *J. exp. Psychol.*, 39, 575–579.

SHEFFIELD, V. F. (1949) Extinction as a function of partial reinforcement and distribution of practice. *J. exp. Psychol.*, 39, 511–525.

SHEFFIELD, V. F. (1950) Resistance to extinction as a function of the distribution of extinction trials. *J. exp. Psychol.*, 40, 305–313.

SHIPLEY, W. C. (1939) The effect of a short rest pause on retention in rote series of different lengths. *J. gen. Psychol.*, 21, 99–117.

SHURRAGER, P. S., and CULLER, E. (1938) Phenomena allied to conditioning in the spinal dog. *Amer. J. Physiol.*, 123, 186–187.

SHURRAGER, P. S., and CULLER, E. (1940) Conditioning in the spinal dog. *J. exp. Psychol.*, 26, 133–159.

SIEGAL, P. S. (1946) Alien drive, habit strength and resistance to extinction. *J. comp. Psychol.*, 39, 307–318.

SIEGAL, P. S., and STEINBERG, M. (1949) Activity level as a function of hunger. *J. comp. physiol. Psychol.*, 42, 413–416.

SIMS, V. M. (1928) The relative influence of two types of motivation on improvement. *J. educ. Psychol.*, 19, 480–489.

SKAGGS, E. B. (1920) The relative value of grouped and interspersed recitation. *J. exp. Psychol.*, 3, 424–446.

SKINNER, B. F. (1931) The concept of the reflex in the description of behavior. *J. gen. Psychol.*, 5, 427–458.

SKINNER, B. F. (1933) The rate of establishment of a discrimination. *J. gen. Psychol.*, 9, 302–350.

SKINNER, B. F. (1935) Two types of conditioned reflex and a pseudo-type. *J. gen. Psychol.*, 12, 66–77.

SKINNER, B. F. (1937) Two types of conditioned reflex: A reply to Konorski and Miller. *J. gen. Psychol.*, 16, 272–279.

SKINNER, B. F. (1938) *The behavior of organisms*. New York: Appleton-Century-Crofts.

SKINNER, B. F. (1950) Are theories of learning necessary? *Psychol. Rev.*, 57, 193–216.

SMITH, A. C. (1908) The limits of educatability in Paramecium. *J. comp. Neurol. & Psychol.*, 18, 499–510.

SMITH, F. L. (1949) *Generalization gradients of antedating and perseverating tendencies in the linear maze*. Ph.D. dissertation, The Johns Hopkins University.

SMITH, M. F. (1939) The establishment and extinction of the token-reward habit in the cat. *J. gen. Psychol.*, 20, 475–486.

SMITH, M. H., JR. (1946) The effect of extinction of a generalized response on the reconditioning of the original response. *Amer. Psychologist.*, 1, 449.

SMITH, M. H., JR. (1949) Spread of effect is the spurious result of nonrandom response tendencies. *J. exp. Psychol.*, 39, 355–368.

SMOKE, K. L. (1932) An objective study of concept formation. *Psychol. Monogr.*, 42, No. 191.

SNODDY, G. S. (1935) *Evidence for two opposed processes in mental growth*. Lancaster, Pa.: Science Press.

SOLOMON, R. L. (1948a) Effort and extinction rate: A confirmation. *J. comp. physiol. Psychol.*, 41, 93–101.

SOLOMON, R. L. (1948b) Influence of work on behavior. *Psychol. Bull.*, 45, 1–40.

SONES, A. M., and STROUD, J. B. (1940) Review with special reference to temporal position. *J. educ. Psychol.*, 31, 665–676.

SPAET, T., and HARLOW, H. R. (1943) Problem solution by monkeys following bilateral removal of the prefrontal areas: II. Delayed reaction problems involving use of the matching-from-sample method. *J. exp. Psychol.*, 32, 424–434.

SPENCE, K. W. (1937a) The differential response in animals to stimuli varying within a single dimension. *Psychol. Rev.*, 44, 430–444.

SPENCE, K. W. (1937b) Analysis of formation of visual discrimination habits in the chimpanzee. *J. comp. Psychol.*, 23, 77–100.

SPENCE, K. W. (1940) Continuous vs. non-continuous interpretation of discrimination learning. *Psychol. Rev.*, 47, 271–288.

SPENCE, K. W. (1942a) The basis of solution by chimpanzees of the intermediate size problem. *J. exp. Psychol.*, 31, 257–271.

SPENCE, K. W. (1942b) Theoretical interpretations of learning. In F. A. Moss (Ed.), *Comparative psychology* (2d Ed.). New York: Prentice-Hall.

SPENCE, K. W. (1945) An experimental test of the continuity and non-continuity theories of discrimination learning. *J. exp. Psychol.,* 35, 253–266.

SPENCE, K. W. (1947) The role of secondary reinforcement in delayed reward learning. *Psychol. Rev.,* 54, 1–8.

SPENCE, K. W. (1950) Cognitive vs. stimulus-response theories of learning. *Psychol. Rev.,* 57, 159–172.

SPENCE, K. W., BERGMANN, G., and LIPPITT, R. (1950) A study of simple learning under irrelevant motivational-reward conditions. *J. exp. Psychol.,* 40, 539–551.

SPENCE, K. W., and LIPPITT, R. O. (1940) Latent learning of a simple maze problem with relevant needs satiated. *Psychol. Bull.,* 35, 429.

SPENCE, K. W., and LIPPITT, R. O. (1946) An experimental test of the sign-Gestalt theory of trial and error learning. *J. exp. Psychol.,* 36, 491–502.

SPENCE, R. B. (1928) Lecture and class discussion in teaching educational psychology. *J. educ. Psychol.,* 19, 454–462.

SPENCER, E. M. (1941) The retention of orally presented materials. *J. educ. Psychol.,* 32, 641–655.

SPITZER, H. F. (1939) Studies in retention. *J. educ. Psychol.,* 30, 641–656.

SPOONER, A., and KELLOGG, W. N. (1947) The backward conditioning curve. *Amer. J. Psychol.,* 60, 321–334.

SPROW, A. J. (1947) Reactively homogeneous compound trial-and-error learning with distributed trials and terminal reinforcement. *J. exp. Psychol.,* 37, 197–213.

STEPHENS, J. M. (1934a) The influence of punishment on learning. *J. exp. Psychol.,* 17, 536–555.

STEPHENS, J. M. (1934b) Further notes on punishment and reward. *J. genet. Psychol.,* 44, 464–472.

STEPHENS, J. M. (1941) The influence of symbolic punishment and reward upon strong and weak associations. *J. gen. Psychol.,* 25, 177–185.

STEPHENS, J. M. (1951) Spontaneous schooling. A neglected feature in theories of education. *Sch. & Soc.,* 73, 337–341.

STEVENS, S. S. (1951) Mathematics measurement and psychophysics. In S. S. Stevens (Ed.), *Handbook of experimental psychology.* New York: Wiley.

STEVENS, S. S., and DAVIS, H. (1938) *Hearing.* New York: Wiley.

STONE, G. R. (1948a) A note on Postman's review of the literature on the law of effect. *Psychol. Bull.,* 45, 151–160.

STONE, G. R. (1948b) The effect of negative incentives in serial learning: III. Fixation due to an isolated verbal punishment. *J. gen. Psychol.,* 38, 207–216.

STRANGE, J. R. (1950a) Latent learning under conditions of high motivation. *J. comp. physiol. Psychol.,* 43, 194–197.

STRANGE, J. R. (1950b) *The effect of an irrelevant drive on the reaction tendency specific to another drive.* Ph.D. dissertation, the Johns Hopkins University.

STRASSBURGER, R. C. (1950) Resistance to extinction of a conditioned operant as related to drive level at reinforcement. *J. exp. Psychol.,* 40, 473–487.

STROUD, J. B. (1940) Experiments on learning in school situations. *Psychol. Bull.,* 37, 777–807.

STROUD, J. B., and MAUL, R. (1933) The influence of age upon learning and retention of poetry and nonsense syllables. *J. genet. Psychol.,* 42, 242–250.

SWENSEN, E. J., ANDERSON, G. L., and STACEY, C. L. (1949) Learning theory in school situations. *Univ. Minn. Stud. Educ.,* No. 2.

SWIFT, E. J. (1918) *Psychology and the day's work.* New York: Scribner.

TEN CATE, J. (1934) Können die bedingten Reaktionen sich auch ausserhalb der Grosshirnrinde bilden? *Arch. néerl. Physiol.,* 19, 469–481.

THACKER, L. A. (1950) An investigation of non-instrumental learning. *J. comp. physiol. Psychol.,* 43, 86–98.

THISTLETHWAITE, D. (1950) Attitude and structure as factors in the distortion of reasoning. *J. abnorm. soc. Psychol.,* 45, 442–458.

THISTLETHWAITE, D. (1951) A critical review of latent learning and related experiments. *Psychol. Bull.,* 48, 97–130.

THOMPSON, E. (1917) An analysis of the learning process in the snail, *Physa gyrina Say. Behav. Monogr.,* 3, No. 3.

THOMPSON, G. G., and HUNNICUTT, C. W. (1944) Effect of repeated praise or blame on the work achievement of introverts and extroverts. *J. educ. Psychol.,* 35, 257–266.

THORNDIKE, E. L. (1898) Animal intelligence. *Psychol. Rev. Monogr. Suppl.,* 2, No. 8.

THORNDIKE, E. L. (1913) *The psychology of learning* (Vol. II of *Educational psychology*). New York: Teachers College, Columbia University.

THORNDIKE, E. L. (1914) Repetition vs. recall in memorizing vocabularies. *J. educ. Psychol.,* 15, 1–22.

THORNDIKE, E. L. (1916) *Educational psychology, briefer course.* New York: Teachers College, Columbia University.

THORNDIKE, E. L. (1923) The influence of first-year Latin upon the ability to read English. *Sch. & Soc.,* 17, 165–168.

THORNDIKE, E. L. (1932a) Reward and punishment in animal learning. *Comp. Psychol. Monogr.,* 8, No. 39.

THORNDIKE, E. L. (1932b) *The fundamentals of learning.* New York: Teachers College, Columbia University.

THORNDIKE, E. L. (1933) An experimental study of rewards. *Teach. Coll. Contr. Educ.,* No. 580.

THORNDIKE, E. L. (1935) *The psychology of wants, interests and attitudes.* New York: Appleton-Century-Crofts.

THORNDIKE, E. L., BREGMAN, E. O., TILTON, J. W., and WOODYARD, E. (1928) *Adult learning.* New York: Macmillan.

THORNDIKE, E. L., and FORLANO, G. (1933) The influence of increase and decrease of the amount of reward upon the rate of learning. *J. educ. Psychol.,* 24, 401–411.

THORNDIKE, E. L., and RUGER, G. J. (1923) The effect of first-year Latin upon knowledge of English words of Latin derivation. *Sch. & Soc.,* 18, 260–270, 417–418.

THORNDIKE, E. L., and WOODWORTH, R. S. (1901) The influence of improvement in one mental function upon the efficiency of other functions. *Psychol. Rev.,* 8, 247–267, 384–395, 553–564.

THORPE, W. H. (1950) The concepts of learning and their relation to those of instinct. In *Symposia of the Society for Exp. Biol.* London: Cambridge. Vol. IV.

THUNE, L. E. (1950) The effect of different types of preliminary activities on subsequent learning of paired-associate material. *J. exp. Psychol.,* 40, 423–438.

THUNE, L. E., and UNDERWOOD, B. J. (1943) Retroactive inhibition as a function of degree of interpolated learning. *J. exp. Psychol.,* 32, 185–200.

THURSTONE, L. L. (1930) The learning function. *J. gen. Psychol.,* 3, 469–493.

TOLMAN, E. C. (1932) *Purposive behavior in animals and men.* New York: Appleton-Century-Crofts.

TOLMAN, E. C. (1948) Cognitive maps

in rats and men. *Psychol. Rev.,* 55, 189–208.

TOLMAN, E. C. (1949) There is more than one kind of learning. *Psychol. Rev.,* 56, 144–155.

TOLMAN, E. C., and HONZIK, C. H. (1930) Introduction and removal of reward, and maze performance in rats. *Univ. Calif. Publ. Psychol.,* 4, 257–275.

TOLMAN, E. C., HALL, C. S., and BRET-NALL, E. P. (1932) A disproof of the law of effect and a substitution of the laws of emphasis, motivation and disruption. *J. exp. Psychol.,* 15, 601–614.

TOLMAN, E. C., RITCHIE, B. F., and KALISH, D. (1946a) Studies in spatial learning: I. Orientation and the short-cut. *J. exp. Psychol.,* 36, 13–24.

TOLMAN, E. C., RITCHIE, B. F., and KALISH, D. (1946b) Studies in spatial learning: II. Place learning vs. response learning. *J. exp. Psychol.,* 36, 221–229.

TRACY, F. W. (1927) *Experiments on the establishment of conditioned motor responses.* Dissertation, Ohio State University. Cited in E. R. Hilgard and D. M. Marquis (1940).

TRAVIS, R. C. (1937) The effect of the length of the rest period on motor learning. *J. Psychol.,* 3, 189–194.

TROWBRIDGE, M. H., and CASON, H. (1932) An experimental study of Thorndike's theory of learning. *J. gen. Psychol.,* 7, 245–258.

TRYON, R. C. (1940a) Genetic differences in maze learning in rats. *39th Yearb. nat. Soc. Study Educ.* Bloomington, Ill.: Public School.

TRYON, R. C. (1940b) Studies in individual differences in maze ability: VII. The specific components of maze ability and a general theory of psychological components. *J. comp. Psychol.,* 30, 283–336.

TRYON, R. C. (1942) Individual differences. In F. A. Moss (Ed.), *Comparative psychology* (2d Ed.). New York: Prentice-Hall.

TSAI, L. S. (1927) The relation of retention to the distribution of relearning. *J. exp. Psychol.,* 10, 30–39.

TSAI, L. S. (1930) Gradual vs. abrupt withdrawal of guidance in maze learning. *J. comp. Psychol.,* 10, 325–331.

TWINING, P. E. (1940) The relative importance of intervening activity and lapse of time in the production of forgetting. *J. exp. Psychol.,* 26, 483–501.

ULMER, G. (1939) Teaching geometry to cultivate reflective thinking: An experimental study with 1239 high school pupils. *J. exp. Educ.,* 8, 18–25.

UNDERWOOD, B. J. (1945) The effect of successive interpolations on retroactive and proactive inhibition. *Psychol. Monogr.,* 59, No. 3.

UNDERWOOD, B. J. (1948a) Retroactive and proactive inhibition after 5 and 48 hours. *J. exp. Psychol.,* 38, 29–38.

UNDERWOOD, B. J. (1948b) "Spontaneous recovery" of verbal associations. *J. exp. Psychol.,* 38, 429–439.

UNDERWOOD, B. J. (1948c) Spontaneous recovery of verbal association as a function of number of extinction periods. *Amer. Psychologist,* 3, 248.

UNDERWOOD, B. J. (1949) *Experimental psychology.* New York: Appleton-Century-Crofts.

UNDERWOOD, B. J. (1950) Proactive inhibition with increased recall-time. *Amer. J. Psychol.,* 63, 594–599.

VANDELL, P. A., DAVIS, R. A., and CLUGSTON, H. A. (1943) The function of mental practice in the acquisition of motor skills. *J. gen. Psychol.,* 29, 243–250.

VAN ORMER, E. B. (1932) Retention after intervals of sleep and of waking. *Arch. Psychol., N.Y.,* 21, No. 137.

VEN, C. D. (1921) Sur la formation d'habitudes chez les astéries. *Arch. néerl. Physiol.,* 6, 163–178.

VON FRISCH, K. (1950) *Bees, their vision, chemical senses and language.* Ithaca, N.Y.: Cornell University Press.

WADE, M. (1947) The effect of sedatives upon delayed responses in monkeys following removal of the prefrontal lobes. *J. Neurophysiol.,* 10, 57–61.

WALKER, E. L. (1948) Drive specificity and learning. *J. exp. Psychol.,* 38, 39–49.

WALLEN, R. (1942) Ego-involvement as a determinant of selective forgetting. *J. abnorm. soc. Psychol.,* 37, 20–39.

WARD, L. B. (1937) Reminiscence and rote learning. *Psychol. Monogr.,* 49, No. 220. .

WARDEN, C. J. (1924) The relative economy of various modes of attack in the mastery of a stylus maze. *J. exp. Psychol.,* 7, 243–275.

WARDEN, C. J., JENKINS, T. N., and WARNER, L. H. (1936) *Comparative psychology:* Vol. III, *Vertebrates.* New York: Ronald.

WATSON, G. (1939) Work satisfaction. In G. W. Hartmann (Ed.), *Industrial conflict.* New York: Cordon.

WATSON, J. B. (1924) *Psychology from the standpoint of a behaviorist* (2d Ed.). Philadelphia: Lippincott.

WATSON, J. B., and RAYNOR, R. (1920) Conditioned emotional reactions, *J. exp. Psychol.,* 3, 1–14.

WEBB, W. B. (1949) The motivational aspect of an irrelevant drive in the behavior of the white rat. *J. exp. Psychol.,* 39, 1–14.

WEBB, W. B. (1950) A test of "relational" vs. "specific stimulus" learning in discrimination problems. *J. comp. physiol. Psychol.,* 43, 70–72.

WELCH, L., and LONG, L. (1943) Comparison of the reasoning ability of two age groups. *J. genet. Psychol.,* 62, 63–76.

WENDT, G. R. (1936) An interpretation of inhibition of conditioned reflexes as competition between reaction systems. *Psychol. Rev.,* 43, 258–281.

WENDT, G. R. (1937) Two and one half year retention of a conditioned response. *J. gen. Psychol.,* 17, 178–180.

WHEELER, R. H. (1940) *The science of psychology* (2d Ed.). New York: Crowell.

WHITELY, P. L., and BLANKENSHIP, A. B. (1936) The influence of certain conditions prior to learning upon subsequent recall. *J. exp. Psychol.,* 19, 496–504.

WHITING, J. W. M., and MOWRER, O. H. (1943) Habit progression and regression—a laboratory study of some factors relevant to human socialization. *J. comp. Psychol.,* 36, 229–253.

WHITTEMORE, I. C. (1924–1925) The influence of competition on performance: An experimental study. *J. abnorm. soc. Psychol.,* 19, 236–253.

WILCOX, M. J. (1917) Does the study of high school Latin improve high school English? *Sch. & Soc.,* 6, 58–60.

WILLIAMS, R. J., BERRY, L. J., and BEERSTECKER, E. (1949) Biochemical individuality: III. Genetotrophic factors in the etiology of alcoholism. *Arch. Biochem.,* 23, 275–290.

WILLIAMS, S. B. (1938) Resistance to extinction as a function of the number of reinforcements. *J. exp. Psychol.,* 23, 506–522.

WILLIAMS, S. B. (1943) A note on approach-approach conflict in rats. *J. comp. Psychol.,* 35, 269–274.

WING, K. G. (1946) The role of the optic cortex of the dog in the retention of learned responses to light: Conditioning with light and shock. *Amer. J. Psychol.,* 59, 583–612.

WING, K. G. (1947) The role of the optic cortex of the dog in the retention of learned responses to light: Conditioning with light and food. *Amer. J. Psychol.* 60, 30–67.

WING, K. G., and SMITH, K. U. (1942) The role of the optic cortex in the dog in the determination of the functional properties of conditioned reactions to light. *J. exp. Psychol.,* 31, 478–496.

WISCHNER, G. J. (1947) The effect of punishment on discrimination learning in a "non-correction" situation. *J. exp. Psychol.,* 37, 271–284.

WISCHNER, G. J. (1948) A reply to Dr. Muenzinger on the effect of punishment on discrimination learning in a non-correction situation. *J. exp. Psychol.,* 38, 203–204.

WITMER, L. R. (1935) The association value of three-place consonant syllables. *J. genet. Psychol.,* 47, 337–359.

WOLFE, J. B. (1934) The effect of delayed reward upon learning in the white rat. *J. comp. Psychol.,* 17, 1–21.

WOLFE, J. B. (1936) Effectiveness of token rewards for chimpanzees. *Comp. Psychol. Monogr.,* 12, No. 60.

WOLFE, J. B., and KAPLON, M. D. (1941) Effect of amount of reward and consummative activity on learning in chickens. *J. comp. Psychol.,* 31, 353–361.

WOLFLE, H. M. (1930) Time factors in conditioned finger withdrawal. *J. gen. Psychol.,* 4, 372–378.

WOLFLE, H. M. (1932) Conditioning as a function of the interval between the conditioned and original stimulus. *J. gen. Psychol.,* 7, 80–103.

WOODROW, H. (1927) The effect of type of training upon transference. *J. educ. Psychol.,* 18, 159–172.

WOODROW, H. (1940) Interrelation of measures of learning. *J. Psychol.,* 10, 49–73.

WOODROW, H. (1946) The ability to learn. *Psychol. Rev.,* 33, 147–158.

WOODWORTH, R. S. (1938) *Experimental psychology.* New York: Holt.

WOODWORTH, R. S., and SELLS, S. B. (1935) An atmosphere effect in formal syllogistic reasoning. *J. exp. Psychol.,* 18, 451–460.

WORCHEL, P., and NARCISO, J. C. (1950) The nature of the memory decrement following electroconvulsive shock. *J. comp. physiol. Psychol.,* 43, 325–328.

WYLIE, G. E. (1928) *Whole vs. part method of learning as dependent upon practice.* Ph.D. dissertation, University of Chicago.

WYLIE, H. H. (1919) An experimental study of transfer of response in the white rat. *Behav. Monogr.,* 3, No. 16.

YERKES, R. M. (1901) The formation of habits in the turtle. *Pop. Sci. Mon.,* 58, 519–525.

YERKES, R. M. (1903) The instincts, habits and reactions of the frog: I. Associative processes of the green frog. *Psychol. Rev. Monogr. Suppl.,* 1, 579–597.

YERKES, R. M. (1912) The intelligence of earthworms. *J. Anim. Behav.,* 2, 332–352.

YERKES, R. M. (1943) *Chimpanzees.* New Haven: Yale University Press.

YERKES, R. M., and DODSON, J. D. (1908) The relation of strength of stimulus to rapidity of habit-formation. *J. comp. Neurol. & Psychol.,* 18, 459–482.

YERKES, R. M., and HUGGINS, G. (1903) Habit formation in the crawfish, *Cambarus affinis. Psychol. Rev. Monogr. Suppl.,* IV.

YUM, K. S. (1931) An experimental test of the law of assimilation. *J. exp. Psychol.,* 14, 68–82.

ZEAMAN, D. (1949a) An application of sER quantification procedure. *Psychol. Rev.,* 36, 341–350.

ZEAMAN, D. (1949b) Response latency as a function of the amount of reinforcement. *J. exp. Psychol.,* 39, 466–483.

ZEAMAN, D., and HOUSE, B. J. (1950) Response latency at zero drive after varying number of reinforcements. *J. exp. Psychol.,* 40, 570–583.

ZEIGARNIK, B. (1927) Das Behalten erledigter und unerledigter Handlungen. *Psychol. Forsch.,* 9, 1–85.

ZELLER, A. F. (1950a) An experimental analogue of repression: I. Historical summary. *Psychol. Bull.,* 47, 39–51.

ZELLER, A. F. (1950b) An experimental analogue of repression: II. The effect of individual failure and success on memory measured by relearning. *J. exp. Psychol.*, 40, 411–422.

ZIRKLE, G. A. (1946) Success and failure in serial learning: II. Isolation and the Thorndike effect. *J. exp. Psychol.*, 36, 302–315.

ZUBIN, J. (1932) *Some effects of incentives: A study of individual differences in rivalry.* New York: Teachers College, Columbia University.

# AUTHOR INDEX

## A

## B

## C

# SUBJECT INDEX

## A

Activity, 85–86
Age and learning ability, 295–299
Alcoholism, 99
Alternation problems, 257–259, 290
Amoeba, 279
Amount of material, 168, 171
Amphibia, learning in, 287
Annelids, 281–285
Anticipation, 131, 139–141, 163–164
  method of, 135–137
Anticipatory behavior, 305
Ants, learning in, 286
Anxiety, 110ff., 119–120, 122–124, 305, 319
  (See also Punishment)
Arithmetic, methods of teaching, 236–238
Associations in verbal learning, remote, 139–141
  backward and forward, 139–140
  theories of, 140–141
Audiogenic seizures, 308–310, 312–313
Auditory presentation, 244–245
Aussage experiment, 184–185
Autonomic nervous system, 303–305
Autonomy, functional, 97, 121
Avoidance conditioning, 37–39, 110–111, 304–305
  two-factor theory of, 304–305

## B

Backward associations, 139–140
Backward conditioning, 82–83
Ballard-Williams effect, 174–175
Bees, communication in, 285–286
Behavior, anticipatory, 305
  symbolic (see Symbolic behavior)
Behavior of Organisms, 186
Blocks, 165

## C

Carnivores, problem solving in, 264–265
Central nervous system, 327–336
Cerebral cortex, 182, 290–291, 327–336
Chordata, 286
Classical conditioning, 65n.
Cockroaches, retention in, 192
Coelenterata, 280–281
Cognitive theory, 37
Comparative studies (see Phylogeny of learning)
Competition, 57–60, 167–168, 202–204
  (See also Proactive inhibition; Retroactive inhibition)
Concept formation, 269–271
Conditioned emotions, 302–305
Conditioned inhibition, 56–57
Conditioned response, 16, 173–174, 283, 325–326
  delayed, 81
  trace, 81, 163
Conditioned stimulus, 16, 65–66, 80, 327
Conditioning, 16, 21–22, 324–330
  anxiety and, 110–111, 119–120, 304–305
  avoidance (see Avoidance conditioning)
  backward, 82–83
  classical, 65n.
  under curare, 328–329
  first-order, 22
  higher order, 22
  instrumental, 65n.
  physiology of, 324–330
  simultaneous, 83
  spinal, 329–330
  time intervals in, 80–83
Conflict, 315–319
  analysis of, 316–317
  anxiety and, 319
  approach-approach, 318–319
  approach-avoidance, 317–318